GREAT AMERICAN
EATING EXPERIENCES

Front cover: (top left) blueberry pancakes; (top right) bacon cheeseburger; (bottom) the Kutztown Folk Festival in Kutztown, Pennsylvania   Back cover: (left to right) varieties of chili peppers; crab shack dining; grilled corn

GREAT AMERICAN
EATING EXPERIENCES

Local Specialties, Favorite Restaurants, Food Festivals, Diners, Roadside Stands, and More

FOREWORD BY
Andrew Nelson, contributing editor, *National Geographic Traveler* magazine

NATIONAL GEOGRAPHIC

WASHINGTON, D.C.

CONTENTS

Foreword by Andrew Nelson 6

NORTHEAST
8–45

MID-ATLANTIC
46–85

SOUTH
86–127

MIDWEST
128–163

GREAT PLAINS
164–199

ROCKY MOUNTAINS & SOUTHWEST
200–237

WEST
238–277

Index 278 • Illustrations Credits 285

Pages 2–3: Florida grows more oranges than any other state in the United States.
Opposite: Martha Lou's Kitchen, Charleston, South Carolina

FOREWORD

In New Orleans, a city provisioned with great chefs, it is not unusual to find one seated at your table and not cooking for it. So it was recently, in the kitchen of a Creole cottage, where I met Cory Bahr. Cory, 39, is a rising chef from Monroe, Louisiana, the owner of two restaurants, and a proponent of what's called North Delta cuisine—menus composed from the wild game, fish, fruits, and vegetables of the alluvial Mississippi, a location that crosses three states and is infused with the traditions of France, Spain, the Congo, and Native American tribes. Interest in regional food is growing mightily, he says, and to find it, order it, and eat it is to celebrate the uniqueness of the country.

"Good food doesn't leave where it came from," Cory tells me. "It has a sense of place—starting with local ingredients, harvested in season, cooked and served with respect for the memories of countless meals before yours."

The evidence is in the pages you are about to turn. In *Great American Eating Experiences,* you will be served a richly illustrated banquet of delicious fare originating from across the 50 states, in small towns and city neighborhoods where tradition, creativity, and inspiration have created foods found nowhere else. Think Brooklyn egg cream; Pennsylvania pepper pot soup; or Hawaiian poke, a dish made of cubes of marinated raw fish, on rice.

You'll uncover our rich immigrant heritage, from Creole jambalaya to Minnesota's Swedish lutefisk to Venezuelan stews ladled from Portland, Oregon's food carts. You'll discover the roots of beloved regional brands like California's In-N-Out burger, Chicago's Frango mints, and Detroit's Vernors ginger ale, along with the surprising origin of well-known treats: thank you, Somerville, Massachusetts, for Marshmallow Fluff!

Tasty meals are one of travel's great rewards. Consult these chapters before heading out on the road so that you can order the lobster rolls at Red's Eats on your way through Wiscasset, Maine, or the bison burgers at the Slippery Otter Pub when you're in West Yellowstone, Montana, or the salsa and chips at El Coronado on a visit to Safford, Arizona.

Lively and mouthwatering, this book celebrates in words and photos the richness of our nation's edible bounty. So go ahead. Place your order. America is waiting.

—Andrew Nelson

Steamed dumplings, a Chinese-American food staple

NORTHEAST

Fresh shellfish and dairy products form the heart of many northeastern recipes—but legendary dishes like New York pizza, Boston cream pie, and even the hamburger originated here as well.

MAINE
10–14

NEW HAMPSHIRE
14–16

VERMONT
16–21

MASSACHUSETTS
21–28

RHODE ISLAND
28–30

CONNECTICUT
31–35

NEW YORK
35–45

A Maine specialty: lobster rolls—long, golden buns filled with fresh lobster meat

The Chauncey Creek Lobster Pier in Kittery Point is a seasonal must for Maine lobster.

★MAINE★

01 LOBSTER

Knowing how to eat a whole lobster is a skill Mainers seem to be born with, which doesn't make it any less messy. Don the requisite plastic bib, grab a claw cracker to get at that tasty claw meat, and dig in. Sucking the meat from the legs is required—and delicious.

The meaty bottom-feeders bring out the masses along the Atlantic coast: Some 70,000 people visit the Maine Lobster Festival in Rockland the first weekend of August. Come with an appetite—the festival serves up more than 17,000 pounds of whole crustaceans, steamed bright red, and hundreds of pounds of lobster salad and lobster rolls: knuckle, tail, and claw meat with a light touch of mayo in a grilled hot dog bun (mainelobsterfestival.com; Harbor Park, Rockland, ME; GPS 44.1011, -69.1084).

Where to Try It

For less of a crowd but no less lobster, head toward the ocean and Maine's almost 3,500-mile coastline. You can get a whole steamed lobster almost anywhere

Basic Ingredient

For visitors, **wild Maine blueberries**—in pies, ice cream, jams, and wine—are synonymous with warm summer days. But it's the region's long, harsh winters and thin, acidic soil that give the lowbush berries their tiny size and potent blueberry punch. Maine is the world's largest producer of wild blueberries, upwards of 90 million pounds annually in recent years.

in the state, but none better than at an outdoor table next to a stack of lobster traps in a centuries-old village.

» Local (seasonal) top spots include Chauncey Creek Lobster Pier in Kittery Point (*chaunceycreek.com; 16 Chauncey Creek Rd., Kittery Point, ME; GPS 43.0845, -70.6894*); Five Islands Lobster Company in Georgetown (*fiveislandslobster.com; 1447 Five Islands Rd., Georgetown, ME; GPS 43.8238, -69.7095*), on the deep, cold waters of Sheepscot Bay; and Thurs-ton's Lobster Pound on Mount Desert Island (*thurs tonslobster.com; 9 Thurs-ton Rd., Bernard, ME; GPS 44.2392, -68.3527*).

» The lobster rolls at Red's Eats in Wiscasset are capable of causing summertime traffic jams on Maine's scenic, coastal Route 1. The hour-plus-long wait is part of the authentic Maine experience at this tiny red-and-white shack, which has been serving up the most iconic of Maine foods for more than 60 years (*41 Water St., Wiscasset, ME; GPS 44.0026, -69.6641*).

02 BLUEBERRY PIE

There's only one thing every pie maker in the state of Maine can agree on: The secret to a Maine blueberry pie—the state's official dessert—is piles of wild Maine blueberries, which are barely a third of the size of typical supermarket blues. The crust of a Maine-made blueberry pie can use butter, shortening, or even lard. It can have a lattice top, double crust, or some fancy combination of the two. It can be served with ice cream or without. Just don't mess with the filling: wild Maine blueberries—the more the better—some sugar, and maybe a squeeze of lemon, dash of cinna-mon, or dusting of tapioca, flour, or cornstarch. But

Blueberry pie

not too much. A Maine blueberry pie should taste like the pure sweet, tart, and juicy bounty of summer.

Where to Try It

» August's blueberry harvest is a statewide celebration. Visit the Wilton Blueberry Festival (*wiltonbbf.com; 25 Pleasant View Heights, Wilton, ME; GPS 44.6274, -70.1875*), the Machias Wild Blueberry Festival (*machiasblueberry.com; 9 Center St., Machias, ME; GPS 44.7159, -67.4581*), the Union Fair & Maine Wild Blueberry Festival (*union fair.org; Fairgrounds Ln., Union, ME; GPS 44.3120, -69.2738*), or the Range-ley Lake Blueberry Festival (*rangeleymaine.com; Rangeley, ME, GPS 44.9637, -70.6407*).

» You could eat a whole pie's worth of slices and not hit all the state's top blueberry pie spots, but that doesn't mean you shouldn't try. Start with Pie in the Sky in Cape Neddick (*pieintheskymaine .com; 1 River Rd., Cape Neddick, ME; GPS 43.1939, -70.6206*) and work your way up the coast to Two Fat Cats in Portland (*twofatcatsbakery.com; 47 India St., Portland, ME; GPS 43.6617, -70.2545*), Quietside Café and Ice Cream Shop in Southwest Harbor (*360 Main St., Southwest Harbor, ME; GPS 44.2794, -68.3262*), and Helen's Restaurant in Machias (*helensrestaurant machias.com; 111 Main St., Machias, ME; GPS 44.7193, -67.4509*).

03 STEAMERS

Eating steamers—the large, soft-shell steamed clams sold almost anywhere you can see the Maine shore-line—takes more finesse than preparing them. The closed clams are simply steamed open in a boiling pot of water (or beer), and then the real fun begins.

◇◇

Around *120 million pounds* of lobster are caught off the coast of Maine each year.

Moxie on ice—its distinct flavor comes from extracts of the gentian root.

> The slightly more formal Waterman's Beach Lobster in South Thomaston serves up a quintessential Maine summer meal of steamers and homemade pie on tablecloth-covered picnic tables at the water's edge *(watermansbeachlobster.com; 343 Waterman Beach Rd., South Thomaston, ME; GPS 44.0203, -69.1261).*
> If you are feeling ambitious, dig for your own clams. State parks allow you to dig up to a peck of two-inch clams. Wolfe's Neck Woods State Park in Freeport offers occasional classes on clamming *(maine.gov/wolfesneckwoods; 426 Wolfe's Neck Rd., Freeport, ME; GPS 43.8177, -70.0931).*

04 MOXIE

Moxie was invented in Massachusetts and is bottled in New Hampshire, but no place loves it more than Maine, which named this 130-year-old patented medicine turned soda its official soft drink in 2005. A favorite of Calvin Coolidge, Ted Williams, and *Mad* magazine, the brand advertises itself as "distinctively different." Even the locals call it an acquired taste, making the bittersweet drink flavored with gentian root a must-try for visitors with, yes, moxie. (The brand is credited as the source of the word that now means courage and daring.)

Where to Try It
> Each July, the town of Lisbon hosts the three-day Moxie Festival. Highlights include the Moxie recipe contest and Moxie Chug-n-Challenge. The reigning chugging champion downed ten cans in two minutes *(moxiefestival.com; Lisbon, ME; GPS 43.9961, -70.0609).*
> Hard to find almost anywhere else in the country, Moxie is a fixture on the shelves of Maine supermarkets. For an out-of-state Moxie fix, order a case online at *drinkmoxie.com.*

Order steamers by the pound. Your clams will be served with a bowl of watery clam broth, plenty of melted butter, and an empty bucket for the shells and such. Next, pluck a clam from its open shell with one hand and with the other, shuck off and discard the tough black membrane covering the siphon (or neck). Holding the clam by the siphon, dunk it in the clam broth to rinse off any sand and then dip it in the melted butter. Eat the clam whole and repeat. Some hardy Mainers will even drink the broth when the clams are gone and the sand has settled to the bottom.

Where to Try It
> The Beach Plum Lobster Farm in Ogunquit is about as basic as you can get—lobsters, steamers, a soda vending machine, outdoor-only seating—so stake out a spot at a picnic table for a steamer feast *(615 Main St., Ogunquit, ME; GPS 43.2628, -70.5986).*

05 WHOOPIE PIES

It's nearly impossible to resist Maine's official treat: the homemade whoopie pie. Two cocoa-y cookies as large as hamburger buns and so fluffy that they could almost be called cakes are sandwiched around a thick layer of vanilla frosting that oozes from the sides with every bite. Food historians trace the origins of the whoopie pie to the Pennsylvania Dutch, and the name to the shouts of delight that follow someone finding one in a lunch box. But Maine has made a mission of claiming the decadent dessert as its own since Labadie's Bakery in Lewiston began making whoopie pies in 1925.

Where to Try It
» Labadie's Bakery still makes whoopie pies. If you can't get to the small bakery in Lewiston, order online, and it's an easy website to remember (whoopiepies.com; 161 Lincoln St., Lewiston, ME; GPS 44.0924, -70.2192).
» Cranberry Island Kitchen in Freeport is the destination for gourmet whoopie pies, in shapes like maple leaves and pumpkins, stuffed with maple cream cheese, raspberry, and orange Creamsicle frostings (cranberry islandkitchen.com; 174 Lower Main St., Freeport, ME; GPS 43.8482, -70.1133).
» Sometimes the best whoopie pies can be found in the most unexpected places. One top Mainer recommendation is Nina's Variety in Falmouth, a pizza joint that bakes up one batch of the coveted cookies each day— go early (125 Bucknam Rd., Falmouth, ME; GPS 43.7297, -70.2414).
» Maine is also home to the annual Maine Whoopie Pie Festival in Dover-Foxcroft each June (mainewhoopiepie festival.com; Dover-Foxcroft, ME; GPS 45.1834, -69.2271).

06 PLOYES
Even some Maine natives will be stumped by ployes. These thin, springy buckwheat pancakes—the name rhymes with "toys"—are indigenous to a narrow stretch of northern Maine along the New Brunswick border settled by French Acadians. Nutty and yellow with a hint of green, ployes are cooked in a very hot skillet on one side only, making the bottom crisp and the top full of holes to catch butter or sauce. Ployes aren't meant to be sweet breakfast food. Instead they are lathered with cretons, an Acadian pork spread; used to sop up stew; or drizzled with maple syrup or molasses for dessert.

Where to Try It
» Sixth-generation Bouchard Family Farms in Fort Kent is the epicenter of the Maine ploye. The farm grows and mills its own (gluten-free) buckwheat and sells packaged ploye mix made with buckwheat and wheat flour, baking powder, and salt (ployes.com; 3 Strip Rd., Fort Kent, ME; GPS 47.2065, -68.5631).
» Fort Kent is also home to the Ploye Festival, a family event touting the world's largest ploye held each August in conjunction with a muskie fishing derby (ployes.com; Fort Kent, ME; GPS 47.2494, -68.5999).
» Unassuming Dolly's Restaurant in nearby Frenchville is the spot for made-to-order ployes and Acadian chicken stew (17 Rte. 1, Frenchville, ME; GPS 47.3525, -68.3606).

07 POTATOES
The potato is king in Aroostook County, Maine's sparsely populated, ruggedly scenic northernmost edge. Irish immigrants imported the spud to the rich soil and cool climate of Aroostook in the early 1800s. Today, the county is no longer the dominant potato producer it was in the 1940s, but the potato remains a staple of Maine culture—many Aroostook schools close for "harvest break" in September and October— and of its dinner tables. Baked is the most common potato preparation, of course, but thrifty Mainers have found many uses for potatoes over the years, from doughnuts to vodka to their needhams, a quirky dessert and must-have Maine potato treat that's a mixture of coconut and potato dipped in chocolate.

Where to Try It
» Needhams' origins are murky, but their flavor—which isn't potato-like—is a nostalgic treat. True needhams are

Whoopie pies

not always easy to find. Hunt for Linda's Gourmet Chocolates in Maine stores for a classic take (lindasgourmet chocolates.com). Dean's Sweets in Portland does a modern version of the needham made with Maine potato vodka (deanssweets.com; 475 Fore St., Portland, ME; GPS 43.6562, -70.2540).

» Maine Distilleries turns the lowly Maine Yukon gold, white, and russet potatoes into elegant Cold River Vodka, described as earthy with hints of caramel. It's available in many of the state's liquor stores.

» Potato is also a key ingredient in some Maine doughnuts. Nobody does it better than the Holy Donut in Portland. There are lines out the door for a bite of the dark chocolate–potato–sea salt version (theholydonut .com; two locations).

★NEW HAMPSHIRE★

08 FRENCH-CANADIAN FARE

A little more than a century ago, New Hampshire was dotted with Little Canadas, neighborhoods throughout the state where Quebecois settled to work in the thriving mills. French was widely spoken and French-Canadian dishes were standard fare. Today, it's harder to find classics like *poutine* (a messy and indulgent pile of french fries, topped with squeaky cheese curds and a rich chicken gravy) and *tourtière* (a simple, hearty dish of pork and mashed potatoes in a flaky crust) on restaurant menus south of the border—but they are worth seeking out.

Where to Try It

» Poutine has undergone a recent revival in trendy bars around the country—Parmesan and rosemary fries with sherry demi-glace, for example—but you'll find the real thing at Manchester's Chez Vachon, where breakfast poutine (the fixings and fried eggs on home fries) or a poutine burger (everything piled on a beef patty) is as newfangled as it gets (chezvachon.com; 136 Kelley St., Manchester, NH; GPS 42.9951, -71.4784).

» The Red Arrow Diner doesn't list tourtière on its menu. Instead, the homey French-Canadian dish is described simply as "pork pie." There's a hint, though, that this will be the tourtière old-timers remember: "Memere's Recipe," it says, using the French-Canadian

The Red Arrow Diner, one of the few places in New Hampshire you'll still find French-Canadian pork pie

endearment for grandmother. This tastes like home and holidays to many Granite Staters (*redarrowdiner.com; flagship location: 61 Lowell St., Manchester, NH; GPS 42.9934, -71.4614*).

09 CORN CHOWDER

Corn chowder might not be as flashy as famed clam chowder, but it tastes like cool fall evenings to a generation of New Hampshire dwellers who remember mom making this rich dish with the last of the native ears from the roadside stand. Corn anchors the chowder, but a little lobster is an acceptable (and tasty) addition. After all, New Hampshire does have a 13-mile Atlantic coastline.

Where to Try It

>> Every year at June's Prescott Park Chowder Festival, the corn version of the creamy soup gets equal billing with the king of all New England "chowdahs": clam. (The festival also allows the occasional bowl of tomato-based Manhattan clam chowder, usually outlawed in these parts.) Sample many different takes on New England chowder—fancy with scallops, spicy, vegetarian—at the festival in Portsmouth (*prescottpark.org; 105 Marcy St., Portsmouth, NH; GPS 43.0758, -70.7530*).
>> The "famous" corn chowder on the menu of West Ossipee's Yankee Smokehouse truly is—though a bowl of the chunky chowder is a formidable appetizer for the restaurant's signature rack of ribs (*yankeesmokehouse .com; Rtes. 16 & 25, West Ossipee, NH; GPS 43.8197, -71.2025*).
>> Homegrown New Hampshire chain the Common Man dresses up its corn chowder with lobster—and serves it with a side of corn bread. The Common Man Company

New Hampshire's state fruit, the pumpkin

Store in Ashland also sells a country corn chowder mix (add your own bacon and lobster) for those craving a taste of New England to go (*thecman.com; multiple locations*).

10 PUMPKINS

The pumpkin won a landmark victory in 2006 when it was named New Hampshire's state fruit, over protests from the state's apple growers. Throughout New Hampshire, fall is marked with a trip to the pumpkin patch to pick out the perfect jack-o'-lantern-to-be and smaller, sugar pumpkins for pumpkin pie making. The squash also tempts by finding its way into treats from pancakes and beer to the now ubiquitous pumpkin spice latte.

Where to Try It

>> The mid-October Milford Pumpkin Festival is the destination for all things pumpkin: the pumpkin weigh-in (winners top 1,300 pounds), the pumpkin catapult, the pumpkin lighting, and, of course, the pumpkin pie competition (*milfordpumpkinfestival .org; Union Square, Milford, NH; GPS 42.8354, -71.6490*).
>> Parker's Maple Barn is both a sugar-house, producing its own maple syrup over a wood fire, and one of the state's most popular breakfast spots. The Mason restaurant is particularly known for its stack of pumpkin pancakes, available year-round (*parkersmaplebarn .com; 1316 Brookline Rd., Mason, NH; GPS 42.7411, -71.7203*).
>> Everybody makes pumpkin beer, but Smuttynose Brewing Company, based in

Basic Ingredient

🌾🌾 Every August, New Englanders await the appearance of roadside stands piled high with **native sweet corn**. Everyone has a preferred variety—tender white kernels, plump yellow kernels, or "butter and sugar," a mosaic of white and yellow kernels—and a system for choosing the freshest, fullest ears. Just drop a couple dollars in the honor box before you go.

Hampton, uses actual pumpkin in their seasonal Pumpkin Ale, a practice that dates back to the New England colonies (smuttynose.com; 105 Towle Farm Rd., Hampton, NH; GPS 42.9456, -70.8547).

11 APPLE CIDER

You can buy apple cider in any grocery store, but that is not New Hampshire apple cider. Proper New Hampshire apple cider is nothing but apples, picked in a small hillside orchard and pressed there on an aging cider press. The taste of the fresh, sweet, tart liquid—pressed from apples like the McIntosh—gulped in the sunshine of an October day is the taste of fall in New Hampshire.

Where to Try It

Each fall, New Hampshire cider lovers share tips on which local farms still grow their own apples and press their own cider.

The best pairing with a cup of cider: a warm apple cider doughnut

» Check out the press behind the farm stand at Tenney Farm in Antrim (tenneyfarm.com; 1 Main St., Antrim, NH; GPS 43.0347, -71.9401), which has been making unpasteurized cider since the 1970s, or at Meadow Ledge Farm in Loudon (meadowledgefarm.com; 612 Rte. 129, Loudon, NH; GPS 43.3129, -71.4302), where you can pick your own apples and a buy gallon of orchard-pressed cider. And the Carter Hill Orchard in Concord produces enough fresh cider to sell at its own farm store and through local grocers (carterhillapples.com; 73 Carter Hill Rd., Concord, NH; GPS 43.2322, -71.6105).

» Apple cider means apple cider doughnuts, light, airy, tangy from apple cider, and still warm from the fryer. These sweet treats are the real reason New Hampshirites make an autumn ritual of apple picking. Most orchards sell them, but the truly devoted make the annual trek to the Chichester Country Store, which produces as many as 12,000 doughnuts a week from scratch to keep up with the demand. Here you can get maple frosted, blueberry, and pumpkin varieties, but there's no improving on the original, dusted with sugar (257 Main St., Chichester, NH; GPS 43.2553, -71.3761).

» At Farnum Hill Ciders in Lebanon, fresh sweet cider is just the beginning of the story. Here, the apple growers transform most of their harvest—unusual apples like Esopus Spitzenburg and Kingston Black—into hard cider, showing off a whole new side of the apple. Hard cider was once common in New England, and Farnum Hill Cider, which has been selling hard cider since the 1990s, is among those leading its resurgence (poverty laneorchards.com; 98 Poverty Ln., Lebanon, NH; GPS 43.6253, -72.2955).

★VERMONT★

12 VERMONT CHEESE TRAIL

From Jacksonville in southern Vermont to Enosburg Falls, nearly at the Canadian border, Vermont is home to 45 cheesemakers, producing far more than just the state's signature white cheddar. (Cheddar is naturally butter-colored; other regions add a vibrant red fruit-derived dye called annatto to produce the orangish color often associated with cheddar.) Along the Vermont Cheese Trail you'll find dozens of farms and production facilities open for tasting and touring,

Shelburne Farms on Lake Champlain makes its cheddar cheese with raw milk from brown Swiss cows.

offering scores of cheese varieties from blue to chèvre. (Another 15-plus are open by appointment only.)

Where to Try It

A map produced by the Vermont Cheese Council winds you through the state's most picturesque scenery and tastiest snacks *(vtcheese.com).* Among the notable Cheese Trail stops:

» Shelburne Farms on the shores of Lake Champlain is an agricultural wonderland. Summertime tours show off the working farm and cheesemaking facilities. Taste the farm-made cheddars in the Welcome Center, and then stroll the ten-mile trail system to work up an appetite for seconds. For the kids, try a visit to the educational farmyard, where you can milk a cow, collect eggs, and spin wool. Time your visit for July's Vermont Cheesemakers Festival, a feast of local foods

(shelburnefarms.org; 1611 Harbor Rd., Shelburne, VT; GPS 44.3957, -73.2474).

» Cheesemaking in Grafton dates from 1892, and Grafton Village Cheese carries on the tradition. It's known for its bold, cloth-bound cheddar and its own creations

Basic Ingredient

In the 1940s, more than 11,000 family dairy farms dotted the state of Vermont. Today, there are fewer than 1,000, but **dairy**—mostly from the state's 130,000-plus cows, though goats and sheep also graze the Vermont hillsides—remains the state's number one agricultural product, and the key ingredient in its well-known cheeses and ice creams.

The first recorded apple-seed planting in the United States was in 1629 in the *Massachusetts Bay Colony.*

such as sweet and nutty alpine-style Bear Hill; tender, creamy sheep's-milk Bismark; and buttery, farmers-style Vermont Leyden (*graftonvillagecheese.com; 400 Linden St., Brattleboro, VT; GPS 42.8641, -72.5684*).

13 MAPLE SYRUP

There is a fifth season in Vermont: sugaring season. As the state's short winter days warm and lengthen into spring in late March and early April, the maple sap begins to flow. At hundreds of sugarhouses across the state, trees are tapped and sap is boiled, releasing maple-scented steam and reducing 40 gallons of sap into a gallon of pure Vermont maple syrup. (Less romantically, but more efficiently, some sugarhouses rely on modern techniques such as pumping and reverse osmosis instead of the tap-and-bucket method.)

Vermont produces 40 percent of the country's rich, sweet syrup—more than a million gallons in the brief three- to four-week season—to be bottled for breakfast and baking.

But the sweetest taste of this Vermont specialty is fresh from the sugarhouse, where "sugar on snow" is a seasonal treat: Still-warm maple syrup drizzled over snow to create a chewy maple taffy that is sometimes served with something salty, like pickles or saltines, to complement the maple sweetness (*vermontmaple.org*).

Where to Try It

» The annual Vermont Maple Festival, held in St. Albans in late April, is a celebration of all things maple—including the end of the hectic sugaring season—with

Vermont sugarhouses produce more than a million gallons of maple syrup during the spring sugaring season.

syrup tastings and, of course, a pancake breakfast (*vtmaplefestival.org; St. Albans, VT; GPS 44.8107, -73.0836*).

» For an in-season visit to a sugarhouse, drive up to the Luce family's Sugarbush Farm in central Vermont for a tour and a walk on a nature trail past the farm's sugar maple trees. Call ahead to make sure you visit on a day when the family is doing sap boiling (*sugarbushfarm .com; 591 Sugarbush Farm Rd., Woodstock, VT; GPS 43.6650, -72.4673*). The Bragg Farm in East Montpelier also offers free sugarhouse tours, and the Bragg family still uses the traditional method of hanging buckets from trees and using wood fires to cook the sap down into pure maple syrup (*braggfarm.com; 1005 Rte. 14, East Montpelier, VT; GPS 44.2812, -72.4733*).

» Year-round, the New England Maple Museum shows off the history and process of maple-syrup making in Vermont (*maplemuseum.com; 4578 U.S. 7, Pittsford, VT; GPS 43.7143, -73.0365*).

Ben & Jerry's factory sign

14 BEN & JERRY'S ICE CREAM

The world has Ben and Jerry—Ben Cohen and Jerry Greenfield—to thank for Chocolate Chip Cookie Dough ice cream, which debuted in 1991. And for Cherry Garcia (cherry-flavored ice cream with cherries and fudge), Chubby Hubby (vanilla malt ice cream with peanut butter, fudge, and peanut-fudge-covered pretzels), and Chunky Monkey (banana ice cream with fudge and walnuts). From their start in a Burlington gas station turned ice cream parlor in 1978 (a plaque on the sidewalk marks the original location), the pair built a uniquely Vermont company. Around one in every 100 Vermont households once held stock in the famously liberal ice-cream maker that endeavored to spread "peace, love, and ice cream" around the world (it was sold to giant Unilever in 2000). The original location and flower child vibe may be gone, but the ice cream lives on.

Where to Try It

» Ben & Jerry's Waterbury factory is a destination for ice-cream lovers. Tour the production line, taste the newest flavors in development, and wander the bucolic grounds to the Flavor Graveyard, where aficionados mourn the passing of concoctions like nut-studded Wavy Gravy—it was retired in 2001 (*benjerry.com; 1281 Waterbury-Stowe Rd., Waterbury, VT; GPS 44.3529, -72.7402*).

★MASSACHUSETTS★

15 CLAMBAKES

The New England clambake, an all-afternoon team effort, starts with gathering seaweed and large stones and digging a deep pit in the beach sand. The stones are heated in the pit with the help of a wood or charcoal fire lit on top of them. Once the fire burns out, piles of local seafood—live lobsters, clams, mussels—potatoes, and corn on the cob get layered with wet seaweed on top of the sizzling rocks. The

Ben & Jerry's Waterbury factory turns out *120,000 pints* of ice cream every day.

whole thing is then covered to steam until done while the cooking crew relaxes with a brew and awaits the feast. Sadly, you don't see that many clambakes these days. Rules against bonfires on the beach have turned the tradition into the still tasty and fun clam *boil*, where all the cooking is done in a large pot, but a few Massachusetts communities, especially on Cape Cod, maintain the clambake tradition. Check the pages of the local newspapers come summer in search of a public clambake.

Where to Try It

» Francis Farm in Rehoboth has been hosting clambakes since 1890. Widely known for its private wedding clambakes, the farm also hosts several public bakes each summer. The only concession to the modern-day demands of catering a massive party is the lack of a sandy pit for cooking (*francisfarm.net; 27 Francis Farm Rd., Rehoboth, MA; GPS 41.8398, -71.2200*).

» The Chatham Bars Inn clambake is served at 6 p.m., but you'll want to be on the private beach in Chatham

by 4:30, when the four-foot-deep pit is prepared with 1,800 pounds of rocks, tangles of freshly harvested seaweed, and enough seafood to fill the inn's extravagant buffet table (alongside dozens of other dishes for the seafood-phobic). You can eat in the more formal dining room, but this dinner is best enjoyed on the deck (*chathambarsinn.com; 297 Shore Rd., Chatham, MA; GPS 41.6850, -69.9523*).

» Technically, Bill Smith's Martha's Vineyard Clambake Company does clam boils, but who wants to quibble? The caterer packs kettles to go along with all the fixings and a propane burner for outdoor cooking for as few as six people (*mvclambake.com*).

16 CRANBERRIES

In Massachusetts, cranberries are much more than a Thanksgiving side dish. They are a thriving industry, with 14,000 acres of the tart and finicky fruit growing in southeastern Massachusetts and along Cape Cod where cranberry farming got its start in the 19th century.

In this region of cranberry bogs, you'll find the fruit in everything from juice and jelly to candles and cocktails. And in the fall, the masses of vibrant red ripe cranberries floating in the cobalt blue bogs rival any leaf peeping the New England mountains have to offer.

Where to Try It

» Some of the world's largest cranberry companies sponsor the annual Cranberry Harvest Celebration, held each Columbus Day weekend in Wareham. The highlight of the lively fair: the cranberry bogs. Take a tour of the bogs on foot—or by helicopter for a bird's-eye view of the massive operation (*cranberryharvest.org; 158 Tihonet Rd., Wareham, MA; GPS 41.7867, -70.7180*).

» Small Flax Pond Farms in Carver grows cranberries and Christmas trees. In the fall, you can see the whole process of the harvest, from the flooded bogs to the antique cranberry separator, which shakes the cranberries to separate the ripe ones. (Ripe cranberries bounce.) In the gift shop, it's cranberry everything: cranberry honey, cranberry taffy, cranberry trail mix, and, of course, the little fresh fruits themselves (*flaxpondfarms.com; 58 Pond St., Carver, MA; GPS 41.8988, -70.7577*).

An annual Cape Cod tradition

Boston cream pie was invented at Parker's Restaurant in the 1850s, and you can still go there for a slice.

» Want to be a cranberry farmer? Mayflower Cranberries will assign you a 100-square-foot plot in Brown Swamp Bog growing intensely red, slightly sweet Early Black cranberries. All season you'll receive updates on your cranberries, but you have to show up in the fall to hand-scoop your own 30 pounds of the crimson harvest (*mayflowercranberries.com; 72 Brook St., Plympton, MA; GPS 41.9492, -70.7909*).

17 BOSTON CREAM PIE

There's a bit of a lie in the name "Boston cream pie." The decadent dessert isn't a pie at all. It's a cake—two layers of golden sponge cake separated by a thick layer of rich, eggy pastry cream, all draped in chocolate and sometimes etched with white icing. The story is that the dessert has been so (mis)named since October 1855 or '56, when it was first introduced at the opening of Parker's Restaurant in Boston's Parker House hotel. At that time, the words "pie" and "cake" were used interchangeably, and the dessert was especially lavish

Specialty of the House

Dunkin' Donuts has some 11,000 locations in 36 countries, but it all started in Quincy, Massachusetts, in 1948. The original location was retro-renovated in 2011, bringing back the doughnut counter of old—but not the ten-cent coffee (*dunkindonuts.com; flagship location: 543 Southern Artery, Quincy, MA; GPS 42.2529, -70.9929*).

since chocolate icing was an unusual indulgence. Massachusetts's official dessert can still be found on restaurant menus throughout the state and in doughnut form in many bakeries.

Where to Try It

» The original is baked up daily at Parker's Restaurant, still serving it in the downtown Boston hotel now known as the Omni Parker House. You can also get it to go in the hotel's gift shop (*omnihotels.com; 60 School St., Boston, MA; GPS 42.3578, -71.0602*).

Woodman's in Essex, Massachusetts, created the fried clam, and still serves them up alongside steamed clams and corn.

» The old-school, red-and-white Lyndell's Bakery sign has come to mean Boston cream for many in Somerville. The bakery—almost as old as the original Boston cream pie—offers a classic pie, an individual-size pie, and the now famous Boston cream doughnut *(lyndells.com; 720 Broadway, Somerville, MA; GPS 42.3999, -71.1130).*

» Mike's Pastry is a Boston North End institution for all things Italian pastry—and Boston cream pie. There's nothing fancy here, just airy sponge cake and rich chocolate icing, in that unmistakable blue-and-white Mike's pastry box wrapped in yards of baker's twine *(mikespastry.com; flagship location: 300 Hanover St., Boston, MA; GPS 42.3642, -71.1130).*

18 BOSTON BAKED BEANS

For a certain generation, the rich, sweet, and salty smell of Boston baked beans conjures memories of

Saturday night dinners at home or the regular church supper. It's harder to find the old-fashioned bean preparation on menus in Beantown these days. But traditionalists still seek out those pea-size navy beans seasoned with salt pork and molasses, most properly prepared in a ceramic bean pot handed down through the generations. Or if they can't find them outside, they make them at home. Leftover baked bean sandwiches are another Massachusetts favorite.

Where to Try It

» The long, communal tables of Durgin-Park in Boston's Faneuil Hall have seen hundreds of thousands, if not millions, of bean suppers. The restaurant has been serving old-school New England fare since the 19th century. Its baked beans are seasoned with a touch of dry mustard heat and served in a custom bean pot *(durgin-park.com; Faneuil Hall, 4 S. Market St., Boston, MA; GPS 42.3600, -71.0543).*

» Baked beans and brown bread are the draw at Nason's Stone House Farm in West Boxford, in business since 1956. For nearly every holiday—even Father's Day—there's a poster board or whiteboard sign reminding customers to order their baked beans in advance so they don't miss out *(276 Washington St., West Boxford, MA; GPS 42.7099, -71.0805)*.

19 CLAM SHACKS

As the story goes, we have Lawrence "Chubby" Woodman of Essex, Massachusetts, to thank for the fried clam and the phenomenon that is the New England clam shack. Chubby opened a small concession stand on Main Street in 1914, selling homemade potato chips and fresh clams he dug up on the nearby beaches. Business was a little slow—until July 3, 1916, when a fisherman jokingly suggested that Chubby fry clams in the lard meant for potato-chip making. He did, debuting the cornmeal-dipped New England fried clam the next day, on the Fourth of July. Five generations later, Woodman's of Essex is still frying up that hot, crisp, sweet, and briny taste of New England summer, and rustic clam shacks like Woodman's have become a staple of coastal New England from Bar Harbor, Maine, to New London, Connecticut.

Where to Try It

» At century-old Woodman's of Essex, of course, for clam strips or, even better, whole belly clams *(woodmans.com; 121 Main St., Essex, MA; GPS 42.6306, -70.7748)*.
» Woodman's isn't the only exit on Massachusetts's now-famous "clam highway," a stretch of Route 133 through the North Shore that is home to the Clam Box of Ipswich *(clamboxipswich.com; 246 High St., Ipswich, MA; GPS 42.6959, -70.8667)*—the building shaped like a cardboard clam box—and J.T. Farnham's *(88 Eastern Ave., Essex, MA; GPS 42.6329,*

-70.7629). There's so much debate over which is best, you should probably sample them all.
» If you can see the ocean in New England, you probably aren't far from the nearest clam shack. If you find yourself near the Kennebunkport, Maine, beaches, head to the Clam Shack at the edge of the bridge over the Kennebunk River. Just follow the eager seagulls that circle overhead *(theclamshack.net; 2 Western Ave., Kennebunk, ME; GPS 43.3609, -70.4784)*. On sheltered Nanaquaket Pond in Tiverton, Rhode Island, Evelyn's Drive In is the destination. Grab a seat on the patio for dinner and you'll get a spectacular sunset to go along with light and crispy fried clams *(evelynsdrivein.com; 2335 Main Rd., Tiverton, RI; GPS 41.6161, -71.2002)*. And in the working shipyard of Noank, Connecticut, Costello's Clam Shack moves the line of clam seekers quickly, going through 100 gallons of whole belly clams a week at the peak of the summer season *(costellosclamshack .com; 145 Pearl St., Noank, CT; GPS 41.3195, -71.9896)*.

20 MARSHMALLOW FLUFF

Massachusetts is serious about Marshmallow Fluff, invented in Somerville before World War I and still produced in the original factory location in East Lynn. Well, at least as serious as one can be about a sticky, sugar shock of airy spreadable marshmallow celebrated each fall at the What the Fluff? Festival. Think Fluff-inspired crafts, an ongoing campaign to have the Fluffernutter (a Fluff and peanut butter sandwich, a must-have in Massachusetts lunch boxes) named the state's official sandwich, and a highly competitive and inventive cook-off. Recent winners have included the erupting Fluff volcano cake, baklaFluff, and chicken wings with Fluff barbecue sauce.

Where to Try It

» As anyone who was once a kid knows, Marshmallow Fluff is probably available in

Continued on p. 28

The chocolate chip cookie was invented in the 1930s at the now gone *Toll House Inn* in Whitman, Massachusetts.

Ice cream—an American treat so iconic that it's hard to imagine a summer's day in the Northeast without it

GREAT AMERICAN EATING EXPERIENCES
Ice Cream & Soda Fountains

Americans love a frosty treat. Ice cream, fro-yo, custard, sherbet—however you scoop it, the average American now eats about 28 pounds of it a year. The Northeast and New England have a special culture of these kinds of treats. Maybe it's because the summers are short, the dairies plentiful, or because soda fountains—from which many specialty frosty treats and drinks originated—numbered in the hundreds here in the 1800s. But the oldest ice-cream brands in the United States started in the Northeast, and different corners of the region are devoted to their own eclectic takes on frozen or frothy desserts.

» Ice Cream
America's oldest ice-cream company, Bassetts, started in 1861 when Lewis Dubois Bassett cranked

out his first batch in Salem, New Jersey, with a mule-turned churn. His green tomato flavor didn't prove a classic, but Bassetts Ice Cream now serves more than 40 other varieties, including decadent Guatemalan Ripple, Irish Coffee, and Rum Raisin. The original store in Philadelphia is still open, with a fifth generation of Bassetts behind the counter *(bassettsicecream.com; flagship location: 45 N. 12th St., Reading Terminal Market, Philadelphia, PA; GPS 39.9535, -75.1593)*. Also homegrown in Philadelphia: Breyers, which started in 1866 with a simple, hand-churned gallon of milk, cream, sugar, and vanilla. Those are the same ingredients in classic Breyers ice cream today *(breyers.com; multiple locations)*. And of course, Vermont lays claim to specialty ice-cream maker Ben & Jerry's, which serves up scoops of imaginative flavors like Coconut Seven Layer Bar and Strawberry Cheesecake in its Waterbury factory (see p. 21).

>> Frappes & Cabinets

In Massachusetts and parts north, a frappe (rhymes with "snap") is a rich concoction of milk, syrup, and ice cream. Well-loved Herrell's Ice Cream gets the balance of ingredients right—even if some of the independently owned stores call it a milkshake *(herrells .com; multiple locations)*. (Real New Englanders consider a milkshake to be just milk and syrup beaten until frothy.)

The cabinet is the frappe of Rhode Island: milk, syrup, and ice cream. Most authentic in this state devoted to coffee milk (see pp. 28–29) is the coffee cabinet. Try the old-fashioned delight at the throwback Delekta Pharmacy in Warren *(496 Main St., Warren, RI; GPS 41.7293, -71.2822)*.

>> Black-and-White Shake

Not to be troubled by New England's provincial definition, New York puts ice cream in its milkshakes—and other things, too, from booze to espresso to candy. Try the black-and-white shake. This perfect pairing—vanilla ice cream, milk, and chocolate syrup—gets an extra squeeze of gooey syrup around the inside of the glass and a hint of malt at top-notch shake makers like Island Burgers and Shakes *(islandburgersandshakes.com; flagship location: 766 9th Ave., New York, NY; GPS 40.7642, -73.9881)*. NYC-born sensation Shake Shack makes a ridiculously thick version with its house-made vanilla custard. Standing in line at the original Madison Square Park location adds to the experience *(shakeshack.com; flagship location: Madison Square Park, New York, NY; GPS 40.7414, -73.9882)*.

>> Awful Awful

That's *awful* big and *awful* good, an apt description of the silky, signature ice-cream drink at Newport Creamery, which has been scooping ice cream in Rhode Island since 1940. "It's a drink," the retro red-and-white cups read at its 11 locations—and a delicious one made with whole milk, flavored syrup, and a secret-recipe ice milk *(newportcreamery.com; flagship location: 208 W. Main Rd., Middletown, RI; GPS 41.5112, -71.3028)*.

>> Egg Cream

The first thing to know: The egg cream has neither egg nor cream. The very New York drink is made with milk, seltzer water, Fox's U-Bet chocolate syrup, and a practiced hand that can transform the three ingredients into a chilly, velvety froth. The staff at Ray's Candy Store in the city's East Village has had the magic touch for 40-plus years *(rayscandystore .com; 113 Avenue A, New York, NY; GPS 40.7263, -73.9837)*. Retro-style Brooklyn Farmacy & Soda Fountain, which opened in 2010, has less practice but no less skill or enthusiasm. Every receipt reads "DRINK MORE EGG CREAMS" *(brooklynfarmacyand sodafountain.com; 513 Henry St., Brooklyn, NY; GPS 40.6840, -73.9993)*.

An egg cream—a strawberry one—at Brooklyn Farmacy & Soda Fountain

Quahog clams

your local grocery store (as well as in stores in Canada, the United Kingdom, France, Germany, Holland, Israel, South Africa, Belgium, and the United Arab Emirates). If not, you can buy it online (*marshmallowfluff.com*).
» Don't miss the annual What the Fluff? Festival in Somerville's Union Square held in September (*unionsquaremain.org; Somerville, MA; GPS 42.3876, -71.0995*).

★RHODE ISLAND★

21 QUAHOGS & STUFFIES

First, the quahog. These large, hard-shell clams—pronounced ко-hog—are native to Rhode Island's Narragansett Bay. The oversize mollusks in their purple-streaked shells aren't suited to slurping at the

raw bar or battering whole at the clam shack; their meat is too tough. So Rhode Island's fishing families created the stuffie (aka the stuffed clam, though you'll rarely see it called that), a frugal way to make use of the easily harvested quahog crop. At its simplest, the stuffie is nothing more than a chopped quahog mixed with its own liquor, some extra clam juice, and lots of bread or cracker crumbs, and piled back into its own shelf before being baked to a sizzling golden brown. But since its advent a century ago, the stuffie has become much more—a point of Ocean State pride.

Where to Try It

» Casual Amaral's Fish and Chips in Warren is known for its stuffed quahog, seasoned lightly with onion and celery, baked to a crisp, and served with a wedge of lemon (*amaralsfishandchips.com; 4 Redmond St., Warren, RI; GPS 41.7302, -71.2757*).
» Rhode Island's large Portuguese population introduced that country's cured meats to the stuffie, to great effect. At Narragansett's Champlin's Seafood, linguica sausage and paprika add a colorful and spicy kick to the traditional (*champlins.com; 256 Great Island Rd., Narragansett, RI; GPS 41.3772, -71.5127*).
» Hot sauce is a favorite addition to any stuffie, but Anthony's Seafood in Middletown offers the choice of a mild roasted pepper stuffie or a hotter cherry pepper version—both also available to go from the restaurant's fish counter (*anthonysseafood.net; 963 Aquidneck Ave., Middletown, RI; GPS 41.5143, -71.2820*).

22 COFFEE MILK

Coffee milk—the official beverage of Rhode Island—isn't difficult to make: Combine ice-cold milk with a generous pour of coffee syrup. Stir. Drink.

The trick is choosing the syrup. Are you an Autocrat devotee? The sweet, subtle coffee syrup is the dominant brand in the state now. Or are you an Eclipse advocate? The longtime Autocrat rival has a stronger coffee flavor with vanilla undertones. Adventurous types buck tradition ever so slightly and go for relative newcomer Morning Glory, a deeply coffee-flavored, small-batch syrup made of nothing more than cane sugar, water, and coffee. Its most radical quality is really just that it isn't Autocrat or Eclipse.

Rhode Island's signature clam cakes are dipped in corn fritter batter and deep-fried to a golden brown.

Where to Try It

» The coffee milk's natural habitat is the uniquely Rhode Island, family-owned Olneyville New York System restaurants, a winner of the James Beard Foundation America's Classics award. Wash down a hot wiener—a thin hot dog with mild mustard, yellow onion, celery salt, and a spiced meat sauce—with a coffee milk at the flagship Providence location (olneyvillenewyorksystem.com; 18 Plainfield St., Providence, RI; GPS 41.8164, -71.4440).

» Try another coffee syrup newcomer—Dave's Coffee—at Dave's Coffee shop in Providence. The baristas will whip up a coffee milk latte with the store's own hand-roasted, cold-brew syrup (davescoffeestore.com; 341 S. Main St., Providence, RI; GPS 41.8214, -71.4044).

» Do your own taste test with mail-order coffee syrups from Morning Glory (morninggylorysyrup.com) and Autocrat and Eclipse (littlerhodyfoods.com).

23 CLAM CAKES

Rhode Island clam cakes are properly ordered alongside Rhode Island clam chowder, both unheard of elsewhere. Clam cakes are fried delights, crunchy on the outside and fluffy on the inside. Large chunks of clams are suspended in the light corn fritter batter to make a golden, lumpy ball for dipping in clam chowder, a clear, brothy version that tastes of clams and the ocean.

Where to Try It

» Summer-only Aunt Carrie's in Narragansett claims to be the originator of the Rhode Island clam cake when, some four generations ago, thrifty Aunt Carrie added clams gathered by her children at the Point Judith beach into her corn fritters. The smell that drew fishermen to the beach shack where her husband first sold them still draws crowds to today's much expanded

Quahogs might alternately be called *littlenecks, cherrystones, or chowders,* depending on their size.

restaurant in the same location (*auntcarriesri.com; 1240 Ocean Rd., Narragansett, RI; GPS 41.3728, -71.4850*).

» Follow the hungry beachgoers straight from East Matunuck State Beach to the take-out window at Cap'n Jack's for an order of handmade beignet-light clam cakes, with clam juice in the batter. The restaurant can sell 10,000 during a sunny summer week (*capnjacksrestaurant.com; 706 Succotash Rd., South Kingston, RI; GPS 41.3842, -71.5254*).

» Flo's Clam Shack got its start in a renovated chicken coop at Island Park in 1936. The original location in Portsmouth has been knocked down by hurricane after hurricane, but Flo's is still frying up quahog-stuffed clam cakes. The Island Park location is takeout only; a second restaurant location in Middletown overlooks Easton Beach (*flosclamshacks.com; 4 Wave Ave., Middletown, RI; GPS 41.4901, -71.2849*).

24 JOHNNYCAKES

The unmistakable johnnycake is a crisp cornmeal cake made with Rhode Island white cornmeal, though the name is forever in dispute. Is it properly johnnycake or jonny cake, with a space and no "h"? The recipe is contentious, too. Should a johnnycake be made with boiling water, into a thick fritter, as it is on the West Bay, or should it be made with cold milk, into a thin pancake, as it is on the East Bay?

Where to Try It

» At Kenyon's Grist Mill, Rhode Island flint corn is ground between two enormous granite millstones, as it has been for more than a century. Visit on one of the mill's occasional tour dates to see the production process, sample Kenyon's own johnnycakes, and pick up a bag of johnnycake corn meal from the mill store to make your own—East Bay– or West Bay–style (*kenyons gristmill.com; 21 Glen Rock Rd., West Kingston, RI; GPS 41.5042, -71.6084*).

» Get your thick West Bay–style johnnycakes, crunchy on the outside, doughy on the inside, and slathered

with butter, at East Greenwich's Beacon Diner, which has been serving them up for nearly 50 years (*2934 S. County Trail, East Greenwich, RI; GPS 41.6166, -71.4910*).

» There's nothing doughy about the thin, lacy East Bay–style johnnycakes at Commons Lunch, where the kitchen turns out hundreds of the plate-size johnnycakes every morning. Get them topped with butter and syrup or bacon and an egg over easy (*48 Commons, Little Compton, RI; GPS 41.5094, -71.1707*).

25 FROZEN LEMONADE

The first thing you need to know about Rhode Island's tart and icy frozen lemonade: Don't ask for a spoon or a straw. Frozen lemonade is to be licked, sipped, slurped, and squeezed; any means necessary, however messy, to extract every drop of sunshine-yellow frozen lemonade from its waxed paper cup is considered acceptable. Icier than Philadelphia's water ice and slushier than Boston's Italian ice, frozen lemonade is a thirst-quenching Rhode Island summer essential.

Where to Try It

» Del's frozen lemonade got its start in 19th-century Naples, Italy, with the DeLucia family. Several generations later, Angelo DeLucia put the family recipe to work in the first outpost of Del's in Cranston in 1948. Today, the franchise has dozens of locations and food trucks across Rhode Island and is the benchmark for frozen lemonade in the Ocean State (*dels.com; multiple locations*).

» You can't miss Mr. Lemon. A grinning lemon holding a stop sign decorates the side of this small, seasonal, take-out-only storefront on an otherwise residential street. You should stop for the classic frozen lemonade or one of the other crazy colors and flavors, like watermelon, vanilla, or tutti-frutti. Can't decide? You can mix them (*32 Hawkins St., Providence, RI; GPS 41.8468, -71.4278*).

★ CONNECTICUT ★

26 APIZZA

In 1925, Frank Pepe opened a restaurant on Wooster Street in New Haven's tiny Little Italy. The Italian baker was not selling pizza. He was selling "apizza" (pronounced ah-BEETS), a style that would become the only way to make pizza in New Haven. Pepe's apizza is a relative of the Italian Neapolitan pie, thin crusted, with an uneven, roundish shape, baked in a coal-fired oven. The crust comes out chewy and charred. The plain is topped with nothing more than tomato sauce, garlic, and olive oil with a dusting of pecorino and oregano. You have to request mozzarella. Today, customers line up outside Pepe—or one of its equally storied competitors—for the famous apizzas, washed

Specialty of the House

Many Connecticut family recipes call for **Pepperidge Farm breads.** The company was created by a Connecticut mom in 1937— she was inspired to produce preservative-free breads for her asthmatic son—and is still based there. Its white bread is *the* white bread of the Louis' Lunch (see pp. 32–33) original hamburger and its stuffing is a must-have ingredient of New England's beloved "stuffie" clams (see p. 28).

down with a locally made Foxon Park birch beer.

Where to Try It

» White clam apizza is the thing at Frank Pepe Pizzeria Napoletana. Although the restaurant had long served

Connecticut's distinctive, thin-crust apizza pie is oven baked and comes with cheese only if you ask for it.

fresh-shucked Rhode Island littleneck clams on the half shell as an appetizer, they didn't find their way onto pizza, with grated cheese, garlic, olive oil, and oregano, until the 1960s *(pepespizzeria.com; flagship location: 157 Wooster St., New Haven, CT; GPS 41.3030, -72.9169).*

» Sally's Apizza opened in 1938, just one block away from the famed Pepe, with Pepe's nephew in the kitchen. The friendly rivalry continues more than 75 years later. Each has its devotees—and a fair number of pizza tourists who have lunch at Pepe and dinner at Sally's *(sallysapizza.com; 237 Wooster St., New Haven, CT; GPS 41.3031, -72.9200).*

» Modern Apizza—despite its name, more than 80 years old—is a consistent local favorite in the New Haven pizza wars *(modernapizza.com; 874 State St., New Haven, CT; GPS 41.3139, -72.9129).*

27 HAMBURGER

Louis' Lunch claims to be the inventor of that all-American staple, the hamburger, but you might not recognize the lean grilled burger, sandwiched, as it always has been, between two pieces of toasted white bread. Since 1900, the Lassen family has been serving the burger served medium rare (though you can request otherwise) and sliced in half on the diagonal. Onions, tomato, and Velveeta-style cheese spread are acceptable toppings. Ketchup is not. ("Don't even ask!" one sign says.)

Where to Try It

» Taste the original at tiny Louis' Lunch in New Haven. The current space is actually much larger than the original lunch wagon or the original storefront four blocks

It's a sticking point, but Louis' Lunch in New Haven—the inside pictured here—claims to have invented the hamburger in 1900.

Shucking oysters (beware the sharp, strong shells) involves a steady hand, a sharp knife, and a ready appetite.

away (louislunch.com; 261 Crown St., New Haven, CT; GPS 41.3065, -72.9304).

» Connecticut is also home to two very different but equally loved cheeseburgers: Ted's Restaurant in Meriden and Cromwell is the standard-bearer of the steamed cheeseburger, said to have been invented by the now defunct Jack's Lunch in Middletown. As the name suggests, the burger is made by steaming loosely packed beef patties and, separately, white cheddar cheese, both of which are then piled into a kaiser roll (tedsrestaurant.com; flagship location: 1046 Broad St., Meriden, CT; GPS 41.5469, -72.7835).

» Shady Glen in Manchester boasts the Bernice Original, a burger topped with four slightly overlapping slices of American cheese. The cheese on top of the burger melts, while the cheese that falls on the cooktop crisps, creating a large halo of cheese around the burger (840 Middle Turnpike E., Manchester, CT; GPS 41.7860, -72.4845).

28 OYSTERS

Blue Points are easily the most famous of Connecticut's centuries-old oyster industry—medium, firm, and briny treats harvested in the Long Island Sound—but other, lesser known varieties raised in the cool waters off the Connecticut coastline shouldn't be overlooked on the state's raw bar menus. Look for briny, crisp Copps Island oysters and full, firm Mystics.

Where to Try It

» Connecticut's annual Milford Oyster Festival celebrates the wealth of East Coast oysters, harvested from Maine to Virginia. Even though oyster lore holds that you should only eat the shellfish in months with an *r*, the Milford Oyster Festival has been an August highlight for 40 years. And the choicest of the 30,000 oysters (and clams) served on the half shell during the daylong event are those marked with a "CT"

Americans eat *three hamburgers a week* per capita—or more than 50 billion annually.

Tackle a quarter-pound hot lobster roll at Abbott's Lobster in the Rough on Connecticut's Mystic River.

(milfordoysterfestival.org; 2 Broad St., Milford, CT; GPS 41.2214, -73.0520).

» Do it up in style with a dozen oysters or a towering display from the raw bar at upscale oyster bars like the Oyster Club in Mystic (oysterclubct.com; 13 Water St., Mystic, CT; GPS 41.3529, -71.9720) and Max's Oyster Bar in West Hartford (maxrestaurantgroup.com/oyster; 964 Farmington Ave., West Hartford, CT; GPS 41.7620, -72.7428). Or keep it totally casual at a waterside spot like Lenny & Joe's Fish Tale in New Haven (ljfishtale.com; 501 Long Wharf Dr., New Haven, CT; GPS 41.2966, -72.9145).

» For oysters anywhere, Copps Island Oysters delivers by the dozen, overnight (coppsislandoysters.com).

29 HOT LOBSTER ROLLS

Don't expect a cold, mayo-kissed Maine lobster roll in Connecticut. Here, a lobster roll is properly served warm with piles of lobster meat fresh from the pot in a griddle hot dog roll, all doused with drawn butter. Milford claims to be the birthplace of the hot lobster roll, though no one can say why Connecticut stands apart in its hot lobster roll love.

Where to Try It

» Seasonal, seaside Abbott's Lobster in the Rough in Noank offers a "famous" and "original" lobster roll that breaks the rules. A full quarter-pound of butter-drenched warm lobster is piled not on a hot dog roll but on a sesame-seed-topped hamburger roll. Judging from the crowds, no one objects to the twist. Still hungry? There is a one-pound roll, too (abbottslobster.com; 117 Pearl St., Noank, CT; GPS 41.3212, -71.9886).

» A whisper of lemon juice sets apart the sizable hot lobster roll (on a well-grilled sub roll) at Branford's seasonal Lobster Shack, a cash-only stand at the

In the 1930s, New York City had around *1,500 kosher Jewish delis*. There are now only about two dozen.

water's edge with a corral of umbrella-shaded picnic tables (lobstershackct.com; 7 Indian Neck Ave., Branford, CT; GPS 41.2734, -72.8117).

» The Lobster Landing in Clinton looks the part: a century-old shack, with the sign askew on a working dock. Seating is limited to picnic tables and patio furniture at the seasonal spot. The foil-wrapped lobster roll tastes the part, too—a lengthy roll, filled with lobster, generously topped with butter (152 Commerce St., Clinton, CT; GPS 41.2691, -72.5284).

★ NEW YORK ★

30 NEW YORK CITY DELIS

The Jewish delicatessen is quintessential old New York. The best haven't changed a bit in decades—or at least give that appearance. On the menu: hand-carved pastrami on rye, never less than three inches thick; buckets of sweet-sour pickles; schmaltzy chopped liver; and smoked fishes.

Where to Try It

» Katz's Delicatessen in New York City can trace its history back to 1888. You can see decades of it on the cafeteria's walls in framed photos of family and celebrities, and in neon signs and quaint slogans like "Send a Salami to Your Boy in the Army." And you can taste it in the pastrami, cured and smoked up to 30 days and hand-sliced to order (katzsdelicatessen.com; 205 E. Houston St., New York, NY; GPS 40.7222, -73.9874).

» Manhattan's flagship Second Avenue Deli is between Lexington and Third. The kosher deli relocated in 2007 after more than 50 years. Everything made the move, from the brown-and-blue tiling to the matzo ball soup recipe (with matzo balls the size of baseballs in rich chicken broth), along with much of the devoted clientele (2ndavedeli.com; flagship location: 162 E. 33rd St., New York, NY; GPS 40.7452, -73.9792).

» The restaurant Barney Greengrass has been "the Sturgeon King" for more than a century. It offers everything a Jewish *appetizing* shop—a place devoted to food one eats with bagels—must, but it's the smoked sturgeon, nova lox, and whitefish that guarantee the line out the door for brunch or provisions (barneygreengrass.com; 541 Amsterdam Ave., New York, NY; GPS 40.7880, -73.9745).

31 BAGELS

Describing the ultimate New York bagel is a task for Goldilocks: crisp on the outside, without being crunchy; dense on the inside without being heavy; plump, without being oversize. It is a bread that shouldn't be bready.

How? Well, some will say it's the New York water that turns this simple combination of flour, yeast, salt,

A bagel with the works at Russ & Daughters in New York City

Katz's Delicatessen has been serving New Yorkers their beloved pastrami sandwiches for well over a century.

and barley malt syrup into the perfect New York City bagel, boiled, baked, and—most important—served fresh, with a schmear of cream cheese.

But while New Yorkers are certain to agree that the world's best bagels are from New York—everything else is just "a roll with a hole"—they will never agree on which New York bagels are the best.

Where to Try It

>> The smell of baking bagels drew the crowd to the original location of Ess-a-Bagel each morning; the Gramercy neighborhood panicked when the nearly 40-year-old location closed in 2015. But a second location, just blocks away, still bakes up the signature almost oversize bagels with a perfectly crackly crust (*ess-a-bagel.com; 831 3rd Ave., New York, NY; GPS 40.7562, -73.9703*).

>> Absolute Bagels on the Upper West Side hand-rolls bagels so bulbous the hole sometimes becomes nothing more than a belly button. Golden, chewy egg bagels are a top choice of the regulars

Basic Ingredient

Ask any New Yorker what makes the city's bagels and pizza better (and their hair straighter) and they'll tell you it's the **New York City water.** True? Scientists are uncertain, but bakers who want to replicate the Big Apple taste have gone so far as to doctor their H_2O with calcium, magnesium, and other additives to mimic the slightly acidic NYC tap water.

(*absolutebagels.com; 2788 Broadway, New York, NY; GPS 40.8025, -73.9674*).

>> There might be no greater New York bagel authority than the city's century-old Russ & Daughters (*russand daughters.com; 179 E. Houston St., New York, NY; GPS 40.7225, -73.9883*) which chooses Brooklyn's Bagel Hole (*bagelhole.net; 400 7th Ave., Brooklyn, NY; GPS 40.6648, -73.9835*) to bake the bagels for its "Classic" sandwich of smoked salmon and cream cheese.

Cheesecake comes in all colors, flavors, and toppings at Junior's in Brooklyn, New York.

32 CHEESECAKE

New York cheesecake is not just a cheesecake made in New York, no matter how tasty. New York cheesecake is a hefty, ivory slice of ultracreamy, velvety, and dense decadence, a sweet-tangy balance of sugar and cream cheese on a thin, buttery graham cracker crust. You'll find it not just in the city that made it famous but on menus across the country. You can dress it up with strawberries or flavor it with peanut butter, cappuccino, or Irish coffee. Just don't skimp on the portion.

Where to Try It

≫ The most well-known New York cheesecake has been found at Junior's in Brooklyn for 60-plus years, long before the Big Apple borough was a foodie destination. The flashy facade of its flagship Flatbush bakery is a beacon for lovers of sweet, rich cheesecake (*juniorscheesecake.com; flagship location: 386 Flatbush Ave. Ext., Brooklyn, NY; GPS 40.6901, -73.9819*).

≫ Eileen Avezzano began baking cheesecakes in her New York apartment in 1973. Just a couple of years later, Eileen's Special Cheesecake opened for business in then not-so-trendy SoHo, quickly earning "best of" accolades for its silky and surprisingly light cheesecakes in all kinds of flavors, from pumpkin to piña colada (*eileenscheesecake.com; 17 Cleveland Pl., New York, NY; GPS 40.7216, -73.9972*).

≫ A relative newcomer to the cheesecake contest, the Upper East Side's Two Little Red Hens' elegant and statuesque cheesecake wows with its deep golden brown crust that hides a dense, sweet-tart interior. No fancy flavors here, just pure New York–style goodness (*twolittleredhens.com; 1652 2nd Ave., New York, NY; GPS 40.7775, -73.9517*).

33 BLACK-AND-WHITE COOKIES

The black-and-white cookie is a staple of New York delis, bakeries, bodegas, and a memorable *Seinfeld* episode that coined the catchphrase "Look to the cookie."

When we look to the cookie, we find something that is more cakelike, a circle of soft vanilla crumb topped edge to edge with chocolate frosting or fondant on exactly one half and vanilla on the other. Seinfeld and many a New York kid would advise eating it as strategically—and probably as messily—as possible so that each bite is a combination of vanilla and chocolate.

Black-and-white cookies—a yin and yang of chocolate and vanilla icing

Where to Try It

≫ Old-fashioned Glaser's Bake Shop in Manhattan's Yorkville neighborhood bakes a plain cookie that is the perfect vehicle for the rich chocolate and vanilla frosting. The hand-frosted treats don't always give equal space to the light and the dark, so you can pick your own balance of flavors (*glasersbakeshop.com; 1670 1st Ave., New York, NY; GPS 40.7776, -73.9485*).

≫ Nussbaum & Wu Bagel & Bakery's elegant black-and-white cookies are covered in neat and smooth fondant. The Manhattan eatery also makes the treat with a mocha half that looks almost gold paired with the chocolate (*nussbaumwu.com; 2897 Broadway, New York, NY; GPS 40.8061, -73.9657*).

≫ William Greenberg Desserts bakes up a black-and-white cookie so robust that it's almost a mini-cupcake. The slightly lemony cookie is incredibly tender and the rich, creamy frosting would be at home on a birthday cake (*wmgreenbergdesserts.com; flagship location: 1100 Madison Ave., New York, NY; GPS 40.7786, -73.9607*).

≫ New York City may claim the black-and-white cookie, but upstate there's a confection called the half-moon

Continued on p. 42

The pizza goes flat into the oven—but not always. America's pizzas may be oven baked, pan baked, or grilled, depending on the region.

GREAT AMERICAN EATING EXPERIENCES
Pizza Pies

Pizza seems uncomplicated: crust, sauce, cheese, maybe some toppings. But if you are from Trenton, New Jersey, you know that, unequivocally, the tomato sauce goes on top. You also call the pizza pie a tomato pie. In Chicago, you are convinced that a pizza pie should, in fact, resemble a pie—one to two inches thick with a flaky, buttery crust. In New York, thin crust—no butter!—is the only proper pizza base.

Ever since the Neapolitans invented the modern version of pizza in the 1800s, regional *pizzaioli* (pizza makers) have been reinventing it. The only common ingredient besides a crust: pride. Each region is absolutely certain its version is the best.

» New York Style
The original New York–style pie is an Americanized version of a Neapolitan pie. Lombardi's Pizza in Manhattan's Nolita neighborhood claims the distinction of being the first of the New York pizzerias, opening in 1905 *(firstpizza.com; 32 Spring St., New York, NY; GPS 40.7214, -73.9945)*. Order by the slice—the proper unit of New York pizza, eaten folded—and eat with your hands (especially if you are the mayor or running for president!) at classics like Joe's Pizza *(joespizzanyc.com; flagship location: 7 Carmine St., New York, NY; GPS 40.7306, -74.0022)*.

» Chicago Style
In Chicago, pizza pie has a buttery, flaky crust with a crisp, almost fried exterior (see pp. 145, 148). Cooked in a cake-style heavy iron pan, the crust has towering sides, the better to hold layers of cheese,

meats, vegetables, and tomato sauce. The deep-dish pizza got its start at Pizzeria Uno—different from the nationwide chain of the same name (*pizzeriaunochicago.com; 29 E. Ohio, Chicago, IL; GPS 41.8923, -87.6269*). The chef who helped create the dish there later opened his own restaurant, Lou Malnati's Pizzeria, sparking an enduring rivalry (*loumalnatis.com; flagship location: 6649 N. Lincoln Ave., Lincolnwood, IL; GPS 42.0022, -87.7256*).

» St. Louis Style

For something completely different, try St. Louis-style pizza, an unleavened cracker-like crust loaded with toppings (see p. 162). The sauce is slightly sweet and seasoned with oregano; the cheese is not mozzarella but processed Provel, with a slightly nutty flavor and an almost magic ability to melt; and the pizza is cut not into slices but squares. Imo's Pizza, which popularized the St. Louis style, is ubiquitous (*imos pizza.com; multiple locations*). Or go upscale with a St. Louis pie at Italian-Spanish Guido's, where Provel is an option, not a requirement (*guidosstl.com; 5046 Shaw Ave., St. Louis, MO; GPS 38.6176, -90.2704*).

» New Haven Style

There's no such thing as New Haven–style pizza. That's New Haven–style *apizza*—thin-crusted and charred, hot from the coal-fired oven (see pp. 31–32). Frank Pepe Pizzeria Napoletana in New Haven, Connecticut, started the trend in 1925 (*pepespizzeria.com; flagship location: 157 Wooster St., New Haven, CT; GPS 41.3030, -72.9169*). The newer, hipper Bar offers its own twist on New Haven's signature pie, with an even thinner, more flexible and less charred crust and a gamut of possible toppings including mashed potatoes, meatballs, or fresh littleneck clams (*barnightclub .com; 254 Crown St., New Haven, CT; GPS 41.3062, -72.9303*).

» Providence Style

Grilled pizza was born in Providence, Rhode Island, in 1980 at Al Forno restaurant (*alforno.com; 577 S. Water St., Providence, RI; GPS 41.8173, -71.4006*). It was one of those happy culinary accidents. The owners, disappointed that the restaurant's architecture prevented them from installing a brick oven, began to experiment with cooking pizzas over a wood-fired grill (they now use hardwood charcoal), which produced a thin, chewy, and slightly smoky crust that they topped with a light hand. Although the style is a rare find outside the city limits, it continues to thrive in Providence pizza joints like Bob & Timmy's, which isn't afraid to pile on the toppings (*bobandtimmys.com; flagship location: 32 Spruce St., Providence, RI; GPS 41.8240, -71.4245*).

» Trenton Style

The Trenton tomato pie has pizza's traditional round shape, but the thin, almost crackery crust is topped first with cheese then with tomato sauce (see pp. 55–56). There is much dispute over who makes the most authentic tomato pie, but Papa's Tomato Pies—believed to be the country's oldest continuously operated pizzeria—is a serious contender (*papastomatopies.com; 19 Robbinsville Allentown Rd., Robbinsville, NJ; GPS 40.2153, -74.6240*). Its longtime competitor De Lorenzo's Tomato Pies is less than a mile away (*delorenzostomatopies.com; 2350 Rte. 33 #105, Robbinsville, NJ; GPS 40.2193, -74.6273*).

Chicago deep-dish pizza layers its cheese, veggies, meats, and tomato sauce within a crust a couple inches thick.

Charlie the Butcher's beef on weck sandwiches are always served on a salty roll and with a pickle.

that may have inspired the Big Apple favorite. Utica's Hemstrought's Bakery, the originator of the half-moon, closed several years ago, but Holland Farms Bakery & Deli in Yorkville continues the tradition: a *chocolate* cookie with chocolate and vanilla frosting *(holland farms.com; 50 Oriskany Blvd., Yorkville, NY; GPS 43.1136, -75.2714).*

34 NEW YORK HOT DOGS

The all-beef, natural-casing, so-called kosher-style hot dog seasoned with salt, garlic, and paprika has been the New York standard since Nathan's, the country's longest continuously operated hot dog stand, opened its doors on Coney Island in 1916. Start with the right dog, and the rest is up to you. You can griddle it à la Nathan's for a nice snap when you bite into it, or boil it as the ubiquitous street cart vendors do with their not-so-appetizingly named "dirty water dogs."

Toppings range from mustard and sauerkraut to bacon and potato chips. And don't expect to find the misleadingly named Coney Island dog, topped with chili-like meat sauce, mustard, and onions. That's not a New York specialty; it's a Michigan one (see p. 139).

Where to Try It

>> There are now hundreds of Nathan's Famous across the United States and around the world. But the original at the corner of Surf and Stillwell Avenues in Coney Island remains a mecca for hot dog lovers. Order a grilled dog with sauerkraut and mustard and a side of crinkle fries *(nathansfamous.com; flagship location: 1310 Surf Ave., Brooklyn, NY; GPS 40.5752, -73.9815).*
>> Papaya King was the original, a 1930s Upper East Side juice bar that later added hot dogs. The King's contribution to the New York hot dog scene was stewed red onion sauce, made with onions, tomatoes, and vinegar, served atop a grilled dog in a toasted bun and washed down with a tropical juice *(papayaking.com; flagship*

Sixty-nine hot dogs in ten minutes is the record at Nathan's annual Hot Dog Eating Contest in Coney Island, New York.

location: *179 E. 86th St., New York, NY; GPS 40.7791, -73.9541*). The King spawned countless imitators, including Gray's Papaya on Broadway, founded by a former King employee in the 1970s, which has gained its own cult following (*grayspapayanyc.com; 2090 Broadway, New York, NY; GPS 40.7783, -73.9816*).

» Hot dogs may be a German import to New York, but the city's other immigrant groups have transformed the hot dog into something entirely new. AsiaDog in Brooklyn adds the flavors of China, Korea, Vietnam, and Japan. Forget sauerkraut: think kimchi, curry, pâté, and seaweed instead (*asiadognyc.com; 899 Bergen St., Brooklyn, NY; GPS 40.6773, -73.9573*).

35 BEEF ON WECK

Beef on weck is western New York's shorthand for a sandwich that's so much more than three short syllables. The "beef": thinly sliced, slow-roasted, hand-carved, rosy-rare roast beef. The "weck": a soft, fluffy, golden-domed *kümmelweck*, a roll liberally coated in crunchy kosher salt and pungent, licorice-scented caraway seeds. The beef is folded onto the bottom of the roll, and the underside of the top of the roll is dipped lightly in the meat's juices. Serve with a heaping spoonful of horseradish and a pickle, please.

Where to Try It

» You can find Charlie carving the roast beef at Charlie the Butcher in Buffalo. He's Charlie W. His father was Charlie J. His grandfather, Charlie E. All butchers. The family has been cutting meat for customers since 1914 and Charlie's beef on weck—with extra au jus—is the must-order. Celebrate your birthday at Charlie's with a freebie (*charliethebutcher.com; flagship location: 1065 Wehrle Dr., Williamsville, NY; GPS 42.9494, -78.7450*).

» According to local lore, a tavern owner invented beef on weck, with its salty roll, to encourage patrons to drink more. It might have been a spot like Bar Bill Tavern in East Aurora, a comfortable, casual, and always-packed pub. Get there early: they only serve beef on weck until 9 p.m. (*barbill.com; 185 Main St., East Aurora, NY; GPS 42.7675, -78.6279*).

» Schwabl's has been serving the Buffalo region since 1837. On almost every table, you'll see the restaurant's sizable beef on weck with a side of German potato salad and a jar of horseradish (*schwabls.com; 789 Center Rd., West Seneca, NY; GPS 42.8393, -78.7534*).

36 ORANGE COUNTY APPLE PIE TRAIL

New York is plenty proud of its apples—more than ten million apple trees bear fruit each fall. But Orange County, in the state's Hudson Valley, knows there is something better than a fresh-picked apple: fresh-baked apple pie. (The state produces enough apples annually to bake 500 million pies!) The Orange County Apple Pie Trail—really four wanders, through each quadrant of the county—starts just 60 miles from Times Square and tours through many of the state's most scenic orchards and vineyards (*www.orangetourism.org/themed-adventures*).

Where to Try It

Highlights along the Apple Pie Trail:

» Soons Orchards in New Hampton is home to Scotty's Country Kitchen, where the farm's apples and fresh-pressed cider are sandwiched in hand-rolled dough to create mile-high pies (*soonsorchards.com; 23 Soons Cir., New Hampton, NY; GPS 41.4026, -74.4035*).

» Pennings Farm in Warwick is home to a pub and grill (serving the orchard's own hard cider) and a farm market that offers five different varieties of apple pie during the holidays (*penningsfarmmarket.com; 161 Rte. 94, Warwick, NY; GPS 41.2356, -74.3831*).

» This is the Apple Pie Trail, and Warwick's Masker Orchards delivers on that promise, but the real treat at the 100-plus-year-old farm is the apple blossom, an individual-size pie of diced apples wrapped in a sweet-salty pastry shell dotted with sugar (*maskers.com; 45 Ball Rd., Warwick, NY; GPS 41.2428, -74.3475*).

Specialty of the House

The "buffalo" in **buffalo wings** is not meant to indicate "spicy," but refers to the city in New York State where the wings were invented in the 1960s. Credit goes to the Anchor Bar, which 50 years later is still serving up buckets of fried, hot sauce–doused wings (*anchorbar.com; flagship location: 1047 Main St., Buffalo, NY; GPS 42.9534, -78.8183*).

A stack of Nathan's hot dogs is bound for the annual Hot Dog Eating Contest in Coney Island, New York.

MID-ATLANTIC

Maryland crab, Virginia ham, Delaware chicken, Pennsylvania Dutch dishes, and Old World colonial cooking have all shaped mid-Atlantic cuisine.

PENNSYLVANIA
48–55

NEW JERSEY
55–61

DELAWARE
61–64

MARYLAND
65–71

DISTRICT OF COLUMBIA
71–76

VIRGINIA
76–80

WEST VIRGINIA
80–85

Head to Maryland, unofficial kingdom of the crab, to get soft-shells coated in cornmeal, deep-fried, and served with lemon.

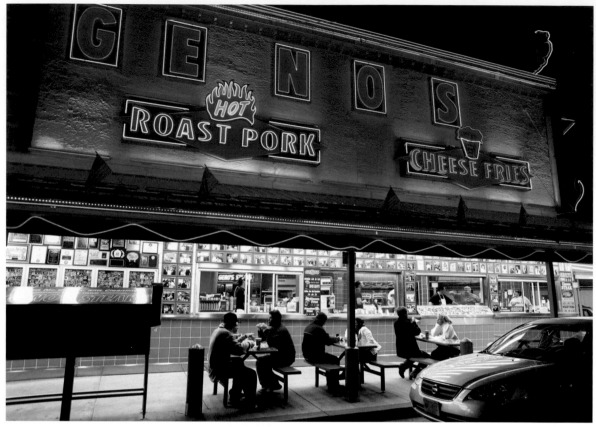

Geno's Steaks has been vying for more than 50 years for the title of Philadelphia's best cheesesteak maker.

★ PENNSYLVANIA ★

37 CHEESESTEAK

For decades, two Philadelphia legends have battled for the title of best cheesesteak in town: Pat's King of Steaks versus Geno's Steaks. Handily enough, the two shops are right across the street from each other.

Pat and Harry Olivieri were brothers and South Philadelphia hot dog vendors when one day in 1930, Harry decided to sub a dog with some beef on the grill for his own lunch. A customer who saw the sandwich asked if he could have one, too. Word spread, and soon the Olivieris opened Pat's King of Steaks (named for Pat, who was older) to sell the sandwiches. They eventually added cheese, and a legend was born.

In 1966, Joey Vento opened Geno's Steaks across the street and also began serving cheesesteaks. For half a century, the two restaurants have been locked in a friendly rivalry—though Joey insisted that the addition of cheese to the sandwich was his brain-child. Now run by the descendants of their respective founders, both shops sizzle 24 hours a day, producing the finest of Philly cheesesteaks: thin-sliced rib eye, grilled onions, and cheese (provolone or American cheese is traditional, but Cheez Whiz is the standout favorite). And most Philly cheesesteaks are served on long rolls from Philadelphia's Amoroso's bakery.

Where to Try It

≫ Try to choose between the aforementioned standard-bearers (or not, and have both): Pat's King of Steaks (*patskingofsteaks.com; 1237 E. Passyunk Ave., Philadelphia, PA; GPS 39.9332, -75.1592*) and Geno's Steaks (*genosteaks.com; 1219 S. 9th St., Phila-delphia, PA; GPS 39.9338, -75.1588*), diagonally across the street.

» Along with Pat's and Geno's, Jim's Steaks South Street is considered one of the Big Three. The location at 400 South St. is the most popular, with lines stretching out the door and around the corner *(jims southstreet.com; 400 South St., Philadelphia, PA; GPS 39.9415, -75.1493)*.

» Other Philly hot spots that serve a mean cheesesteak are John's Roast Pork *(johnsroastpork.com; 14 E. Snyder Ave., Philadelphia, PA; GPS 39.9211, -75.1450)*, opened in 1930, a favorite of South Philadelphia dockworkers; Dalessandro's Steaks & Hoagies *(dalessandros.com; 600 Wendover St., Philadelphia, PA; GPS 40.0295, -75.2059)*; and McNally's *(mcnallystavern.com; 8634 Germantown Ave., Philadelphia, PA; GPS 40.0771, -75.2089)*, famed for the Schmitter—its cheesesteak variation that adds grilled salami, grilled tomatoes, and special sauce.

38 PENNSYLVANIA PEPPER POT SOUP

The winter of 1777 was brutal for Gen. George Washington and his Continental Army. For months the soldiers camped in Valley Forge, outside of Philadelphia, suffering lack of food and shelter, while they waited for spring to battle the British. According to legend, Washington commanded his baker general to create a dish that would "warm and strengthen the body of a soldier and inspire his flagging spirit." The cook improvised a stew using vegetable scraps, the few spices he had at hand, and tripe, the stomach lining of a cow. The savory stew reportedly revived and sustained the downtrodden army through that dark winter, helping lead to its eventual victory in the American Revolutionary War.

In truth, this patriotic tale is likely apocryphal. It's more probable that slaves or freedmen in Philadelphia

Philadelphia's City Tavern Restaurant, where you can still get pepper pot soup

brought the spicy broth from the Caribbean to America.

Regardless, pepper pot soup became a wildly popular, iconic Philadelphia dish. Nineteenth-century street hawkers chanted, "All hot! All hot! Pepper pot! Pepper pot!" to entice passersby. An 1811 painting of the Philadelphia Market depicts a cook ladling out the stew to eager customers. Campbell's Soup produced a canned version, and Andy Warhol featured it in his famed 1960s silkscreen paintings.

Alas, true pepper pot with tripe has all but disappeared. Campbell's discontinued its version, and hardly any restaurants still offer it, even in Philadelphia. Many Pennsylvanians who remember the soup from their youth keep the tradition alive by making their own.

Where to Try It

» The historic City Tavern Restaurant in downtown Philadelphia is one of the few restaurants with pepper pot still on the menu—although without the distinctive tripe. It serves a tasty West Indies version with spicy beef, taro root, and greens *(citytavern.com; 138 S. 2nd St., Philadelphia, PA; GPS 39.9471, -75.1445)*.

» The food company Bookbinder Specialties sells a canned seafood pepper pot soup that can be ordered online. Its thick, spicy, tomato based stew contains cod, carrots, onions, and macaroni *(bookbinderspecialties.com)*.

» Occasionally, a Philly restaurant will revive pepper pot. Check out *philly .eater.com* for such announcements. Recently, Davio's briefly offered a special of the classic (tripe and all) for $11 a bowl *(davios.com; 111 S. 17th St., Philadelphia, PA; GPS 39.9510, -75.1688)*.

» To make the soup yourself, you can find a recipe on Philadelphia's JNA Institute of Culinary Arts website *(culinaryarts.com)*.

In Philly cheesesteak parlance, *"whiz wit"* means with Cheese Whiz and fried onions.

39 PRETZELS

Both soft and hard pretzels are a legacy of the Pennsylvania Dutch, who sell their hand-rolled creations in countryside bakeries and farmers markets. The first American pretzels were reportedly sold in Philadelphia as early as the 1820s, but they went large-scale in the 1850s, the story goes, when bread baker Ambrose Roth was given a pretzel recipe by a passing traveler in return for a hot meal. Roth passed it on to his apprentice, Julius Sturgis, who went on to establish the country's first commercial pretzel bakery. Pretzels have been big business in Pennsylvania ever since—the state produces 80 percent of the nation's pretzels.

Philadelphians adore the city's soft pretzels, which are shaped in a figure eight. The pretzels, sold on street corners, are usually lightly salted and topped with yellow mustard. National brand Auntie Anne's *(auntieannes.com)* got its start in 1988 when Anne Beiler began selling her pretzels in a Pennsylvania farmers market.

Where to Try It

≫ In Philadelphia, look for pretzels being sold on the street during rush hour, either out of metal lunch carts or from vendors who've packaged them in brown paper bags. You can also head for downtown's Reading Terminal Market to pick up big, brown, salty, soft pretzels at Miller's Twist stall *(millerstwist.com; 51 N. 12th St., Philadelphia, PA; GPS 39.9539, -75.1594).*

≫ The Julius Sturgis Pretzel Bakery in Lititz is still run by Sturgis's descendants. Visitors can tour the 19th-century pretzel bakery and get a hands-on lesson in pretzel twisting *(juliussturgis.com; 219 E. Main St., Lititz, PA; GPS 40.1565, -76.3013).*

≫ Sample hand-rolled, freshly made Amish pretzels at bakeries such as Stoltzfus Bakery in Ardmore

Hershey's Chocolate World, mecca of America's chocolate lovers, offers tours of the hallowed candy factory.

(120 Coulter Ave., Ardmore, PA; GPS 40.0077, -75.2860), right outside Philadelphia; and at Hammond Pretzel Bakery (hammondpretzels.com; 716 S. West End Ave., Lancaster, PA; GPS 40.0301, -76.3240) and Immergut Hand-Rolled Soft Pretzels (3537 Old Philadelphia Pike, Intercourse, PA; GPS 40.0384, -76.1086), both in Lancaster County.

40 HERSHEY'S & PENNSYLVANIA CHOCOLATE

After discovering chocolate making during the 1893 World's Columbian Exposition in Chicago, candymaker Milton S. Hershey decided to experiment with adding chocolate coating to his caramels. He soon jumped entirely into the business of chocolate, prophetically declaring, "Caramels are only a fad. Chocolate is a permanent thing."

Hershey built his new factory among the rolling farmlands near his hometown in rural central Pennsylvania, close to many dairy farms that could provide the milk essential for his process of making milk chocolate.

The first Hershey's milk chocolate bar was produced in 1900; the first Hershey's Kiss debuted in 1907. The town he helped to develop adopted his name, and as the headquarters of the Hershey Company, Hershey, Pennsylvania, is frequently called "Chocolatetown, U.S.A." and "the sweetest place on Earth."

Where to Try It

≫ Hershey is 15 miles east of Harrisburg. As part of the many attractions of Hershey's Chocolate World, visitors can tour the immense factory, taste chocolate from around the globe, and create their own candy bars. Be sure to look for the town's iconic Hershey's Kiss–shaped lampposts (hersheys.com; 251 Park Blvd., Hershey, PA; GPS 40.2882, -76.6604).

≫ Hershey's isn't the only homegrown candy company in Pennsylvania. Wilbur Buds were invented in 1894. Stop by the Wilbur Chocolate Company candy store and museum in Lititz to sample the bite-size chocolates

Specialty of the House

Reese's Peanut Butter Cups, enormously popular throughout the country, also got their start in Hershey, Pennsylvania. Harry Burnett Reese began working for the Hershey Company as a dairyman in 1917 and built a factory in 1926 to produce his own candies. The rationing of sugar during World War II led him to focus his resources on his most popular confection: the peanut butter cup.

shaped like flower buds (wilburbuds.com; 48 N. Broad St., Lititz, PA; GPS 40.1585, -76.3080).

≫ Daffin's Candies sells gourmet chocolates at its Factory Chocolate Shoppe in Farrell and other Pennsylvania retail shops (daffins.com; 7 Spearman Ave., Farrell, PA; GPS 41.2033, -80.5021). Meanwhile, Sarris Candies' Chocolate Factory and Ice Cream Parlour covers a full city block in Canonsburg (sarriscandies.com; 511 Adams Ave., Canonsburg, PA; GPS 40.2655, -80.1734).

41 POTATO CHIPS

Pennsylvanians are fiercely opinionated about their favorite chips. Walk into any supermarket in the state,

Continued on p. 54

Hershey's made *more than a billion* chocolate ration bars for U.S. troops during World War II.

A dish born of Dutch frugality, scrapple is baked in loaves, sliced, and fried in pans until it's crispy and hot.

GREAT AMERICAN EATING EXPERIENCES
Old-Fashioned Scrapple

Throughout the mid-Atlantic states, you'll find scrapple alongside your breakfast eggs, or smothered in syrup, ketchup, or apple butter.

Scrapple is not for the squeamish. Traditional recipes that go back to the Pennsylvania Dutch boil together minced pork trimmings, pork broth, cornmeal, buckwheat flour, and spices, most commonly sage, thyme, and black pepper. The trimmings can include virtually anything from the pig—heart, liver, even the snout. The resulting mush is poured into loaf pans, baked into a spongy loaf, sliced, and panfried until crispy.

The dish was a child of economy. The Pennsylvania Dutch believed nothing should go to waste. Not even offal. Instead of tossing scraps of meat and organs left over after butchering hogs, Amish farmers transformed them into scrapple (as in "scraps").

Some of the most well-known commercial producers are Delaware's RAPA Scrapple (*rapa-scrapple.my shopify.com*) and Habbersett (*habbersett-scrapple .myshopify.com*), and Lancaster County, Pennsylvania's Stoltzfus Meats (*stoltzfusmeats.com*), each with its own recipes. Which is best is a subject of fierce debate among area scrapple aficionados.

Local butchers also make and sell their own scrapple, and taste can vary widely depending on who makes it and what, exactly, they throw into it.

≫ Pennsylvania
For home-cooked Amish country scrapple, head to Lancaster County for the real deal. At the White Horse Luncheonette in Gap, a favorite local Amish gathering place, try the breakfast platter with

creamed chipped beef, scrapple, sausage gravy, and eggs (*5562 Old Philadelphia Pike, Gap, PA; GPS 40.0343, -76.0021*).

Philadelphians quickly embraced the savory pork loaf in the 18th century, and it's still wildly popular in the city today. Historic Reading Terminal Market, housing several merchants selling authentic Pennsylvania Dutch foods, celebrates a biennial Scrapplefest, with all-day scrapple tastings and cooking demonstrations. Year-round, the market's Down Home Diner serves market visitors a perfect Philly breakfast of scrapple, eggs, and toast (*readingterminalmarket .org; 12th & Arch Sts., Philadelphia, PA; GPS 39.9533, -75.1591*).

≫ Delaware

Bridgeville, Delaware, home to the nation's largest producer, RAPA Scrapple (*rapa-scrapple.myshopify .com*), goes all out with its annual Apple Scrapple Festival each October. For more than 20 years, the festival has celebrated the area's famed food product with a full weekend of activities, including all-you-can-eat scrapple breakfasts, scrapple carving, and scrapple chunkin'—a shot put–style contest where participants fling packages of scrapple as far as they can (*applescrapple .com; Bridgeville, DE; GPS 38.7427, -75.6047*).

Restaurants statewide have scrapple on hand. For stellar egg, cheese, and scrapple breakfast sandwiches, check out Crystal Restaurant in Rehoboth (*37300 Rehoboth Ave., Rehoboth, DE; GPS 38.7136, -75.0952*).

Even Delaware breweries are getting in on the scrapple action. In Georgetown, the meat company Kirby & Holloway collaborates with 16 Mile Brewery to produce beer-infused scrapple by blending Old Court Ale into its product (*16milebrewery.com; 413 S. Bedford St., Georgetown, DE; GPS 38.6788, -75.3781*). Or take the reverse approach at the Dogfish Head craft brewery in Milton with the new RAPA Scrapple–infused brew named Beer for Breakfast (*dogfish.com; 6 Village Center Blvd., Milton, DE; GPS 38.7706, -75.3109*).

≫ New Jersey

New Jerseyans love their processed meats (see p. 60) and they are a fixture on the menu in the state's famed diners (see pp. 56–57). The Edison Family Restaurant in Edison is the rare diner that makes its own scrapple (*edisonfamilyrestaurant.net; 1900 Oak Tree Rd., Edison, NJ; GPS 40.5731, -74.3608*). In Malaga, at Pegasus Restaurant you can order scrapple with Belgian waffles (*pegasusrestaurant.org; 455 Delsea Dr., Malaga, NJ; GPS 39.5726, -75.0540*). In Mickleton, pick up fresh scrapple to fry at home from Haines Pork Shop, which has quite the history. Enterprising Rachel Haines began making scrapple in the late 1800s to earn money after the Civil War, and her great-great-great-granddaughter still follows her original recipe (*hainesporkshop.com; 521 Kings Hwy., Mickleton, NJ; GPS 39.7893, -75.2404*).

Delicious, versatile scrapple can be served alongside everything from eggs to apples to beer.

Pennsylvania Dutch treats abound at the Kutztown Folk Festival.

(utzsnacks.com); superthin Herr's Crisp 'n Tasty (herrs.com); and Middleswarth's much touted barbecue flavor (middleswarthchips.com). Dieffenbach's (dieffenbachs.com) boasts old-fashioned chips cooked in lard, and Hartley's (hartleyspotatochips.com) has been making kettle-cooked chips since 1935.

» Some markets sell homemade potato chips, including the Allentown Fairgrounds Farmers Market (fairgroundfarmersmkt.com; 17th & Chew Sts., Allentown, PA; GPS 40.6008, -75.4942) and the Lancaster County Farmers Market in Wayne (lancastercountyfarmersmarket.com; 389 W. Lancaster Ave., Wayne, PA; GPS 40.0448, -75.4002).

42 PENNSYLVANIA DUTCH/AMISH FOOD

Shoofly pie, spaetzle, sauerkraut. These are among the simple comfort foods, passed down from generation to generation, that are the staples of Pennsylvania Dutch kitchens.

"Dutch" is an archaic term used to describe people who speak Germanic languages, and this group includes Amish and Mennonite communities that have lived in Pennsylvania for more than 300 years. Their New World history dates back to the early 1700s, when they fled to the colonies to escape persecution in Europe for their Anabaptist beliefs.

Pennsylvania Dutch cooking emphasizes fresh produce grown in the region like asparagus, potatoes, cherries, sweet corn, apples, and lima beans.

and the snack aisle will blow you away. Pennsylvania has a wealth of potato chip brands, with several regional companies (including Hanover's Utz) and more than a dozen smaller companies that make chips for local markets. Hence, the "potato chip belt," a cluster of producers in south-central Pennsylvania that has earned York County, Pennsylvania, its proud moniker as the "snack food capital of the world."

It all comes down to the spuds. Only certain types, chipping potatoes, have the special characteristics to make chips, and Pennsylvania grows more than almost any other state. During the 20th century, families began frying and distributing their own chips, and many of the brands continue to carry their names: Herr's, Martin's, Good's, King's.

Where to Try It

» Choose your favorites by stopping by just about any Pennsylvania supermarket and select several bags to sample the state's chips. Among them: salty Utz chips

Specialty of the House

✕ Although **whoopie pies** are most commonly associated with New England, especially Maine (see pp. 12–13), the Pennsylvania Dutch make a strong case for having created the chocolate cake sandwich with cream filling from leftover cake batter. The annual Whoopie Pie Festival, held at the Hershey Farm Restaurant & Inn in Lancaster County, features more than 100 different whoopie pie flavors and an eating contest (whoopiepiefestival.com; 240 Hartman Bridge Rd., Ronks, PA; GPS 39.9999, -76.1841).

Among the favorite dishes commonly found at regional dining tables are the aforementioned gooey, molasses shoofly pie; spaetzle, a German side dish of tiny noodles or dumplings; and sauerkraut, thin-sliced, brined and fermented cabbage often served alongside pork.

Where to Try It

» Lancaster County is the heart of Pennsylvania Amish country. The area boasts many restaurants serving authentic Pennsylvania Dutch dishes. The award-winning Plain & Fancy restaurant, in the picturesque town of Bird-in-Hand, offers an Amish Farm Feast where diners eat family style, sharing a host of traditional dishes including chicken potpie and shoofly pie (*plainandfancyfarm.com; 3121 Old Philadelphia Pike, Bird-in-Hand, PA; GPS 40.0392, -76.1417*).

» Other standouts include Hometown Kitchen in Quarryville (*eatathometown.com; 18 Furnace Rd., Quarryville, PA; GPS 39.9374, -76.0850*) and Dienner's Country Restaurant in Ronks (*dienners.us; 2855 Lincoln Hwy. E., Ronks, PA; GPS 40.0159, -76.1589*).

» Head to the summertime Kutztown Folk Festival for a traditional Pennsylvania Dutch ox roast—a 1,200-pound animal cooked all day over a spit and then carved up and served to festivalgoers (*kutztownfestival.com; 225 N. Whiteoak St., Kutztown, PA; GPS 40.5184, -75.7844*).

★ NEW JERSEY ★

43 SALTWATER TAFFY

Sticky, chewy, gooey, colorful bits of delight: No food symbolizes the Jersey Shore's carnival atmosphere more than saltwater taffy, a boardwalk staple for more than 100 years.

The simple ingredients include sugar, salt, corn syrup, butter, water, and flavoring—but no actual seawater, as popular fancy might suppose. According to

Saltwater taffy

legend, a boardwalk candy shop was flooded by ocean water one day in the 1880s. When a child walked in the next morning asking for taffy, the owner joked: "You mean saltwater taffy?" And the name stuck.

Several long-standing companies now offer dozens of flavors—chocolate (the most popular), strawberry, Creamsicle, blue raspberry, peanut butter, and root beer, to name a few.

Where to Try It

» Shriver's Salt Water Taffy & Fudge is the oldest business on the Ocean City, New Jersey, boardwalk—it opened in 1898. It offers 70 flavors, and visitors can watch the taffy being made through a floor-to-ceiling glass window (*shrivers.com; 852 Boardwalk, Ocean City, NJ; GPS 38.2752, -74.5710*). Fralinger's Original Salt Water Taffy is another 100-plus-year-old Ocean City candy and taffy shop (*fralingers.com; 1100 Boardwalk, Ocean City, NJ; GPS 39.2738, -74.5761*).

» In Atlantic City, the star is James' Candy Company (*jamescandy.com; 1519 Boardwalk, Atlantic City, NJ; GPS 39.3567, -74.4268*), dating back to the 1880s.

44 TOMATO PIE

In Trenton, they like to make their pizzas backward. Cheese and toppings go on first, and then comes the tomato sauce. But this is no ordinary sauce—you need thick hunks of seasoned, crushed plum tomatoes that gather in little mounds on the pizza. For tomato pie, the rich, flavorful tomatoes are the star attraction (see p. 41).

The dish originated in the early 20th century, in pizzerias founded by Italian immigrants in Trenton's Chambersburg neighborhood. Papa's Tomato Pies, which opened in 1912, was one of the early purveyors of the dish (*papastomatopies.com; 19 Robbinsville Allentown Rd., Robbinsville, NJ; GPS 40.2153, -74.6240*).

In summer, Shriver's boardwalk shop in Ocean City, New Jersey, churns out *2,200 pounds* of saltwater taffy daily.

Although Papa's and some of Trenton's other beloved pizzerias have migrated to the suburbs, the shops still keep to their cherished recipes and turn out tasty, piping hot tomato pies.

Where to Try It

» Besides Papa's, De Lorenzo's is the other heavyweight in tomato pies, and has been serving its crispy-crust specialty topped with bold, juicy tomatoes since 1938 (*delorenzostomatopies.com; 2350 Rte. 33 #105, Robbinsville, NJ; GPS 40.2183, -74.6273*; and *delorenzospizza.com; 147 Sloan Ave., Hamilton, NJ; GPS 40.2495, -74.6892*).
» In Bordentown, just outside Trenton, Palermo's Restaurant & Pizzeria serves pies with sweet tomatoes seasoned with oregano (*palermostomatopie.com; flagship location: 674 Rte. 206S, Bordentown, NJ; GPS 40.1696, -74.7001*).
» Pete's Steak House and Tavern in Hamilton offers authentic tomato pies that you can order with sausage (*petessteakhouse.com; 523 Whitehorse Ave., Hamilton, NJ; GPS 40.1978, -74.6997*).

45 DINERS

New Jersey is known as the "diner capital of the world" and for good reason: There are some 600 diners here, more than in any other state in the nation. You can find them everywhere, from big cities and small towns to country roads and along highways.

These simple, classic American restaurants are woven into the very fabric of New Jersey's history and culture. Positioned between the buzzing East Coast metropolises of Philadelphia and New York City, New Jersey diners were destined to thrive as way stations for hordes of hungry travelers.

Beginning as lunch wagons around 1910, diners gradually evolved into iconic narrow, stainless steel–sided structures sporting brilliant neon signs. Although many Jersey diners have now adopted a

House-made desserts—classic New Jersey diner offerings

Hiram's Roadstand in Fort Lee, New Jersey, has been in the business of selling hot dogs since 1930.

more traditional restaurant design, they still serve as prime community hangouts and offer menus packed with all-American staples, from a full breakfast menu to milkshakes, cheeseburgers, and ice-cream sundaes. Every New Jerseyan has a favorite diner.

Where to Try It

» The rather upscale Americana Diner in East Windsor is frequently named as New Jersey's best diner. It has a stylish art deco–inspired, 1950s-retro design, and its homemade breads take the form of fluffy Belgian waffles or bagels deluxe with house-smoked salmon (americanadiner.com; 359 U.S. 130, East Windsor, NJ; GPS 40.2757, -74.5349).

» Mustache Bill's Diner, on the Jersey Shore in Barnegat Light, serves juicy hamburgers and homemade potato salad and coleslaw, as well as seaside entrées such as scallops and grilled shrimp (8th St. & Broadway, Barnegat Light, NJ; GPS 39.7583, -74.1071).

» Be sure to try the famous homemade pasta salad at the Mark Twain Diner & Restaurant in Union made from a secret recipe. The desserts are also baked in-house—don't miss the cheesecake or the nut horns, crispy pastries stuffed with almond paste (marktwaindinernj.com; 1601 Morris Ave., Union, NJ; GPS 40.6923, -74.2542).

» The Tropicana Diner & Bakery in Elizabeth lives up to its name with island-themed decor (including palm tree murals) and plenty of Caribbean seafood specialties along with straight-up diner fare (tropicanadiner.com; 545 Morris Ave., Elizabeth, NJ; GPS 40.6737, -74.2236).

» Locals rave about the fresh-baked goods and huge portions at Mastoris in Bordentown. Get the French toast, made with the diner's own cheese bread (mastoris.com; 144 U.S. 130, Bordentown, NJ; GPS 40.1543, -74.6990).

46 HOT DOGS

Northern New Jersey is hot dog heaven. The area is full of hole-in-the-wall joints serving thick, juicy hot dogs heaped with toppings.

For over 80 years, New Jerseyans have scarfed down three varieties in particular: rippers, Texas wieners, and the Italian hot dog. Rippers date to 1928, when Royal Rutt, of Rutt's Hut in Clifton began deep-frying his pork and beef hot dogs until they split (or *ripped*). The hot Texas wiener, a chili dog topped with chili sauce, onions, and mustard, was—never mind the name—created in Paterson, New Jersey. And Jimmy Buff's invented the Italian hot dog: a loaf

Vintage cars are a fitting accessory for New Jersey's classic Bendix Diner, built in the 1940s.

of pizza bread stuffed with one or two deep-fried hot dogs and topped with onions, peppers, and fried potatoes.

Where to Try It

» Rutt's Hut in Clifton still uses its original process of frying the dogs and slathers the rippers in its famous relish, made with a secret blend of mustard and spices *(ruttshut.com; 417 River Rd., Clifton, NJ; GPS 40.8270, -74.1238).*

» Check out the following joints for stellar Texas wieners: The Hot Grill in Clifton *(thehotgrill.org; 669 Lexington Ave., Clifton, NJ; GPS 40.8840, -74.1331)*; Hiram's Roadstand in Fort Lee *(1345 Palisade Ave., Fort Lee, NJ; GPS 40.8416, -73.9747)*; and Libby's Lunch in Paterson *(98 McBride Ave., Paterson, NJ; GPS 40.9142, -74.1819).*

» Besides Jimmy Buff's *(jimmybuff.com; multiple locations)*, Tommy's Italian Sausage & Hot Dogs in Elizabeth *(900 2nd Ave., Elizabeth, NJ; GPS 40.6593, -74.2053)* also serves a mighty Italian dog. Instead of grilling the

A Taylor pork roll sandwich

thin-sliced potatoes, the cook drops them in a deep fryer to get them nice and crispy before stuffing them into the pizza bread bun.

47 TAYLOR PORK ROLL

New Jersey may be the Garden State, but that doesn't prevent locals from loving pork roll—cylindrical, processed, and packed pork originally created by Trenton native John Taylor back in 1856. Many North Jersey residents call pork roll Taylor ham, and Trenton remains the world headquarters of the pork roll—it's still made there.

Generally sliced and panfried or grilled, the salty, greasy meat is most commonly eaten as part of a hugely popular breakfast sandwich in New Jersey. Hop off any exit on the Jersey Turnpike and you'll likely have no problem finding a diner, convenience store, or street cart selling a "Taylor ham, egg, and cheese," slices of fried pork roll topped with a fried egg and American cheese, all served on a kaiser roll or bagel.

Where to Try It

» A town landmark since 1929, the Summit Diner in Summit offers up a fabulous breakfast sandwich with crispy pork roll, eggs, and molten cheese on fresh-baked bread *(1 Union Pl., Summit, NJ; GPS 40.7170, -74.3563).*

» Olde Towne Deli in Boonton uses Thumann's Jersey Made pork roll (leaner than Taylor ham) in its sandwiches served on crusty rolls *(205 Main St., Boonton Township, NJ; GPS 40.9030, -74.4075).*

» In Fredon customers at the Fredon Deli can order their pork roll sandwich with additional meats—including scrapple, another Jersey favorite (see pp. 52–53) *(fredondeli.com; 428 Rte. 94, Fredon, NJ; GPS 41.0404, -74.8081).*

» The Bagel Chateau in Westfield goes through about 100 pounds of Taylor ham every week for its best-selling sandwich on a bagel *(bagelchateau.com; 223 S. Avenue E., Westfield, NJ; GPS 40.6499, -74.3400).*

» Trenton recently inaugurated the annual Pork Roll Festival to celebrate its unique culinary contribution. Vendors sell their favorite pork roll creations against a background of live music *(porkrollfestival.com; Trenton, NJ; GPS 40.2184, -74.7626).*

Delaware's fresh oysters are often battered, sizzled up, and eaten on a po'boy.

48 DISCO FRIES

What do you eat if you're from New Jersey and you're hungry for a late-night bite? Disco fries, of course. (So named, some speculate, because the snack is a party favorite.) They're a mainstay on New Jersey diner menus (see pp. 56–57).

Similar to Canadian *poutine* (fries layered with cheese curds and gravy; see p. 14), the calorie-laden—but delicious—grub is composed of french fries smothered in brown gravy and melted cheese. Mozzarella is most common, but you'll also find disco fries topped with cheddar or American.

Where to Try It

» Tick Tock Diner in Clifton serves disco fries 24/7. Slathered with gravy and mozzarella, they're frequently called the best disco fries in New Jersey (*theticktock diner.com; 281 Allwood Rd., Clifton, NJ; GPS 40.8369, -74.1523*).
» Known locally as BLD, Budd Lake Diner also does mozzarella on its disco fries (*120 U.S. 46, Budd Lake, NJ; GPS 40.8821, -74.7316*).
» Locals who swear by Suburban Diner in Paramus cite its disco fries as simply their favorite food

(*suburbandiner17.com; 172 Rte. 17, Paramus, NJ; GPS 40.9324, -74.0702*).
» The Pompton Queen Diner in Pompton Plains boasts a whopping 13-page menu of diner classics, including disco fries, chicken gyros, and banana splits (*pompton queendiner.com; 710 Rte. 23, Pompton Plains, NJ; GPS 40.9747, -74.2885*).

★ DELAWARE ★

49 FRIED OYSTERS

Delaware Bay has long been prime oystering territory. Bordered by Delaware and New Jersey, the bay's prized shellfish have formed an essential part of the area's economy and food supply for over 200 years. Though the once robust oyster population declined sharply during the second half of the 20th century, it is rebounding thanks to restoration efforts.

Oysters from near the mouth of the bay tend to taste briny and nutty, while inner bay oysters have a milder, sweeter flavor. Locals love to down platters of deep-fried, battered oysters, and a favorite sandwich

A heaping, heavy (at least a pound) bucket of Thrasher's famous vinegar-drizzled fries

is a fried oyster po'boy, stuffed with plump shellfish and a variety of toppings.

Where to Try It

» Henlopen City Oyster House in Rehoboth Beach carries fresh oysters for its raw bar, and serves huge, perfectly done fried oysters (*hcoysterhouse.com; 50 Wilmington Ave., Rehoboth Beach, DE; GPS 38.7151, -75.0809*).

» In New Castle, Alex's Seafood Restaurant & Clam Bar is famed for its superfresh seafood, including oysters on the half shell, oyster stew, and a lightly battered oyster sandwich with tartar sauce (*alexsseafood.com; 110 N. Dupont Pkwy., New Castle, DE; GPS 39.6665, -75.6003*).

» For more than 40 years, Feby's Fishery in Wilmington has served fresh-off-the-boat seafood. Keep an eye out for the excellent value daily specials, and try the fried oyster sandwich—or the oysters Rockefeller if you're feeling fancy (*febysfishery.com; 3701 Lancaster Pike, Wilmington, DE; GPS 39.7550, -75.5941*).

» Check out the Northeast Seafood Kitchen in Ocean View, whose ever changing menu sometimes includes baked Sweet Jesus oysters—a special variety cooked with baby kale, smoked ham, and Vermont cheddar (*northeastseafoodkitchen.com; 29 Atlantic Ave., Ocean View, DE; GPS 38.5435, -75.0867*).

Surprise

More than 1,000 miles from New Orleans, you can find **authentic Creole-Cajun cuisine** in the small town of Milton, Delaware. Po'boys Creole & Fresh Catch restaurant isn't much to look at, but the food is a knockout: rich, spiced gumbo, jambalaya, blackened fish, greens, and more. Try the Zydeco po'boy, bursting with a crab cake, fried shrimp, and fried Delaware oysters (*poboyscreole.com; 900 Palmer St., Milton, DE; GPS 38.7887, -75.3104*).

50 VINEGAR FRENCH FRIES

After a long day lounging on Delaware's broad, sandy beaches, the ultimate boardwalk treat is vinegar french fries, a go-to snack with a unique, puckery flair. Crispy on the outside, hot and fluffy on the inside, with a splash of vinegar on top is the way locals like it when it comes to their beloved fries. Inland, vinegar fries are popular, too. Just about every diner and fast-food restaurant in the state places a bottle of vinegar on the table for customers to drizzle on their fried spuds.

Where to Try It

» When it comes to Delaware vinegar french fries, Thrasher's is the gold standard. The iconic shop has been an Ocean City boardwalk staple since 1929, and was so popular that it eventually expanded onto the Delaware shore. Just look for the crowd. You can't go half in—Thrasher's fresh-cut, twice-fried, and vinegar-dunked fries come in buckets, and the smallest size is a pound. And don't even think about adding ketchup: Thrasher's won't provide it. The only sauce allowed here is apple cider vinegar (thrashersrehoboth.com; multiple locations in Delaware).

» DB Fries in Bethany Beach also offers up delicious, piping hot vinegar french fries, along with skillfully prepared fresh seafood. Their version of the fries is simmered in peanut oil, and diners can dump on Cajun seasoning or Old Bay, in addition to the essential vinegar (100 Garfield Pkwy., Bethany Beach, DE; GPS 38.5381, -75.0555).

Surprise

It sounds like a dubious combination: pretzels, cream cheese, and red Jell-O, neatly layered together. But Delaware, especially Sussex County, is crazy for **pretzel salad**. Fans insist that the odd mix makes for a surprisingly tasty side dish. Find it on menus around the state, including at the Georgia House (eatgh.com; multiple locations).

51 FROZEN CUSTARD

Delaware's extensive boardwalks attract hordes of strolling beachcombers scarfing down the refreshing, special treats of summer. And nowhere is frozen custard, born at the beach, more beloved.

Among the most popular boardwalk stops is the dessert's originator, Kohr Brothers Frozen Custard. In 1919, ice-cream vendors Archie, Elton, and Lester Kohr first discovered that adding egg yolks to their ice-cream recipe made for a silky, creamy frozen dessert that stayed chilled longer in the warm, salty ocean air. The light, fluffy product "tasted just like a custard," they found. On their first weekend peddling it from their small booth on the Coney Island, New York, boardwalk, the brothers sold more than 18,000 cones at a nickel apiece.

Other ice-cream makers adopted the dessert. Today, you'll find Kohr Brothers and other frozen custard

Frozen custard

stands dotting the mid-Atlantic coast, and Delaware boasts a healthy concentration.

Where to Try It

» Kohr Brothers has several shops in Delaware, including on the mile-long Rehoboth Beach boardwalk, first built in 1873. It also has shops in New Jersey, Maryland, and Virginia (*kohrbros.com; Rehoboth boardwalk stand: 111 S. Boardwalk, Rehoboth Beach, DE; GPS 38.7129, -75.0757*).

» Dickey's Frozen Custard serves generous portions of rich, creamy custard in Bethany Beach, known as the "quiet resort" because most beachgoers head to Rehoboth (*seasonal; 97 Garfield Pkwy., Bethany Beach, DE; GPS 38.5388, -75.0545*).

» In New Castle, the Dairy Palace dishes up frozen custard each summer from late March to early October (*2 Jay Dr., New Castle, DE; GPS 39.6862, -75.5941*).

Chicken and slippery dumplings are a Delaware classic.

52 CHICKEN DISHES

Delaware is a chicken-loving state. It's true the mascot and state bird of the Blue Hen State is more symbolic than real—it traces its origin to fighting gamecocks that Delaware Revolutionary War soldiers supposedly carried into battle, and it isn't officially recognized as a breed.

But even with the blue hen relegated to nostalgic lore, poultry is a big deal in Delaware. The big and juicy broiler chicken makes up a fat 70 percent of the state's annual agricultural production, and Sussex County, Delaware, remains the largest broiler-producing county in the United States.

According to legend, in the 1920s a Sussex County woman ordered 50 chicks to sell as meat—and mistakenly received 500. The enterprising farmwife made such a profit off her big chickens that within a few years she'd built a shed to hold 10,000 of them. And so was born Delaware's chicken market.

All sorts of chicken dishes anchor Delaware menus, but a local favorite is chicken and dumplings. The soothing stew combines simmered chicken, celery, onion, and gravy with slippery dumplings—thin, large rectangles cut from dough and dropped into the boiling broth. It's the ultimate in comfort food.

Where to Try It

» Rudy's Family Restaurant in Harrington serves all-you-can-eat chicken-and-dumpling meals on Wednesdays and Sundays, and they offer many other chicken dishes, including a broiled half spring chicken served with scampi sauce (*rudysofharrington.com; 17064 S. Dupont Hwy., Harrington, DE; GPS 38.9255, -75.5682*).

» Hall's Family Restaurant, in Wyoming, Delaware, is a must for hearty home-cooked food, especially its chicken and dumplings, meatloaf, and sauerkraut, and homemade pies. Devoted regulars pop in for meals several times a week (*108 N. Railroad Ave., Wyoming, DE; GPS 39.1200, -75.5584*).

» In Bridgeville, Jimmy's Grille is acclaimed for its down-home cooking and offers chicken and slippery dumpling specials half the week. Don't miss the fried chicken—another house specialty—and the massive cinnamon rolls (*jimmysgrille.org; 18541 S. Main St., Bridgeville, DE; GPS 38.7282, -75.5923*).

Maryland's market-fresh crab cakes are mixed with seasonings like Old Bay and Worcestershire sauce.

★ MARYLAND ★

53 CRAB CAKES

Crab cakes are, without question, Maryland's favorite food. Residents adore the state's plump patties, made with blue crabs fished mostly from the Chesapeake Bay. Fresh crabmeat is mixed with ingredients like bread crumbs, onions, eggs, mayonnaise, Worcestershire sauce, and Old Bay seasoning, made into patties, and then broiled, sautéed, or breaded and deep-fried. Served on a platter or in a sandwich, the thick, moist cakes don't stay around for long.

Where to Try It

≫ Baltimore is the epicenter of Maryland crab cake culture. Near the Inner Harbor, Faidley Seafood's golden, delicately spiced crab cakes define the dish for Baltimoreans (faidleyscrabcakes.com; 203 N. Paca St., Baltimore, MD; GPS 39.2919, -76.6222). Find Faidley Seafood in the bustling, 200-plus-year-old Lexington Market (lexingtonmarket.com).

Continued on p. 68

Basic Ingredient

Translated from Latin and Greek, the **blue crab**'s scientific name, *Callinectes sapidus,* means "savory beautiful swimmer." Male crabs have blue claws; females have red-tipped ones. The blue crab ranges from Nova Scotia to Uruguay along the Atlantic coast, and forms the most economically valuable fishery in the Chesapeake Bay. Fishermen usually catch them with simple gear like a hand line or a dip net.

Bottles of hard cider stand at the ready at Harvest Moon Cidery in Cazenovia, New York.

GREAT AMERICAN EATING EXPERIENCES
Hard Cider

The once common pleasure of drinking a glass of sparkling, hard cider that pretty much vanished with Prohibition is making a big comeback in the hills and orchards of the mid-Atlantic, Northeast, and Midwest.

The American tradition of fermenting apples into hard cider started with the earliest English settlers in the 17th century. The English carefully transported saplings and seeds to the New World for the express purpose of making cider, a staple of daily colonial life when water was often considered unsafe to drink and beer was harder to make. Hard cider could be found on every family table, and homesteads throughout the original colonies had orchards to grow multiple apple varieties for baking, eating, and pressing and fermenting into cider.

Today, artisanal producers in apple country are rediscovering surviving varieties of heirloom cider apples. Their ciders vary widely in flavor, depending on the blend of apples, ranging from dry to sweet, still to sparkling, with about half the alcohol content of wine.

›› Virginia
Virginia, whose apple legacy stretches back to Thomas Jefferson (he planted some 18 varieties of apples), is helping revive hard cider. Not far from

Monticello outside Charlottesville, Albemarle Cider-Works orchard has a tasting room where you can try Jupiter's Legacy cider, named for the Jefferson slave in charge of Monticello's cider production (*albemarleciderworks.com; 2545 Rural Ridge Ln., North Garden, VA; GPS 37.9665, -78.6500*).

Virginia Cider Week in Richmond celebrates the hard stuff in November with tastings and workshops (*ciderweekva.com*). While you're there, visit Blue Bee Cider in the heart of downtown Richmond's Old Manchester district, an urban orchard with tastings of its hard ciders (*bluebeecider.com; 212 W. 6th St., Richmond, VA; GPS 37.5256, -77.4414*).

» New York

The second largest apple producer in the country, New York has more hard cider makers than any other state and is known for its tart cider apples. Dozens of cideries now produce more than 200 kinds.

The state's burgeoning craft cider movement is so big that it throws three weeklong parties to celebrate. At Cider Week Hudson Valley in June there are cider tastings and meals that pair hard ciders with special entrées and cheeses (*ciderweekhv.com*). October's Finger Lakes Cider Week hosts special cider-centric dinners and tastings around the region (*ciderweekflx.com*). And at November's New York Cider Week, there are tastings of top regional craft ciders in bars, restaurants, and shops across the metro area (*ciderweeknyc.com*).

And aside from festivals, plan a visit to Wassail, New York City's first cider bar. It features a wide variety of domestic and imported hard ciders, but with a special focus on New York and New England varieties (*wassailnyc.com; 162 Orchard St., New York, NY; GPS 40.7210, -73.9885*).

» Michigan

Michigan is famed for its apples, with more than nine million apple trees covering 36,500 acres. These days, many Michigan small producers are joining the hard cider movement.

Scrumpy—a traditional English farmhouse style of cider—has been pressed and produced at the family-owned Almar Orchards in Flushing, Michigan, since the 1800s. Today, the family bottles organic J.K.'s Scrumpy (*organicscrumpy.com*) with apples from the same orchards (*almarorchards.com; 1431 Duffield Rd., Flushing, MI; GPS 43.0274, -83.9112*). You can try Virtue Cider's Old World, farmhouse-style hard ciders at its bottle shop and tasting room in Fennville (*virtuecider.com; 2170 62nd St., Fennville, MI; GPS 42.5768, -86.1517*). Tandem Ciders in Suttons Bay leads the charge in cider production in northern Michigan's Leelanau Peninsula. Visit its tasting room for a sip of hard ciders like Smackintosh and Pretty Penny (*tandemciders.com; 2055 N. Setterbo Rd., Suttons Bay, MI; GPS 45.0111, -85.6577*).

» New England

New England was America's first center of hard cider and has been at the forefront of its rebirth. Farnum Hill is virtually synonymous with New Hampshire cider (see p. 16), while Vermont is home to national brand Woodchuck Hard Cider, based in Middlebury. Its new cider house welcomes visitors with a tour of the cidery and free drink samples; the brand's Amber Draft Cider is considered one of the best mass-produced hard ciders (*woodchuck.com; 1321 Exchange St., Middlebury, VT; GPS 44.0358, -73.1663*).

Hard cider's return to the foodie scene couldn't happen without orchards.

» Just up the coast in Middle River, By the Docks Restaurant & Lounge serves mega crab cakes in a dining room with a model lighthouse (bythedocks.com; 3321 Eastern Blvd., Middle River, MD; GPS 39.3373, -76.4046).

54 SOFT-SHELL CRABS

Contrary to common misperception, soft-shell crabs aren't a separate species but rather blue crabs that have just molted. The variety is only available from May to September, during the crabs' molting season. Harvested before their new shells harden, they're a famous Maryland delicacy. Instead of having to laboriously pick out the crabmeat, soft-shell aficionados happily crunch down on the entire crustacean—legs and all. Those not put off by the spiderlike appearance of the crab (this would include just about everyone in Maryland) enjoy the soft-shells best broiled in garlic butter or deep-fried and served on a roll.

Where to Try It

» Smith Island has been home to Chesapeake Bay watermen for 13 generations, and one of the island's specialties is soft-shell crab. Head to the Drum Point Market in Tylerton for a crispy, soft-shell po'boy (drumpointemarket.com; 21162 Center St., Tylerton, MD; GPS 37.9683, -76.0228).

» The soft-shell crabs at Catonsville Gourmet in Catonsville are lightly tempura-battered, fried, and then drizzled with a Creole mustard (catonsvillegourmet.com; 829 Frederick Rd., Catonsville, MD; GPS 39.2712, -76.7350).

» In Annapolis, Lemongrass offers its fried crabs with either a chili, basil, and garlic sauce; a black bean,

Forks and knives are not essential—or even advisable—at many Maryland crab houses.

mushroom, and ginger sauce; or with a choice of curries (*lemongrassannapolis.com; 167 West St., Annapolis, MD; GPS 38.9773, -76.4995*).

» Mike's Crab House in Riva has a waterfront location on the Chesapeake Bay's scenic South River, and dishes up soft-shell crabs in season as part of its extensive menu (*mikescrab house.com; 3030 Riva Rd., Riva, MD; GPS 38.9540, -76.5738*).

This way to Cantler's Riverside Inn in Annapolis, Maryland

55 CRAB HOUSES

One of the best things to do on a hot summer day in Maryland is head to a great waterside crab shack and dig in to a seafood meal.

The state's many crab houses are a world unto themselves: rustic, casual, lined with communal tables. Crabs, of course, are the star attraction. Tables are often covered by heavy brown paper to accommodate mounds of fresh-caught blue crabs. The crustaceans come in heaps and are steamed whole in their shells; tenacious diners pick out every last morsel of crabmeat by hand.

Crabs share some of the spotlight with other locally sourced seafood menu items caught in the Atlantic or Chesapeake Bay, including fish, shrimp, scallops, mussels, oysters, and clams.

Where to Try It

» The Cantler's Riverside Inn is an Annapolis institution. Founder and owner Jimmy Cantler was once a Chesapeake waterman, and for nearly 40 years, his authentic crab house has been hugely popular with locals for its laid-back atmosphere and Jimmy's unique seafood seasoning. Besides the fresh blue crabs, try the seared ahi tuna with seaweed salad (*cantlers.com; 458 Forest Beach Rd., Annapolis, MD; GPS 39.0032, -76.4579*).

» Baltimore's boat-shaped Captain James Seafood Palace has a floating deck overlooking the harbor. Order the all-you-can-eat special that comes with medium-size crabs, crab soup, and corn on the cob (*captainjameslanding.com; 2127 Boston St., Baltimore, MD; GPS 39.2840, -76.5863*).

» Head far off the beaten track to tiny Hoopers Island on Maryland's Eastern Shore to find Old Salty's. Delightfully housed in a converted 1920s schoolhouse, the restaurant serves up massive crab cakes and Ocean City, Maryland, sea scallops (*oldsaltys.com; 2560 Hoopers Island Rd., Fishing Creek, MD; GPS 38.3240, -76.2315*).

Surprise

Maryland isn't just about seafood—locals are also wild for grilled, rare beef. Roadside stands across the state serve up **pit beef**, lean-cut top round grilled over charcoal. Cooks carve thin, juicy slices from the roast and pile them high on sandwiches with horseradish, mayo, and raw onion. Dig in at Pioneer Pit Beef in Woodlawn (*N. Rolling & Johnnycake Rds., Woodlawn, MD; GPS 39.3070, -76.7538*).

56 SMITH ISLAND CAKE

Maryland's official dessert, Smith Island cake, is named for the tiny island in the Chesapeake Bay where it originated in the 1800s. It's a wonder of baked architecture—ten buttery, pancake-thin layers stacked high with chocolate frosting between every tier. Island bakers pour each layer into individual pans, bake them simultaneously, and then quickly assemble the delectably moist cake. Traditional yellow cake with homemade fudge icing will always

Moist, buttery layers slathered with chocolate frosting stack up into a Smith Island cake.

be the favorite of islanders, though other flavors include banana, coconut, and red velvet.

Where to Try It

» To get a proper Smith Island cake, hop on the ferry to the island and visit the Smith Island Baking Company, in Ewell, Maryland. It's the island's only bakery and the primary source of authentic Smith Island cakes. The company also ships them nationwide; or you can order online (smithislandcake.com; 20926 Caleb Jones Rd., Ewell, MD; GPS 37.9948, -76.0302).
» Classic Cakes owner Dana Evans grew up on Smith Island, and her Salisbury, Maryland, bakery sells nine-layer cakes in many flavors (classicsmithislandcakes .com; 1305 S. Division St., Salisbury, MD; GPS 38.3381, -75.5987).

57 ROCKFISH

The rivers and streams feeding the Chesapeake Bay form the spawning grounds for the silver-flanked rockfish, which then spends most of its life out in the Atlantic Ocean. Marylanders love to grill the firm, white fillets or stuff them with crabmeat. Also known as striped bass, they are prized among bay anglers for their size and tenacious fighting ability.

Where to Try It

» The historic Treaty of Paris Restaurant in Annapolis dates back to the Revolutionary War and offers rockfish topped with lump crabmeat in a light white sauce (historicinnsofannapolis.com; 16 Church Cir., Annapolis, MD; GPS 38.9784, -76.4922).

The largest rockfish caught in the Chesapeake Bay clocked in at *67 pounds 8 ounces*.

» The farm-to-table menu of Baltimore's Woodberry Kitchen features fresh-caught rockfish in multiple dishes, including as a starter mixed with mustard greens and pickled cauliflower *(woodberrykitchen.com; 2010 Clipper Park Rd., Baltimore, MD; GPS 39.3320, -76.6456)*.

» At Carrol's Creek Cafe, you can enjoy rockfish on a bed of sautéed spinach, risotto, and jumbo lump crab while sitting outside on the deck, with views of Spa Creek and downtown Annapolis beyond *(carrolscreek .com; 410 Severn Ave., Annapolis, MD; GPS 38.9717, -76.4833)*.

★ DISTRICT OF COLUMBIA ★

58 ETHIOPIAN FOOD

Tens of thousands of Ethiopians now call Washington, D.C., home, forming a vibrant community that some say is second in size only to Addis Ababa's. Civil war, political repression, famine, and the hope for a better life caused hundreds of thousands of Ethiopians and Eritreans to leave their countries between the 1970s and 1990s. Immigrants and refugees immigrated to the District, lured by relatives or friends who had moved to the city for university studies.

The new arrivals brought their home cuisine with them, and many entered the restaurant industry. Thick, spicy stews made with beef, lamb, lentils, potatoes, or carrots, ladled atop *injera*, a spongy sourdough flatbread, mark Ethiopian food. Diners use their hands to eat, scooping up the savory sauces with pieces of injera. Coffee—which may have originated in Ethiopia—is traditionally served after a large meal.

Where to Try It

» The Adams Morgan neighborhood, along D.C.'s 18th Street corridor, is the historic center of the city's Ethiopian restaurant community. Pop into Keren Restaurant on Florida Avenue for a delicious Eritrean breakfast of *fūl* (mashed fava beans topped with tomato, onion, jalapeño, yogurt, olive oil, and berbere, a chili-like spice) *(kerenrestaurant.com; 1780 Florida Ave. NW, Washington, DC; GPS 38.9168, -77.0413)*.

» As rents climbed in Adams Morgan in the 1990s, Ethiopian entrepreneurs began buying and revitalizing properties in the U and H Street neighborhoods. Etete *(eteterestaurant.com; 1942 9th St. NW, Washington, DC; GPS 38.9168, -77.0243)* offers a tasty vegetarian platter with injera, while the signature dish of Dukem Restaurant *(dukemrestaurant.com; 1114–1118 U St. NW, Washington, DC; GPS 38.9168, -77.0279)* is *doro wot*—braised chicken and hardboiled eggs simmered in a thick berbere sauce.

» Sleek Ethiopic Restaurant in the city's burgeoning Atlas District presents delightfully spicy dishes with lamb and yellow lentils *(ethiopicrestaurant.com; 401 H St. NE, Washington, DC; GPS 38.8999, -76.0004)*.

» To sample several different places, try the Little Ethiopia Food Tour from DC Metro Food Tours *(dcmetro foodtours.com)*, a leisurely guided walking trip along

Ethiopian food at Washington, D.C.'s Ethiopic Restaurant

The lunchtime crowd in downtown D.C. throngs Farragut Square and its selection of food trucks.

U Street to Ninth Street NW that explores Ethiopian cuisine and history.

59 HALF-SMOKES

In this city of international travelers and tastes, half-smokes are one of the few foods natively born and bred. The coarsely ground and smoked half-beef, half-pork sausages, flecked with red pepper and piled with any number of toppings (eggs, cheese, onions, chili, you name it), emerged sometime in the 1930s or '40s and quickly became a beloved local snack. They've been described as a cross between a kielbasa and a jumbo hot dog, with spices similar to the Colombian chorizo. But as the name imparts, it's all about the smoke: Smoking the sausages before grilling them gives them a distinct woody flavor.

Where to Try It

» Roadside stand Weenie Beenie, just outside the District in Arlington, Virginia, opened in 1950 and claims to be the home of the original half-smoke. Sample its fully loaded option topped with a runny egg while listening to the Foo Fighters' song "Weenie Beenie"—lead singer Dave Grohl used to live nearby in Alexandria (2680 S. Shirlington Rd., Arlington, VA; GPS 38.8438, -77.0861).

» Iconic D.C. institution Ben's Chili Bowl on U Street has been serving chili half-smokes to customers since 1958. Its quintessential version is a charred spicy half-smoke on a hot dog bun topped with homemade chili, mustard, and diced white onions (benschilibowl.com; 1213 U St. NW, Washington, DC; GPS 38.9172, -77.0287).

» DC-3 on Capitol Hill (eatdc3.com; 423 8th St. SE, Washington, DC; GPS 38.8830, -76.9952) serves a simple version with onions, relish, and yellow mustard, while Bold Bite's Union Station location (boldbite.net; 50 Massachusetts Ave. NE, Washington, DC; GPS 38.8979, -77.0060) offers a wide array of half-smoke options (including one with guacamole) in the food court of D.C.'s historic train station.

» ChurchKey (churchkeydc.com; 1337 14th St. NW, Washington, DC; GPS 38.9085, -77.0313) and Meats & Foods (meatsandfoods.com; 247 Florida Ave. NW, Washington, DC; GPS 38.9138, -77.0156) make their

Half-smokes on the grill at the D.C. classic Ben's Chili Bowl in the city's U Street neighborhood

The Pleasant Pops food truck in D.C. passes a frozen pop to a hungry biker.

half-smokes in-house. ChurchKey's comes with home-made Old Bay pork rinds and spicy pickles, while Meats & Foods tops theirs with onions, beef chili, and seared cheddar.

60 FOOD TRUCKS

Downtown Washington, D.C., is a neat, compact city, where pedestrians flood the streets during the lunch hour looking for a quick bite. By the mid-2000s, the city's army of office workers and Capitol Hill staffers yearned for better street food—more ethnic varieties, seasonal foods, and healthy options. Change fittingly arrived during President Obama's first Inauguration. During that frigid January weekend in 2009, the Fojol Brothers food truck debuted its quirky mix of Indian and Asian dishes on the National Mall.

Spurred on by the rise of Twitter, with which trucks can report their location and movements in real time, more trucks swiftly followed, offering diverse ethnic eats ranging from Mexican to Vietnamese and Korean to Peruvian. Today, roughly 100 trucks roam the District's streets, staking out prime spots during the lunch-hour rush and populating hip late-night neighborhoods to catch the hungry after-hours crowd.

Where to Try It

» Websites such as Food Truck Fiesta *(foodtruckfiesta .com)* and Roaming Hunger *(roaminghunger.com/dc)* track the city's food trucks daily, mapping their locations based on their Tweets. There's also an iPhone app, TruckToMe *(trucktome.com)*.

» Truckeroo is a monthly festival held April through October at the corner of Half Street and M Street SE, across from the Navy Yard metro station. It brings together more than 20 food trucks for a full day of live music, games, and tasty eats *(fairgroundsdc.com /truckeroo; 1201 Half St. SE, Washington, DC; GPS 38.8750, -77.0071)*.

» Locals' favorite trucks include Chatpat Truck for Indian food *(chatpattruck.com)*, TaKorean for Korean tacos *(takorean.com)*, Pho Junkies for Vietnamese noodle soup, Red Hook Lobster Pound for buttery lobster rolls *(redhooklobsterdc.com)*, Rito Loco for immense burritos *(ritoloco.com)*, Halal Grill for juicy gyro and chicken pita sandwiches, and Goodies *(mmmgoodies .com)* for delectable custard and milkshakes.

★VIRGINIA★

61 CORN PUDDING

Corn pudding has been a Virginia staple since colonial times. Today, the rich, thickly textured blend of creamed corn, cornstarch, eggs, milk, and sugar is guaranteed to make an appearance at Virginia family gatherings, holidays, and potluck dinners.

Early settlers quickly adopted corn, which had long been an important part of Native Americans' diet. The hardy crop was relatively easy to grow and better suited to the hilly terrain of Appalachia than wheat or

Corn pudding, a 250-year-old Virginia specialty

barley. Corn could be eaten all year long, either fresh in summer or dried and ground into meal for winter, and settlers added it to many dishes. Due to the long English tradition of enjoying savory custard puddings, corn pudding was a natural development.

In Virginia households, it's been served for centuries with little change in ingredients or preparation, and it is an essential side dish for the Thanksgiving meal today.

Where to Try It

» Gadsby's Tavern, in historic Old Town Alexandria, was founded circa 1792 and was a favorite of Thomas Jefferson and George Washington. It still serves period dishes, including corn pudding, gentleman's "pye" (pie made with game), and English trifle *(gadsbystavern restaurant.com; 134 N. Royal St., Alexandria, VA; GPS 38.8056, -77.0435).*

» Family-owned and operated since 1947, Mrs. Rowe's Restaurant in Staunton, Virginia, offers corn pudding along with its home-style fare like fried chicken and biscuits and gravy *(mrsrowes.net; 74 Rowe Rd., Staunton, VA; GPS 38.1256, -79.0340).*

» On historic Tangier Island in the Chesapeake Bay, Hilda Crockett's Chesapeake House serves its corn pudding hot *(chesapeakehousetangier.com; 16243 Main St., Tangier Island, VA; GPS 37.8252, -75.9916).*

62 VIRGINIA HAM

Like corn pudding (see above), salt-cured Virginia country ham is a culinary mash-up of New World and Old. Native Americans had long preserved venison and fish through smoking, a very different process from the sun drying that Jamestown colonists had used on meat back home in England. The settlers soon adopted the Indian method for hogs they imported to the colony. Farmers would rub the meat with salt (obtained from evaporated seawater), allow it to age for several months, and then smoke the pork over hickory and oak fires.

Nowadays, proper Virginia ham preparation adheres closely to the traditional methods. Packed in salt by hand, the hams can be aged from 45 days to a year before hickory smoking, imparting a robust flavor.

Virginia Smithfield hams hang outside the Taste of Smithfield Restaurant in . . . you guessed it, Smithfield.

Where to Try It

» Smithfield, Virginia, is known as the "ham capital of the world." The colonial town, not far from the historic Jamestown settlement, produces what many consider to be the finest of Virginia country hams. A ham can only earn the coveted moniker "Genuine Smithfield Ham" if it's been processed, smoked, and cured (for a minimum of six months) within the town limits. Visit the Genuine Smithfield Ham Shoppe in the Taste of Smithfield Restaurant (217 Main St., Smithfield, VA; GPS 36.9812, -76.6327) to sample a slice. Then stop by the Smithfield Inn (smithfieldinn.com; 112 Main St., Smithfield, VA; GPS 36.9821, -76.6318) to try one of its special ham rolls, made with thin-sliced Smithfield ham tucked into rolls baked fresh every morning by the same cook for nearly 50 years.

» Edwards Virginia Smokehouse has been smoking, dry curing, and aging ham in the town of Surry since 1926. Founder S. Wallace Edwards (his direct descendants still run the business) started out selling the Wigwam country ham, a salt-cured, hickory-smoked ham aged for a full year and glazed with brown sugar. It's still available on the smokehouse's online store, along with other premier Virginia hams, from Surryano ham—a hand-cured, smoked meat from spotted heritage breed hogs—to brown sugar–cured Virginia bacon and sage-flavored Berkshire sausage (edwardsvaham.com).

Surprise

Crabs and oysters aren't the only seafood in the Chesapeake Bay. The waters are also the summer home of large, stingray-like **cownose rays**. Enterprising restaurants have begun offering the lean, protein-rich meat to adventurous eaters. The Conch & Bucket in Hampton serves ray in multiple ways, including applewood-smoked or braised in a spicy Thai curry (13 E. Queens Way, Hampton, VA; GPS 37.0260, -76.3437).

63 PEANUTS

Virginia peanuts are so distinctive that an entire variety was named after the state. Known for their large size, crunchy texture, and high quality, they've been called the Cadillac of peanuts. Most often grown in the flat, sandy soil of southeastern Virginia, especially Southampton County, Virginia peanuts have the biggest kernels of the four major peanut varieties—significantly larger than the well-known Runners grown in Georgia, which are primarily used to make peanut butter. Virginians love to snack on their peanuts roasted in the shell, or make them into inventive dishes such as peanut pie and peanut soup.

Where to Try It

» The historic Virginia Diner first opened in a refurbished railroad car in 1929. Although it's since transformed into a full-size restaurant in Wakefield, the diner still features antique peanut vendor roasters and offers buckets of free peanuts to customers. Don't miss the delectable peanut pie (vadiner.com; 408 County Dr. N., Wakefield, VA; GPS 36.9736, -76.9890).

» Peanut soup was a favorite colonial dish. Try the creamy soup at the Mount Vernon Inn Restaurant (mountvernon.org; 3200 Mount Vernon Memorial Hwy., Mount Vernon, VA; GPS 38.7110, -77.0871), on the grounds of George Washington's estate in Mount Vernon, and at the King's Arms Tavern (colonialwilliams burg.com; 416 E. Duke of Gloucester St., Williamsburg, VA; GPS 37.2713, -76.6955) in Colonial Williamsburg, which originally opened in 1772.

» The family-owned Hubbard Peanut Company has been producing home-cooked, superlarge Virginia peanuts for more than 60 years; visit the website to order online (hubspeanuts.com).

64 BRUNSWICK STEW

The town of Brunswick, Georgia, may claim to have invented Brunswick stew in the late 19th century, but Virginians insist it isn't so. They say a hunting

A bowl of peanut soup—made from a colonial recipe—at the King's Arms Tavern in Williamsburg, Virginia

party on the banks of Virginia's Nottoway River created the dish in 1828, when the camp cook stirred together an impromptu concoction of onions, bread crumbs, and squirrel.

Nowadays, chicken has replaced squirrel, but the stew—a richly seasoned, savory blend of potatoes, corn, onions, lima beans, tomatoes, and butter beans in thick tomato broth—is still cherished throughout Virginia. Communities frequently band together to cook it in massive quantities in huge cast-iron pots. Making the stew is an arduous process that requires hours of nonstop stirring as ingredients are slowly added. No matter how long it takes, stew masters agree: The dish isn't done until the stirring paddle can stand up in the middle.

Where to Try It

» The small town of Alberta in Brunswick County, Virginia, hosts the annual Taste of Brunswick Festival (*tasteofbrunswickfestival.com; Brunswick County, VA; GPS 36.8389, -77.9167*) every October. You can taste the entries from its Brunswick Stew Cook-Off. Richmond also holds a Brunswick Stew Festival (*virginia.org; 100 N. 17th St., Richmond, VA; GPS 37.5339, -77.4284*) every fall at the 17th Street Farmers Market, where you can buy sample- or quart-size portions of stew from different makers.

» The Alberta General Store's specialty is sweet-and-spicy "Unkol" Chuck's Brunswick stew. The shop also sells take-out frozen stew (*albertageneralstore.com; 106 W. 1st Ave., Alberta, VA; GPS 36.8643, -77.8863*).

Thick, hot, tomatoey Brunswick stew

> ### *Basic Ingredient*
>
> 🌾 Virginia's seven distinct **American viticultural areas** (AVAs), or grape-growing wine regions, contain the fifth most wineries in the country. The area's sandy loam and mild climate produce world-class vintages. Rich American history goes along with them: Two state AVAs encompass George Washington's birthplace and Thomas Jefferson's Monticello plantation.

65 APPLE TASTING AT MONTICELLO

Virginia's apple roots go deep, and a Founding Father deserves the credit. Thomas Jefferson was an avid horticulturalist who loved growing apples, especially for pressing into hard cider (see pp. 66–67).

Today, Monticello, Jefferson's Virginia plantation, maintains his legacy by carefully cultivating little-known apple varieties. Every October, it hosts an annual Apple Tasting at Tufton Farm, one of Jefferson's original quarter farms, which borders the plantation. Participants can sample, taste, and rate their favorite apples, and hear apple experts expound on the history and culture of *pomme* varieties rarely seen in modern grocery stores (*monticello.org; 931 Thomas Jefferson Pkwy., Charlottesville, VA; GPS 37.9954, -78.4287*).

It takes approximately *540 peanuts* to make one 12-ounce jar of peanut butter.

Fresh apple dumplings, one of the delicious products of Virginia's fall apple harvest

Where to Try It

In the fall, you can celebrate the apple harvest at other Virginia orchards and towns:

» It's over a century old, and Carter Mountain Orchard is just down the hill from Monticello. It's a great place to pick your own apples in the fall, though weekends can be crowded. Also on sale in the orchard's country store: apple butter, doughnuts, jams, and, of course, apple pie *(cartermountainorchard.com; 1435 Carters Mountain Trail, Charlottesville, VA; GPS 37.9917, -78.47143).*

» Virginia apples are also the star attraction at the Apple Dumpling Festival, which is held every fall in historic downtown Stuart. Vendors peddle delicious fresh apple dumplings, as well as apple pies and apple butter *(townofstuartva.com; Stuart, VA; GPS 36.6381, -80.2695).*

★WEST VIRGINIA★

66 PAWPAW

Also known as the American custard apple or West Virginia banana, the pawpaw is the United States' effort at a mango—a creamy, green-on-the-outside, yellowy orange inside, tropical-tasting fruit. Thomas Jefferson planted pawpaw trees at his Monticello home in Virginia, and George Washington loved eating them chilled for dessert.

Pawpaws are in season for only a short time in September and October, and they don't last long—once they're fully ripe, they'll stay good for only a couple of

Virginia's most famous heirloom apple is the Albemarle pippin, a juicy dessert apple grown by George Washington and Thomas Jefferson.

days. They're best eaten fresh, baked into pies, cakes, and bread, or made into chilled desserts such as custard, ice cream, and smoothies.

Where to Try It

❯ Ellen's Homemade Ice Cream in Charleston, West Virginia, offers a seasonal pawpaw flavor September through October that's wildly popular with local residents (*ellensicecream.com; 225 Capitol St., Charleston, WV; GPS 38.3506, -81.6344*).

❯ The annual Ohio Pawpaw Festival is held each September in Albany, Ohio, just 20 miles from the border with West Virginia. The three-day celebration features creative culinary inventions like pawpaw mustard, pawpaw tamales, and even pawpaw wheat beer (*ohiopawpawfest.com; 5900 U.S. 50, Albany, OH; GPS 39.2402, -82.1903*).

❯ Chris Chmiel sells fresh pawpaws in season plus pawpaw jam, chutney, and frozen pulp year-round from Integration Acres, his Albany, Ohio, farm (*integrationacres.com; 9794 Chase Rd., Albany, OH; GPS 39.2046, -82.1199*).

67 RAMPS

Ramps, also known as wild leeks, are a member of the lily family, along with scallions, onions, and garlic—but with an even stronger flavor than those pungent plants. The cooked greens can add a potent kick to many dishes.

The colloquial term "ramps" comes from the word "ramson," the common name of the European variety. The prized wild plants primarily grow in the remote,

higher elevations of the Appalachian Mountains, especially in the Monongahela National Forest. April is ramp season in Appalachia, and in Richwood, West Virginia, in the heart of Monongahela, it's time for the annual Feast of the Ramson. Celebrated for nearly 80 years, the festival dishes up savory ramps along with ham, potatoes, corn bread, and dessert, plus plenty of heritage crafts and bluegrass music (*richwood chamberofcommerce.org; 1 E. Main St., Richwood, WV; GPS 38.2234, -80.5293*).

Where to Try It

Other ramp-centric celebrations in Appalachia:

❯ Find ramps in season at the Wild Ramp, a farmers market in Huntington. Its recently inaugurated ramp festival, Stink Fest, features ramp dishes from local vendors and live music, plus an appearance by Stinky, the mascot (*wildramp.org; 555 14th St. W., Huntington, WV; GPS 38.4111, -82.4792*).

❯ Towns and community organizations throughout the region host ramp dinners during high ramp season. Check *kingofstink.com* for a list. Standouts in West Virginia include the Annual Ramp Dinner in Colliers, held in 165-year-old St. John's Church (*St. John's & Eldersville Rds., Colliers, WV; GPS 40.3492, -80.5487*); the activity-filled Ramps & Rail Festival in Elkins (*315 Railroad Ave., Elkins, WV; GPS 38.9252, -79.8509*); and the Wild Wonderful Bluegrass, Sports, and Ramps Bingo in Buckhannon (*25 N. Kanawha St., Buckhannon, WV; GPS 38.9952, -80.2308*).

68 PEPPERONI ROLLS

Step into any gas station or convenience store in West Virginia, and you'll likely spot the unofficial state

Wild leeks—or as they're known in Appalachia, ramps

West Virginia Golden Delicious
apples are sold at farmers markets
both in the state and regionally.

snack: pepperoni rolls. Immigrant Italian bakers in the 1920s and '30s created the rolls as a quick and easy, nonperishable lunch for coal miners.

Still a favorite throughout the region, the traditional pepperoni roll is simply a soft, warm handful of dough baked around sticks or slices of spicy pepperoni. Some bakers like to add provolone or hot pepper jack cheese.

Where to Try It

» The Country Club Bakery in Fairmont, West Virginia, may have invented the snack. The bakery turns out as many as 900 dozen rolls a day, five days a week (*1211 Country Club Rd., Fairmont, WV; GPS 39.4718, -80.1708*).

» Northern West Virginia is home to several Italian bakeries that produce top-rated pepperoni rolls, including Tomaro's in Clarksburg (*tomarosbakery .com, annasofglenelk.com; 411 N. 4th St., Clarksburg, WV; GPS 39.2838, -80.3380*); Colasessano's Pizza

Surprise

In West Virginia, a **squirrel** isn't just a cute critter; it's on the menu. The state's squirrel-hunting season runs from September to January, and bushy-tailed game yields a rich, chewy meat. At November's Squirrel Fest at Bigg Riggs Farm near Romney, West Virginia, devotees savor caramel-colored squirrel gravy and meat ladled over biscuits and baked potatoes (*biggriggsfarm.com; 47 Industrial Park Rd., Romney, WV; GPS 39.3544, -78.7563*).

in Fairmont (*colasessanos.com; 141 Middletown Cir., Fairmont, WV; GPS 39.4942, -80.1422*); and in Morgantown, Chico Bakery (*407 Beechurst Ave., Morgantown, WV; GPS 39.6398, -79.9594*) and Nonna's Bakery & Deli (*nonnasbakery.com; 511 Burroughs St., Morgantown, WV; GPS 39.6574, -79.9705*).

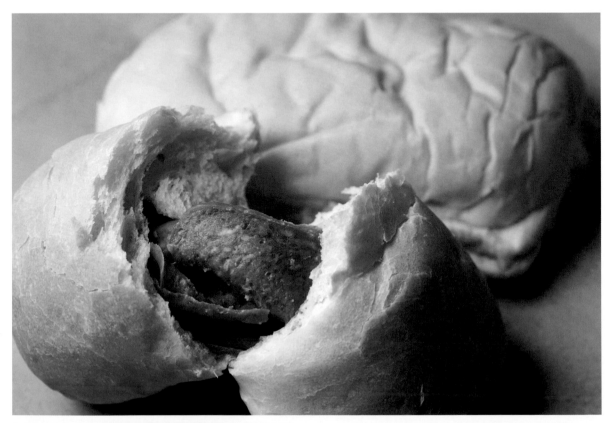

A pepperoni roll, the Italian-invented, West Virginia–adored snack

69 GOLDEN DELICIOUS APPLES

The Golden Delicious apple is the stuff of West Virginia lore. Sometime in the late 1800s to early 1900s, a mysterious, lone seedling was discovered on a farm in Clay County, West Virginia. The tree eventually bore big yellow apples of a kind never seen before. Eventually deemed a whole new variety of apple, it was propagated, improved, and designated the Golden Delicious.

The original tree is now long gone, but the West Virginia apple, perfect for snacking with its mellow, sweet flavor and crisp flesh has spread throughout the world.

Where to Try It

» The Clay County Golden Delicious Festival has celebrated its native fruit for more than 40 years. Each September, the town of Clay hosts a celebration with baking contests, a parade, quilt show, and 5K run, while festivalgoers munch on buckets of Golden Delicious apples (claygoldendeliciousfestival.com; Clay, WV; GPS 38.4601, -81.0842).
» Find Golden Delicious apples in the fall season at farmers markets throughout the state, such as Mountaineer Country Farmers Market in Morgantown (26 Gladesville Rd., Morgantown, WV; GPS 39.4881, -79.9201). Or pick your own at spots such as Orr's Farm Market in Martinsburg (orrsfarmmarket.com; 682 Orr Dr., Martinsburg, WV; GPS 39.4354, -78.0469) or Ridgefield Farm & Orchard in Harpers Ferry (ridgefieldfarm.com; 414 Kidwiler Rd., Harpers Ferry, WV; GPS 39.3562, -77.7924).

70 PRESTON COUNTY BUCKWHEAT FESTIVAL

Buckwheat, once an essential crop in the United States, has largely disappeared from fields and tables. Although only a small amount is still grown in Preston County, West Virginia—once the heart of the historical buckwheat belt—locals are still wild for homemade buckwheat pancakes. The county's annual Buckwheat Festival dates to 1938. Each year, around 100,000 people descend upon the small town of Kingwood during the final weekend of September for festivities, including three parades, the coronation of King Buckwheat and Queen Ceres (goddess of agriculture), and endless stacks of buckwheat pancakes.

These aren't your ordinary flapjacks. Old-fashioned buckwheat cakes are slowly fermented with a sour starter and sizzled fast on a griddle. The thin, dense cakes can range from slightly sour to strongly acidic in taste, and are usually doused with syrup, applesauce, or squirrel or sausage gravy. You can get local buckwheat flour at the festival too, so you can whip up your own treats throughout the year (buckwheatfest.com; Kingwood, WV; GPS 39.4694, -79.6888).

Where to Try It

Other places to try all things buckwheat:
» Becky's Cafe is the only restaurant in Kingwood that serves buckwheat cakes year-round, and always has three batches of starter going at once: sweet, medium sour, and sour (Kingwood, WV; GPS 39.4603, -79.6878).
» Melanie's Family Restaurant in Aurora serves buckwheat cakes from fall until spring, with a surprise ingredient in the batter that adds to the flavor: coffee (25164 George Washington Hwy., Aurora, WV; GPS 39.3254, -79.5360).

Basic Ingredient

The main ingredient in West Virginians' favorite pancakes has an ancient origin: **Buckwheat** was first planted as early as 5,000 or 6,000 years ago, likely in China. Now only a minor crop in the United States, buckwheat is making a comeback. Buckwheat boosters tout it as a healthy alternative to wheat. It's one of the best sources of protein in the plant kingdom and contains all eight essential amino acids.

Buckwheat is a three-sided, teardrop-shaped seed that's actually _classified as a fruit,_ not a grain.

SOUTH

Fried chicken and biscuits might be its signature, but Cajun and Creole cooking, barbecue, Cuban dishes, and soul food show the South has food in its blood.

NORTH CAROLINA
88–89

TENNESSEE
109–114

SOUTH CAROLINA
89–94

ALABAMA
114–115

GEORGIA
94–99

MISSISSIPPI
115–117

FLORIDA
99–104

ARKANSAS
117–120

KENTUCKY
104–109

LOUISIANA
121–127

Fried chicken, attributed especially to Kentucky, is a dish you'll find on almost any true southern menu.

Fried oysters battered in cornmeal—a classic Carolina Calabash-style food

★NORTH CAROLINA★

71 CALABASH-STYLE SEAFOOD

The cooking style associated with the small fishing town of Calabash has three key ingredients: fresh-off-the-boat seafood, a deep-fried cornmeal coating, and either an all-you-care-to-eat buffet or piled-high platters. And while Calabash-style restaurants are ubiquitous along U.S. 17 between Calabash and Myrtle Beach, South Carolina, fish camps and families in the North Carolina namesake town have been cooking Calabash-style fried oysters, shrimp, and flounder since the 1930s.

Today, the small fishing village of Calabash, which immodestly bills itself as the "seafood capital of the world," reels in visitors with no less than a dozen seafood restaurants. The town may share its name with the crooked-neck gourds grown in the region, but for seafood lovers the word "calabash" means heaping helpings of fried seafood. And, it isn't really Calabash-style unless the meal includes hot hush puppies (golf ball–size fried cornmeal and flour fritters).

Where to Try It

» Beck's Restaurant in Calabash is Calabash-style royalty. Opened by Ruth Beck around 1940 as either the first or second seafood restaurant in town (Beck's sister Lucy Coleman opened the other, Coleman's Original), Beck's serves just about everything under the sea from catfish to clams *(becksrestaurant.com; 1104 River Rd., Calabash, NC; GPS 33.8905, -78.5683).*

» Ella's of Calabash opened in 1950 as the third jewel in the Beck-Coleman family triple crown of Calabash-style seafood restaurants. The must-try are the hush puppies, served with honey butter *(ellasofcalabash.com; 1148 River Rd., Calabash, NC; GPS 33.8868, -78.5681).*

» The Calabash Fishing Fleet runs an outdoor Water-front Seafood Shack on the docks. Order fresh local and wild-caught seafood cooked in the local style. Or visit the retail market next door to buy seafood to cook at home *(calabashfishingfleet.com; 9945 Nance St., Calabash, NC; GPS 33.8860, -78.5670).*

72 CHEERWINE

Despite the name, this bubbly, black cherry fusion of fruit, fizz, and caffeine is a nonalcoholic soda, not a wine. The liquid candy concoction was invented in Salisbury, North Carolina, in 1917 by the Carolina Beverage Corporation, which remains among the nation's oldest continuously operated and family-owned soft drink operations.

Originally bottled under the company's Mint Cola Bottling Company, Cheerwine quickly became the company's top seller. By 1924, the group's name was changed to Cheerwine Bottling Company, and the self-proclaimed "legend" (printed on every Cheerwine bottle and can) was born.

The so-called "nectar of North Carolina" wasn't available outside of the state until the 1990s. Even though cans and bottles are scheduled to be available in all 50 states by 2017 (the 100th anniversary), Cheerwine's amped-up carbonation (part of the soda's secret sauce) makes the fountain version the one to try. Drink it ice cold to taste the candy "crunch" in the crystallized ice.

Where to Try It

» 12 Bones Smokehouse in Arden has diet and original Cheerwine on tap. Order at the counter and fill up the red plastic Cheerwine logo tumbler with ice and soda while you wait for your ribs, pulled chicken or pork, or sliced beef brisket *(12bones.com; 3578 Sweeten Creek Rd., Arden, NC; GPS 35.4802, -82.5174).*

» Get Cheerwine delivered to your door, or find your closest Cheerwine retailer (packaged and fountain drinks) at *cheerwine.com.*

★ SOUTH CAROLINA ★

73 GULLAH/GEECHEE CULTURAL HERITAGE CORRIDOR

Everyone from the early French Huguenot settlers to African slaves left a culinary legacy in South Carolina's Low Country. Some of these dishes qualify as soul food (see pp. 118–119); others are considered Gullah, and most are composed of some mix of seafood, rice or grits, and tomatoes or corn.

Gullah, also known as Geechee, is a unique African-American cultural and linguistic heritage that was born along the coastal Low Country, including the state's Sea Islands. The Gullah language, a Creole blend of English and African languages, developed out of necessity in the 1700s. Enslaved West and Central Africans who were thrown together in holding pens and on coastal rice plantations created the rhythmic lingua franca—a hypnotic, haunting, and melodic mix of words and shouts—to communicate.

The remoteness of the Low Country helped preserve the language and culture and Gullah/Geechee people who live there today are direct descendants of the slaves. They carry on their traditions, which include cooking Gullah recipes like Ol' Fuskie fried crab rice, okra pilau, sticky-bush blackberry dumplings, and Frogmore stew, made with shrimp, sausage, and corn on the cob.

Some of these Gullah dishes are regulars on Low Country menus. Others, including sweet potato bread pudding and tater pone (a kind of sweet potato corn bread),

Calabash-style hush puppies get their name from cooks who fed the cornmeal treats to their dogs to *"hush the puppies."*

A plateful of Gullah bounty at Dye's Gullah Fixin's on Hilton Head

Gullah/Geechee heritage. Try the squash casserole (gullahgrubs.com; 877 Sea Island Pkwy., St. Helena Island, SC; GPS 32.3973, -80.5763).

» Enjoy plenty of shrimp and okra gumbo, conch stew, and bread pudding at the Original Gullah Festival in Beaufort's Waterfront Park over Memorial Day weekend (theoriginalgullahfestival .org; 803 Greene St., Beaufort, SC; GPS 32.4312, -80.6731) or the Taste of Gullah food fair in February at Hilton Head (gullahcelebration.com; Hilton Head, SC; GPS 32.1786, -80.7283).

» Located in an elegantly restored 1888 Victorian home, Poogan's Porch has been a Charleston favorite since 1976 for authentic and local Low Country cuisine. Reservations are strongly suggested, as is sharing an order of pimento cheese fritters with green tomato jam (poogansporch .com; 72 Queen St., Charleston, SC; GPS 32.7781, -79.9319).

» The Old Post Office Restaurant on Edisto Island serves a mix of locally sourced items, including Low Country classics like shrimp and grits, crab cakes, and fried oyster cocktail (theoldpostoffice restaurant.com; 1442 Rte. 174, Edisto Island, SC; GPS 32.5600, -80.2796).

are harder to find. The best way to try both Gullah/ Geechee cuisine and classic Low Country dishes like Hoppin' John (a black-eyed peas and rice dish traditionally served on New Year's Day) is to explore the Gullah/Geechee Cultural Heritage Corridor. It extends north and south of U.S. 17, 425 miles along the Atlantic coast and 30 miles inland (nps.gov/guge).

Where to Try It
Stop off at these eateries along the Heritage Corridor:

» Dye's Gullah Fixin's on Hilton Head Island is a tiny, family-owned restaurant tucked away in a business park. Reservations are required—owner and head chef Dye Scott-Rhodan makes everything from scratch, so she needs to know how much corn bread and macaroni and "chez" to make (dyesgullahfixins.com; 840 William Hilton Pkwy., Hilton Head, SC; GPS 32.1745, -80.7332).

» Gullah Grub Restaurant & Catering is on St. Helena Island, home of the Penn Center (penncenter.com), the only national historic landmark district dedicated to

74 BOILED PEANUTS
Whether you call them goober peas, groundnuts, or the more pedestrian boiled peanuts, South Carolina's official state snack is rooted in resourcefulness. In the 1800s, farmers in South Carolina and across the South

Specialty of the House
Called "pimento cheese with soul," **Palmetto Cheese** is a Pawleys Island, South Carolina, original. First created by Sea View Inn co-owner Sassy Henry and produced in small batches by family friend Vertrella Brown (that's her face on the label), the chunky spread is a blend of sharp cheddar cheese, Hellman's mayonnaise, pimentos (red cherry peppers), and Sassy's secret seasonings. But the cheese itself is a secret no longer: It's sold in 35 states, D.C., and Puerto Rico (pimentocheese.com).

started boiling any unsold, freshly harvested peanuts so they wouldn't go to waste. Salted water helped preserve the peanuts, which were boiled in-shell over an open fire.

The resulting soggy shell snack is an acquired taste: hot, a bit slimy, and often requiring spitting (shells are easier to open with your teeth). The best ones are boiled and sold at roadside stands from May to November.

Where to Try It

» At the annual South Carolina Peanut Party in Pelion each August, local Ruritan club members boil and sell 50 bushels of local peanuts. Before the boiling begins, a local minister blesses the pots (scpelionpeanutparty .com; Pelion, SC; GPS 33.7608, -81.2488).

» Thomas Scott sells hot boiled peanuts throughout the Charleston, West Ashley, and Mount Pleasant area. Look for his trailer most Thursdays through Sundays at the Festival Centre lot in North Charleston, or call Scott at 803-496-6512 (5101 Ashley Phosphate Rd., N. Charleston, SC; GPS 32.9142, -80.1048).

» The Lee Brothers Boiled Peanut Catalogue ships five-pound packs of small-batch boiled peanuts, plus Roddenbery's canned green boiled peanuts, and a boil-your-own-peanuts kit—all you need to add is the flame, water, and salt (boiledpeanuts.com).

75 SHE-CRAB SOUP

This savory, bisque-like Low Country delicacy deserves special mention since it's widely regarded as a Charleston classic. The soup's name comes from the she-crab's (female) red-orange roe (eggs), the original recipe's key ingredient. Today, it's illegal to harvest mature she-crabs with fertilized roe, so fresh white meat from male and immature female blue crabs is used instead. Some recipes include unfertilized roe or crumbled egg yolk to re-create the original look. Mace (the membrane surrounding nutmeg) or Old Bay seasoning, warm sherry, and Worcestershire sauce help mimic the tanginess and pale orange color previously provided by the roe.

Where to Try It

» Amen Street Fish & Raw Bar in Charleston ladles out she-crab soup by the cup or bowl. Located in a historic mercantile building rebuilt after the city's devastating earthquake in 1886, the restaurant has indoor and

Boiled peanuts—perhaps an acquired taste, but the South loves them and sets up roadside stands to sell them

Bowens Island Restaurant, on the watery outskirts of Charleston, South Carolina, has local roasted oysters on the menu.

outdoor seating plus an all-local raw bar *(amenstreet .com; Rainbow Market, 205 E. Bay St., Charleston, SC; GPS 32.7802, -79.9273).*

» Weekdays, head to the bar at 82 Queen in Charleston where you can get she-crab soup by the cup or bowl. Or pair it with the side salad and half sandwich for the Chef's Trio *(82queen.com; 82 Queen St., Charleston, SC; GPS 32.7779, -79.9325).*

76 SHRIMP & OYSTERS

In coastal Carolina, the most virgin of seafood is raw oysters, slurped down right out of the shell. But if you want your seafood cooked, the Low Country version of a backyard barbecue is a shrimp boil or an old-school oyster roast. The boil is simply a big batch of fresh corn on the cob, local shrimp, red potatoes, and smoked sausage, and spices all tossed together in a pot. The roast is reserved for shellfish season (October 1–May 15) when hand-harvested oysters are available by the bushel.

A piece of sheet metal or metal grill is the cooktop, propped up on cement blocks over a fire. The oysters sit on top and are covered with a wet burlap sack to steam, a rudimentary cooking method that slightly opens the shells.

The hot, roasted oysters are then shoveled onto a table where diners deploy shucking knives to scoop out the meat. There's little else to it, except maybe cocktail or hot sauce, saltine crackers, napkins, and beer. There are invariably some minor scratches or

Basic Ingredient

From black-eyed to washday, monkey tail to polecat, summer **field peas** have provided cheap, filling fare for generations of rural Southerners. Traditionally hulled by hand, simmered in a pot with a ham hock, and served with a hunk of corn bread, the humble and hearty field peas are enjoying newfound fame on foodie menus.

burns during the shucking frenzy, but it's rarely bad enough to postpone the eating.

Where to Try It

» The annual Low Country Oyster Festival held each January at Boone Hall Plantation in Mount Pleasant is the world's largest event of its kind. Some 80,000 pounds of oysters are shucked and slurped. Ride the festival shuttle from downtown Charleston *(charleston restaurantassociation.com; 423 King St., Charleston, SC; GPS 32.8474, -79.8263).*

» October's Beaufort Shrimp Festival is held downtown on the Beaufort waterfront. There's shrimp prepared any way you'd like it, plus bags of wild-caught South Carolina shrimp to cook at home *(mainstreetbeaufort .com; Beaufort, SC; GPS 32.4310, -80.6740).*

» Bowens Island Restaurant is a no-frills, family-owned fish camp tucked in the marshy outskirts of Charleston. The upstairs, ramshackle dining room and decks hold graffiti-covered picnic tables. The downstairs cinder block Oyster Room is where (in season, generally October 1–May 15) steam pots of local oysters are cooked. Get there before the doors open at 5 p.m. so you don't have to wait an hour to get a table *(1870 Bowens Island Rd., Charleston, SC; GPS 32.6754, -79.9646).*

77 GRITS

People either "get" grits or they don't. And, if they do, well, they can't get enough: with butter and salt for breakfast; topped with cheese or gravy and paired with shrimp, sausage, or eggs; or baked with butter, egg, and cheese into a soufflé-like dish.

Smooth, creamy, and nutrient-rich grits are basically ground whole corn kernels or hominy (dried corn soaked in a mineral solution to remove the hulls). Grits can be coarse, medium, or finely ground, and made from white or yellow mill corns. Purists prefer real stone-ground grits (some call them speckled, for their dappled appearance). Regular grits take about 40 minutes to boil, quick grits (finely ground) whip up in about 10. And instant grits? Aficionados agree—they're not worth the minute of microwaving required.

Where to Try It

» The World Grits Festival held each April in St. George celebrates the small town's collective appetite for grits. According to the locals, more grits are consumed per capita here than anywhere else in the world. The event includes the opportunity to roll in grits because . . . why not *(worldgritsfestival.com; 110 S. Parler Ave., St. George, SC; GPS 33.1834, -80.5743).*

» The exterior mural on the red clapboard siding of the Hominy Grill in Charleston says all you need to know: "Grits are good for you." And these grits (cheese and deep-fried cheese) are some of the best in town *(hominygrill.com; 207 Rutledge Ave., Charleston, SC; GPS 32.7888, -79.9469).*

» The Greg and Betsy Johnsman family uses heirloom corn and antique gristmills to make their Geechie Boy Mill grits and cornmeal. Visit the family's Edisto Island farm market or order online *(geechie boymill.com; 2995 Rte. 174, Edisto Island, SC; GPS 32.5974, -80.3476).*

» A bit deeper south, Alabama has its own take on the dish: Chef-owner and Birmingham native Frank

Shrimp and grits at Hominy Grill in Charleston

Stitt elevated baked grits to an art form in 1982 when he opened his Highlands Bar and Grill in the city's Five Points South neighborhood. The dish is the restaurant's signature appetizer and is served with a rich cream sauce with grated cheese, white wine, and hot sauce, and then topped with mushrooms and country ham *(highlandsbarandgrill.com; 2011 11th Ave. S., Birmingham, AL; GPS 33.5005, -86.7955)*.

★GEORGIA★

78 PECANS

American Indians were eating and trading pecans long before the first European settlers arrived. And although the nuts didn't catch on as a cash crop in Georgia until the late 1800s, the state has been the nation's top producer for the last half century. Georgia's annual pecan harvest—an estimated 88 million pounds—would be enough to make about 176 million pecan pies.

Where to Try It

» Roadside pecan stands pop up throughout southern Georgia during pecan season (October–December). Look for temporary stands near exit ramps off I-75

A Georgia pecan pie

between Macon and the Florida border. Or visit a year-round stand such as Marks Melon Patch on U.S. 82 near Sasser *(marksmelonpatch.com; 8580 Albany Hwy., Dawson, GA; GPS 31.7070, -84.3368)*.

» The Peachtree Café and Bakery at Lane Southern Orchards in Fort Valley serves pecan-crusted catfish, pecan pie, and fresh cinnamon bread with pecans. The Lanes harvest their pecans October through January, but pecan recipes are featured in the café year-round *(lanesouthernorchards.com; 50 Lane Rd., Fort Valley, GA; GPS 32.5556, -83.8276)*.

» Wade Plantation Pecans in Screven County sells its homegrown pecan products online. Buy pecan halves, pieces, or meal to make your own sweets. Or order a whole southern, cinnamon, or chocolate pecan pie; and gift tins filled with pecan brittle, toffee, or chocolate-covered pecans *(wadepecans.com)*.

79 COCA-COLA

You'd be hard-pressed today to find a place in the world where Coca-Cola isn't sold or served. But there's only one birthplace of "the Real Thing," and that's Atlanta. Local pharmacist John Stith Pemberton combined coca wine (from the leaves of the coca shrub) and kola (from the African kola nut) into a soda fountain tonic in 1886. He first sold the drink (syrup mixed with carbonated water) for five cents a glass at his neighborhood pharmacy. Although Pemberton initially touted Coca-Cola's potential health benefits such as headache relief and even curing morphine addiction, those claims were unfounded—though it's true that his earliest versions of the beverage contained small amounts of cocaine.

Where to Try It

» World of Coca-Cola in Atlanta is the cathedral of Coke. Visit the second-floor "Taste It!" exhibit for unlimited, free (with a museum ticket) samples of several Coca-Cola trademark brands, plus more than 60 international products such as Beverly, a nonalcoholic Italian aperitif *(worldofcoca-cola.com; 121 Baker St. NW, Atlanta, GA; GPS 33.7628, -84.3929)*.

Georgia peaches—after they're plucked off the tree, they show up in everything from pies and jams to ice cream.

» West Egg Café in Atlanta's Westside Provisions District bakes a daily batch of Coca-Cola cupcakes and serves Mexican Coke floats mixed with soft serve vanilla ice cream that's made in-house *(westeggcafe.com; 1100 Howell Mill Rd., Atlanta, GA; GPS 33.7848, -84.4120).*
» The Coca-Cola Company collects and shares recipes infused with Coke products on its website. Learn how to use Coca-Cola as a sweetener in everything from traditional southern gelatin salads to barbecue sauce *(coca-colacompany.com/food/recipes).*

80 PEACHES

Franciscan monks are credited with planting Georgia's first peach trees on coastal St. Simons and Cumberland Islands in 1571. But it wasn't until post–Civil War Reconstruction in the late 1800s that Georgia

began building its reputation as the Peach State. It was then that peach grower Samuel Henry Rumph, known as the father of the Georgia peach industry, invented the mother of all Georgia peaches, a firm, yellow-fleshed peach variety named Elberta after his wife. Rumph also invented the ice-filled train cars that could safely ship them to East Coast cities, and most of the 40 commercial varieties grown in the state today were bred from Elberta. Fresh Georgia peaches are harvested and available at state fruit farms mid-May to August.

Where to Try It

» Built in 1936, Dickey Farms in Musella is the oldest peach packinghouse in continuous operation in Georgia. Visit during the summer harvest season to buy peaches by the bag or bushel, and foods ranging from ice cream and cobbler to jams and salsa

Continued on p. 98

More than 10,000 Coca-Cola soda products
are consumed *every second of every day* worldwide.

Pork ribs, one of many kinds of barbecue the South serves up

GREAT AMERICAN EATING EXPERIENCES
Southern Barbecue

Barbecue could be a honing device in the South. One taste of the local barbecue will tell you where you are. Chopped pork with a tomato-free vinegar sauce? Chances are you're in eastern North Carolina. Tangy dry-rub baby backs? You're likely in Memphis.

Which state is the birthplace of barbecue? Truth is, people have been slow roasting meat over fire ever since there's been fire. But below the Mason-Dixon Line, barbecue is often considered a basic food group.

≫ Kentucky Style
The state's signature barbecue is in Owensboro and it's mutton, a one- to five-year-old ewe producing tasty, tender meat. Early Welsh settlers raised lots of sheep, which is one theory why barbecued mutton is

served at summer picnics hosted by the city's Catholic parishes (and open to all).

Sample fresh-from-the-pits mutton at the city's International Bar-B-Q Festival held each May *(bbqfest .com; Owensboro, KY; GPS 37.7748, -87.1135)*. Any day of the week, try the mutton (sliced or chopped) at the Moonlite Bar-B-Q Inn, an Owensboro tradition since 1963 *(moonlite.com; 2840 W. Parrish Ave., Owensboro, KY; GPS 37.7566, -87.1487)*.

≫ Memphis Style
Blues and barbecue—both tender, smoky Memphis hallmarks. The signature barbecue is pork (ribs or pulled), and the style is dry-rub served "wet" (with sauce) or "dry" (no sauce). Go dry; the tangy Memphis seasoning blend is flavor enough.

The charcoal-broiled pork ribs at the legendary Rendezvous restaurant in Memphis define the word "barbecue" for many (hogsfly.com; 52 S. 2nd St., Memphis, TN; GPS 35.1434, -90.0519). Or order a pulled pork sandwich and add the sweet coleslaw on top at the original Central BBQ location in midtown Memphis (cbqmemphis.com; flagship location: 2249 Central Ave., Memphis, TN; GPS 35.1257, -89.9870).

›› East Tennessee Style

Two major interstates (I-75 and I-40) converge in Knoxville, which may have influenced the region's quirky blend of barbecue meats and styles, and the city's fast-and-loose way of presenting and dressing it. Local pit masters mix it up with dry-rub St. Louis–cut pork spare ribs, chopped pork butt, hand-pulled chicken, and Tennessee beef brisket.

For total South-in-your-mouth barbecue, devour a Dead End BBQ Mac-Attack sandwich: pulled pork or chicken, red sauce, caramelized onions, and macaroni and pimento cheese on grilled sourdough (deadendbbq.com; 3621 Sutherland Ave., Knoxville, TN; GPS 35.9467, -83.9801). At the original Sweet P's Barbeque & Soul House, get messy with the BBQ burrito: a flour tortilla stuffed with barbecue pork or chicken, pintos, slaw, cheddar cheese, and BBQ sauce (sweetpbbq.com; 3725 Maryville Pike, Knoxville, TN; GPS 35.8736, -83.9428).

›› North Carolina Style

When it comes to barbecue, North Carolina is a house divided. Eastern barbecue is whole hog with a peppery, vinegar-based sauce. Western, or Lexington-style, barbecue typically is made from just pork shoulder. The sauce is still vinegary, but there's ketchup and maybe Worcestershire sauce mixed in.

The king of eastern style is, appropriately, King's Restaurant in Kinston, run by the King family since 1936 (kingsbbq.com; multiple locations). For the best of the western style, order

An eastern North Carolina–style BBQ sandwich, with slaw

the chopped BBQ sandwich at Lexington Barbecue, known as "the Monk," a nod to founder Wayne Monk (lexbbq.com; 100 Smokehouse Ln., Lexington, NC; GPS 35.8341, -80.2675).

›› South Carolina Style

The real deal here is whole hog, slow cooked overnight in a pit. The pulled pork is served as a mouthwatering mound or stuffed in a hamburger bun. And the sauce varies depending where in South Carolina you are: mustard in the midlands, vinegar and pepper on the coast, heavy tomato sauce in the western mountains, and light tomato sauce in the northeast and upper middle part of the state.

Sample the barbecue and all the sauces at the Festival of Discovery BBQ & Blues held in Greenwood each July. About 90 teams compete in the festival's Kansas City Barbeque Society BBQ and Hash Cook-Off (festivalofdiscovery.com; Greenwood County, SC; GPS 34.1917, -82.1614). At Scott's Bar-B-Que in Hemingway, pile on the pork—pulled, with fried pork skins on the side (thescottsbbq.com; 2734 Hemingway Hwy., Hemingway, SC; GPS 33.7433, -79.4750).

›› Kansas City Style

Kansas City has its own style of the southern staple—barbecue slow smoked over wood and then drowned in a thick tomato or molasses-based sauce served spicy or sweet (see p. 163). The classic KC joint Arthur Bryant's has been smoking barbecue for nearly 100 years, with an original "rich and spicy" barbecue sauce that's become legend. Joe's Kansas City Bar-B-Que (joeskc.com; multiple locations) is the outgrowth of an amateur barbecue team that got so good (and won so many competitions) that they started their own restaurant. Two decades later, the barbecue counter started inside a KC gas station by Jeff and Joy Stehney is a full-fledged restaurant that TV's Anthony Bourdain named one of "13 places to eat before you die."

(gapeaches.com; 3440 Musella Rd., Musella, GA; GPS 32.7978, -84.0288).

» Located only five minutes west of I-75, Lane Southern Orchards in Fort Valley (see p. 94) is a little peach theme park of sorts. Tour the peach-packing operation (mid-May–August) or the orchards (June–July); sample Ms. Caroline Lane's sweet Georgia peach cobbler at the Peachtree Café and Bakery, or buy some fresh or pickled peaches to take with you (lanesouthernorchards.com; 50 Lane Rd., Fort Valley, GA; GPS 32.5556, -83.8276).

» Held every June in Peach County, the weeklong Georgia Peach Festival includes the baking—and eating—of the world's largest peach cobbler. The 11-by-5-foot dessert uses 75 gallons of fresh peaches. Festival events are held in Peach County's two cities, Fort Valley and Byron (gapeachfestival.com; Byron and Fort Valley, GA).

Blackberry cobbler, a simple, summertime Georgia dessert

81 FRUIT COBBLERS

A cobbler is a pie's country cousin: a syrupy jumble of bubbling fruit and sugary biscuit crust that couldn't be neatly sliced if you tried. Baked in a deep-dish casserole and filled with whatever fresh fruit is in season (such as peach, pear, cherry, blueberry, blackberry, or apple), the cobbler is a simple summer dessert. What makes any cobbler southern is the scoop of vanilla ice cream on top. The resulting melt makes the whole mess even sloppier—and more delicious.

Where to Try It

» Mary Mac's Tea Room opened in 1945 and was designated as "Atlanta's Dining Room" in 2011 by the Georgia House of Representatives. The last of the 1940s woman-owned Atlanta restaurants, or "tea rooms," specializing in southern comfort foods, Mary Mac's bakes a flaky crust cobbler packed with cinnamon-spiced fresh peaches. À la mode is $1 extra, and worth every slurp (marymacs.com; 224 Ponce De Leon Ave. NE, Atlanta, GA; GPS 33.7729, -84.3800).

» Clarkson-based Ivy's Heavenly Cobbler (heavenlycobbler.com) bakes the homemade peach cobbler served at Twisted Soul in Decatur (twistedsoulkitchenandbar.com; 314 E. Howard Ave., Decatur, GA; GPS 33.7720, -84.2921). To have a pan-size Ivy's cobbler (assorted fruit flavors available) shipped to your door, order online, or call or text Ivy's at 404-664-2091.

» "Come for the shoes, stay for the cobbler" is the motto at the family-owned Donovan's Irish Cobbler in Woodstock. The "shoes" are the Donovan's

Stone crabs' distinctive black-tipped claws are delicious dipped in warm butter or mustard sauce.

specialty horseshoe sandwiches (Texas toast plus meat, fries, and cheese sauce; see p. 148). The cobbler (which is worth staying for) may be peach, blueberry, or whatever's in season (*donovansirishcobbler.com; 1025 Rose Creek Dr., Woodstock, GA; GPS 34.1270, -84.5734*).

see p. 148

★FLORIDA★

82 STONE CRAB

Fall in South Florida means one thing: The Florida stone crabs are back. From October 15 to May 15, the stone crabs, or, more precisely, their oversize and distinctive black-tipped claws, can be harvested. And all of the nation's commercial stone crab fishing takes place in warm Florida waters, from the state's northwest Gulf Coast region down to the Keys.

Florida stone crab claws are coveted for their rich, sweet-tasting meat. Strict state laws dictate how the claws can be harvested: Only claws measuring at least 2.75 inches long can be taken, and the live stone crab (with one or two claws missing) must be released back in the water, where the claw will regenerate. Eat each claw like a local: cold, cracked open with a mallet or hammer, and dipped in warm butter or mustard sauce.

Where to Try It

≫ Joe's Stone Crab in Miami Beach is the undisputed king of the crabs. Joe Weiss—the restaurateur credited with figuring out the crabs were worth cooking and eating—opened his legendary restaurant in 1913. In season, Joe's sells fresh stone crab claws with mustard sauce (and bibs) three ways: online for overnight shipment, in the dining room, and at the restaurant's laid-back

Basic Ingredient

Alligator is exotic meat traditionally associated with Cajun cuisine. Although gator hunters have gained fame on reality TV, most meat eaten in the United States is raised on commercial alligator farms in Florida, Georgia, Louisiana, and Texas. The prime cut is the mild-flavored tail meat. With no carbs and little fat, it's gaining favor as the "other white meat."

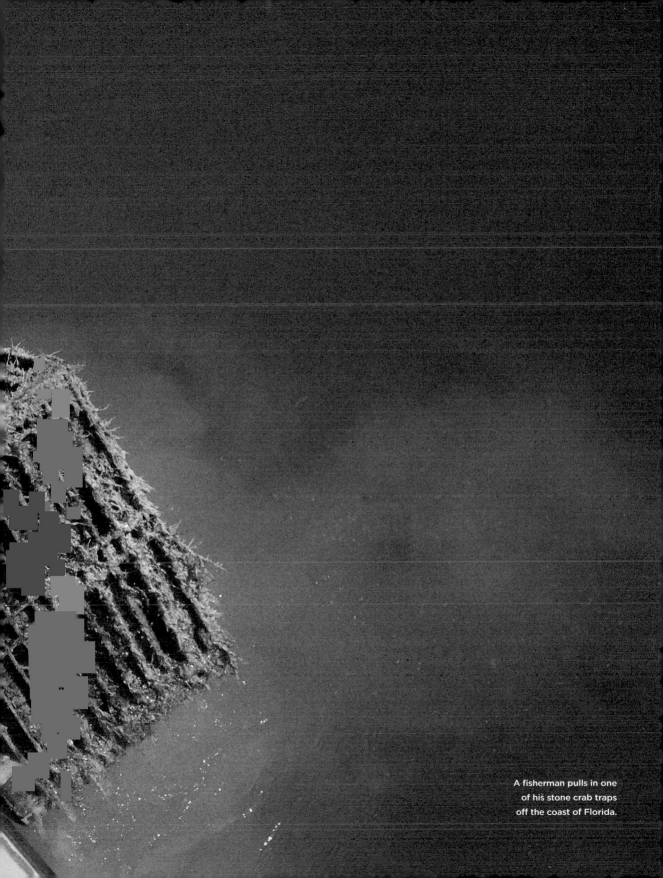

A fisherman pulls in one
of his stone crab traps
off the coast of Florida.

Joe's Take Away. Joe's is open year-round, but the fresh crabs are available October 15 through May 15 and Thanksgiving Day (*joesstonecrab.com; 11 Washington Ave., Miami Beach, FL; GPS 25.765, -80.1352*).

» All-you-can-eat stone crab is reason number one to try Billy's Stone Crab Restaurant in Hollywood (Florida, that is). Number two is the view of the Intracoastal Waterway. Sit on the dock or by the windows in the upstairs dining room (*crabs.com; 400 N. Ocean Dr., Hollywood, FL; GPS 26.0145, -80.1177*).

» October's Stone Crab Festival on the Naples waterfront kicks off with a mayoral "cracking of the stone crab" (*stonecrabfestival.org; Naples, FL; GPS 26.1427, -81.7903*). The three-day event includes stone crab specials at the community block party, and fresh stone crab dinners at Kelly's Fish House Dining Room (*kellys fishhousediningroom.com; 1302 5th Ave. S., Naples, FL; GPS 26.1414, -81.7897*).

83 KEY LIME PIE

Florida's official state pie is made with key limes, a tart fruit that's roughly the size of a golf ball, has a yellow rind when ripe, and today is actually very sparsely grown in the United States, though southern Florida and the Keys historically propagated it. The lime juice (also yellow) is mixed with egg yolks and sweetened condensed milk to make the pie's thick and creamy filling, and poured into a graham cracker crust. A whipped meringue is spread on top, and the whole shebang is baked and then chilled. Many recipes and restaurants substitute the juice from larger (and more readily available) Persian limes. One good rule of thumb to test whether it's the real deal: If the filling is lime green, it's not authentic key lime pie.

Where to Try It

» Key Lime Republic in Key West bakes homemade key

True key lime pie is always yellow.

lime pies daily. Watch the pies being made, and buy a slice or a whole pie to go (*keylimerepublic.com; 412 Greene St.; Key West, FL; GPS 24.5586, -81.8058*).

» Kermit's Key West Key Lime Shoppe sells authentic key lime at two Key West locations. Eat a slice of pie or a chocolate-dipped key lime pie–on-a-stick in the shaded patio of the original Kermit's on Elizabeth Street or on the front porch of the smaller Duval Street shop (*keylimeshop.com; flagship location: 200 Elizabeth St., Key West, FL; GPS 24.5605, -81.8028*).

» The annual Key Lime Festival in Key West around July 4 includes pie-cooking demonstrations and competitions and the requisite key lime pie–eating contest. Plus, there's ample opportunity to sample the goods along with key lime cocktails and locally distilled key lime rum (*keylimefestival.com; Key West, FL; GPS 24.5591, -81.8045*).

» The Florida Key Lime Pie Company sponsors January's annual Florida Key Lime Pie Festival in Port Canaveral (*floridakeylimepiefestival.com; Port Canaveral, FL; GPS 28.4065, -80.6176*), and runs a retail store in Cocoa (*flkeylimepies.com; 340 King St., Cocoa, FL; GPS 28.3560, -80.7301*). Visit the festival or the store to buy key lime pie in a cup, jar, or coconut shell; on a stick; or by the slice or whole pie (traditional and deep-dish).

84 CUBAN SANDWICHES & SPECIALTIES

Florida is home to nearly 70 percent of the approximately 1.9 million Cubans living in the United States. And South Florida's vibrant Cuban neighborhoods, most notably Miami's Little Havana, are lined with mom-and-pop bodegas, cafés, and *cafecitos* (walk-up coffee windows).

On restaurant menus, look for the classic *Cubano* sandwich (ham, roast pork, Swiss cheese, mustard, and pickles on Cuban bread) or the *medianoche* (a Cuban sandwich on sweet yellow bread). Also be sure to try Cuban specialty dishes such as *mariquitas* (a plantain chip appetizer served with a dip) or *croquetas* (plump and crunchy cigar-shaped finger foods filled with meat or fish and cheese).

Where to Try It

» Enriqueta's Sandwich Shop in Miami serves authentic stuffed and pressed Cuban sandwiches (among other menu items). The hole-in-the-wall café is packed at lunch. Order at the walk-up window and ask for extra napkins *(186 NE 29th St., Miami, FL; GPS 25.8039, -80.1915).*
» Visit Islas Canarias Café & Bakery in West Dade (Islas Canarias has a sit-down restaurant less than a mile north) for *croquetas jamón o pollo* (ham or chicken croquettes). Eat in, or order to go at the walk-up window *(islascanarias restaurant.com; 3804 SW 137th Ave., Miami, FL; GPS 25.7323, -80.4166).*
» Miami's landmark Versailles Restaurant is on Calle Ocho (Eighth Street), cultural and culinary hub of Miami's Cuban community. Sample a variety of Versailles specialties that includes *ropa vieja* (shredded beef in tomato sauce), fried pork chunks, ham croquettes, sweet plantains, and Cuban tamales *(versaillesrestaurant.com; 3555 SW 8th St., Miami, FL; GPS 25.7650, -80.2528).*
» The National Cuban Sandwich Festival held every March in Tampa's historic Ybor City neighborhood includes the Big City2City Smackdown: Cuban sandwiches (and samples) from restaurants around the United States *(thecubansandwichfestival.com; Tampa, FL; GPS 27.9613, -82.4386).*

Miami's Versailles Restaurant is a must for sampling Cuban specialty dishes.

85 FLORIDA ORANGES & CITRUS

Perhaps no other state is as closely linked to a drink as Florida is to orange juice. Most years, Florida produces around 65 percent of U.S. citrus, and 90 percent of that is made into the country's OJ. But oranges aren't the Sunshine State's only commercial citrus crop: Florida farmers also harvest grapefruit, tangerines, tangelos, and other specialty fruits.

Where to Try It

» The old-school Orange Shop in Citra has been selling seasonally fresh citrus products on U.S. 301 since 1936.

All the fruit is grown locally in Marion County and the Indian River area. Buy in store or online *(floridaorange shop.com; 18545 U.S. 301, Citra, FL; GPS 29.4178, -82.1098).*
» Tom and Lynda Mack, owners of Svrlinga Groves (established in 1911) in Zellwood, sell their tree-ripe citrus, citrus juice candies, and citrus marmalades and jellies online *(florida-citrus.com).*
» Florida Orange Groves Winery in St. Petersburg produces more than 40 different wines, including several citrus varietals. Tour the winery, visit the tasting room, and then buy a bottle of Orange Sunshine Dry or Sweet, Tangier Tangerine, Key Limen, or another citrus wine to take home *(florida wine.com; 1500 Pasadena Ave. S., St. Petersburg, FL; GPS 27.7532, -82.7378).*

Florida grapefruit

86 REEF, TROPICAL & SALTWATER CATCH

With more than 80 types of seafood harvested off Florida's coasts and raised in commercial aquaculture farms, a bounty of fresh, local seafood is available any month of the year. Depending on the season, the daily catch could include reef fish like amberjack, grouper, and snapper; or saltwater catch like swordfish, mullet, snapper, and flounder. Plus, nearly 85 percent (or more) of the tropical and subtropical U.S. catch like tilapia, pink shrimp, pompano, spiny lobster, Spanish mackerel, and stone crab is caught here.

Where to Try It

» The fall Florida Seafood Festival held in Apalachicola features "Caught Fresh, Served Fresh" seafood. Items such as smoked mullet and fried shrimp are prepared by local residents and sold on the festival's Food Row to support local nonprofits (*floridaseafoodfestival.com; 1 Bay Ave., Apalachicola, FL; GPS 29.7241, -84.9814*).
» Hosted by the Florida Keys Commercial Fishermen's Association, January's annual Florida Keys Seafood Festival in Key West showcases the local Monroe County fresh catch. Florida specialty dishes include pink shrimp, ceviche, and grilled Florida spiny lobster (*fkcfa.org; Bayview Park, Key West, FL; GPS 24.5570, -81.7888*).
» Waterfront Capt. JB's Fish Camp Seafood Restaurant in New Smyrna Beach serves all the local fish in the sea, plus the ones in the river, too. Most items are available grilled, blackened, broiled, or Cajun fried. Or bring in your catch, and they'll cook it (*jbsfishcamp .com; 859 Pompano Ave., New Smyrna Beach, FL; GPS 28.9468, -80.8382*).
» The specialty of the house at Miami's ultrahip Area 31 is local, sustainable seafood. Choose one of the daily wood-grilled catches such as snapper and swordfish, and request a table on the terrace of the restaurant (on the 16th floor in the EPIC Hotel) overlooking Biscayne Bay and the Miami River (*area31restaurant.com; EPIC Hotel, 270 Biscayne Boulevard Way, Miami, FL; GPS 25.7702, -80.1896*).

Surprise

Blend the culinary influences of South Florida's cultural melting pot and the result is **Floribbean, or New World, cuisine.** The colorful fusion of fresh Florida fish, fruits, and vegetables; bold and flavorful spices; and Caribbean, pan-Latin, Indio-Asian, and southern cooking methods produces dishes like pan-roasted red snapper on coconut-jasmine rice, and Brazilian creamy, cracked conch chowder served at Miami Culinary Institute restaurant Tuyo (*tuyomiami.com; 415 NE 2nd Ave., Miami, FL; GPS 25.7785, -80.1901*).

» Reef fish like fresh grouper are one of the many local catches delivered daily to the Sanibel Fish House on laid-back Sanibel Island. Order the grouper crunchy (dipped in a cornflake batter and fried), broiled plain, or stuffed with crabmeat and scallops (*sanibelisland fishhouse.com; 1523 Periwinkle Way, Sanibel, FL; GPS 26.4424, -82.0540*).

★KENTUCKY★

87 MINT JULEPS & DERBY FARE

At the famed "Run for the Roses," held annually since 1875 and the oldest continuous sporting event in the United States, it's all about the horses, the hats—and the mint juleps. The Kentucky-bourbon-infused drink is as much part of the tradition as the Derby's storied steeds. On Kentucky Derby weekend, nearly 120,000 juleps are served in traditional, frosted silver julep cups garnished with a sprig of fresh mint. The pretty packaging along with the mint julep's simple sugar, bourbon, and mint recipe masks the potency of the genteel southern cocktail.

At the track and at Derby-watching parties everywhere, the menu of the day

Mint julep

Burgoo, a mutton-and-vegetable-based stew, is classic fare on Kentucky Derby day.

also typically includes three Kentucky staples: burgoo (a thick, throw-everything-into-a-pot stew traditionally made with mutton and vegetables); Benedictine (a mint green, cucumber and cream cheese spread) or finger sandwiches; and the original Derby-Pie, a gooey, sweet, chocolate chip and walnut concoction trademarked and baked exclusively by Kern's Kitchen in Louisville.

Where to Try It

» The Kentucky Derby Museum's Derby Café at Churchill Downs in Louisville serves a Triple Crown of Salads (Benedictine, country ham, and creamy chicken), burgoo with corn bread, Derby-Pie topped with fresh whipped cream, and a mint julep served in a souvenir tumbler. Open year-round, except for holidays and, somewhat ironically, Derby week (derbymuseum.org;

Churchill Downs, 704 Central Ave., Louisville, KY; GPS 38.2055, -85.7709).

» Anderson County, self-proclaimed "burgoo capital of the world," hosts a Burgoo Festival each September in Lawrenceburg. Cook-off competitors stir up simmering pots of the stew to sample (kentuckyburgoo.com; Lawrenceburg, KY; GPS 38.0360, -84.8968).

» Proof on Main in Louisville stocks more than 75 Kentucky bourbons, including special barrels of the Woodford Reserve used to make mint juleps (proof onmain.com; 702 W. Main St., Louisville, KY; GPS 38.2570, -85.7618).

» Fresh-baked Derby-Pies from Louisville's Kern's Kitchen can be triple-wrapped and shipped directly to your door (derbypie.com). Order a classic full pie or an individual-size tart online from authorized Derby Traditions (derbytraditions.com).

88 APPALACHIAN APPLE STACK CAKE

Precisely how and when the first apple stack cake was baked in Appalachia is up for debate. But the cake, an old-timey special occasion dessert baked by the region's early mountain pioneers, is most closely associated with the Bluegrass State. Local lore says when Appalachian settlers served stack cake at a family wedding, neighbors brought the layers and the hosts supplied the filling.

Also known as Kentucky pioneer washday cake, dried apple cake, and gingerbread stack cake, the "cake" actually is a stack of slim ginger and sorghum dough layers. The filling spread between them is typically apple butter, apple preserves, or dried apples. The result is a thick, moist cake that's slightly sweet and very filling (and low in fat).

Where to Try It

» An Appalachian apple stack cake is time-consuming

Basic Ingredient

🌾🌾🌾 In country kitchens across Kentucky and Tennessee, the syrup on your pancakes or simmered into your beans is more likely to be **sweet sorghum** than molasses or maple. Produced from sorghum grass grown across the nation's arid sorghum belt—from South Texas to South Dakota—the amber-colored syrup pulls double duty as a sweetener and natural health supplement. A spoonful is packed with nutrients such as iron, calcium, and potassium.

to make, so it's not commonly found on restaurant menus. Kroger grocery store bakeries throughout eastern Kentucky and eastern Tennessee often carry the dessert *(kroger.com; multiple locations)*. You also may be able to special order a Kentucky-made stack cake from a local bakery.

The ginger and sorghum dough layers of an Appalachian stack cake are usually spread with an apple filling.

» For a homemade version, you can tackle the cake yourself with the recipe found at *bravetart.com/recipes/applestackcake*, the blog of Kentucky pastry chef Stella Parks.

89 BEER CHEESE TRAIL

Clark County restaurateur Johnnie Allman is considered the founding father of central Kentucky beer cheese. In the 1930s, Allman first served "snappy cheese" with crackers as a complimentary appetizer at his Driftwood Inn on the Kentucky River. The original spicy, sharp cheddar cheese spread recipe has been copied, adapted, and expanded (there's beer cheese soup, chili, burgers, and more) over the years. So, despite claims by different vendors, there's no one true Kentucky beer cheese. Instead, all variations share two key traits: beer in the recipe and enough kick (created by ingredients such as garlic, cayenne pepper, and horseradish) to inspire tasters to douse their flaming taste buds with a cold beer.

The best way to experience the range of Kentucky beer cheeses is to follow the Beer Cheese Trail through Winchester, in Clark County. You'll get a sampling of beer cheese relish trays at eight different restaurants along the way. Fill your cheese log (available at any trail location) with stamps from each place to earn an official Beer Trail T-shirt (*beercheesetrail.com; multiple locations*).

Where to Try It

Other worthy, off-the-trail destinations for Kentucky beer cheese:

» Howard's Creek Authentic Beer Cheese can be ordered online packaged in a pail, plastic container, or ceramic crock. Based on the original snappy cheese recipe, the creamy sharp cheddar blend has a cayenne kick (*howardscreek.com*).

Beer cheese spread on a baguette

» The hole-in-the-wall Wunderbar! in Covington serves its *sriracha*-spiced beer cheese warm. Pair it with a plump, plate-size Bavarian pretzel baked in-house and big enough for three (*wunderbar covington.com; 1132 Lee St., Covington, KY; GPS 39.0768, -84.5150*).

» Main Street in Winchester's historic downtown district is renamed Beer Cheese Boulevard the second weekend of every June during the city's annual Beer Cheese Festival, offering lots of opportunities to sample all kinds of the cheese, along with music and local crafts (*beercheesefestival.com; Winchester, KY; GPS 37.9863, -84.1805*).

90 HOT BROWN

The signature sandwich of Louisville's elegant Brown Hotel and, arguably, of the city is the often imitated but never duplicated Hot Brown. Baked with a bubbly blend of creamy Mornay sauce and Romano cheese (and garnished with crispy bacon) the open-faced turkey sandwich on thick-cut toast was invented in the 1920s by Brown Hotel chef Fred K. Schmidt. He concocted the hot and filling dish as an after-hours snack for the hotel's famished dinner-dance crowd. Then, as now, the Hot Brown is intended to be eaten with a knife and fork, both to savor the flavors and keep your clothes clean.

Where to Try It

» The Brown Hotel's Lobby Bar and J. Graham's Café both serve the original recipe Hot Brown. For a twist on the real deal, try the Hot Brown casserole at the café's all-you-care-to-eat Sunday buffet (*brownhotel.com; 335 W. Broadway, Louisville, KY; GPS 38.2464, -85.7574*).

The bacon on the Hot Brown was suggested by the Brown Hotel's 1920s-era maître d' to *add color to the sandwich.*

The lobby of the Brown Hotel, where Kentucky's signature Hot Brown sandwich was born

» Stella's Kentucky Deli in Lexington is a little, farm-to-table café housed in a cheery yellow Victorian house with a bright red awning. There's a traditional Hot Brown on the menu, plus a herbivore version made with grilled fresh vegetables and chopped tomatoes (stellaskentuckydeli.com; 143 Jefferson St., Lexington, KY; GPS 38.0528, -84.5019).

» At the Whistle Stop in Glendale, owners Mike and Lynn Cummins make their country kitchen version of the Kentucky Hot Brown with turkey and ham. Hold on to your glass of sweet tea when the CSX train rumbles by outside (whistlestopky.com; 216 E. Main St., Glendale, KY; GPS 37.6015, -85.9057).

91 KENTUCKY FRIED CHICKEN

Americans have the interstate system to thank, or not, for the nation's first, and most widely recognized fried chicken chain. A couple of decades before finding fame as the Colonel (a title awarded by the state commission in recognition of his contribution to Kentucky cuisine), Harland Sanders opened a gas station in Corbin on U.S. 25, the main north–south route through eastern Kentucky. Ever the entrepreneur, Sanders quickly recognized the need to feed passing motorists. He started serving food out of the back of the service station, and then added a café (it burned down in 1939 and was rebuilt along with an adjacent motel).

Between pumping gas and preparing meals, Sanders started tinkering with a pressure-frying method to fast-fry his chicken. By the time I-75 was completed in the 1950s and highway traffic was rerouted away from the Sanders Café, Sanders was ready to take his fried chicken—coated in a thin batter with 11 herbs and spices—on the road. Although the first Kentucky Fried Chicken (now KFC) franchise opened in 1952, the North American rollout didn't begin in full force

KFC's handwritten secret recipe of 11 herbs and spices is kept inside a *state-of-the-art vault* in Louisville, Kentucky.

until 1956. The signature paper bucket premiered the following year *(kfc.com; multiple locations)*.

Where to Try It

» Founded in 1968 by Harland Sanders and his wife Claudia, the Claudia Sanders Dinner House in Shelbyville originally was called the Colonel's Lady. The original recipes for fried chicken and fried chicken livers are "finger lickin' good," but mind your manners. This is an elegant southern manor: stately columns, white tablecloths, and linen napkins *(claudiasanders.com; 3202 Shelbyville Rd., Shelbyville, KY; GPS 38.2160, -85.2786)*.

» Harvest in Louisville serves "rustic regional" cuisine including buttermilk fried chicken served with a drunken pork biscuit hoecake. This is not the KFC recipe, but consider it authentic Kentucky fried chicken, since 80 percent of the restaurant's ingredients are locally sourced within a 100-mile radius of Louisville *(harvestlouisville.com; 624 E. Market St., Louisville, KY; GPS 38.2532, -85.7409)*.

No one fries chicken quite like Kentucky, home to Colonel Sanders and KFC.

» The World Chicken Festival held each September in London honors Laurel County's fried fowl heritage. Kentucky Fried Chicken was invented nearby, and Lee Cummings, Colonel Sanders's nephew and co-founder of the Lee's Famous Recipe Chicken restaurant chain, launched his career here. Some 7,000 festival chicken dinners are fried annually in what's billed as the world's largest stainless steel skillet: a 700-pound pan that can cook 600 chicken quarters at a time *(chickenfestival.com; 140 Faith Assembly Church Rd., London, KY; GPS 37.1484, -84.1130)*.

★TENNESSEE★

92 BENTON'S BACON & SWAGGERTY'S PORK

Tiny Madisonville in southeast Tennessee may be pickup-truck country, but its signature brand—Benton's Smoky Mountain Country Hams, in business since 1947—is the Rolls-Royce of bacon. Everything from cupcakes to cocktails infused with Benton's bacon appears on upscale menus in places like New York and L.A. Locals prefer their slow-cured Benton's bacon and ham in a warm, buttermilk biscuit.

Up the road an hour or so in the foothills of the Smokies, Swaggerty's Farm (started in 1930) is to breakfast sausage what Benton's is to bacon. Today, a third generation of the Swaggerty family still produces the all-pork sausage (rolls, patties, and links) on their Kodak farm *(swaggertys.com)*.

Where to Try It

» Visit Allan Benton's roadside store on U.S. 411 in Madisonville to buy whole hams or packages of sliced country ham and bacon. No extra charge for the aromas wafting out from the small woodstove smokehouse *(bentonscountryhams2.com; 2603 U.S. 411, Madisonville, TN; GPS 35.5610, -84.2976)*.

» The menu at hipster-cool Knox Mason in downtown Knoxville celebrates hyperlocal southern ingredients, including Swaggerty's Farm breakfast sausage and warm Benton's bacon vinaigrette *(knoxmason.com; 131 S. Gay St. #101, Knoxville, TN; GPS 35.9683, -83.9204)*.

» Don't forget to ask for a side of fresh country sausage patties from local Swaggerty's Farm when you order the Farmhouse Special Breakfast (two eggs to order, home fries, grits, cinnamon apples, biscuit and gravy) at the Applewood Farmhouse Grill in Sevierville *(applewoodfarmhouserestaurant.com; 220 Apple Valley Rd., Sevierville, TN; GPS 40.7144, -74.0060).*

93 BISCUITS & CORN BREAD

Plenty of Tennesseans would argue that on the eighth day, God made biscuits and corn bread. Cheap, filling, and requiring few ingredients (basically flour or cornmeal, buttermilk, baking powder, and shortening or lard), these two quick breads are the staff of southern life.

Tennessee is the birthplace of biscuit and corn bread royalty: White Lily flour *(whitelily.com)*, founded in Knoxville in 1883 and milled there until 2008; and Martha White flour *(marthawhite.com)*, introduced by Nashville's Royal Mill in 1899 (and named after the founder's daughter). Hot corn bread squares made with White Lily buttermilk white cornmeal mix or from a Martha White quick mix (such as Cotton Country, buttermilk, or sweet yellow) regularly accompany bowls of beans and plates of barbecue.

Where to Try It

» The International Biscuit Festival and the aroma of fresh-baked biscuits draws more than 20,000 people into downtown Knoxville each May. Biscuit-based events include a contest with several categories, including sweet and savory, and samples for nibbling *(biscuitfest.com; Knoxville, TN; GPS 35.9639, -83.9188).*

» Nashville institution the Loveless Cafe has earned fame among regular folk and country music stars for its plates of fresh, warm biscuits that accompany every meal, from country-fried steak and eggs to southern fried chicken. If you must, order online

Sevierville, Tennessee's Applewood Farmhouse Grill serves pork sausage from Swaggerty's Farm.

Crumbly corn bread with butter accompanies many a home-cooked meal in Tennessee.

instead: the All-Time Favorites package includes a two-pound package of biscuit mix, three two-ounce jars of Tennessee-made preserves, and a pound of applewood smoked country bacon (lovelesscafe.com; 8400 Rte. 100, Nashville, TN; GPS 36.0352, -86.9720). » The National Cornbread Festival in South Pittsburg holds a National Championship Cook-Off that requires participants to use Martha White cornmeal and cook their entries in a Lodge cast-iron skillet (the century-plus-old cookware manufacturer is based in town). And perhaps best yet, for those who wish to taste rather than cook, $4 buys you a stroll down Cornbread Alley to sample nine inventive corn bread creations like cheesy skillet corn bread, smoked sausage and green onion corn bread, or (for the sweet tooth) coconut almond corn bread bars or brown sugar corn bread

(nationalcornbread.com; 221 S. Cedar Ave., South Pittsburg, TN; GPS 35.0127, -85.7042).

94 MOONPIES, GOO GOO CLUSTERS & OTHER SWEETS

MoonPies may be Tennessee's most famous confection. Yet, as legend goes, it was a Kentuckian who inspired the chocolate-dipped, marshmallow-filled graham cracker cookie creation. According to company lore, in 1917 a coal miner requested a snack "as big as the moon" that could fit in a lunch pail. The Chattanooga Bakery obliged, and the MoonPie was born.

About 20 miles east of the MoonPie factory, the McKee family has produced Tennessee's Little Debbie

If you're out of buttermilk, you can simply *add vinegar* to regular milk to produce the acidity necessary to make biscuits.

The Loveless Cafe in Nashville, Tennessee, serves hearty southern fare like fried chicken with fresh biscuits.

brand snack cakes since 1960. Named after the founder's granddaughter (that's her image on the logo), the cakes come in an assortment of flavors, including top-sellers Oatmeal Creme Pies, Swiss Rolls, and Nutty Bars *(littledebbie.com; multiple locations)*.

Not to be outdone by Chattanooga, Nashville lays claim to the Goo Goo Cluster, billed as the world's "first-ever combination candy bar." Born in 1912 at the Standard Candy Company, the sticky-sweet mound of peanuts, nougat, caramel, and marshmallow covered with milk chocolate broke new ground in candy-making. Previously, mass-produced confections only featured one main ingredient.

Where to Try It

» At the flagship MoonPie General Store in Chattanooga, buy MoonPies by the carton or sit at the counter to wash down a MoonPie single-decker, double-decker, or mini with an RC Cola *(moonpie.com; flagship location: 429 Broad St., Chattanooga, TN; GPS 35.0514, -85.3110)*.

» Deep-fried Goo Goo Clusters are the signature treat at the ten-day Tennessee State Fair held each September in Nashville *(tnstatefair.org; Nashville, TN; GPS 36.1306, -86.7658)*.

MoonPies

95 CATCH & COOK RESTAURANTS

"You hook 'em, we'll cook 'em!" That's the upbeat mantra of restaurants along Alabama's 46 miles of Gulf of Mexico coast, plus the Intracoastal Waterway that separates coastal beaches from the mainland. Depending on the season and whether you take a deep-sea fishing trip out of Gulf Shores or Orange Beach or drop a line off the fishing pier at Gulf State Park *(alapark.com/gulf-state-park; 20115 Rte. 135, Gulf Shores, AL; GPS 30.2674, -87.6360)*, your catch could include red snapper, triggerfish, amberjack, and king mackerel, among others.

Your catch secured, bring your haul to one of several catch-and-cook restaurants in Orange Beach or Gulf Shores. While you swap fish tales with your dining companions, the chef will prepare your catch (typically blackened, broiled, or fried), and add fries, hush puppies, coleslaw, or other landlubber sides.

Where to Try It

» Shipp's Harbour Grill in Orange Beach offers a regular and gourmet ($12 and up) "You Hook It, We Cook It" menu option that includes salad and sides. Best seats in the house are outside on the covered porch overlooking the boats *(shippsrestaurant.com; 27842 Canal Rd., Orange Beach, AL; GPS 30.2954, -87.5506)*.

» Bring your cleaned catch to Mikee's in Gulf Shores, choose a cooking style (fried, broiled, blackened, pan grilled, or sautéed), and the kitchen crew do the rest. Your meal will include corn fritters, hush puppies, potatoes, and vegetables *(mikeesseafood.com; 205 E. 2nd Ave., Gulf Shores, AL; GPS 30.2503, -87.6877)*.

96 SOUTHERN-STYLE POTATO SALAD

No self-respecting 'Bama tailgate picnic would be complete without enough southern-style potato salad to go around twice. Served cold by the scoopful, the chunky, melt-in-your mouth side dish looks similar to traditional yellow German potato salad. Both include potatoes and some sort of mustard, but the similarities stop there. True southern-style potato salad has

This red snapper caught in the Gulf off the Alabama coast is headed for a catch-and-cook restaurant.

a surprising spicy-sweet flavor (from Creole or Dijon mustard, plus sweet pickles or pickle relish), and it includes mayonnaise, chopped celery or celery seed seasoning, and chopped boiled eggs.

Where to Try It

» Homewood Gourmet, a restaurant and caterer in Homewood, prepares and sells southern-style potato salad by the pint, as a side, or as a scoop on the trifecta Salad Sampler Plate (homewoodgourmet.com; 1919 28th Ave. S., Homewood, AL; GPS 33.4808, -86.7878).

» Publix grocery store locations throughout Alabama sell southern-style potato salad in the deli. Buy a cold 8-, 16-, or 32-ounce container to bring to a picnic (publix.com; multiple locations).

★ MISSISSIPPI ★

97 FRIED CATFISH

Fly over Humphreys County and you might think the farmers below are growing infinity pools. As far as the eye can see, neat rows of watery rectangles glimmer across the pancake-flat Mississippi Delta. Those are commercial catfish ponds, and this is catfish farm country. The county's heavy clay soil is ideal for building watertight ponds—that's one big reason why Mississippi is the nation's top producer of farm-raised catfish.

A health-conscious case can be made for broiling, baking, and sautéing your catfish. Those all are fine

More than 600 fried green tomato slices are served daily at Alabama's Irondale Cafe (irondalecafe.com), inspiration for the novel and 1991 movie *Fried Green Tomatoes.*

options, but they won't fly at a Delta fish fry. Try the real deal: fried catfish coated in yellow cornmeal and seasonings. Add hush puppies, and for goodness sakes, wash it down with a mason jar full of sweet tea.

Where to Try It

» Taylor Grocery & Restaurant, also called "that catfish place," in Taylor is only open Thursday to Sunday. Order the all-you-can-eat catfish dinner for what'll seem like a week's worth of fried catfish (whole or fillets), hush puppies, and sides like fried okra *(taylorgrocery.com; 4-A Depot St., Taylor, MS; GPS 34.2726, -89.5882).*

» The World Catfish Festival in Belzoni each March celebrates the city's 1976 title as "farm-raised catfish capital of the world." Events include a catfish fry, live blues and gospel music, and a catfish-eating contest *(belzonims .com; Belzoni, MS; GPS 33.1767, -90.4895).*

98 MISSISSIPPI MUD PIE

Named for the sticky, ultra-chocolaty filling thought to resemble the banks of the muddy Mississippi River, mud pie, or cake, is four luscious desserts in one. The crust typically is some sort of crushed cookie (Oreos or chocolate graham crackers); the two-layer filling is part chocolate pudding, part flourless chocolate cake; and the topping is straight off an ice-cream sundae—whipped cream, drizzled chocolate, and nuts.

Where to Try It

» Housed in a circa 1737 home, Biloxi's iconic Mary Mahoney's Old French House features homemade

The facade of Taylor Grocery & Restaurant, humble home to generous fried catfish dinners

Mississippi mud pie (along with pecan, key lime, and lemon meringue) on its extensive menu. Reserve a table in the ivy-walled, outdoor courtyard (*mary mahoneys.com; 110 Rue Magnolia, Biloxi, MS; GPS 30.3943, -88.8887*).

» Roux 61 Seafood & Grill in Natchez is a roadside restaurant and watering hole off the beaten tourist path. Its take on Mississippi mud pie is built on a dense chocolate cake base and topped with decadently rich fudge icing (*roux61.com; 453 U.S. 61, Natchez, MS; GPS 31.4925, -91.3670*).

» The Crown Restaurant in Indianola is a café-gift shop that feels a bit like eating at grandma's house. Best of all: its self-serve dessert table (including its version of Mississippi mud pie) in the back. When you're finished eating, tell the gift shop cashier what you had. She'll tally the tab (*thecrownrestaurant.com; 112 Front St., Indianola, MS; GPS 33.4518, -90.6516*).

99 CHEESE STRAWS

Well-mannered Mississippi hosts (are there any other kind?) roll out plates of cheese straws like welcome mats. The crunchy snack is made with cheddar cheese, soft pastry dough, butter, and spicy cayenne pepper. The flaky dough is twisted, rolled, or cut into thin strawlike or crinkle-cut french fry shapes.

Where to Try It

» Indianola Pecan House in Indianola, hometown of legendary bluesman B. B. King, is a Mississippi Delta must-stop on U.S. 82 between Greenwood and Greenville. Buy cheese straws in the store as road snacks, and order more online to eat when you return home (*pecanhouse.com; 1013 U.S. 82 E., Indianola, MS; GPS 33.2756, -91.1809*).

» Look for the blue-and-white tins of cheese straws in the take-out section of both Primos Café locations (*primoscafe.com*): Flowood (*2323 Lakeland Dr., Flowood, MS; GPS 32.3289, -90.1229*) and Ridgeland (*515 Lake Harbour Dr., Ridgeland, MS; GPS 32.4135, -90.1167*).

» The Mississippi Cheese Straw Factory in Yazoo City is owned and operated by the Yerger family,

Cheese straws, a crunchy southern snack staple

fifth-generation Mississippians who built a mail-order business based on an old family cheese straw recipe. Go online to check out the offering of ten flavors, including lemon and key lime (*mscheesestraws .com; 741 E. 8th St., Yazoo City, MS; GPS 32.8559, -90.3997*).

★ARKANSAS★

100 FRIED DILL PICKLES

Bernell "Fatman" Austin is credited with creating the fried dill pickle in 1963 in Atkins. His drive-in restaurant was just across the road from the Atkins Pickle Plant, which produced a steady supply of pickles. Business at the plant generated a fair number of

Continued on p. 120

You can find a *species of catfish* in every state in the United States except Alaska and on every continent except Antarctica.

Barbecued pork and collard greens are classic, hearty soul food fare in the South.

GREAT AMERICAN EATING EXPERIENCES
Soul Food

Yes, soul food is country cooking. And, yes, it is rooted in the South. But soul food adds a uniquely African-American dimension: It feeds the body and the soul and is linked to African-American culture, descent, and history. Soul food provides sustenance, offers comfort, and builds community.

And although soul and southern foods share common ground (including an affinity for frying any-thing), what gives a dish "soul" is a deep connection to the African-American slave experience, and the later migration of those people out of the South and into northern cities and elsewhere in the country.

To find soul food at its root, you'll want to travel all over the South. With hearty mainstays like smoth-ered pork chops, no one ever walks away from soul food hungry.

» Alabama

The Heart of Dixie is home to straight-up soul food, no frills. Look for the hand-painted sign outside Eagle's Restaurant in North Birmingham advertising pig feet, pig ears, chitterlings, and oxtails (cow tail). The vinyl booths hold only about 30 people total. Get there before noon for the lunch plate—choices include fried chicken, steamed cabbage, and can-died yams *(eaglesrestaurant.com; 2610 16th St. N., Birmingham, AL; GPS 33.5437, -86.8310)*. Or grab a plastic tray and join the cafeteria line at Mrs. B's Home Cooking in Montgomery. Mrs. B cooks up com-fort foods like oxtails, sweet potatoes, and collard greens. Plates include corn bread and a glass of fruit punch or sweet tea—all for about $10 *(17 Cullman St., Montgomery, AL; GPS 32.3762, -86.3331)*.

» Georgia

Time hasn't changed Georgia's soul food meccas. Busy Bee Café opened in Atlanta in 1947. New owners over the years haven't messed with a good thing. The menu has always remained pure soul: pork chops fried in peanut oil or smothered in gravy, neck bones and greens, oxtails with gravy over white rice, and more (thebusybeecafe.com; 810 M. L. King Jr. Dr. NW, Atlanta, GA; GPS 33.7544, -84.4140). And tradition is a staple at Macon's H & H Restaurant, where owner Mama Louise started dishing out fried chicken, succotash, and other soul food staples in 1959. Regular patrons have included the Allman Brothers Band. Mama sold the place in 2014, but most of her recipes—and Allman Brothers memorabilia—remain (807 Forsyth St., Macon, GA; GPS 32.8356, -83.6348).

» The Carolinas

Whether you're north or south, the Carolinas are fertile soul food grounds. In North Carolina, Pan Pan Diner has been Durham's signature soul food place since the 1970s. New owners and a move to the Northgate Mall have changed things up a bit, but it's still worth a stop for the history and the pig feet and chitterlings (1058 W. Club Blvd. #528, Durham, NC; GPS 36.0194, -78.9100). Over at La' Wan's in Charlotte, choose a stick-to-your-ribs house favorite, such as BBQ grilled turkey ribs, southern fried chicken, or fried pork chops. For somewhat lighter fare, try the broiled catfish (lawans.com; 7520 S. Tyron St. #19, Charlotte, NC; GPS 35.1509, -80.9266). And Nana's Soul Food Kitchen in Charlotte serves up smothered chicken and pork chops, collard greens, yams, and much more (nanassoulfoodkitchen .com; flagship location: Shops at Lake Pointe, 2908 Oak Lake Blvd. #106, Charlotte, NC; GPS 40.7144, -74.0060).

The traditional main meal in South Carolina is dinner, eaten at midday. The feasting can commence at Martha Lou's Kitchen in Charleston, which serves southern dinner on weekdays from 12 p.m. to 5 p.m. The cheery pink meat-and-two diner (where you pick a meat and two sides) is hard to miss—or forget; you'll feel full the rest of the day. Options include "mystery meat," giblet rice, and bread pudding (marthalouskitchen.com; 1068 Morrison Dr., Charleston, SC; GPS 32.8097, -79.9454). At Bertha's Kitchen in Charleston, check the whiteboard for the day's choices (an assortment of fried meats, plus sides like lima beans and okra soup). The corn bread is sweet, just like the price: around $6 for lunch (2332 Meeting Street Rd., North Charleston, SC; GPS 32.8381, -79.9607).

» Tennessee

Tennessee soul food is about its famed fried chicken, and you can start your day out with a breakfast of just that, plus waffles, at tiny Miss Polly's Soul City Cafe (154 Beale St., Memphis, TN; GPS 35.1399, -90.0528). At the original Swett's in Nashville, a fixture since 1954, soulful eats also mean meat-and-three plates, served from two cafeteria lines: one with down-home dishes (such as country fried steak, okra, and candied yams), the other with barbecue, including pork shoulder and chicken wings (swetts restaurant.com; flagship location: 2725 Clifton Ave., Nashville, TN; GPS 36.1583, -86.8181).

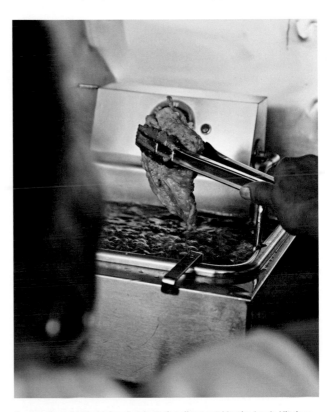

Scrumptious fried chicken is what's for dinner at Martha Lou's Kitchen in Charleston, South Carolina.

Fried pickle chips, an Arkansas delicacy

and *2125 Harkrider St., Conway, AR; GPS 35.1074, -92.4421).*

101 POSSUM PIE

Rest easy. No marsupials are killed to make Arkansas's unofficial state pie. The three-layer dessert gets its name from "playing possum," that is, appearing to be something it's not. To look at it, you wonder, is it a pie, is it a cake, is it a custard? Even food snobs find the creamy combo of vanilla and chocolate custard topped with whipped cream (can you say "Cool Whip"?), sprinkled with pecans, and all layered inside a pecan or graham cracker crust irresistible.

Where to Try It

» Sassy's Red House in Fayetteville slices generous squares of Terri's possum pie, a mixed chocolate and vanilla pudding variation layered high on a pecan crust *(sassysredhouse.com; 708 College Ave., Fayetteville, AR; GPS 36.0737, -94.1572).*
» PattiCakes Bakery *(patticakesbakery.net)* makes the daily batch of from-scratch possum pie served at Stoby's Restaurant in Conway. Order a slice or split a whole pie with the table *(stobys.com; 805 Donaghey Ave., Conway, AR; GPS 35.0888, -92.4542).*

passing motorists, too, so Austin decided to lure them into his restaurant by creating his signature recipe: large pickles sliced lengthwise, rolled in a secret-recipe breading, deep-fried, and served with homemade ranch dipping sauce.

Where to Try It

» Munch on a big and crunchy fried dill and watch, or enter, the pickle-eating contests at Atkins's Picklefest held each May *(peopleforabetteratkins.org; Atkins, AR; GPS 35.2483, -92.9375).*
» Eat My Catfish, with locations in Benton and Conway, serves appetizer fried pickle chips *(eatmycatfish.com; 1205 Military Rd. #7, Benton, AR; GPS 34.5741, -92.5781;*

Surprise

Chocolate gravy and biscuits is the Arkansas equivalent of pancakes and syrup. Filling, sweet, and easy to make with basic ingredients, the stick-to-your-ribs breakfast is particularly popular with kids, since it looks and tastes like dessert. And "chocolate" isn't a code word. This is the real thing: a thick, warm cocoa powder and sugar-based sauce made with milk, vanilla, eggs, and lots of butter.

Billions of bowls around the globe are filled with rice from Arkansas, home to the world's *largest rice miller.*

102 CAJUN FOOD

The terms "Cajun" food and "Creole" food often get blended together like sausage and seasonings in a pot of gumbo. The lines between the two may have blurred over the years, but these are two distinct cuisines with separate traditions, flavors, and dishes.

Cajun food emerged from the South Louisiana swamps and bayous settled by French-Canadian Acadians. Commonly considered "country" food (the Acadians had a knack for using every part of a pig), authentic Cajun is big on pork, particularly boudin sausage; rice; cayenne pepper and paprika; and onion, garlic, bell pepper, and celery. The roux, the fat-and-flour thickener used in the cuisine's sauces and bases, is thick and dark hued.

Where to Try It

» Merci Beaucoup in Natchitoches puts a Cajun spin on all of its creative menu items. Try the Cane River Jambalaya: a mouthwatering blend of black-eyed peas, Cajun stewed tomatoes, seasonings, and ground beef ladled over rice and served with a side of warm corn bread (mercibeaucouprestaurant.com; 127 Church St., Natchitoches, LA; GPS 31.7607, -93.0870).
» Prejean's, billed as one of the world's first Cajun-themed restaurants, is located in Lafayette in the heart of Louisiana's French Cajun Country. In addition to serving up award-winning Cajun specialties like chicken and sausage gumbo, the restaurant stages live Cajun musical acts for its diners seven days a week (prejeans.com; 3480 NE Evangeline Thwy., Lafayette, LA; GPS 30.3062, -92.0280).
» Mulates Restaurant, directly across the street from the convention center in New Orleans, is popular with tourists, but that shouldn't stop you from sampling its authentic Cajun dishes (try the jambalaya or the red beans and rice, served with smoked ham shank) or dancing to the live Cajun music (mulates.com; 201 Julia St., New Orleans, LA; GPS 29.9446, -90.0650).

Luckily, possum pie contains no actual opossum.

103 CREOLE FOOD

Authentic French-Creole dishes (such as oysters Rockefeller and *pommes de terre soufflées*—hollow, twice-fried potato puffs) are considered more genteel than their Cajun country counterparts. Creole culinary roots are planted in French, West African, Caribbean, Portuguese, Spanish, and Native American traditions. The Creole roux tends to be thinner and lighter in color than the Cajun version.

Where to Try It

» Dooky Chase's Restaurant, a New Orleans landmark since 1941, serves a weekday lunch buffet and Friday dinner showcasing the recipes of matriarch Leah Chase, aka the "queen of Creole cuisine." Everyone who's anyone, it seems, has dined at Dooky's, from the Jackson Five to President Kennedy (dookychaserestaurant.com; 2301 Orleans Ave., New Orleans, LA; GPS 29.9682, -90.0785).
» Jolie's Louisiana Bistro in Lafayette has Cajun art on the walls and a locally sourced Creole menu that features dishes like redfish LaFreniere and cioppino stew. Chef Greg Doucet

specializes in the New Orleans–style dishes you'd find at white tablecloth restaurants in the city *(jolieslouisiana bistro.com; 507 W. Pinhook Rd., Lafayette, LA; GPS 30.2080, -92.0108).*

» Commander's Palace—an imposing blue-and-white Victorian mansion in New Orleans' Garden District—is known for its haute Creole cuisine, such as crawfish étouffée, turtle soup, Creole gumbo, and Creole bread pudding soufflé. The Sunday jazz brunch is a must *(commanderspalace.com; 1403 Washington Ave., New Orleans, LA; GPS 29.9289, -90.0842).*

Surprise

New Orleans' *ya-ka-mein,* or "yock," soup is a distinctly Chinese/Cajun mash-up. Thought to have arrived with Chinese railroad workers in the mid-1800s, the traditionally African-American beef broth dish is mild and flavorful. Recipes vary; however, typical ingredients include spaghetti, Cajun seasonings, soy sauce, and hard-boiled eggs. You'll also hear it called "old sober" for its purported effectiveness as a hangover cure.

104 PO'BOY SANDWICHES

The common denominator of any New Orleans' po'boy (named for the free "poor boy" sandwiches served to the city's striking transit workers in 1929)

A classic New Orleans–style fried shrimp po'boy

starts with Cajun- or Creole-seasoned seafood or meat inside crusty French bread. From there, all bets are off. Po'boys can be "undressed" (plain); "dressed" with lettuce, sweet pickle, mayo, hot sauce, and sliced tomato; smeared with mustard instead of mayo; with or without cheese; and on lightly toasted or grilled bread.

The classic po'boy is served toasted, dressed, and stuffed with fried Gulf oysters or shrimp. And the city's thriving Vietnamese community brings its own French-Indochina po'boy, or *bánh mì,* to the table. Built on the same baguette foundation, the Vietnamese-style sandwich typically is filled with sliced pork, pork meatballs, Chinese sausage, or ham, and served with butter, mayonnaise, pickled root vegetables, and sliced jalapeños.

Where to Try It

» Arrive early and prepare to wait (it's worth it) at Guy's Po-Boys in New Orleans. The cash-only shop is open 11 a.m. to 4 p.m. There are enough po'boys here to eat a different kind every day of the week. Save at least one day for the catfish. And order a small unless you intend to share *(5259 Magazine St., New Orleans, LA; GPS 29.9206, -90.1126).*

» Bevi Seafood Company in Metairie serves fresh-off-the-boat shrimp and oyster po'boys and other varieties for around $10. Or try a pricier boy—the fried green tomato and shrimp remoulade—that seems more rich than po' *(beviseafoodco.com; 4701 Airline Dr., Metairie, LA; GPS 29.9760, -90.1823).*

» November's Oak Street Po-Boy Festival in Uptown New Orleans attracts nearly 60,000

Café Du Monde in New Orleans serves only beignets, which you should have with chicory coffee or café au lait.

sandwich lovers and more than 40 vendors selling a dizzying array of delicious po'boys stuffed with everything from German goulash to fried Maine lobster (poboyfest.com; Oak St., New Orleans, LA; GPS 29.9495, -90.1324).

105 BEIGNETS

French Acadians may have introduced these fritter-like, fried dough squares to New Orleans. Served hot and typically in orders of three, beignets are to be savored in a café, not devoured as a quick snack. The eating of beignets (always plural, because it is impossible to eat just one) is a two-step process. First, take a moment to inhale the intoxicating aroma of powdered sugar dusting the still warm beignets. Second, take a bite and chase it with a sip of café au lait. Repeat.

Where to Try It

» At New Orleans' flagship Café Du Monde location, opened in 1862 in the historic French Market, beignets aren't simply the signature food. They're the only food. The only decision you have to make is what to drink: dark roasted coffee and chicory (hot or iced); milk (chocolate or white); orange juice; or a soda (cafedu monde.com; 800 Decatur St., New Orleans, LA; GPS 29.9575, -90.0618).

» Big Easy Beignets and Donuts Café in Denham Springs serves baskets of beignets by the dozen and to-go cups filled with smaller beignet bites. It's open until noon (31799 Rte. 16, Denham Springs, LA; GPS 30.5288, -90.9567).

» At the New Orleans' Foodfest, a weeklong celebration of hometown American fare, beignets are fried up

Specialty of the House

More meal than sandwich, the **muffuletta** is a New Orleans original. Central Grocery says it invented it in 1906 and still serves it. The Frisbee-size sandwich is stacked with Sicilian cold cuts inside a round, soft sesame bun. But it's the topping that gives the muffuletta its signature taste: a spicy Creole-Italian olive-veggie salad (923 Decatur St., New Orleans, LA; GPS 29.9589, -90.0611).

Beignets, fresh from the fryer and soon to be dusted with powdered sugar—and devoured

at the street festival and downed by the dozen at the Beignet Eating Contest. The event is held in March in the French Quarter (*nolafoodfest.com; French Market, New Orleans, LA; GPS 29.9560, -90.0602*).

106 KING CAKE

Mardi Gras season begins on January 6, the Christian feast day of the Epiphany, or Three Kings' Day. According to the Bible, that's the day when the three wise men saw the baby Jesus for the first time. To honor the kings (and likely, to feed the public's need to ingest as many sweets as possible before Lent), New Orleans introduced its own oval version of a traditional French *galette des rois* (cake of kings) in the 1800s.

Originally made of basic dough, the round, hand-braided cake now can be ordered with fillings such as apple, cream cheese, and chocolate. The cinnamon-flavored cakes are glazed on top and decorated with sugar in Mardi Gras's signature colors of green (faith), gold (power), and purple (justice). But the best part is what's hidden inside: a tiny, plastic toy baby, meant to symbolize the Christ Child. Tradition dictates that whoever gets the slice of cake with the bonus baby must host the Mardi Gras party (or at least bring a king cake) next year. King cake season ends Mardi Gras Day, or Fat Tuesday. However, some bakeries will bake and ship king cakes year-round.

King cake

Specialty of the House

A banana surplus inspired the 1951 creation of New Orleans' famous, flaming **bananas Foster**. Owen Brennan, owner of Owen Brennan's Vieux Carré Restaurant on Bourbon Street (now just Brennan's), was stuck with too many ripe bananas and asked his French-Creole chef Paul Blangé for help. The resulting sliced banana dessert, flambéed tableside with rum, banana liqueur, and vanilla, remains Brennan's most requested menu item (*brennansneworleans.com; 417 Royal St., New Orleans, LA; GPS 29.9562, -90.0667*).

Where to Try It

» Joe Gambino's Bakery in Metairie has been supplying New Orleans with sweet Danish dough king cakes since 1949. Traditional single-filling and double-filling cakes are baked, sold, and shipped daily year-round (*gambinos.com; flagship location: 4821 Veterans Memorial Blvd., Metairie, LA; GPS 30.0063, -90.1916*).

» Manny Randazzo King Cakes in Metairie only makes one thing: fresh-baked king cakes. The bakery opens a temporary storefront in mid-December and sells the cakes January 3 through Lundi Gras (the day before Fat Tuesday). Or order online any day of the year (*randazzo kingcake.com; 3515 N. Hullen St., Metairie, LA; GPS 30.0121, -90.1574*).

» Launched in 2014, January's daylong King Cake Festival at Champions Square in New Orleans pits the city's bakeries against each other in a battle of sugary, braided, baked dough. Buy a tasting ticket to sample the entries (*kingcakefestival.org; Champions Sq., New Orleans, LA; GPS 29.9450, -90.0786*).

107 CRAWFISH BOIL

Just over half the year (January or February until about July) is live crawfish season. For locals, this means it's time for a weekend, weeknight, or every night crawfish boil. Equal parts meal and social event, a basic crawfish boil involves cooking up a big pot of potatoes, corn on the cob, Cajun sausage and spices, onions, and a sack (about 30 pounds) of mini-lobster-like crawfish, or mudbugs (never "crayfish").

Facing your first heap of mudbugs can be intimidating. A basic attack plan goes like this: Break off the crawfish head and suck out the yellow-orange "fat" (forgetting it's actually an organ that works like a liver), twist off the tail, pinch the tail meat between your teeth, and pull. You'll be left with a tender piece of tail meat that can be eaten as is or dunked in a mild or Cajun spicy dipping sauce. *C'est bon.*

Where to Try It

» The Galley Seafood in Metairie is a local, family-owned favorite during crawfish season for two big reasons: heaping helpings of fresh crawfish and few tourists. In season, skip the printed menu and order the boiled crawfish platter (*thegalleyseafood.com; 2535 Metairie Rd., Metairie, LA; GPS 29.9812, -90.1512*).

» During crawfish season, New Orleans' legendary Maple Leaf Bar holds Sunday night boils with live music. Seither's Seafood (*seitherssea food.com*) caters with a mind toward experimentation (think quirky additions like frog legs or duck liver), and results have done nothing but increase attendance (*mapleleafbar.com; 8316 Oak St., New Orleans, LA; GPS 29.9490, -90.1321*).

» The take-out joint J & J Seafood in Gretna is a local favorite for boiled crawfish and the usual sides—potatoes, corn, sausage—along with the more unusual accompaniment of turkey necks (*632 Franklin Ave., Gretna, LA; GPS 29.9329, -90.0497*).

» The Louisiana Crawfish Festival in Chalmette, held annually in March, is a four-day crawfish feast. Try them boiled, baked in bread and pie, simmered in jambalaya and pasta sauce, and more (*louisianacrawfishfestival.com*).

» Host your own crawfish boil by ordering fresh live or cooked, farm-to-table crawfish plus local dipping sauces (and free crawfish boil recipes) from

A crawfish boil fresh from the pot

cajuncrawfish.com or the Louisiana Crawfish Company (lacrawfish.com).

Basic Ingredient

Crawfish are freshwater crustaceans historically found in Louisiana's swamps and marshes. Since 2005, however, hurricanes, oil spills, droughts, and development have destroyed or damaged natural crawfish habitats. Today, 85 percent of the nation's crawfish crop is raised in man-made ponds on Louisiana's more than 1,200 commercial crawfish farms.

It takes about *seven pounds of live Louisiana crawfish* to get a pound's worth of peeled tail meat.

MIDWEST

Eastern Europeans and Scandinavians helped shape hearty, flavorful midwestern cooking, while orchards and farms bring bountiful corn, cherries, and cheese.

MICHIGAN
130–134

OHIO
134–136

INDIANA
136–140

WISCONSIN
140–144

ILLINOIS
144–151

MINNESOTA
152–156

IOWA
156–159

MISSOURI
159–163

The Coney dog, smothered in chili and white onions, is Detroit's hot dog—courtesy of Greek immigrants.

There are cherries galore at the summertime National Cherry Festival in Traverse City, Michigan.

★ MICHIGAN ★

108 CHERRY PIE

Around 70 percent of America's tart cherries are grown in Michigan, so the state's beloved cherry pies tend to run more sour than supersweet. Because of their sharp, tart flavor, Michigan cherries are best savored in jams, juices, and pie fillings rather than nibbled fresh from fruit stalls or produce stands.

Early 18th-century French settlers brought the first cherry pits to Detroit and other Great Lakes settlements via the St. Lawrence River. But the region's modern fruit-growing trend didn't emerge until the mid-1800s, when cherry farming took root around Traverse City in northern Michigan. By the end of the century, tart cherries had overtaken their sweeter cousins as the predominant variety grown in Michigan, especially the Montmorency cherry, which has been popular since Roman times.

Cultivation spread along the state's western lakeshore and by 1910, Traverse City had staged its first "blessing of the blossoms" ceremony in springtime. The self-billed "cherry capital of the world," the lakeside city soon instituted other cherry-centric celebrations, including an annual Cherry Queen pageant and National Cherry Festival—and of course, it has numerous bakeries specializing in tart cherry pies.

Where to Try It

» In early July, the eight-day National Cherry Festival attracts half a million people to Traverse City for events like the Cherry Pie Bike Ride (all participants get a free slice of cherry pie), orchard tours, cherry pie–eating contests, and the Make & Bake cherry pie workshop for children (cherryfestival.org; 250 E. Front St., Traverse City, MI; GPS 44.7656, -85.6238).

» Grand Traverse Pie Company makes eight different kinds of Montmorency cherry pie, including cherry-rhubarb, cherry-peach, and cherry-apple (gtpie.com; flagship location: 525 W. Front St., Traverse City, MI; GPS 44.7637, -85.6320).

» The Cherry Hut in Beulah, started life in 1922 as a roadside pie stall and moved to its present spot in 1937. In addition to awesome cherry pie, the restaurant and shop (open seasonally) offer cherry chicken salad, dried cherries, cherry jam, and cherry salsa (*cherryhutstore.com; 211 N. Michigan Ave., Beulah, MI; GPS 44.6353, -86.0886*).

109 PASTIES

The humble pasty, a D-shaped crust stuffed with beef, sliced rutabaga, carrot, onion, and potato, is a beloved comfort food of Michigan's Upper Peninsula.

Its history goes back to the 19th century, when Cornish miners who came from England to work in copper and iron mines introduced the pocket-size pie to the northern Great Lakes region. Miners' wives would stamp each pie with an initial. Later, other ethnic groups adapted the lunch box staple, folding in their own culinary traditions. Modern versions feature pork and chicken instead of beef, and breakfast and vegetarian versions are available, too.

Eating them fresh from the oven is heaven, but pasties also travel well and make a perfect snack for UP hiking, biking, or boating excursions.

Where to Try It
» Founded in 1946 to serve miners in the area, Lawry's Pasty Shop in Ishpeming and Marquette makes traditional pasties, although they do vary in size from 17-ounce giants to bite-size minis (*lawryspasties.com; multiple locations*).
» Grab a window table with views of Portage Lake and order a plate of freshly made pasties with a side of coleslaw at Suomi Home Bakery & Restaurant in Houghton on Michigan's Keweenaw Peninsula (*54 Huron St., Houghton, MI; GPS 47.1222, -88.5683*).
» Dobber's Pasties in Iron Mountain and Escanaba offers one of the wider ranges of the little pie—beef,

A Michigan pasty

Surprise
Who knew the Finns had their own version of the pancake? The breakfast dish called ***pannukakku*** (literally, "pancake") is a simple baked combination of egg, milk, flour, and sugar. Cafe Rosetta in Calumet, on Michigan's Upper Peninsula, offers them with berry sauce or maple syrup (*caferosetta.com; 104 5th St., Calumet, MI; GPS 47.2447, -88.4524*).

chicken, veggie, ham and cheese, and breakfast pasties, as well as a unique pizza pasty stuffed with pepperoni, sausage, provolone, mozzarella, and tomato sauce (*dobberspasties.com; flagship location: 827 N. Lincoln Rd., Escanaba, MI; GPS 45.7556, -87.0772*).

110 CUDIGHI

Like other immigrants to Michigan's Upper Peninsula, Italian miners brought along foods from the old country—in this case spicy pork sausages, which later became the cornerstone of a local sub sandwich called the *cudighi*.

Pronounced koo-duh-ghee, the dish consists of a grilled sausage patty, melted mozzarella cheese, marinara sauce, and onion between halves of French bread, though variations abound. The sausage is usually well seasoned with cinnamon, cloves, and other spices. Although the sandwich has spread across the peninsula, the Marquette area on Lake Superior remains a particular cudighi hot spot.

Where to Try It
» Purists flock to Ralph's Italian Deli in Ishpeming for original-style

One of the ***world's largest ever cherry pies***—nearly 6 yards in diameter and weighing more than 14 tons—was baked in Traverse City, Michigan, in 1987.

A marinara-drenched, onion-topped *cudighi* sandwich

cudighi (*ralphsitaliandeli.com; 601 Palms Ave., Ishpeming, MI; GPS 46.5038, -87.6657*).

» Vango's Pizza & Cocktail Lounge in Marquette offers several versions, among them a cudighi "with the works" that includes mushrooms and green peppers (*vangospizza.com; 927 N. 3rd St., Marquette, MI; GPS 46.5520, -87.3949*).

» On Iron Street in the old mining town of Negaunee, Tino's Bar & Pizza offers an outstanding cudighi with the works (mushrooms and green peppers) plus extra toppings if you want them (*220 Iron St., Negaunee, MI; GPS 46.4989, -87.6091*).

111 GROUND BOLOGNA SANDWICHES

Processed meat forced through a grinder and spread on two pieces of white bread may not sound romantic, but it's mighty tasty: The ground bologna sandwich is a longtime Michigan favorite. The classic version contains Koegel's ring bologna (from Flint, Michigan) mixed with diced sweet pickles, Spanish onions, mayonnaise, mustard, and salt.

You can switch out the old-school meat for whatever bologna catches your fancy: turkey, garlic, jalapeño, and more. The same is true for the other ingredients and the kind of bread you put them on.

Modern chefs have even tried to morph the humble bologna sandwich into a gourmet dish with highbrow ingredients like duck, veal, nutmeg, and white wine.

Where to Try It

» Nehring's Market in the Flint suburb of Burton, makes its own ground bologna sandwich spread ready to slap between two slices (*3517 Belsay Rd., Burton, MI; GPS 42.9760, -83.5932*).

» Close to the Koegel's factory, Colony's Quality Meats in Grand Blanc sells the ring bologna that goes into the classic spread (*colonysqualitymeats.com; 311 E. Grand Blanc Rd., Grand Blanc, MI; GPS 42.9252, -83.6325*).

112 GREAT LAKES WHITEFISH

Found throughout the Great Lakes region, whitefish is one of lakeshore Michigan's most popular dishes, partly because its subtle flavor doesn't taste "fishy" to diners who normally don't love seafood. Chefs along the Lake Michigan coast prepare it all sorts of ways, from grilling, poaching, and frying to making it the principal ingredient in tacos, chowder, and cakes. Whitefish are still a vital part of the state's commercial fishery, and an important summer sport-fishing species. Although they've been caught in sizes up to 15 pounds, the average whitefish runs around 4 pounds.

Where to Try It

» An authentic working fishing village, Leland, sits at the outlet of the Leland River into Lake Michigan. Whitefish features on the menu of several local eateries including the Cove, which offers smoked whitefish pâté, whitefish stuffed with crab and shrimp, baked almond whitefish, campfire whitefish with roasted peppers and onions, and garlic Parmesan whitefish (*thecoveleland.com; 111 River St., Leland, MI; GPS 45.0231, -85.7612*).

» The Fish Monger's Wife, a family restaurant in Muskegon, specializes in fresh, local, sustainable, and wild whitefish (*thefishmongerswife.net; 2127 W. Sherman Blvd., Muskegon, MI; GPS 43.2054, -86.2964*).

» For an upscale Italian take on Great Lakes whitefish, dine at the elegant Chianti restaurant inside the Mission Point Resort on Mackinac Island. Dine on crab cakes with whitefish caviar or semolina-dusted whitefish with asparagus risotto on the terrace overlooking Lake Huron, and complement your meal with one of the house's signature martinis (*missionpoint.com; 6633 Main St., Mackinac Island, MI; GPS 45.8509, -84.6062*).

113 VERNORS GINGER ALE

"Detroit's drink" somehow managed to weather modern mergers in the beverage industry to emerge recently as a popular retro soda in Michigan and beyond. Michigan-made Vernors ginger ale blends the flavors of tangy ginger, caramel, and vanilla with a secret recipe of 19 herbs, spices, and other ingredients.

Company legend holds that Detroit pharmacist James Vernor was so enchanted by a ginger ale imported from Ireland that he decided to make his own version for the pharmacy soda fountain. But the Civil War came along and Vernor went off to fight, leaving his brew in an oak barrel. When he returned four years later, he discovered that his ginger ale tasted pretty swell after all that aging. (More likely, he created the recipe much later, around 1880.)

No matter, the drink quickly caught on with folks throughout the Midwest and Vernor closed his pharmacy and opened a full-blown bottling plant in downtown Detroit.

The brand's beloved mascot—a red-haired gnome called Woody—was retired in the 1980s, but he was "rehired" in the wave of nostalgia that revived Vernors in the early aughts. Now, in addition to drinking it straight or mixing it with various spirits, Motor City residents have put Vernors ginger ale to use as a glaze on salmon, ham, and other dishes.

Where to Try It

» Flint-based Halo Burger still makes its Boston coolers (a Detroit original that may be named after the city's Boston Boulevard and is like an ice-cream float) with Vernors ginger ale (*haloburger.com; multiple locations*).
» Kerby's Koney Island chain features Boston coolers at their 25 locations in southern Michigan (*kerbyskoneyisland.com; multiple locations*).
» In addition to supermarkets, Vernors is available at more than 200 7-Eleven stores in Michigan, which also offer the unique Vernors Slurpee—the chain's first regionally flavored Slurpee (*7-eleven.com; multiple locations*).

114 PICKLES

Motorcar production may have largely moved across the pond, but Michigan still makes a pretty mean pickle. With dozens of farms growing cucumbers,

It's an unlikely claim to fame, but Michigan is the biggest producer of pickles in the United States.

Skyline Chili, one of the first places in Cincinnati to sell the city's distinctive chili, and still a great place to try it

especially in the counties around Saginaw Bay, the Wolverine State ranks number one in U.S. pickle production. Although big companies like Vlasic (founded in the 1920s in Detroit) still dominate the industry, small artisanal pickle makers are revolutionizing the fermented cucumber scene.

Where to Try It

» Based in an old automotive axle plant in Detroit, McClure's is known for its garlic dills and spicy pickles laced with cayenne and habanero peppers. McClure's pickles (*mcclurespickles.com*) are among the many locally made items found at Pure Detroit clothing and gift stores (*puredetroit.com; multiple locations*).
» True to its name, Pickles & Rye Deli in West Bloomfield Township serves fried pickles with sweet serrano aioli dipping sauce (*picklesandryedeli.com; 6724 Orchard Lake Rd., West Bloomfield Township, MI; GPS 42.5387, -83.3605*).

★OHIO★

115 CINCINNATI CHILI

Cincinnati's hometown dish is a chili all its own: a heaping pile of heavily spiced ground beef served atop spaghetti.

According to local jargon, that's a two-way. Add a mountain of shredded cheddar cheese and it's a three-way. A four-way can mean an added topping

Cincinnati residents eat more than two million pounds of chili, about the *weight of 500 cars,* each year.

of either kidney beans or chopped onions; beans *and* onions is a five-way.

Then there's the distinctive flavor of the tomato sauce–simmered beef: spicy (but not too hot), sweet, bright, and warming all at once.

Cincinnati chili dates back to the early 1920s with a Macedonian immigrant, Athanas "Tom" Kiradjieff, and his brother, John, who owned a small Cincinnati restaurant called Empress Chili. The two drew upon the culinary traditions of their native country to create a uniquely spiced chili using bay leaf and oregano, but also adding allspice and cinnamon, flavorings common in eastern Mediterranean dishes.

How the spaghetti came into the picture remains a mystery, but soon other chili parlors in Cincinnati, like Skyline—founded in 1949 by a former Empress employee—and Gold Star followed suit.

Empress has closed its Ohio locations today, and the city's loyalties are split between Skyline and Gold Star. Each place has its own distinctive take on the chili, and the recipes are top secret.

Where to Try It

» Greek immigrant Nicholas Lambrinides sparked a fierce chili rivalry when he left Empress and opened Skyline; the chili here is darker and sweeter than others—some even think it might contain chocolate. Today, there are dozens of Skyline eateries in Ohio and other nearby states *(skylinechili.com; multiple locations)*.

» Founded in 1965 by four brothers from Jordan, Gold Star is a thriving chain that got its start in Cincinnati and now has locations across Ohio and in Indiana and Kentucky. Its chili is redolent of cumin and paprika *(goldstarchili.com; multiple locations)*.

» Price Hill Chili, a family-owned Cincinnati diner, offers a slightly more upscale venue than the city's rival chains. The chili here is less spicy than at other eateries *(pricehill chili.com; 4920 Glenway Ave., Cincinnati, OH; GPS 39.1190, -84.5992)*.

116 BUCKEYE CANDY

Who can resist a confection that evokes a little state pride? The buckeye (which is also a nickname for the state of Ohio and the mascot of Ohio State University) is named for its resemblance to the two-toned nut of Ohio's state tree, the buckeye. These bonbons consist of a ball of sweet peanut butter dough that's partially dipped in melted chocolate. That's where the buckeye nut analogy comes in—the tiny exposed circle of peanut butter on the candy looks like the pale brown patch on each nut. These easy-to-make candies are a favorite Ohio confection both home-made and store-bought.

Where to Try It

» A family-owned chocolatier and ice-cream company since 1935, Malley's Chocolates in Lakewood makes buckeyes with premium milk chocolate *(malleys .com; flagship location: 14822 Madison Ave., Lakewood, OH; GPS 41.4776, -81.8012)*.

» Esther Price has been an Ohio institution since 1952, and makes candy that uses locally made butter in its creamy buckeyes *(www.estherprice .com; multiple stores in Ohio and select Kroger stores)*.

» The Buckeye Chocolate Company in Middlefield makes both milk and dark chocolate buckeyes *(buckeyechocolate.com; 15010 Berkshire Industrial Park, Middlefield, OH; GPS 41.4601, -81.1054)*.

Ohio buckeyes

117 SAUERKRAUT BALLS

In Akron, it's not uncommon to start a meal with an appetizer of deep-fried sauerkraut balls. Kraut mixed with minced ham or sausage, parsley, and other seasonings is rolled into golf ball–size spheres, then breaded and deep-fried. The resulting orbs are crisp and toasty on the outside, tart and tangy on the inside, and need little embellishment—though they're often served with cocktail sauce or mustard. The origin of these zesty little balls is murky, but most people credit Polish or German immigrants with coming up with them sometime in the mid-20th century.

Though the tradition was born in Akron, the rest of the Buckeye State has since caught on. Today, you'll find frozen versions in local grocery stores and homemade sauerkraut balls in restaurants throughout Ohio.

Where to Try It

» The company that helped popularize sauerkraut balls more than any other is Ascot Valley Foods (formerly Or Derv Foods), a 50-plus-year-old brand that makes three varieties (all with ham) to sell at restaurants and grocery stores across the state *(ascotvalleyfoods.com).*
» At Schmidt's in Columbus, sauerkraut balls take on a different quality: Mixed with crumbed bratwurst, yellow onions, and spicy brown mustard, the balls are breaded, deep-fried, and served with a half-mustard, half-mayo dipping sauce *(schmidthaus.com; 240 E. Kossuth St., Columbus, OH; GPS 39.9462, -82.9909).*
» You might be inclined to take the food at Hey Hey Bar and Grill in Columbus for generic pub fare, but you'd be wrong. The house-made sauerkraut balls, mixed with ground sausage, cream cheese, and mustard, are sweet and tangy *(heyheybarandgrill.com; 361 E. Whittier St., Columbus, OH; GPS 39.9441, -82.9871).*

⋆INDIANA⋆

118 MITCHELL'S PERSIMMON FESTIVAL

If you haven't yet tried a persimmon, it's time to take the plunge. These orange, plum-size fruits grow wild in southern Indiana. The supersweet fruit features in a range of local food specialties, including persimmon pudding (actually more like cake that has been sweetened with the persimmon's lush pulp), breads, and cookies.

Persimmon passion peaks every year in September during the fruit's namesake festival in Mitchell, Indiana *(persimmonfestival.org).* Expect a seriously small-town scene, complete with a parade, a candlelight tour of the town's historic area, and shows featuring antique cars and farm equipment. Not surprisingly, the festival's main event is the persimmon pudding competition, which usually draws between 100 and 200 participants every year. Plus, plenty of vendors offer tastes of persimmon pudding and persimmon ice cream.

Where to Try It

» Apart from the festival, sweet-tart persimmon preserves (and more than 100 other jams, relishes, and fruit butters) are available year-round at the rustic roadside stand Gnaw Bone Sorghum Mill in picturesque Brown County, about an hour south of Indianapolis. If you swing by, sample the persimmon pudding and fudge *(4883 E. Rte. 46, Nashville, IN; GPS 39.1615, -86.3178).*

Persimmons

119 HOOSIER SUGAR CREAM PIE

This simple but ingenious pie made with just flour, butter, cream, vanilla, and salt has a special place in the hearts of Hoosiers. State legislature has even named it Indiana's official pie.

Thought to have originated in Amish and possibly Quaker communities in Indiana in the early to mid-1800s, Hoosier sugar cream pie was a dessert born out of necessity during winter months when fresh fruit was unavailable. You'll also hear it called finger pie, likely because cooks sometimes used their fingers to mix the filling into the crust.

While slight variations on the pie exist today (some recipes require cooking the filling on the stovetop before baking; others use a pinch of nutmeg or cinnamon), most of the Hoosier pies you'll find at small-town cafés and restaurants throughout the state stay true to the original.

Where to Try It

» Winchester's Wick's Pies Inc., one of the most influential and respected pie makers in Indiana, has a sit-down restaurant with 30 pie flavors to choose from. What you want, of course, is their famous sugar cream pie, which hews to a 19th-century family recipe

The Blue Gate Restaurant in northern Indiana serves up sugar cream pie among its spread of desserts.

(wickspies.com; 100 N. Cherry St., Winchester, IN; GPS 40.1723, -84.9745).

» Shapiro's Delicatessen, Indianapolis's most beloved deli since 1905, rarely disappoints; neither will the sugar cream pie, which follows the head baker's family recipe (shapiros.com; multiple locations).

» Lisa's Pie Shop in Atlanta, Indiana, sells classic sugar cream pie as well as seasonal fruit versions with raspberry, strawberry, and peach (lisaspies.com; 5995 U.S. 31, Atlanta, IN; GPS 40.2175, -86.1276).

» Blue Gate Restaurant, part of the sprawling Amish Riegsecker Marketplace in northern Indiana, has a traditional from-scratch sugar cream pie on the menu, made without spices and with a homemade crust. It's served with a scoop of vanilla ice cream (riegsecker.com; Farmhouse Riegsecker Market, 195 N. Van Buren St., Shipshewana, IN; GPS 41.6761, -85.5803).

Basic Ingredient

Indiana sits in a sweet spot when it comes to **cantaloupes**. Its melon season peaks in summer when most southern cantaloupes are just about over and it's a little early to pick them up north. Indiana is the country's third largest grower of the melon (after California and Arizona), grown mostly on farms in the southwestern part of the state.

120 TIPTON COUNTY PORK FESTIVAL

For one weekend in September every year, Tipton, a central Indiana town of about 5,000 people, swells greatly as visitors come streaming in to feast on all things pork. Pork burgers, pork ribs, pulled pork, bacon burgers, and more—it's all made with meat raised by local pork farmers. The festival got its start in 1969 when the spouses of Tipton pork farmers

Continued on p. 140

Happy anticipation at American Coney Island in Detroit, home of the Coney dog

GREAT AMERICAN EATING EXPERIENCES
Hot Dog Heaven

Though many consider the hot dog to be the purview of New York (specifically, Coney Island, where it was allegedly first hawked in 1916 for five cents a pop; see p. 42), the Midwest has put its own stamp on the beloved American dog, as have other, prideful places like New Jersey (see pp. 57, 60) and Rhode Island. And though hot dogs are a quintessentially American food, the influence of early 20th-century immigrant populations are to thank for the creation of many of these signature dogs.

» Chicago Style
In Chicago, German immigrants get credit for first selling frankfurters between buns from pushcarts in the early 20th century. And Chicagoans invented the iconic dragged-through-the-garden dog.

The creation is an all-beef wiener nestled into a poppy seed bun and amped up with sweet relish, a pickle spear, hot pickled peppers (sport peppers), tomato wedges, diced onions, and a dash of celery salt and mustard.

The unique combo reflects the rich ethnic makeup of the city. The preference for all-beef is likely due to eastern European Jewish immigrants. And all those embellishments were gifts from Italian and Greek immigrants.

Don't even think about defiling your dog with ketchup at these classic spots: Gold Coast Dogs (goldcoastdogs.net; multiple locations), Superdawg Drive-In (superdawg.com; 6363 N. Milwaukee Ave., Chicago, IL; GPS 41.9967, -87.7870), the Wiener's Circle (2622 N. Clark St., Chicago, IL; GPS 41.9301, -87.6438), Gene and Jude's (geneandjudes.com; 2720 River Rd., River Grove, IL; GPS 41.9299, -87.8466), and Jimmy's Red Hots (jimmysredhots.com; 4000 W. Grand Ave., Chicago, IL; GPS 41.9064, -87.7265).

>> Detroit Style

Greek immigrants in Detroit launched another locally cherished hot dog variation called the Coney Island, a beef-and-pork or all-beef dog tucked into a steamed bun and coated with a meaty, bean-less chili, a squirt of yellow mustard, and a shower of chopped white onions. In the 1920s, when Detroit was a booming auto town, Coneys were the fuel that ran the city—cheap, filling, on-the-go meals for tired assembly-line workers. The rivalry between two of the city's most famous Coney spots—American Coney Island (americanconeyisland.com; 114 W. Lafayette Blvd., Detroit, MI; GPS 42.3313, -83.0485) and Lafayette Coney Island (118 W. Lafayette Blvd., Detroit, MI; GPS 42.3314, -83.0487) runs deep. American Coney Island was founded by brothers Bill and Gust Keros around 1917; they eventually had a family fallout, and Bill left the business to open up his own shop, Lafayette, right next door.

Though Detroit is most famous for Coneys, Flint, Michigan, also lays claim to the tradition, though the chili used in this city tends to be thicker and extra beefy. Angelo's Coney Island, open since 1949, is a must-try (angelosconeyisland.com; multiple locations).

>> Kansas City Style

Kansas City, Missouri, meanwhile, has its own regional hot dog riff. That is, its baseball stadium does. At Kauffman Stadium, Royals fans scarf down hot dogs that take a cue from a Rueben sandwich—a wiener garnished with melted Swiss and a tangle of sauerkraut, on a sesame seed bun (Kauffman Stadium, 1 Royal Way, Kansas City, MO; GPS 39.0510, -94.4806).

>> Rhode Island Style

Plenty of places outside the heartland have their own fierce loyalties to local hot dog traditions.

Order a "hot dog" in Rhode Island and you'll get a variety of the hot wiener known as the New York System, popularized by Greek immigrants in the early 20th century. Ask for yours "all the way" to get a true mouthful: a sausage (usually made of pork and veal) cut to about four inches and cooked slowly on a griddle, and then tucked into a steamed bun, smeared with mustard, and topped with a thin meat sauce, chopped onions, and celery salt. Because the wieners are small, it's customary to eat several in one sitting. You'll feel frozen in time at these old-school Providence locales: Olneyville New York System (olneyvillenewyorksystem.com; multiple locations) and Sparky's Coney Island System (122 Taunton Ave., East Providence, RI; GPS 41.8198, -71.3770).

A classic Chicago hot dog, with its signature pickle spear topping

were exploring ways to promote the pork industry. Today, it's a highly anticipated event for Hoosiers near and far.

Don't miss the inch-thick pork chops, charred to perfection on-site in three giant cookers—there's a reason the crowd goes through ten tons of the juicy chops. Feel free to "pig" out—you can work it off later in the evening, when big-name country music acts hit the stage (*tiptoncountyporkfestival.com; Tipton, IN; GPS 40.2815, -86.0407*).

Where to Try It

» Indianapolis pork lovers who can't make it to Tipton in the fall have another year-round option for succulent pork sandwiches: the Steer-In Diner, a pork standby since 1960 and one of the best places in the state for tenderloin sandwiches. Theirs are made with massive slabs of juicy meat coated with intensely crunchy, peppery breading (*steerin.net; 5130 E. 10th St., Indianapolis, IN; GPS 39.7818, -86.0823*).

121 FRIED CORNMEAL MUSH

A humble dish eaten throughout the world, cornmeal mush gets special treatment in Indiana and throughout the Midwest, where love for the homey breakfast dish runs deep.

Cornmeal mush, fried in butter

At first, it looks a lot like polenta: ground cornmeal slow cooked in boiling water. Once cooked, though, the cornmeal is poured into a pan and chilled; when it has set, it's sliced into squares, floured, and fried in butter, oil, or bacon fat until it takes on a gorgeous golden crust. Often served with maple syrup alongside sausage or bacon, fried mush can be hard to find these days, except at a handful of home-style cafés and Amish restaurants.

Where to Try It

» The fried mush at Das Dutchman Essenhaus, an Amish restaurant in Middlebury, Indiana, is chilled overnight, then sliced and fried in canola oil the next morning. One of the most popular breakfast items on the menu, it's served with maple syrup. Or choose the headcheese fried mush with tomato gravy, a savory, flour-thickened tomato-based sauce typical in Amish cuisine (*essenhaus.com; 240 U.S. 20, Middlebury, IN; GPS 41.6674, -85.7226*).

» Cornmeal mush may not be homemade at midwestern chain Bob Evans (*bobevans.com; multiple locations*) or Lincoln Square Pancake House (*eatatlincolnsquare.com; multiple locations*), with locations throughout Indianapolis, but the simple fact that it's on the menu, alongside eggs, sausage, and bacon, is a throwback to another time.

⋆ WISCONSIN ⋆

122 KRINGLE

In and near lakeside Racine, the top choice for morning pastries and dessert is *kringle*. This ultrasweet, delicious flaky Danish ring is large, flat, oblong shaped, and made from dozens of layers of yeast dough that are filled with fruit, nuts, chocolate, and other fillings. Typically, the treats measure about 14 by 10 inches and yield 12 or so servings.

Danish immigrants, who started arriving in Racine in the mid-1800s, brought kringle with them. By the turn of the century, several versions of the pastry were popping up at bakeries throughout the city.

Time-consuming and labor-intensive, kringles are rarely made at home. In fact, the entire process—which involves mixing the dough, letting it rest, and stretching it until it's very, very thin—takes up to three days. The original kringles were pretzel shaped (*kringle* is Danish for "pretzel" and the pastries are still pretzel shaped in Denmark).

As for the fillings, the most traditional are almond paste and pecans, but you can find everything from cream cheese to chocolate-caramel-pecan. Racine's kringle bakeries do a brisk business year-round, but orders really pick up over Christmas.

Where to Try It

>> O & H Danish Bakery in Racine, named for founders Christian Olesen and Harvey Holtz, has been a family-run labor of love since 1949. Bakers work by hand and machine to turn out thousands of light, fresh-tasting kringles a day (*ohdanishbakery.com; flagship location: 1841 Douglas Ave., Racine, WI; GPS 42.7446, -87.7961*).

>> Thirty varieties of moist, flaky kringle are on offer at Racine's Larsen's Bakery; among the most popular are apple, cherry, and apricot (*larsenkringle.com; 3311 Washington Ave., Racine, WI; GPS 42.7184, -87.8189*).

>> The golden, tender kringles at Lehmann's Bakery in Sturtevant just a few miles from Racine have been made the same way since the 1930s. Today, more than 36 flavors are available; all are finished with a honey glaze and a thin layer of white icing (*lehmannsbakery.com; multiple locations*).

>> For a taste of kringle farther afield, pop into Madison, Wisconsin's beloved Lane's Bakery & Coffee, a family-owned spot since 1954 with stellar kringles,

The flaky, sweet pastry ring known as the *kringle*

doughnuts, and cakes (*lanesbakerymadison.com; 2304 S. Park St., Madison, WI; GPS 43.0407, -89.3954*).

123 CHEDDAR CHEESE & CHEESE CURDS

For cheese lovers, Wisconsin is the place to be. "America's Dairyland" produces more than 600 varieties, leading the country in cheese production. Wisconsin's cheesemaking tradition started off as a way to preserve excess milk.

Of all the state's cheeses, rich and nutty cheddar is among the most popular. Nearly 600 million pounds of Wisconsin cheddar is produced each year. The cheese, which becomes sharper and more crumbly with age, can be either golden orange or white; golden versions get their color from the addition of annatto, a tasteless, odorless vegetable dye.

Cheese curds, a byproduct of the cheddar-making process, are sold fresh at Wisconsin grocery stores as well as creameries and cheese shops. About the size of a walnut, curds are salty, but mild, with a springy texture. Oh, and when you bite into one, it squeaks. Cheese curds can also be found beer battered and deep-fried, which renders the cheese on the inside melty—and completely irresistible.

Where to Try It

>> Four hundred fifty local farms produce cheese for the Ellsworth Cooperative Creamery, a dairy cooperative in western Wisconsin and Minnesota. The group is known for its excellent cheese curds—160,000 pounds are batched each day and sold in the cooperative's two retail shops in Ellsworth and Comstock, Wisconsin, and in area groceries *(ellsworthcheese.com; multiple locations)*.

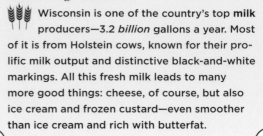

Basic Ingredient

Wisconsin is one of the country's top **milk** producers—3.2 *billion* gallons a year. Most of it is from Holstein cows, known for their prolific milk output and distinctive black-and-white markings. All this fresh milk leads to many more good things: cheese, of course, but also ice cream and frozen custard—even smoother than ice cream and rich with butterfat.

>> Mullins Cheese in small-town Mosinee is run by fourth-generation cheesemakers who sell a wide variety of Wisconsin cheeses, including creamy cheddar, Colby, Gouda, and brick, a Wisconsin-invented cheese a bit like German *Bierkäse* (beer cheese). Also on sale: just-made cheese curds *(mullinscheese.com; 598 Seagull Dr., Mosinee, WI; GPS 44.7176, -89.6959)*.

>> On nights when the Packers are playing, the Village Inn Sports Bar & Grill, a popular sports bar in Hudson,

Cheese curds can be taken to a whole new level of delicious when they're battered and deep-fried.

Wisconsin, right on the Minnesota border, goes through dozens of pounds of cheese curds. Choose from two kinds—lightly battered and beer battered (village innsportsbar.com; 723 6th St. N., Hudson, WI; GPS 45.0028, -92.7550).

124 FISH FRIES

Equal parts social event and meal, fish fries are a fun and inexpensive way to kick off the weekend all over Wisconsin.

A fish fry dinner on Friday night is a long-standing Wisconsin tradition.

Usually on Friday nights, the best fish fries feature local freshwater catch like perch, walleye, smelt, and bluegill, lightly breaded and panfried. Traditional sides like french fries, potato salad, coleslaw, and bread usually accompany the fish. The beverage of choice: beer.

Attended by everyone from families to farmers to college students, fish fries are a tradition that likely began sometime in the 19th century with the arrival of Catholic Irish, Polish, and German immigrants (among others) who abstained from eating meat on Fridays.

These days, some Wisconsin residents like to rotate between different fish fries each Friday, but most are loyal to one or two spots, where they have been coming since they were kids.

Where to Try It

» Cliff's Boathouse Cafe in Racine is one of the few places that still advertises an all-you-can-eat fish fry menu. Cod is usually the fish of choice, and the secret-recipe potato pancakes are not to be missed (cliffsboathouse.com; 301 Hamilton St., Racine, WI; GPS 42.7354, -87.7838).

» The owner of K. K. Fiske on Washington Island, off the tip of Door County, is a commercial fisherman; locally caught whitefish and burbot are among the fish typically featured (1177 Main Rd., Washington Island, WI; GPS 45.3718, -86.9311).

» In 1962, the Friday fish fry at picturesque Wendt's on the Lake, steps from Lake Winnebago, was only 99 cents. That's not true anymore, but the family-owned spot still serves up fried smelt at its weekly fry (wendtsonthelake.com; N9699 Lake Shore Rd., Van Dyne, WI; GPS 43.8832, -88.4686).

125 SUPPER CLUBS

With their old-timey ambience, warm service, and giant, sizzling steaks, it's no surprise that supper clubs—traditionally the venue of choice for the 60-and-up set—are enjoying a comeback in the state.

Historically found roadside (and announced by a giant neon sign) among northern Wisconsin's woods and lakes, supper clubs with wood-paneled walls, low lighting, and massive meal portions offered a relaxing

Each year, Wisconsin makes *enough cheddar cheese* to cover a football field *and* reach the top of a 15-story building.

The HobNob supper club, 1937

way to cap off a long day of fishing or hunting. Though supper clubs exist in parts of Minnesota and Iowa as well, nowhere else is the tradition so firmly embedded in the state's identity as in Wisconsin.

Despite the name, supper clubs are anything but exclusive—the term is a vestige of the Prohibition era, when they were an all-in-one evening out, with dinner, dancing, and booze.

These days, the custom of making a meandering evening out of a supper club visit lives on, though usually without the dancing. Those in the know always order a brandy old-fashioned sweet, Wisconsin's trademark cocktail. Dinner starts with a relish tray, a platter of raw and pickled veggies, often served on a lazy Susan. The meal quickly leads to more carnivorous fare, like Flintstone-size prime ribs, buttery lobster tails, and skewered shrimp. A unique finish to the meal comes in the form of an ice-cream cocktail: the grasshopper, with vanilla ice cream and crème de menthe.

Where to Try It

» In the northern Wisconsin woods of Rhinelander, Rob Swearingen's Al-Gen Dinner Club is a log cabin with

---

Basic Ingredient

🌾 An abundance of choice wheat, along with a large German immigrant population, helped crystallize the strong **beermaking** tradition in Wisconsin. By 1860, nearly 200 breweries were thriving in Wisconsin; Pabst and Miller, both founded in Milwaukee, are still major brands. Today, the state is also home to a rising crop of innovative craft breweries.

---

taxidermy-covered walls, stiff drinks, and reliably good food (*3428 N. Faust Lake Rd., Rhinelander, WI; GPS 45.6312, -89.3709*).

» Toby's Supper Club in Madison dates back to the 1940s. Today, it's known equally for its tender steaks and its fresh-tasting fried perch (*tobyssupperclub.com; 3717 S. Dutch Mill Rd., Madison, WI; GPS 43.0440, -89.3027*).

» The HobNob's menu consists mostly of two sections: steaks and chops, and seafood; you can't go wrong with either. This lakeside spot in Racine features live music on the weekends (*thehobnob.com; 277 S. Sheridan Rd., Racine, WI; GPS 42.6631, -87.8089*).

★ ILLINOIS ★

126 MORTON PUMPKIN FESTIVAL

Anyone who loves pumpkin pie needs to know about Morton. This small town in central Illinois is where they make Libby's canned pumpkin—that Thanksgiving meal staple.

In 1929, Libby's was started in Eureka, Illinois, and later put down roots in Morton. Today, Morton is home to several thousand acres of pumpkin-dotted fields and Libby's only canning plant.

If you want to soak up the town's pumpkin pride, get yourself to the annual Morton Pumpkin Festival, which has been held during September harvest time for nearly 50 years (*mortonpumpkinfestival.org; Morton, IL; GPS 40.6135, -89.4653*). Prepare to feast on all things pumpkin, from pumpkin doughnuts to pumpkin chili; cheer on competitors in a variety of contests (pumpkin decorating is a favorite); and ooh and aah over the giant specimens on display in the Pumpkin Weigh Off (recent winners have clocked in at more than 1,000 pounds). Don't miss the pumpkin pancake breakfast, which starts at 6:30 a.m. sharp Saturday morning (long lines form quickly). For lunch, feast on a brat or tenderloin sandwich (this is the Midwest, after all), then try the pumpkin ice cream, made on-site, for dessert.

Where to Try It

For more Illinois pumpkin:

» Pumpkin pie gets a makeover at Bang Bang Pie & Biscuits, a food truck turned brick-and-mortar spot in

Chicago's trendy Logan Square neighborhood. Available October to December, Bang Bang's pumpkin pies come with a crumbly graham cracker crust and are topped with whipped cream and pumpkin seed brittle (bangbangpie.com; 2051 N. California Ave., Chicago, IL; GPS 41.9191, -87.6971).

127 DEEP-DISH PIZZA

With its extra-thick crust and colossal amounts of cheese, Chicago deep-dish pizza is a perfect early example of America's preference for supersize dishes.

In the early 1900s, there were just a handful of pizza joints in Chicago, serving Neapolitan-style pies to mostly first- and second-generation Italian immigrants. Then entrepreneurs Ike Sewell and Ric Riccardo opened Pizzeria Uno in 1943 and that all changed. Their pizza, which they hoped would appeal to a wider audience and be more filling than the thin version, was nothing like anything Chicagoans had tasted before: a crunchy crust and layers of chunky tomato sauce, cheese, and sausage—all in crazily amped-up proportions. The city was skeptical at first, but the restaurant soon had lines down the block and, in the years that followed, scores of other deep-dish temples joined the dining scene.

Today, pizza purists may question whether the deep-dish is more casserole than pizza, but that's really a technicality—and what's not to love in a thick, cheesy piece of pie? (See also pp. 40–41.)

Where to Try It

» Chicago's original Pizzeria Uno, different from the nationwide chain, is the birthplace of deep-dish pizza (pizzeriaunochicago.com; 29 E. Ohio St., Chicago, IL; GPS 41.8923, -87.6269).

» Lou Malnati's empire of more than 40 Chicago-area restaurants is widely considered to offer one of the most authentic deep-dish options in the city. Lou and his father, Rudy, got their start at the original Pizzeria Uno. Order the Chicago Classic—a crisp, buttery crust topped with plenty of sausage and cheese (loumalnatis .com; flagship location: 6649 N. Lincoln Ave., Lincolnwood, IL; GPS 42.0022, -87.7256).

» At Burt's Place, a legendary spot in suburban Morton Grove, Burt Katz crafts a leaner version of

Chicago deep-dish pizza, one of the first American mega-dishes

Giant pumpkins at the Morton
Pumpkin Festival in Illinois

deep-dish using fresh ingredients purchased that very morning. Baked in steel pans blackened from use over the years, Katz's pizzas have an irresistible crispy ring of Parmesan around the edges and a crisp-bottom crust *(8541 Ferris Ave., Morton Grove, IL; GPS 42.0370, -87.7847)*.

128 HORSESHOE SANDWICH

You'd be hard-pressed to find one elsewhere in the country, but in Springfield, capital of Illinois, the horseshoe sandwich is king. Variations abound, but the original horseshoe was the ultimate open-faced sandwich: two pieces of white toast stacked with a horseshoe-shaped ham steak, a pile of fries, and a Welsh rarebit–style cheese sauce. According to popular legend, chef Joe Schweska came up with the dish in 1928 at Springfield's Leland Hotel (now an office building).

Today, you can order a horseshoe made with everything from a hamburger to a chicken cutlet at pretty much every type of restaurant in Springfield. If you fear heartburn afterward, go for the diminutive pony shoe, made with just one piece of toast. However you order, make sure there's a fork and knife nearby—this isn't the kind of "sandwich" you'll want to grab with your hands.

Where to Try It

» At Darcy's Pint—an Irish pub in Springfield—horseshoes and their spin-offs occupy an entire section of the menu. All "shoes" start with Texas toast; some come stacked high with additional toppings like chili, scallions, or tomatoes *(darcyspintonline.com; 661 W. Stanford Ave., Springfield, IL; GPS 39.7655, -89.6629)*. At historic Charlie Parker's, you can order your horseshoe with walleye *(charlieparkersdiner.com; 700 North St., Springfield, IL; GPS 39.7660, -89.6635)*.

» Also in Springfield, don't miss the breakfast horseshoe at D & J Cafe, a beloved, inconspicuous spot: Picture a base of toast, and then eggs and sausage all topped with sausage gravy, cheese sauce, and a mountain of hash browns *(915 W. Laurel St., Springfield, IL; GPS 39.7829, -89.6675)*.

» 6 Degrees in Chicago's Bucktown neighborhood is the best place to find a horseshoe outside of the state's capital—the owner is a Springfield transplant *(6degreesbucktown.com; 1935 N. Damen Ave., Chicago, IL; GPS 41.9170, -87.6774)*.

129 ITALIAN BEEF SANDWICH

There are so many slices of paper-thin, gravy-dripping roast beef piled into an Italian beef sandwich that you're pretty much guaranteed to make a mess while eating it. No matter—you'll fit right in at the casual "beef stands" unique to Chicagoland (Chicago and environs), most of which are no-frills joints with little more than a stand-up counter for eating.

What makes these massive sandwiches so good? There's the crusty French or Italian roll; the long-cooked, flavorful beef, usually sirloin or rump; the *giardiniera,* a spicy relish of chilies and vegetables that adds crunch and heat; and the jus, or souplike gravy, in which the beef is cooked.

Before ordering, brush up on the local terminology: A dry sandwich means the beef will get a brief swirl in gravy before it's loaded onto the bread; a wet version

Charlie Parker's diner will give you nine choices of meat for your horseshoe.

The Italian beef sandwich at Al's in Chicago—if you believe their story, you're eating the true original.

will get some gravy ladled over the sandwich; and a dipped version means the whole shebang, bread and all, gets dunked in gravy (it's good). Ask for it hot if you want the giardiniera (you do) or sweet if you'd rather have strips of green peppers as a topping.

Where to Try It

>> Al's #1 Italian Beef claims to have invented the Italian beef sandwich in Chicago back in 1938, when the restaurant's founders were looking for ways to stretch meat during the Depression. Today, Al's makes one of Chicago's best Italian beefs—slow-cooked top sirloin folded into same-day-baked bread with a perfect giardiniera (alsbeef.com; flagship location: 1079 W. Taylor St., Chicago, IL; GPS 41.8693, -87.6540).

>> Since 1961, Johnnie's, a bare-bones, roadside stop in Elmwood Park, has been perfecting its Italian beef sandwich: thick shreds of garlic- and black pepper–spiced beef soaked in jus, and topped with a house-made giardiniera of carrots, cauliflower, and sport peppers. Order a zingy Italian ice to go with it (7500 W. North Ave., Elmwood Park, IL; GPS 41.9089, -87.8133).

130 POPCORN

Inseparable from the movies and the munchies, some might call popcorn the bedrock all-American, sit-around-and-snack food. We have the state of Illinois to thank for it.

Popcorn originated in Illinois, but Nebraska leads the nation in production, popping more than *350 million pounds* a year.

In 1893, the debut of two Illinois inventions to the general public set the stage for the age of popcorn: One was Cracker Jack candy, created in Chicago by German immigrant brothers Frederick and Louis Rueckheim; the other was a mobile, steam-powered machine that could pop corn as fast as you could eat it, invented by a confectionery shop owner from Decatur, Illinois, named Charles Cretors. He debuted his revolutionary machine at the World's Columbian Exposition in Chicago, and the public was dazzled. Soon popcorn became a popular snack sold by street vendors all over the city. Cretors went on to design electric poppers, used in movie theaters, which further cemented popcorn in American snack culture.

Where to Try It

» For more than 65 years, Chicago-based Garrett Popcorn has been crafting batches of popcorn the old-fashioned way, using copper kettles. The Garrett Mix, an addictive combo of caramel corn and savory cheese corn—and the company's best seller—is the kind you want (*garrettpopcorn.com; multiple locations*).

» "Nuts on Clark" is a family-owned Chicago institution with stands at all the crowded places—the city's train stations, baseball fields, and airports. It uses locally grown corn in its popcorn, which comes in half a dozen flavors. And as the name suggests, they also sell nuts (*nutsonclark.com; multiple locations*).

» Unlike the city's other major popcorn players, Wells Street Popcorn's snacks are completely nut-free. The shop has locations in Chicago and its suburbs (*wellsstreetpopcorn.com; multiple locations*).

131 STEAK HOUSES

Considering Chicago's role as the country's meat-packing epicenter for nearly a century, it's not surprising that the city is rapturous about good-quality beef. Perhaps that's why steak houses play such an

important role in the city—both in honoring its past and in looking toward the future.

Chicago's steak houses range from clubby, decades-old spots that once served the likes of Frank Sinatra to sleek steak joints with menus that nod to today's culinary landscape (care for some *shishito* peppers with your rib eye?).

Where to Try It

» For the old-school experience, look no further than Gibsons Bar & Steakhouse in Chicago, a 25-year-old joint with wood-paneled walls and white table-cloths. Their flavorful Black Angus steaks come from the Upper Midwest *(gibsonssteakhouse.com; 1028 N. Rush St., Chicago, IL; GPS 41.9013, -87.6281).* Another spot with an old-fashioned feel is Morton's. From the warm onion bread to the delectable wet-aged, charred steaks, eating here always feels like a special occasion *(mortons.com; multiple locations).*
» Want something hipper? With its speakeasy-like space and retro cocktails, Chicago's Bavette's is any-thing but stodgy. The food is serious, though, from the tender rib eye to the rarely seen old Chicago dish, garlicky shrimp de Jonghe *(bavetteschicago.com; 218 W. Kinzie St., Chicago, IL; GPS 41.8893, -87.6349).*

132 FRANGO MINTS

Few American confections inspire the same nos-talgia as Chicago's Frango mints, those delectable chocolate truffles tucked into dark green boxes and historically popular at Christmastime.

From the early 1930s until 1999 (when produc-tion was moved off-site), the treats were made at Chicago's most beloved department store, Marshall Field's, on State Street. They were an iconic sym-bol of the store, and Macy's, which bought Marshall Field's in 2005, has happily carried on the Frango tradition.

A quick Frango primer: The classic mint chocolate variety is essential, but the dark mint chocolate and dark raspberry chocolates are just as tempting.

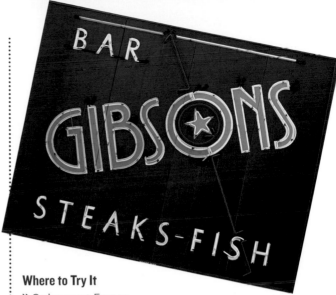

Where to Try It

» Order some Frango cheesecake or Frango mint ice-cream pie at Chicago's Frango Café, on the seventh floor of Macy's historic Marshall Field's building. Don't leave without stocking up on Frango goodies; the store where the chocolates started also sells the complete line of the candy company's products. If you come during the holi-days, be prepared for a crowd *(111 N. State St., Chicago, IL; GPS 41.8838, -87.6275).*
» The bad news is that Frango chocolates are only available from Macy's. The good news: You can order online and have them shipped anywhere in the country *(macys.com).*

Specialty of the House

At almost any restaurant in Chicago's Greektown, you'll find **flaming *saganaki,*** a square slice of Greek sheep's milk cheese fried in olive oil, doused in brandy, and set alight as the waiter exclaims *"Opa!"* Accord-ing to local legend, the appetizer was first served in 1968 at Greektown's famed Parthenon restaurant. Crisp edged and deliciously salty, saganaki always disappears within minutes of the flames being extinguished.

***More than a million pounds** of Frango mints are sold each year.*

The molten-cheese middle of a Juicy Lucy hamburger

blue cheese in its Juicy Lucy. Although its story is less precise, the 5-8 credits itself with inventing the burger in the 1950s (*5-8club.com; 5800 Cedar Ave. S., Minneapolis, MN; GPS 44.8977, -93.2479*).

» To the horror of Southsiders, the Lucy has migrated across the Mississippi to St. Paul, where the Blue Door Pub has elevated the burger to gourmet status with versions like the coconut and ginger-infused Bangkok Blucy; the Erin Go Blucy with Swiss cheese, sauerkraut, and corned beef; and the Breakfast Blucy with bacon and fried egg (*thebdp.com; multiple locations*).

★ MINNESOTA ★

133 JUICY LUCY

The Juicy Lucy is a hamburger—but not just *any* burger, say aficionados on the city's south side, where the dish was born. The Juicy Lucy contains a golden, molten, cheesy core tucked into the middle of a beef burger, and Minneapolitans proudly proclaim the gooey, delicious patty as their own.

A couple of vintage Cedar Avenue eateries—Matt's Bar and the 5-8 Club—have been dueling over who invented the Lucy since the 1950s. The only verdict arising from the long-standing rivalry is that everyone south of Powderhorn Park agrees that more cheese is better than less.

Where to Try It

» Matt's Bar near Powderhorn Park still serves its fat Lucys with the traditional American cheese melted in the middle. Local legend holds that founder Matt Bristol exclaimed, "That's one juicy Lucy!" when he first tasted his creation in 1954. In addition to claiming the Lucy as its own, Matt's has always set itself apart by spelling it "Jucy" instead of "Juicy" (*mattsbar.com; 3500 Cedar Ave. S., Minneapolis, MN; GPS 44.9394, -93.2476*).
» Born as a Prohibition speakeasy, the 5-8 Club offers a choice of American, Swiss, pepper jack, or

134 WILD RICE

For thousands of years, humans have harvested and eaten the wild rice that flourishes in marshy areas of Minnesota. Today, the state leads the nation in the production of natural wild rice.

In addition to its distinctive nutty flavor, wild rice has nutritional virtues: It's high in protein, vitamins, and minerals and lends itself to many culinary uses, from chowders and soups to stuffing and sushi.

The only cereal grain native to North America, wild rice was more than just a food to Minnesota's Ojibwe people. It was also a vital part of their culture, economy, and religion, and the monthlong wild rice harvest season was the apex of every year. After harvesting the rice in canoes (it generally grows in clear, shallow water), the Ojibwe processed the grain in autumn "rice camps" near lakes or

Basic Ingredient

More than 50 kinds of **wild berries** thrive in the Minnesota countryside, from blueberries to partridgeberries. *Wild Fruits of Minnesota: A Field Guide* can help you figure out what you're seeing. And stop by the Minnestalgia Winery in McGregor (*minnestalgiawinery.com; 41640 Rte. 65, McGregor, MN; GPS 46.6169, -93.3171*) to imbibe one of its 11 varieties of berry wine.

streams. The tradition continued well into the 20th century (and still does on reservations) and almost overlapped with the advent of wild rice cultivation in 1950s Minnesota.

Where to Try It

» Harriet Alexander Nature Center in Roseville, Minnesota, hosts a Native American–focused Wild Rice Festival each September where visitors can feast on wild rice pancakes, sausages, and "four sisters" soup made with corn, squash, beans, and wild rice (*wildricefestival.org; 2520 N. Dale St., Roseville, MN; GPS 45.0192, -93.1232*). July's Deer River Wild Rice Festival puts a rural American spin on the rice harvest with a parade, bingo, a beer garden, a tractor pull, and the United Methodist Church Wild Rice Dinner (*wildricefestival.com; Deer River, MN; GPS 47.3328, -93.7930*).
» Year-round, you can sample Mahnomin porridge at Hell's Kitchen in downtown Minneapolis. Made with locally harvested, hand-parched wild rice from the Leech Lake Band of Ojibwe, the breakfast dish is served with heavy cream, roasted hazelnuts, dried blueberries, sweetened cranberries, and pure maple syrup. The restaurant also sells a home porridge kit with most of the fixings (*hellskitcheninc.com; 80 S. 9th St., Minneapolis, MN; GPS 44.9747, -93.2730*).

135 SCANDINAVIAN FOODS

With around a third of the population (1.6 million people) claiming Scandinavian heritage, it's natural that Minnesota would boast its fair share of Nordic foods. From Swedish meatballs to Norwegian *lefse* (flatbread), Scandinavian food has for more than a century been a staple in many Minnesota kitchens.

   More recently, the food of northern Europe has entered the mainstream with a strain of New Nordic cuisine that's featured at trendy restaurants in the Twin Cities area. New Nordic dishes combine fresh, local ingredients with traditional cooking methods, and the result is a little like California cuisine with a Scandinavian bent.

Where to Try It

» A Minneapolis landmark since 1921, Ingebretsen's deli hawks a wide variety of Scandinavian edibles including

---

Basic Ingredient

Minnesota is one of three states (along with Texas and South Dakota) that leads the nation in production of edible **goose,** the fourth most popular American poultry after chicken, turkey, and duck. It was once the most popular Christmas-dinner fowl, but a mid-20th-century marketing push by America's turkey producers pushed the gobbler into first.

---

lefse, Swedish meatballs, blood sausage, *klub* (potato dumplings), *spekekjøtt* (dry-cured meats), lutefisk (dried, salted whitefish), and Danish liver pâté (*ingebretsens.com; 1601 E. Lake St., Minneapolis, MN; GPS 44.9482, -93.2510*).
» Norwegian almond *kringle* cookies, Swedish *limpa* bread, and Finlandia tortes are just a few of the items made fresh every day at the Taste of Scandinavia Bakery & Café in the Twin Cities (*celebrate.tasteofscandinavia.com; multiple locations*).
» The Bachelor Farmer in Minneapolis has a rooftop garden that grows many of the herbs and spices featured on its Nordic-inspired menu. Among the constantly rotating choice of dishes are salt- and sugar-cured salmon, and baked duck egg with fiddlehead ferns and morels. Sunday brunch features a modern take on traditional *smørrebrød*, an open-faced sandwich with cold cuts (*thebachelorfarmer.com; 50 N. 2nd Ave. N., Minneapolis, MN; GPS 44.9857, -93.2687*).
» Open for breakfast and lunch six days a week, Fika café at the American Swedish Institute in Minneapolis goes all out with New Nordic cuisine. Its menu features juniper-spiced

Wild rice grains

Harvesting the rooftop garden at
Minneapolis's Bachelor Farmer restaurant,
which specializes in Nordic food

meatballs, gravlax with herb crème fraîche, and potato sausages with pickled herring (*fikacafe.net; 2600 Park Ave., Minneapolis, MN; GPS 44.9553, -93.2653*).

★IOWA★

136 MUSHROOMS

Come spring, thousands of Iowans head for the woods, dales, and river valleys in search of fresh—and wonderfully edible—mushrooms, or fungi. Several varieties thrive in the Hawkeye State's rich soils and humid continental climate. Morels are the most common, but avid mushroom hunters are also on the lookout for porcini, hen of the woods, goat's beard, coral, puffballs, and oyster varieties.

Several organizations cater to the state's love of fungi. The Iowa-based Prairie States Mushroom Club organizes regular forays to search for mushrooms, and they even have a "SmugMug" page for members to post their mushroom finds. An entire Facebook page is dedicated to "basic talk about morels in Iowa." And Iowa State University maintains a Fungi of Iowa website (*herbarium.iastate .edu/fungi*) with a searchable database created by distinguished mycologists and curators from the university's Ada Hayden Herbarium.

Each variety of mushroom has its culinary peculiarities. Oysters derive their name from a slight shellfish essence. Morels are somewhat nutty in flavor. Often growing to more than ten pounds, hen of the woods are huge and can be parceled out over numerous meals. White, stringy goat's beard, with its uncanny resemblance to vermicelli noodles, goes well in stir-fry dishes.

Although mushrooms can be used in a variety of dishes, purist Hawkeyes prefer them prepared with a light touch—perhaps sautéed in butter or olive oil with a pinch of seasoning—rather than drowned in sauces or mixed with other vegetables.

Where to Try It

» Members of the general public are welcome to join the Prairie States Mushroom Club's forays, workshops, and lectures between May and October each year. Iowa's Wickiup Hill Natural Area (in Toddville), Palisades-Kepler State Park (Mt. Vernon), and Grimes Farm (Marshalltown) are some of the club's regular foraging areas (*multiple locations; iowamushroom.org*).

» Fungi feature in several specialties at Trostel's Dish restaurant in Clive, Iowa, including roasted mushrooms with boursin cheese, duck confit with mushroom onion hash, and lobster risotto with wild 'shrooms (*dishtrostels.com; 12851 University Ave., Clive, IA; GPS 41.6010, -93.7962*).

137 PORK TENDERLOIN SANDWICH

With more than 20 million pigs, double the number of the next most pig populous state, it's no surprise that Iowans love their pork. In particular, they love a pork tenderloin sandwich.

Breaded with flour and eggs and then deep-fried, the boneless meat is prepared in a way similar to Wiener schnitzel, and then it's placed on a roll and topped with various burger-like condiments. Although it was allegedly invented in Indiana, the sandwich has been an Iowa staple for nearly 100 years.

Where to Try It

» Porky's Revenge is the name of the hogzilla-size sandwich at the Lucky Pig Pub & Grill in Ogden, a tenderloin topped with barbecued pulled pork, four strips of bacon, and Swiss cheese (*113 W. Walnut St., Ogden, IA; GPS 42.0393, -94.0290*).

» Pick up a pork tenderloin sandwich to go at the Brick Street Market's Butler Café in Bondurant or purchase your own locally farmed pork products at the meat counter in the market (*thebrickstreetmarket .com; 114 Brick St. SE, Bondurant, IA; GPS 41.6898, -93.4618*).

» Just a mile from the Mississippi River, Breitbach's Country Dining in bucolic Sherrill offers a choice of

At any given time, Iowa's *6,000-plus hog farms* are raising around 20 million pigs, about a third of the U.S. pig population.

Fresh Dutch letters in the classic S shape at Jaarsma Bakery in Pella, Iowa

grilled or hand-battered pork tenderloin sandwiches, as well as pork chops, ham steaks, and pork ribs *(breit bachscountrydining.com; 563 Balltown Rd., Sherrill, IA; GPS 42.6391, -90.8692)*.

» The breaded pork tenderloin sandwich at B&B Grocery Meat & Deli was named "central Iowa's ultimate sandwich" by the Des Moines *Cityview* newspaper *(bbgrocerymeatdeli.com; 2001 SE 6th St., Des Moines, IA; GPS 41.5698, -93.6051)*.

138 DUTCH LETTERS

What's the best letter in the alphabet? In Iowa, the answer would always be *S*, thanks to those delicious butter pastries called Dutch letters.

Packed with almond paste and sprinkled with sugar crystals, the flaky favorites have been an Iowa tradition since late 19th-century Dutch settlers brought the recipe over with them from Holland. Edible letters have a long tradition in Europe. The popular S shape (the one you'll see in Iowa bakeries) derives from the fact that

the pastries were especially popular on Sinterklaas Day (Santa Claus Day, observed on December 6).

Nowadays, Iowa bakeries sell them year-round, catering to sweet-toothed patrons that just don't want to wait for the holidays to roll around again.

Basic Ingredient

Desserts, trifles, casseroles, salads— there's really nothing an Iowa native can't make into a **Jell-O** dish, in combination with other ingredients that may include (but are not limited to) fruits, vegetables, coconut, nuts, Miracle Whip, buttermilk, cottage cheese, or even Coke. But always bonding the entire wiggly heap is Jell-O, in any of its nearly 20 flavors. Lemon-flavored Jell-O, for instance, is blended with pineapple, banana, and marshmallows and topped with Cool Whip, pineapple juice, and cheddar cheese to make a longtime holiday favorite in the Hawkeye State.

Where to Try It

» Established in 1898 by Dutch immigrant Harmon Jaarsma, Jaarsma Bakery (in Pella and Oskaloosa) sells Dutch letters by the dozen and half dozen, as well as other Dutch treats like *speculaas* (spice cookies) and almond-filled *gevulde koek* cookies (*jaarsma bakery.com; 727 Franklin St., Pella, IA; GPS 41.4065, -92.9176*).

» For something savory with your sweet Dutch letters, stroll 130 feet farther east along Pella's Franklin Street to Vander Ploeg Bakery, where the pastries are sold solo or in combo boxes that also include Dutch sausages and spices (*vanderploegbakery.com; 711 Franklin St., Pella, IA; GPS 41.4065, -92.9170*).

139 ESKIMO PIES

The story is now enshrined in Hawkeye State folklore: Onawa resident Christian Kent Nelson invented the Eskimo Pie. Although he was the son of a Danish immigrant dairy farmer, Nelson decided that farming was not in his future and instead became a proprietor of a confectionery shop and the Latin teacher at the local high school.

Sometime in 1921, an eight-year-old came into Nelson's store with enough money to buy either an ice-cream sandwich or a chocolate bar, but not both. The resourceful Nelson set about creating a blend of chocolate, cocoa butter, and vanilla ice cream that would provide both treats in the same bite.

Nelson initially called his frozen novelty the I-Scream Bar, a name changed to Eskimo Pie a year later when he teamed up with local chocolatier Russell Stover to patent, mass-produce, and market the confection.

The original store is gone, but Eskimo Pie has become part of American pop culture, featured in everything from the play *Inherit the Wind* to the long-running *Two and a Half Men* television series. It's even the name of a classic country song by George Jones (though in a play on words, his "Eskimo pie" was a woman, not a dessert).

Where to Try It

» The Monona County Historical Museum in Onawa features an "Eskimo Pies" exhibit with vintage packaging and one of Nelson's original chocolate dipping machines. The museum sometimes sells the chocolate ice-cream bars during the summer (*47 12th St., Onawa, IA; GPS 42.0281, -96.0998*).

» Imitation being the sincerest form of flattery, the Internet is flush with recipes for homemade Eskimo Pies, including one at TasteBook comprising brownie mix, vanilla ice cream, chocolate dipping sauce, and caramel sauce (*tastebook.com*).

140 LOOSE MEAT SANDWICH

As if one state sandwich wasn't enough, Iowa is also stark raving mad for the loose meat variety. Also called a steamed sandwich or a tavern sandwich (because they were traditionally served in bars), the filling is ground beef that is left loose, rather than pressed into a patty.

Loose ground beef tumbles out of a Maid-Rite sandwich.

The lightly seasoned meat is initially fried and then steamed in water before it's placed into a burger bun. Pickles and mustard are the traditional toppings, but modern takes on the loose meat sandwich feature onions, ketchup, cheese, and other add-ons. Purists insist the sandwich should always be presented in waxed paper.

Where to Try It

» Hawkeye butcher Fred Angell supposedly invented the loose meat sandwich in 1926, the same year he opened the first Maid-Rite restaurant in Muscatine. Maid-Rite eateries in Iowa (and elsewhere in the Midwest) serve the original as well as a cheesy version with a choice of Swiss, American, or mozzarella (maid-rite.com; multiple locations).

» Although locals cherish its loose meat sandwiches, Ottumwa's hole-in-the-wall Canteen Lunch in the Alley is also renowned as the inspiration for the fictional Lanford Lunch Box restaurant where Roseanne and her sister worked in the hit 1990s sitcom Roseanne (112 2nd St. E., Ottumwa, IA; GPS 41.0181, -92.4116).

» Another local hangout, the redbrick Miles Inn in Sioux City calls its loose meat sandwich the Charlie Boy. Named after the founder's son, the sandwich comes wrapped in waxed paper with a slice of American cheese (2622 Leech Ave., Sioux City, IA; GPS 42.4876, -96.3747).

★ MISSOURI ★

141 GOOEY BUTTER CAKE

Gooey butter cake is one of those many foods that seem to have been discovered by a fortuitous accident, when things went terribly wrong (but in the end, so very right) in the kitchen.

There are several versions of the cake's genesis story, but the most common is that a 1930s German-American baker accidentally reversed the proportions

St. Louis butter cake, a dubious—but delicious—breakfast food

of butter and flour in a regular cake. The result was a gooey mess that quickly caught on as a novelty food and has now been a St. Louis favorite for at least 80 years.

Served mainly as a coffee cake, this über-rich, über-sweet treat is normally baked in a square or rectangular dish and cut into brownie-like portions. The base of a gooey butter cake contains flour or yellow cake mix, eggs, and lots of butter. Prior to baking, the batter is covered in a sticky mix of cream cheese, eggs, sugar, and vanilla extract. When the cake comes out of the oven, powdered sugar is sprinkled on top. It goes beautifully with morning coffee, but there's no rule—you can munch gooey butter cake at any time of day. And there's a popular Thanksgiving dinner version made with canned pumpkin pie mix, cinnamon, and nutmeg.

Where to Try It

» As the name suggests, Gooey Louie specializes in the sweet, sticky concoction. Besides the original version,

Continued on p. 162

Five different people claim to have *invented the ice-cream cone* and introduced it at the 1904 St. Louis World's Fair.

Trays of golden-baked *kolache,* a pillowy, sweet-filled Czech pastry

GREAT AMERICAN EATING EXPERIENCES

Old Country Cuisine

Midwestern cities large and small were magnets for migrants from eastern and central Europe, including Germany, Czechoslovakia, and Poland, during the late 19th and early 20th centuries. They brought with them a wealth of culinary influences from the old country.

›› Kolache

This pastry pillow or pocket—stuffed with a sweet, gooey poppy seed or fruit filling—originated in Bohemia and is now popular in places where Czech migrants settled in America. *Kolache* are one of several Czech specialties at Sykora Bakery in Cedar Rapids, Iowa's historic Czech Village neighborhood *(sykorabakery.com; 73 16th Ave. SW, Cedar Rapids, IA; GPS 41.9648, -91.6608).* The Agricultural Heritage

Farm in Kewaunee, Wisconsin, hosts a summer Czech & Kolache Festival that includes polka, beer—and, of course, lots of kolache *(agriculturalheritage.org; N2251 Rte. 42, Kewaunee, WI; GPS 44.4051, -87.5433).*

›› Polish Boy (Kielbasa) Sandwich

Ohio gave us inventor Thomas Edison, basketball superstar LeBron James, the term "rock-and-roll," and perhaps crowning all, a sinfully good sandwich called the Polish Boy. Start with a kielbasa, or Polish sausage, load it into a hot dog bun or sub roll, and then smother it with barbecue sauce, coleslaw, and french fries. Seti's Polish Boys food truck in Cleveland makes delicious Polish Boys *(3500 Woodland Ave., Cleveland, OH; GPS 41.4906, -81.6650).* The

Little Polish Diner in Parma, outside of Cleveland, tops its kielbasa with sauerkraut *(5772 Ridge Rd., Parma, OH; GPS 41.4054, -81.7348)*.

» Pierogi

These versatile little dumplings, pervasive throughout Eastern Europe and in urban areas in the American Midwest, usually come crescent shaped and stuffed with all sorts of things—potato, cheese, meat, sauerkraut, even fruit. Chicago's Pierogi Street café is a dumpling hub. Its gourmet pierogi come stuffed with spinach and cheese, braised beef, mushrooms, or spiced onions, among other fillings *(pierogistreet .com; 1043 N. California Ave., Chicago, IL; GPS 41.9006, -87.6966)*. Whiting in northern Indiana livens up its lakeshore summers with a three-day Pierogi Fest that features a dozen variations on the dumpling, as well as the entertainment combo of Mr. Pierogi and the Pieroguettes *(pierogifest.net; Whiting, IN; GPS 41.6798, -87.4945)*.

» Bierkäse

German *Bierkäse,* or beer cheese, is full-flavored white cheddar that doesn't actually contain any beer. Rather, tradition dictates you eat it with, and perhaps dip it in, beer before sliding it down your gullet. Also called *Weisslacker* (literally, "white wash"), the cheese is considered best after six months of aging. You can find one-pound bricks of Wisconsin-made Bierkäse at the West Allis Cheese & Sausage Shoppe in West Allis, Wisconsin *(wacheese -gifts.com; 6832 W. Becher St., West Allis, WI; GPS 43.0065, -87.9990)*, as well as at Bavaria Sausage in Fitchburg, on the outskirts of Madison, Wisconsin *(bavaria sausage.com; 6317 Nesbitt Rd., Fitchburg, WI; GPS 43.0070, -89.4838)*.

» Goetta

A traditional German-American dish popular around Cincinnati, *goetta* is a breakfast sausage loaf. Sliced like meatloaf and often served as a side with eggs, it contains pork and beef bulked up with steel-cut or pinhead oats and flavored with herbs and spices. Opened in 1946, Tucker's Restaurant serves goetta in the historic

German-American ambience of Cincinnati's Over-the-Rhine district *(1637 Vine St., Cincinnati, OH; GPS 39.1142, -84.5164)*. Just across the Ohio River, Anchor Grill in Covington, Kentucky, offers a goetta-and-cheese omelet *(438 W. Pike St., Covington, KY; GPS 39.0785, -84.5172)*.

» Pączki

The Polish Catholic tradition of eating *pączki* the week before Lent jumped the Atlantic with Polish immigrants who flocked to the Great Lakes region. Deep-fried dough encasing a fruity filling, pączki's closest American cousin is the jelly doughnut. Pączki Day on Fat Tuesday is celebrated throughout the Detroit region, but especially in Detroit's Polish Hamtramck community, where New Palace Bakery offers the usual berry jelly–filled pączki and specialty flavors like caramel cream and chocolate marshmallow crunch *(newpalacebakery.com; 9833 Joseph Campau Ave., Detroit, MI; GPS 42.3975, -83.0586)*. Also in Hamtramck, the bar Small's celebrates Fat Tuesday with pączki "bombs"—mini pączki filled with flavored vodkas *(smallsbardetroit.com; 10339 Conant St., Hamtramck, MI; GPS 42.4022, -83.0527)*.

Pierogi, a culinary contribution from eastern Europe

the southwest St. Louis bakery also makes butter cake in chocolate peanut butter, key lime, devil's food, red velvet, and blueberry flavors (gooeylouiecake.com; 6483 Chippewa St., St. Louis, MO; GPS 38.5930, -90.3011).

» Although primarily a chocolate maker, Lake Forest Confections in St. Louis also creates wonderful gooey deep-dish butter cakes (lakeforestchocolates.com; 7801 Clayton Rd., St. Louis, MO; GPS 38.6379, -90.3384).

» Missouri Baking Company, a St. Louis neighborhood bakery since 1924, makes gooey butter cake the way it always has (2027 Edwards St., St. Louis, MO; GPS 38.6161, -90.2752).

142 TOASTED RAVIOLI

Another quirky St. Louis food, toasted ravioli, was invented sometime during the 1940s or '50s at an eatery on The Hill, the city's Italian neighborhood. Several places claim they created it, but many sources credit a restaurant originally called Angelo's Pasta House (now Charlie Gitto's). The story is that a harried cook dropped ravioli into oil instead of water, creating an instant hit and an enduring St. Louis dish.

Back in the day, the dish was nothing more than boiled raviolis "toasted" (fried) in hot grease. In the modern version, frozen uncooked raviolis are breaded, deep-fried, and served with Parmesan cheese and marinara sauce. Chefs can add seasoning as they like.

Where to Try It

» On The Hill, Charlie Gitto's serves what it says is its own original dish as an appetizer (charliegittos.com; flagship location: 5226 Shaw Ave., St. Louis, MO; GPS 38.6178, -90.2735).

Specialty of the House

Don't be misled by the unlovely name "concrete." It describes a rich frozen vanilla custard so thick it won't fall out when you turn the cup upside down. Invented in 1959 by St. Louis custard king Ted Drewes, concretes are now found as far away as Las Vegas (teddrewes.com; flagship location: 6726 Chippewa St., St. Louis, MO; GPS 38.5894, -90.3076).

» The other real contender for inventing toasted ravioli is present-day Mama's (in the 1940s, it was Oldani's Restaurant), also on The Hill. In its version of the story, bartender Mickey Garagiola (brother of baseball legend and St. Louis native Joe Garagiola) first tasted the raviolis and declared them a hit (mamasonthehill.com; 2132 Edwards St., St. Louis, MO; GPS 38.6150, -90.2751).

» In addition to the traditional version of the dish, St. Louis's Zia's restaurant offers a seafood toasted ravioli stuffed with crabmeat and shrimp (zias.com; 5256 Wilson Ave., St. Louis, MO; GPS 38.6157, -90.2750).

143 ST. LOUIS–STYLE PIZZA

Taking its rightful place at the table in the nation's pizza rivalries is the St. Louis–style pie, a variety perhaps less known but no less appetizing than the Chicago or New York heavyweights (see also pp. 40–41).

St. Louis pizza comes with an unleavened, cracker-thin crust and is made with only Provel cheese. Similar to Velveeta, Provel is a processed white-cheese mash-up of provolone, cheddar, and Swiss, and St. Louis traditionalists would not consider making pizza without it. Also, the St. Louis pizza is cut into squares rather than into triangles or wedges. But like its pizza brethren elsewhere, it can be topped with just about anything found in the fridge or pantry.

Where to Try It

» Guido's Pizzeria and Tapas on The Hill bakes its pizzas in a classic stone deck oven. The deluxe pizza comes with pepperoni, sausage, mushrooms, onions, and green peppers; the menu also includes offbeat varieties like chicken alfredo and taco pizzas (guidosstl.com; 5046 Shaw Ave., St. Louis, MO; GPS 38.6176, -90.2704).

» Frank & Helen's Pizzeria in the University City neighborhood near Washington University has been serving St. Louis–style pizza since 1956. Diners can dive into a Provel-only pizza or go gourmet with toppings like artichoke hearts, shrimp pesto, kalamata olives, or sun-dried tomatoes (frankandhelens.com; 8111 Olive Blvd., St. Louis, MO; GPS 38.6737, -90.3466).

» Four blocks from the Missouri River in Jefferson City, Imo's Pizza is the place to munch St. Louis–style pies in the state capital (imospizza.com; multiple locations).

144 LAMBERT'S CAFE'S "THROWED" ROLLS

At Lambert's Cafe in Sikeston, Missouri, a "throwed" roll is exactly what it sounds like—a bread roll that gets hurled across a restaurant.

Norman Lambert, the founder's son, allegedly started the tradition during an especially busy day in 1976 when a hungry customer at a far table suggested he throw the rolls across the dining room because he couldn't wait any longer to eat. Norman obliged and a tradition was born. Today, Jay Leno, Morgan Freeman, and Bob Costas have all been on the receiving end of throwed rolls.

The restaurant is also renowned for "pass arounds," side dishes like macaroni and tomatoes, fried potatoes, and fried okra passed around the dining room in buckets and offered as all-you-can-eats.

Where to Try It

» There are three Lambert's Cafes in Missouri and Alabama, but the Sikeston restaurant is where throwed rolls were born, and the one to visit *(throwedrolls.com; 2305 E. Malone Ave., Sikeston, MO; GPS 36.8878, -89.5464)*.
» If you can't make it to the restaurant to catch a roll, there are several recipes for Lambert's hot yeast rolls online, including one at *grouprecipes.com* from a contributor who claims to have once worked there.

145 KANSAS CITY BARBECUE

So good it's been copied by chefs around the world—and scarfed down by nearly every U.S. president who's visited the Missouri metropolis—barbecue is the king of Kansas City cuisine (see also pp. 96–97).

From vacant lot stalls to gourmet restaurants, Kansas City, Missouri, boasts nearly 100 joints serving barbecued meat the KC way: slow smoked over a wood fire and slathered with a thick, sweet, tangy sauce made with tomatoes, molasses, and whatever secret herbs and spices the cook feels like adding.

Barbecued pork ribs are on most carnivores' must-try list when visiting Kansas City.

Henry Perry, a local African-American chef, kicked off the frenzy around 1908 by selling pork slabs from his alley stand. Today, pork ribs, beef burnt ends, chicken breasts, lamb, and even fish all lend themselves to the storied Kansas City technique.

Where to Try It

» The oldest continuously operated barbecue joint in Kansas City, Arthur Bryant's was founded by Henry Perry's protégé Charlie Bryant and his brother, Arthur, in the 1920s. The original brick eatery at the corner of Brooklyn and 18th is a longtime hangout for jazz musicians, professional ballplayers, and just plain barbecue fanatics *(arthurbryantsbbq.com; flagship location: 1727 Brooklyn Ave., Kansas City, MO; GPS 39.0915, -94.5561)*.
» Started by yet another Perry disciple, Gates Bar-B-Q opened its doors just after World War II and has since expanded to six locations in the Kansas City metro area (on both sides of the state line). Gates sets itself apart from the competition by forgoing the molasses in its barbecue sauce *(gatesbbq.com; multiple locations)*.
» Jack Stack Barbecue, in business since the 1970s and with several locations in Kansas City, is famous for using hickory-fired brick ovens to smoke its meat. The result is tender brisket, ribs, burnt ends, and steak, served with a sweet, tangy sauce and accompanied by hearty, delicious sides like cheesy corn bake or a loaded baked potato *(jackstackbbq.com; flagship location: 13441 Holmes Rd., Kansas City, MO; GPS 38.8827, -94.5861)*.

GREAT PLAINS

The chow on the Great Plains is meat, and preferably red: Beef, bison, and elk are all a main course. Pioneers and German immigrants also left their culinary mark on the region.

NORTH DAKOTA
166–172

SOUTH DAKOTA
172–174

NEBRASKA
174–180

KANSAS
180–183

OKLAHOMA
183–189

TEXAS
189–199

A bison burger, product of the Great Plains, where the giant animals are raised on farms

The thick, chocolate-dipped Red River Valley potato chip known as the Chipper

★ NORTH DAKOTA ★

146 CHIPPERS

About a half century ago, Carol Widman's parents dunked a potato chip in chocolate and discovered a candy creation for the ages: the Chipper. It starts with a thick, rippled chip made from a locally grown Red River Valley potato, which is then hand-dipped in milk or dark chocolate. The product is a thick, bite-size (well, two-bite-size) candied slab that hits all the right flavor notes—sweet, salty, and crunchy—in a single mouthful.

Carol Widman's Candy Shop in Fargo has a following devoted to the treat, which has spawned a raft of imitators (both Trader Joe's grocery stores and Lay's potato chips have wised up with their own versions). Nothing can top the original, though, which you can also get coated in almond bark or peanut butter fudge.

Where to Try It
» The Widman family has three independent shops, and each makes and sells its own Chippers. In Fargo, visit Carol Widman's Candy Shop, or order online *(carol widmanscandy.com; 4325 13th Ave. S., Oak Park Plaza, Fargo, ND; GPS 46.8626, -96.8562)*. One brother runs their parent's former shop in Grand Forks *(106 S. 3rd St., Grand Forks, ND; GPS 47.9240, -97.0289)*, while another brother runs a Widman's in Minnesota *(116 S. Broadway, Crookston, MN; GPS 47.7732, -96.6070)*.
» Chippers have proven so successful that others in North Dakota have gotten into the act. In Fargo and Bismarck, you can pick up the slyly named imitation Chipperz at multiple locations *(chipperzdelights.com)*.

147 BISON BURGERS

You can score a bison burger or steak all over the country these days, but North Dakota is prime grazing ground for the majestic American beasts, and has been for millennia. (And by the way, though we all like to think of the Great Plains as that romantic place "where the buffalo roam," those are *bison* roaming. The buffalo is a different, smaller bovine that lives in Africa or Asia.)

Some complain that bison meat is gamier and drier than beef, but, skeptics, chew on this: It's leaner, required by law to be hormone-free, and bred without antibiotics or steroids. Bison are also grass-fed, meaning they don't spend their days fattening up in crowded feedlots. And the meat has a tender, lighter texture and a sweeter taste than beef that some meat lovers prefer. It's hard to beat an old-fashioned bison burger, but nowadays chefs add the meat to everything from pizza to stews.

Where to Try It

» The hand-pressed burgers at Boots Bar & Grill make a perfect complement to the historic ranching town of Medora, near Theodore Roosevelt National Park. Diners can choose from five different toppings to customize the dry-aged ground meat patty (*bootsbarmedora.com; 300 Pacific Ave., Medora, ND; GPS 46.9150, -103.5286*).
» Fargo's HoDo Lounge and HoDo Restaurant, both in the Hotel Donaldson, offer bison steak and a bison burger. The latter is a thing of beauty. It comes topped with house-made pickles, sweet and spicy shallot jam, aged Wisconsin cheddar, lettuce, and tomato (*hotel donaldson.com; 101 N. Broadway, Fargo, ND; GPS 46.8771, -96.7872*).
» Make sure you're hungry before swaggering into Jack's Steakhouse & Saloon in Bismarck. The burger is a half-pounder, served on a kaiser roll with Thousand Island dressing (*jackssteakhouse.net; 1201 S. 12th St., Bismarck, ND; GPS 46.7920, -100.7730*).

148 GERMAN-RUSSIAN FARE

When immigrants moved onto the lands of the Great Plains, North Dakota attracted a tiny subset of Europeans: Germans who had previously been lured to Russia by Catherine the Great and Alexander I in the late 1700s and early 1800s, and then were expelled or fled a few generations later. North Dakota has more residents of German-Russian descent than any other state, and their influence is still present on menus today.

Two favorite dishes are a rich, creamy potato-and-dumpling soup called *knoephla* and *fleischkuechle,* a fried meat pie.

Knoephla is true comfort food, so thick it borders on stew. The dumplings are dense and chewy, like spaetzle (a traditional German egg noodle or dumpling). Fleischkuechle is a meat lover's dream: a sealed, half-moon pastry shell loaded with ground meat and deep-fried. Eat the pie like a local: Start from the corner and tilt it sideways and away from you as you chomp. Otherwise you'll end up wearing the filling on your shirt.

Where to Try It

You'll find a concentration of German-Russian cafés and restaurants west of Fargo in Emmons, Logan, and McIntosh Counties (*germanrussiancountry.org*).
» Kroll's Diner in Fargo, Bismarck, Mandan, and Minot serves a memorable knoephla (*sitdownandeat.com; multiple locations*). While you're there, go the full monty and pair it with fleischkuechle, which is deep-fried and made daily from a closely guarded recipe.
» Fleischkuechle is on the menu at Bar M Steakhouse in Mandan (*barmsteakhouse.com; 2815 Memorial Hwy., Mandan, ND; GPS 46.8215, -100.8566*). You can also get it ready-to-eat at market deli counters like Krause's Supervalu in Hazen (*krausessupervalu.com; 1221 W. Main St., Hazen, ND; GPS 47.2946, -101.6447*).
» To try fleischkuechle at home, pick up some at the Mandan-based Cloverdale Country Store (*cloverdale countrystore.com; 3017 34th St. NW, Mandan, ND; GPS 46.8573, -100.9317*).

149 JUNEBERRY PIE

It looks like a blueberry, is related to the apple, and wins over pie lovers with a nutty flavor all its own.

The Juneberry, sometimes called the Saskatoon berry or serviceberry, makes a North Dakota summer especially sweet. Once a staple for Native American tribes, the fruit has a sweet almond flavor that comes from its seed. An added bonus: It's rich in antioxidants and iron, and packs almost double the amount of fiber and protein as blueberries. Love of the berry has spread to commercial growers even in places like Michigan and New York.

The native, pea-size Juneberry brightens up everything from scones to smoothies, and even ciders and meat sauces—but it's perhaps at its finest in pie. Recipes often amp up the filling with lemon juice, almond extract, and butter.

Where to Try It

» Lund's Landing, at the Lake Sakakawea marina in Ray, serves a homemade pie year-round. Co-owner Analene Torgerson calls on the area's summertime berry pickers to help her maintain her supply of the chief ingredient (lundslanding.com; 11350 Rte. 1804, Ray, ND; GPS 48.1657, -103.1421).

» On summer Saturdays, you can pick up a pie at Grand Forks' Town Square Farmers Market, where Adrienne Wellman's handmade creations have become a thing of legend (tsfarmersmarket.com; 3rd St. & Demers Ave., Grand Forks, ND; GPS 47.9253 -97.0305). They're also available frozen from local stores and her farm in Cavalier.

» Harvest the berries on your own at you-pick farms like the Juneberry Patch in Velva (1926 U.S. 52, Velva, ND; GPS 48.0785, -101.0090). But don't let the fruit's name confuse you: The best time to pick North Dakota Juneberries is actually mid-July.

150 NORSE NIBBLES

Dust off your horned helmet and bring a Viking-size appetite if you're heading to the Norsk Høstfest. North America's largest Scandinavian festival attracts more than 50,000 visitors every year to the state fairgrounds in Minot, and generally runs late September through early October (hostfest.com; Minot, ND; GPS 48.2315, -101.2637).

As organizers promise: It's "pure Scandimonium!" The five-day celebration includes concerts, dancing, shopping, and even a folk school teaching traditional crafts. But for many the biggest draw is the food.

A third of North Dakotans have roots in Norway—so-called Norwegian Dakotans—so the Norwegian lunch buffet draws crowds with specialties like *lefse,*

Juneberry pie, a North Dakota specialty

Toast Skagen, a Scandinavian appetizer of shrimp and sour cream

a soft flatbread cooked on a griddle; smoked fish; and *rømmegrøt,* a pudding made with sour cream, flour, milk, butter, cinnamon, and sugar. A temporary restaurant, En To Tre, offers a three-course meal each night (reservations required). Other featured countries and cuisines include Iceland, Denmark, Sweden, and Finland.

For those who like grazing, stands serve Swedish meatballs and other less familiar treats: Viking on a Stick, a meatball dipped in pancake batter; Danish *aebelskiver,* an apple popover; and an array of Swedish pastries. And for the brave of stomach, there's also lutefisk, made from cod soaked in lye and boiled or baked until gelatinous. Fairgoers gobble up more than 5,000 servings every year. Let's just say it's an acquired taste.

Where to Try It
» Aside from the festival, during the December holiday season North Side Cafe in Grand Forks usually serves lutefisk and lefse dinners *(3450 Gateway Dr., Grand Forks, ND; GPS 47.9338, -97.07879).* Find Swedish meatballs on special at Thompson's Cafe in Cavalier *(210 W. Main St., Cavalier, ND; GPS 48.7942, -97.6249).*

151 SUMMER SAUSAGE

Long before canning and refrigeration, butchers kept meat from spoiling by packing it in casing and smoking it, nice and slow. The summer sausage, so named because it could be kept during warmer months, became a European specialty.

But North Dakotans like to say they perfected the link, using mixtures of ground pork, beef, venison, and bison. For decades, practically every farmer and butcher had their own recipe, usually with some combination of garlic salt, mustard seeds, black pepper, and sugar, and maybe diced cheese.

Grand Forks, North Dakota, serves up *more than 5,000 pounds* of free fries each September at its French Fry Feed.

Rolling out the dough for *lefse*—a traditional Norse flatbread—at Norsk Høstfest in Minot, North Dakota

But all the sausages shared a distinctive tangy taste, a by-product of the natural fermentation that preserves the meat.

A few butchers and processors continue the tradition. But today's consumers aren't packing summer sausage for arduous, prolonged prairie treks. Instead, they enjoy it on crackers and sandwiches, on picnics and charcuterie boards, and with wine or beer.

Where to Try It

» The biggest name in summer sausage, Cloverdale Country Store, can be found in grocery stores across the state and in its company store in Mandan. It offers several variations of the sausage, including pepper jack and garlic, but the most popular flavor is the Original Tangy, which can make former North Dakota residents teary with homesickness (cloverdalecountrystore .com; 3017 34th St. NW, Mandan, ND; GPS 46.8573, -100.9317).

» Smaller producers include Stan's Supervalu, a family-owned grocery in Wishek that makes and sells Wishek Sausage and ships it to all lower 48 states (wisheksausage.com; 1112 Beaver Ave., Wishek, ND; GPS 46.2590, -99.5506). Myers' Meats & Specialties (myersmeats.com; multiple locations) in Parshall and Garrison offers plain and jalapeño summer sausage, and the Supervalu in Ashley sells an all-beef product (ashleysupervalu.com; 122 W. Main St., Ashley, ND; GPS 46.0345, -99.3736).

Chislic, the South Dakota meat-on-a-stick snack

152 CHISLIC

As any self-respecting snacker knows, whenever you find food on a stick, you're probably onto a good thing. In South Dakota, the food of choice is chislic, a variation on a shish kebab.

The meat, which can be beef, venison, or, preferably, mutton, is cubed, skewered, sometimes marinated in some simple spices, then fried or grilled, and finally de-skewered and served with toothpicks, some saltines, and maybe a dipping sauce.

Chislic is often traced to a single settler, John Hoellwarth, who emigrated from Crimea in the late 19th century and prepared the dish as a snack. The name comes from the name of the Russian dish shashlik, also a meat kebab that likely derived from the Middle East.

Some restaurants get fancy with a range of marinades and dips, but generally chislic is flavored with garlic salt or similar seasonings. It pairs nicely with a cold beer, so it's no surprise that it's a staple of many bars and sporting events.

Where to Try It

» Chislic purists head to Freeman for their fill. Prairie House Restaurant serves mutton chislic, grilled or fried, marinated or plain (prairiehouse freeman.com; 1121 U.S. 81S, Freeman, SD; GPS 43.3438, -97.4204). Neighboring Meridian Corner, a bar and burger joint, also specializes in chislic (43915 U.S. 18, Freeman, SD; GPS 43.2415, -97.4195).

» Elsewhere, Shooters Wood Fire Grill in Rapid City serves breaded and deep-fried sirloin chislic with sweet barbecue sauce (shooters woodfiregrill.com; 2424 W. Main St., Rapid City, SD; GPS 44.0826, -103.2601). Or Schnitz in Menno serves up a sirloin tip chislic (215 S. 5th St., Menno, SD; GPS 43.2396, -97.5780).

» Look for stands selling chislic at festivals and gatherings like the

Turner County Fair in Parker in August (*turner countyfair.com; 680 E. 2nd St., Parker, SD; GPS 43.3975, -97.1287*).

153 KUCHEN

Sara Lee, eat your heart out. *Kuchen,* German for "cake," is a prized treat in South Dakota. So much so, in fact, that the coffeecake-like pie-size pastry was named South Dakota's official dessert in 2000. But people were devoted to the sweet as early as the 19th century, when immigrants began settling the wheat-growing plains of north-central South Dakota, particularly McPherson County.

For many Dakotans, kuchen means home—a dish their mothers or grandmothers made for Christmas and Easter, or pulled from the freezer for company.

Though kuchen preparation varies widely, traditionally it's loaded with fruit, custard, sprinkled with sugar or cheese, and topped with cinnamon. Popular flavors include strawberry, peach, prune, rhubarb, raisin, poppy seed, and apple. Of course, it's also great à la mode.

German immigrants brought *kuchen* to the Great Plains.

Where to Try It

>> Head to Eureka, the town that led the campaign to get kuchen designated the state dessert by bringing samples to legislators in Pierre. Local purveyors include Eureka Kuchen Factory, which, along with traditional flavors, sells chocolate and peanut butter. It also sells seasonal specialty varieties like cranberry and pumpkin (*eurekakuchenfactory.freeservers.com; 1407 J Ave., Eureka, SD; GPS 45.7670, -99.6302*).

>> Pietz's Kuchen Kitchen & Specialties in Scotland runs a busy bakery, distributing its cakes across the state from Sioux Falls to Rapid City (*kuchenkitchen.com; 800 4th St., Scotland, SD; GPS 43.1454, -97.7190*). It also sells its kuchen to tourist hot spots like Cedar Pass Lodge (*cedarpasslodge.com; 20681 Rte. 240, Interior, SD; GPS 43.7478, -101.9452*) in Badlands National Park

and Laughing Water Restaurant (*crazyhorsememorial .org; 12151 Avenue of the Chiefs, Crazy Horse, SD; GPS 43.8364, -103.6234*) at the Crazy Horse Memorial.

154 MENNONITE EATS

In 1959, supporters of the Freeman Academy, a Mennonite school in the tiny town of Freeman, South Dakota, launched a celebration with a mouthful of a name: Schmeckfest, using the German word *schmeck* which means "taste." The event, capped with dinner and a local theater production, serves a cornucopia of dishes that honor the area's three Mennonite ethnic groups: the Swiss, Low Germans, and Hutterites. Schmeckfest runs on two consecutive weekends in late March or April, and thousands descend to watch

◇◇

Thomas Jefferson brought the first ice-cream recipe to the nation—you can sample it at Mount Rushmore, South Dakota.

the show and buy sausage, fruit pockets, peppernuts (spice cookies), and more whipped up on-site by volunteer chefs.

Dinner itself is a grand production. Dishes include specialties like *nudel suppe* (noodle soup), *grüne schauble suppe* (green bean soup), *dämpfleisch* (stewed beef), *käse mit knöpfle* (cheese-stuffed noodles known as cheese buttons), *geschmäcke* (relishes), and *pluma moos* (dried fruit sauce). Eager diners line up outside the school's Pioneer Hall, where they're seated with strangers on long white benches and dine family style.

Meal and show tickets for Schmeckfest become available by November, although you can usually buy tickets there. Saturday nights are most crowded *(schmeckfest.com; Freeman, SD; GPS 43.3471, -97.4380)*.

Kool-Aid

Where to Try It

» Restaurants serving German specialties year-round include Dakota Jo's Cafe *(205 Main St., Tolstoy, SD; GPS 45.2072, -99.6142)*. The hearty daily buffet often features German soups and cheese buttons. You'll find German breads, bratwursts, and dumplings on the menu at Alpine Inn in Hill City *(alpineinnhillcity.com; 133 Main St., Hill City, SD; GPS 43.9328, -103.5756)*.

155 SUNFLOWER SEEDS

Kansas may be the Sunflower State, but South Dakota actually grows more of them.

The state grows more than 600,000 acres of the cheerful, bountiful blossom, making it the biggest producer in the nation. While most of the flowers' seeds are cultivated for oil and bird food, the larger ones, loaded with magnesium and vitamin E, are more popular than ever with health-minded humans (not to mention, they're tasty). In response, seed processors are upping their game, offering a range of sunflower seeds in flavors like barbecue, ranch, and dill pickle.

Sunflower seeds are sold both as shelled kernels and in the hull. Some people enjoy the process of

biting into a jumbo seed to tease out the salty center—and then, of course, spitting out the shell. Seasoned seed-eaters can devour them by the handful, skillfully using tongue and teeth to open each one individually.

Where to Try It

» South Dakota processors package a fresh and addictive product, which can be found in stores across the state.

» Wild Dutchman in Mound City claims to use half the salt of other brands and has a devoted following *(wild-dutchman .com; 11440 302nd Ave., Mound City, SD; GPS 45.6172, -100.1515)*. Others swear by Dakota Style, which also offers flavored kernels as a salad topper, with honey roasted or ranch. They also carry large seeds with dill pickle and barbecue flavoring *(dakotastyle.com; 211 Industrial Dr., Clark, SD; GPS 44.8779, -97.7329)*.

★NEBRASKA★

156 DOROTHY LYNCH DRESSING

Who needs ranch or vinaigrette? The Great Plains has its own dressing mainstay, a creamy, orange, sweet-spicy condiment that tastes like, well, pretty much nothing else.

The dressing's namesake, Dorothy Lynch, created the sauce in the late 1940s while running a restaurant with her husband at an American Legion Club in tiny St. Paul, Nebraska. It was such a hit that customers started bringing empty bottles to fill up and take home. Although some compare it to French dressing, which is oil based, Dorothy Lynch starts with tomato soup and adds celery seeds, vinegar, and spices for a taste that's tangy and sweet, with a touch of sour.

It's now produced in Duncan and distributed in 35 states. While the dressing has an old-fashioned pedigree, it has kept up with the times, adding a fat-free version in 1993 and slightly altering its formula a few years ago to be gluten-free. The company likes to brag that its regular product is lower in fat than most light ranch dressings.

But don't limit Dorothy Lynch to salads. It's an ingredient in recipes for everything from pancakes to chicken tacos, and the Iowa State Fair even runs a Dorothy Lynch recipe contest, proving that love of the dressing has spread well beyond Nebraska's borders.

Where to Try It
» While you're likely to find the wide-mouth plastic bottle in any Nebraska grocery store, the company also sells online (dorothy lynch.com).

Runza, a meat-, onion-, and cabbage-filled sandwich

Where to Try It
» Kool-Aid Days in Hastings has a fun run, a beauty pageant, and concerts. There are also collectible exhibits, photo ops with the Man, drinking contests, and the world's largest Kool-Aid stand (kool-aiddays.com; 301 S. Burlington Ave., Hastings, NE; GPS 40.5879, -98.3899).
» The Hastings Museum features the "Kool-Aid: Discover the Dream" exhibit, and the gift shop sells eccentric items—including purses and wallets—made from the distinctive, shiny Kool-Aid envelopes (hastingsmuseum.org; 1330 N. Burlington Ave., Hastings, NE; GPS 40.6002, -98.3914).

157 KOOL-AID

If the phrase "Oh yeah!" elicits a wave of nostalgia, you probably grew up watching the Kool-Aid Man crash through walls to bring an icy beverage to a group of eager kids. The iconic commercials featuring a friendly, if somewhat clumsy, smiling pitcher literally put a face on a sweet, flavored drink mix that has its roots in Hastings, Nebraska.

The city hasn't forgotten its hometown carafe made-good. The annual August Kool-Aid Days festival honors inventor Edwin Perkins with a parade and plenty of the sweet drink. Perkins started his beverage business in 1927 with a concentrated powder that easily mixed with water. The original six flavors were cherry, grape, lemon-lime, orange, strawberry, and raspberry, with the latter being Perkins's favorite. In 1953, General Foods bought the product, and went on to create an advertising icon that would make Don Draper proud.

158 RUNZA

A homemade pocket bun stuffed with ground beef or pork, onions, cabbage, and secret spices—this is a Runza, a German-Russian meat pie and a Great Plains staple for nearly a century. Runza are very similar—some might say identical—to bierocks, a name more commonly used in Kansas—with one notable difference: Bierocks tend to be round while Runza are rectangular.

Field hands once packed these savory pies as an easily portable meal; now, they're a statewide obsession. Just how popular are Nebraska's meaty Runza sandwiches? An entire fast-food empire is built around them. The Runza restaurant chain started in 1949 as a drive-in specializing in the dish, and now dozens of franchises dot Nebraska, along with Iowa, Kansas, and Colorado. If you're in any doubt as to how

Approximately 17 gallons of Kool-Aid are consumed *every second* during the summer months.

good Runza are, go check out the lunchtime line that forms at the University of Nebraska–Lincoln's Runza outlet in the food court.

Where to Try It

≫ You'll have no problem tracking down a Runza in Nebraska, where tasting only requires pulling up to a drive-through and choosing between an original Runza or variations with cheese, mushrooms, barbecue, and bacon. The website even lists locations near the airports and along I-80—essentially offering to cater the Nebraska portion of your cross-country road trip (runza.com; multiple locations).

≫ Fort Robinson State Park in Lincoln offers a similar sandwich with ground bison (outdoornebraska.ne.gov; 2200 N. 33rd St., Lincoln, NE; GPS 42.6667, -103.4742). Head to 9th Street Tavern & Grill in Omaha for slider-size bites (9thstreettavernandgrill.com; 902 Dodge St., Omaha, NE; GPS 41.2599, -95.9283). Or if you want to do a comparison taste test, Thunderhead Brewing Company in Kearney makes a bierock with ground beef and sauerkraut, served with spicy mustard (thunderhead brewing.com; 18 E. 21st St., Kearney, NE; GPS 40.6968, -99.0809).

159 SWEET CORN

In Nebraska, where the beloved state football team is called the Cornhuskers, residents have a deep connection to the heartland crop. Nothing, they say, matches the taste of freshly harvested sweet corn on

Roasted sweet corn ears, just off the grill

the cob, served piping hot, slathered in butter, and sprinkled with salt.

By late July, produce stands pop up across the region, selling bushels of ears picked that morning. Some farmers immediately bathe the ears in cold water after they're picked to remove field heat and preserve the flavor. And there's no surer sign that fall is on its way than when those corn stands disappear in mid-September.

Where to Try It

≫ If you can time your visit to Grand Island during the Nebraska State Fair in late August and early September, you'll be in corn heaven: corn dogs, stuffed corn torti-llas, and corn served straight-up, with Manny's Sweet Corn–on-a-Stick's ears picked that day. No judgment if you decide to jazz it up with toppers such as maple-chipotle glaze, coconut, or southwestern spices (state fair.org; 501 E. Fonner Park Rd., Grand Island, NE; GPS 40.9059, -98.3289).

≫ Omaha visitors, stop by Lauritzen Gardens' Sweet Corn Festival in August, when you can nibble on corn products and samples and watch corn-cooking demonstrations (lauritzengardens.org; 100 Bancroft St., Omaha, NE; GPS 41.2346, -95.9166). Or buy corn at one of Omaha's favorite stands, Cream of the Crop (76 Cass Court parking lot, Omaha, NE; GPS 41.2632, -96.0321).

≫ Straight-from-the-stalk corn can also be had all over the state at farmers markets in season (nefarmers markets.org/member-markets). The Omaha Farmers Market (omahafarmersmarket.com; 11th & Jackson Sts., Omaha, NE; GPS 41.2544, -95.9306), held in the Old Market, is one of the country's best.

160 REUBEN

Many stars found fame in New York, but the Reuben got its start in the Midwest. The fabled grilled sandwich consists of corned beef, melted Swiss cheese, sauerkraut, and Thousand Island or Russian dressing on dark rye, and owes its existence to a marathon poker game at Omaha's Blackstone Hotel. (It was a prolific place for food: The hotel is also credited with butter brickle ice cream.)

Most food historians agree the sandwich is named for Reuben Kulakofsky, who played a weekly game at the hotel with the owner and friends.

The Reuben sandwich—loaded with corned beef, kraut, and melted cheese—started in Omaha, Nebraska.

One night in the 1920s, Reuben, who owned an Omaha grocery store, ordered a corned beef with cheese and sauerkraut on dark rye. The hotel owner's son, Bernard, was working in the kitchen and legend says he decided to drain the kraut and add the creamy pink dressing. One taste and Reuben and his poker buddies declared it a winner, and the Reuben was added to the hotel menu.

Decades later, a former hotel waitress entered the sandwich in a national contest and its fame was sealed. A recent count found that more than 50 Omaha restaurants serve a version of the sandwich.

Where to Try It

» Omaha is ground zero for Reubens, so you tend to listen when the city's residents say one of the best ones can be found at Crescent Moon Alehouse, just down the street from the sandwich's Blackstone Hotel birthplace (beercornerusa.com; 3578 Farnam St., Omaha, NE; GPS 41.2580, -95.9663).

» Maybe it's because the Reuben pairs so well with beer, but another bar, Sean O'Casey's, is a good place

Surprise

It's not just balls flying through the air at University of Nebraska–Lincoln Cornhuskers football and baseball games. **Fairbury Brand hot dogs** get airtime, too, thanks to a pressurized hot dog–shaped cannon known as Der Viener Schlinger that shoots them into the crowd. The bag-wrapped dogs come complete with a bun, so hungry fans can bite right in.

to try the sandwich; here, they serve it as a fat, double-decker with a rich dressing (seanocaseyspub.com; 2523 S. 140th Ave., Omaha, NE; GPS 41.2819, -96.1325).

» Other contenders include Barrett's Barleycorn Pub & Grill (barrettsomaha.com; 4322 Leavenworth St., Omaha, NE; GPS 41.2527, -95.9780). An upscale version at the Drover substitutes prime rib for the corned beef (droverrestaurant.com; 2121 S. 73rd St., Omaha, NE; GPS 41.2391, -96.0258). Not to be left out, vegetarians get in on the act at Marks Bistro, which uses

Continued on p. 180

Rounding up Texas longhorns—in the 1800s, the steers were driven all the way up the Chisholm Trail to Abilene, Kansas.

GREAT AMERICAN EATING EXPERIENCES
Steak Houses

It all started on the great American range.

Well, almost. Christopher Columbus brought the first cows to the New World, and beef was raised in colonial America.

But the Great Plains has been the nation's center of beef production since the mid-1800s. It was the region's open range and cattle drives that spurred the legend of the iconic American cowboy, celebrated in art, movies, and Pulitzer Prize–winning literature like Larry McMurtry's epic *Lonesome Dove*.

The drives were fueled by simple economics. Texans, struggling after the Civil War, discovered their longhorn cattle would fetch higher prices at railheads in Kansas and Nebraska, so the herds were driven north from Texas along routes like the Chisholm Trail and sold at stockyards. Most of the beef was then shipped east to big cities like Chicago and New York.

Two advancements cut short the storied era: the expansion of railroads into Texas, so that cattle no longer needed to be driven north to railheads, and the end of the open range, which meant the plains were enclosed in barbed wire and the cattle drive trails quite literally fenced off. Today, cattle are raised on farms, and the top three beef producers are Texas, Nebraska, and Kansas, with Oklahoma and South Dakota following close behind.

Not surprisingly, ranchers and cattlemen like a good steak, and know how to prepare one. The region has both clubby brass-and-dark-wood steak houses, where fellow diners are likely feasting on a healthy expense account, along with rustic Old West outposts. Whatever the setting, don't expect cheap prices when you're buying the best.

Tastes differ, but top cuts include tenderloin, rib eye, strip, and T-bone. And although fat has become a dirty word, a good steak requires marbling. Otherwise, the meat will be tough and tasteless. The most expensive steaks are dry-aged to further intensify the flavor, and graded USDA Prime. Order it medium rare, and you can't go wrong.

But that's just the start. A classic menu also offers the simple trifecta of a good steak house meal: baked potatoes, wedge salad with blue cheese dressing and chunks of bacon, and creamed spinach. And you need butter sizzling atop your T-bone and sour cream piled on your potato, to ingest the full experience.

» Steak Showdown in Texas & Oklahoma City

From one-of-a-kind to famous chains, Texas has it all when it comes to great steak houses.

Pappas Brothers in Dallas and Houston are the chain's crown jewels, winning raves from the most discriminating carnivores (pappasbros.com; multiple locations). Or head to Perini Ranch in picturesque Buffalo Gap, Texas, which has catered meals at the White House and serves up a pepper strip and a cowboy rib eye bone-in for even more flavor (periniranch.com; 3002 Rte. 89, Buffalo Gap, TX; GPS 32.2715, -99.8439). Fort Worth was right on the old Chisholm Trail, and for an authentic setting, you can't beat Cattlemen's Steak House in the city's historic Stockyards District (cattlemens steakhouse.com; 2458 N. Main St., Fort Worth, TX; GPS 32.7894, -97.3488). The same holds true at a different Cattlemen's Steakhouse in Oklahoma City, which serves steak for breakfast, lunch, and dinner (cattle mensrestaurant.com; 1309 S. Agnew, Oklahoma City, OK; GPS 35.4523, -97.5548).

» Carnivore Bliss in Nebraska, Iowa & Kansas City

Kansas City is legendary for its beef. Jess & Jim's Steakhouse has been serving steaks in Kansas City, Missouri, since the 1930s (jessandjims.com; 517 E. 125 St., Kansas City, MO; GPS 38.8822, -94.5891).

Elsewhere in the region, rural Nebraska offers several good options. Two family-run and locally sourced, small-town gems: Coppermill in McCook (coppermill steakhouse.com; U.S. 83N & Coppermill St., McCook, NE; GPS 40.2044, -100.6465) and Red Cloud's Palace Steakhouse (125 W. 4th Ave., Red Cloud, NE; GPS 40.0888, -98.5200). In beef-savvy Omaha, Gorat's counts billionaire Warren Buffet as a regular (gorats omaha.com; 4917 Center St., Omaha, NE; GPS 41.2412, -95.9887). Others swear by the Drover and its whiskey-marinated steaks (droverrestaurant.com; 2121 S. 73rd St., Omaha, NE; GPS 41.2392, -96.0258).

Or head north 130 miles to Le Mars, Iowa, where award-winning Archies is renowned for its dry-aged porterhouse cuts (archieswaeside.com; 224 4th Ave. NE, Le Mars, IA; GPS 42.7958, -96.1609).

Grilled skirt steak, one of many cuts you can get in steak houses on the plains.

Burnt ends, once a throwaway, now a savored dish

Surprise

A Kansas steak rivalry wouldn't be surprising, but a **fried chicken face-off**? For nearly 70 years two chicken restaurants in Pittsburg have battled over who's best: Chicken Annie's Original (*chickenanniesoriginal.com; 1143 E. 600th Ave., Pittsburg, KS; GPS 37.4839, -94.6407*) and Chicken Mary's (*1133 E. 600th Ave., Pittsburg, KS; GPS 37.4840, -94.6429*).

tempeh instead of corned beef but doesn't hold back on the kraut or dressing (*marksindundee.com; 4916 Underwood Ave., Upper Omaha, NE; GPS 41.2653, -95.9894*).

★ KANSAS ★

161 BURNT ENDS

Although the name wouldn't suggest it, burnt ends are a delicacy, the tastiest bits of Kansas City–style barbecue. The ends of beef brisket are higher in fat and have to cook longer, eventually charring the outside of the smoked meat. Once considered something to trim away and toss, seasoned "pit masters" and restaurants have turned burnt ends into a featured dish, and barbecue lovers now seek them out.

Burnt ends were first publically embraced by food writer Calvin Trillin. The Kansas City native rhapsodized about the savory scraps in a 1972 *Playboy* story. Until then, if they weren't pitched, they were given to staff or restaurant patrons as free nibbles.

The meat stands up to the tangiest barbecue sauce, and you can get the ends on a sandwich, or served swimming in baked beans and gumbo.

Where to Try It

Burnt ends are served by most barbecue joints in the Kansas City area (both in Kansas and Missouri), but some are especially notable.

» Find them in all their permutations at Burnt End BBQ in Overland Park (*burntendbbqkc.com; 11831 Metcalf Ave., Overland Park, KS; GPS 38.9137, -94.6668*). Its Burnt End Bowl serves its barbecue with hickory pit beans over sweet corn bread and fried onion straws. Or mix it up in a Reuben sandwich on fat Texas toast. Joe's Kansas City Bar-B-Que (*joeskc.com; multiple locations*) only serves burnt ends on Mondays and Saturdays at lunch, and Wednesdays at dinner.

» Other purveyors include Papa Bob's Bar-B-Que in Bonner Springs (*papabobsbbq.com; 11610 Kaw Dr., Kansas City, KS; GPS 39.066, -94.8498*), where you can get burnt ends on sandwiches, in platters, and by the pound; Hillsdale Bank Bar B-Q (*hillsdalebankbarbq.com;*

Kansas' gooey *Valomilk candy* is named for its three primary ingredients: vanilla, marshmallow, and milk chocolate.

201 Frisco St., Hillsdale, KS; GPS 38.6637, -94.8502), where the meat for the ends is pork; and the BBQ Shack in Paola *(thebbqshack.com; 1613 E. Peoria St., Paola, KS; GPS 38.5700, -94.8581),* which serves a hefty half-pound burnt end sandwich.

162 HARVEY HOUSES

Long before Starbucks, McDonald's, and Chipotle lined American freeways, Fred Harvey had figured out how to keep hungry travelers happy.

In 1876, Harvey opened a restaurant in the Topeka train station. It was such a hit that two years later, he built a rail-side hotel and restaurant in Florence, Kansas.

His Harvey Houses, considered the nation's first restaurant chain, catered specifically to western railroad passengers, offering a quick, tasty meal served by friendly "Harvey Girls" in modest, starched uniforms. The company and the Harvey Girls, it was said, civilized the West.

Harvey Houses found success because their competitors were so bad. Most railway eateries were squalid, dirty places serving barely palatable meals. Harvey, by contrast, offered quality and cleanliness at a fair price, insisting his restaurants serve large portions, on china and atop white table linens. The food, delivered by the railway, was astonishingly fresh by the standards of the time, bringing seafood and vegetables to the plains and Southwest.

The waitresses found yet more fame thanks to a lively 1946 musical, *The Harvey Girls,* which starred Judy Garland clad in the classic Harvey Girl outfit. Today, so-called Fred Heads travel the West to visit former Harvey Houses, most of which are empty, abandoned, or repurposed.

Where to Try It

» Sadly, there are no more Harvey Houses, although restaurants do operate in historic Harvey buildings in western national parks, like the El Tovar at Grand Canyon National Park. About the only place to get a Harvey meal today is at the Harvey House Museum in Florence, which serves group tours a five-course feast by women in black-and-white Harvey uniforms *(kansastravel.org/ harveyhousemuseum.htm; 221 Marion St., Florence, KS; GPS 38.2474, -96.9279).*

The Harvey House Museum in Florence, Kansas—the only place left that will serve you a true Harvey-style meal

Elk jerky

(35935 Rte. 4, Alta Vista, KS; GPS 38.8545, -96.4268). You can also find the products at specialty shops like Alma Creamery in Alma, just south of I-70 (509 E. 3rd St., Alma, KS; GPS 39.0128, -96.2837).

» Yoder Meats, with retail stores in Wichita and Yoder, includes elk jerky among its offerings (yodermeatsks .com; multiple locations). And if you provide them with the elk meat, Fritz's Meat & Superior Sausage in Leawood will smoke it into jerky for you (fritzskc meats.com; 10326 State Line Rd., Leawood, KS; GPS 38.9404, -94.6096).

163 ELK JERKY

Here in the heart of beef country, jerky is finding new popularity as a low-fat, high-protein snack, as welcome in car pools as it once was in 18-wheelers. And though beef is still the chewy, protein-packed choice for many, jerky fans are also picking up new varieties, including quite tasty elk.

Elk are related to deer, and the meat tastes similar to venison. It's a healthier option than beef, pork, and even chicken; a red meat that's low in cholesterol and fat. You'll find domesticated herds in counties surrounding Hutchinson in central Kansas.

Jerking is simply a meat preservation technique, developed by South American Indians long before the days of vacuum packing, canning, and refrigeration. Preparation requires pounding meat into thin slices, then smoking, salting, and drying it. The Spanish adopted the practice and it eventually found its way to pioneers and cowboys, who used the technique on beef, bison, pork, deer, turkey, and elk, among other game. While the finished product required prolonged chewing, it provided a compact, lightweight meal far from civilization back then, and it's still a tasty, durable snack today.

Where to Try It
» Prairie Thunder Elk in Alta Vista sells elk sausage, jerky, and snack sticks, and offers tours of its herd

164 POTATISKORV

Swedish cooking isn't just meatballs, pastries, and pancakes. It's *potatiskorv!* Immigrants brought the distinct Swedish sausage with a simple soul to the Plains states in the 19th century and it hasn't really changed much since first arriving in the New World. Its ingredients: ground beef, pork, onions, and shredded potatoes (those were once simply a way to stretch the meat).

This humble link has many names. Swedes called it *värmlandskorv,* but Kansans prefer *potatiskorv, potatis korv,* or sometimes the descriptive "potato sausage." The taste is mild but addictive, and often enjoyed with spicy mustard. Though it was traditionally a specialty

Surprise

When you order ice cream at Kansas State University's student-staffed **Call Hall Dairy Bar** counter, you might be eating someone's final exam. The store at the Department of Animal Sciences and Industry on campus sells more than 30 flavors of ice cream, all produced from K-State farm teaching units (the Dairy Unit houses 200 cows) and processed at the university (asi.k-state.edu; 144 Call Hall, Manhattan, KS; GPS 39.1961, -96.5813).

The nation's first fast-food chain, *White Castle,* sizzled up its first slider in Wichita, Kansas, in 1921.

found on a Christmas Eve smorgasbord, potatiskorv is now an all-season staple.

Where to Try It

» Swedish Crown Restaurant in Lindsborg serves potato sausage with its Swedish Dinner entrée (*theswedish crown.com; 121 N. Main St., Lindsborg, KS; GPS 38.5743, -97.6763*). Or if you prefer to pack up some potatis-korv to go, stop and browse Scott's Hometown Foods' Swedish food selection, which also ships (*scottshome townfoods.com; 215 N. Harrison St., Lindsborg, KS; GPS 38.5756, -97.6673*).

» In nearby Marquette, specialty grocer Piper's Fine Foods (*pipersfinefoods.com; 102 S. Washington, Marquette, KS; GPS 38.5530, -97.8342*) sells the sausage, as does Werner's Fine Sausages (*wernerswurst.com; 5736 Johnson Dr., Mission, KS; GPS 39.0223, -94.6523*) over in Mission, which suggests serving the Swedish link with a Pilsner or American ale.

165 ZWIEBACH

There are two types of *zwiebach,* and you don't want to get them confused. Kansas is known for a soft, sweet dinner roll brought to the region by Mennonites from Russia and western Europe. The other *zwieback,* German for "twice baked," is a crunchy, bland toast, sometimes used for teething babies. And to make matter a bit more confusing, the former is sometimes spelled like the latter . . . but not always.

But once you have a bite of the golden, squishy Mennonite version with its distinctive round bob on the top, your palate will at least have it straight. Made with butter or shortening, it's rich, a little salty, and irresistible when eaten warm with butter and fresh

jelly, or on a picnic with sliced ham. Some even dunk them in coffee, like a doughnut.

The buns are made by placing two rounds of dough on top of each other before baking, giving them a unique shape. Mennonite women traditionally prepared them for weddings, but they also traveled well, so immigrants brought them on the long shipboard journeys to the United States and introduced them to the Great Plains. They're now often made as a weekend treat, or baked for special events.

Where to Try It

» The Breadbasket in Newton sells bags of zwiebach from its bakery. You'll also find the rolls on the Friday and Saturday night German buffet, where they're served with apple butter (*newtonbreadbasket.com; 219 N. Main St., Newton, KS; GPS 38.0446, -97.3456*).

» More places to score some homemade zwiebach are special events, including the Kansas Mennonite Relief Sale (*kansas.mccsale.org, 2000 N. Poplar St., Hutchinson, KS; GPS 38.0804, -97.9283*), held every April at the State Fairgrounds in Hutchinson; Country Threshing Days in late July and early August hosted by the Mennonite Heritage and Agricultural Museum in Goessel (*goesselmuseum.com; 200 Poplar St., Goessel, KS; GPS 38.2482, -97.3430*); and the Kidron Bethel Village Christmas Gift Market (*3001 Ivy Dr., North Newton, KS; GPS 38.0777, -97.3501*) in December in North Newton.

★OKLAHOMA★

166 BRISTOW TABOULEH FEST

Tiny Bristow is a long way from Beirut, but every spring it celebrates Lebanon's signature salad: tabbouleh.

It's no fluke. The Bristow area, with two companies packaging tabbouleh mixes, has been home to Lebanese immigrants for more than a century. While recipes (and its spelling) differ, the dish includes bulgur wheat, finely chopped parsley, mint, tomatoes, lemon juice, and olive oil.

Tabbouleh has a long history in Oklahoma, where it appears alongside cabbage rolls and hummus as side dishes at Lebanese-run steak houses.

Finally, in 2005, Bristow, a town on Route 66 southwest of Tulsa, decided to give the salad the attention

Tabbouleh salad, made of bulgur wheat, parsley, and chopped mint

(cateringtulsa.com; 3823 E. 51st St., Tulsa, OK; GPS 36.0902, -95.9341); and Freddie's Bar-B-Que and Steak House (freddiesbbq .com; 1425 New Sapulpa Rd., Sapulpa, OK; GPS 36.0190, -96.0950), about 15 miles from Tulsa. Freddie's also sells Gourmet Touch Tabouly mix that's made by the owner's family business in Bristow.

» For nearly a half century, Bristow's Bishop Brothers has sold prepared tabbouleh and mixes, also available online (bishoptaboli .com; 113 W. 5th, Bristow OK; GPS 35.8321, -96.3915).

it deserved with a citywide festival complete with a Miss Tabouleh pageant, belly dancers, and a recipe contest. It also has an all-you-can-eat Lebanese lunch prepared by local churches, and the highlight is the tabbouleh bar, where visitors can top off a bowl of the salad with anything from chopped chicken and shrimp to fruit, nuts, tomatoes, and an array of spices. The festival, held on the second Saturday in May, Mother's Day weekend, attracts visitors from across the region (bristowchamber.com; 305 N. Main St., Bristow, OK; GPS 35.8350, -96.3907).

Where to Try It

Oklahoma isn't shy about pairing its other local specialties with tabbouleh:

» If you'd like some Oklahoma barbecue or steak with your Lebanese tabbouleh, you've got plenty of good options. You'll find the salad on the menu at Eddy's Steakhouse of Tulsa (eddysoftulsa.com; 3510 E. 31st St., Tulsa, OK; GPS 36.1184, -95.9375); Jamil's in Tulsa

Specialty of the House

Sonic, the chain that uses carhops to deliver orders to parked customers, started as a root beer stand in the 1950s. The classic meal remains tater tots, cherry limeade, and an extra-long chili-cheese Coney dog. There are now Sonic drive-ins in 44 states, but for nostalgia's sake, visit the very first one, in Stillwater, Oklahoma (sonicdrivein.com; 215 N. Main St., Stillwater, OK; GPS 36.1244, -97.0583).

167 EL RENO FRIED ONION BURGER DAY

Oklahoma's fried onion burger grew out of necessity, as so many beloved dishes do.

Depression-era cooks seeking a way to stretch their budget and larder added shredded onions to the top of ground beef as it fried on the griddle. The quickly caramelizing onions added a sweet taste to a satisfying, greasy burger and it soon developed a following.

The small town of El Reno, a half hour west of Oklahoma City, is the world capital of the humble fried onion burger. Locals say an El Reno chef created it, although there's some disagreement about which one. Today, the town honors the plus-one patty with a festival that features the world's largest fried onion hamburger (250 pounds of beef, 150 pounds of onions, on a 350-pound bun), topped with gallons of pickles and mustard. It's held in early May (elreno burgerday.wordpress.com; 119 S. Rock Island, El Reno, OK; GPS 35.5322, -97.9550).

Where to Try It

» No need for the burger blues if you can't make the May festivities. The sandwich is available year-round all over town. Among El Reno's noteworthy options: Sid's Diner (300 S. Choctaw Ave., El Reno, OK; GPS 35.5312, -97.9551); Robert's Grill (300 S. Bickford Ave., El Reno, OK; GPS 35.5313, -97.9537), which has a tiny counter and dates to the 1920s; and Johnnie's Grill (301 S. Rock Island Ave., El Reno, OK; GPS 35.5312, -97.9523).

» Elsewhere, in Oklahoma City, try Tucker's Onion Burgers (tuckersonionburgers.com; multiple locations).

168 FRIED OKRA

Oklahoma may be located on the plains, but come dinnertime, it acts like it's the South, with a love of fried chicken, sweet tea, and deep-fried okra.

Over the years, the state has added okra to its culinary repertoire, serving it at picnics and church suppers. You'll usually find the vegetable breaded in cornmeal and deep-fried, and served with a side of ranch or buttermilk dressing, which is especially tasty if the coating has been spiced up with black or red pepper.

It has to be said, though, that some diners are okra-phobic, scarred by early exposure to a vegetable that can be slimy, depending on its preparation. Never fear, fried okra's a whole different animal, or plant anyway, with a crunchy, spicy taste that pairs perfectly with barbecue.

The best time to try okra is during the height of summer when the cook has access to fresh pods. Aficionados like their fried okra whole, but others chop it up and serve it as a salad topping. Either will convert haters.

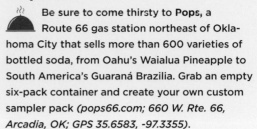

Surprise

Be sure to come thirsty to **Pops**, a Route 66 gas station northeast of Oklahoma City that sells more than 600 varieties of bottled soda, from Oahu's Waialua Pineapple to South America's Guaraná Brazilia. Grab an empty six-pack container and create your own custom sampler pack *(pops66.com; 660 W. Rte. 66, Arcadia, OK; GPS 35.6583, -97.3355)*.

Where to Try It

» Find a good barbecue joint or southern-style restaurant, and you'll find okra. In Oklahoma City, the Drum Room *(drumroomokc.com; 4309 N. Western Ave., Oklahoma City, OK; GPS 35.5148, -97.5300)* serves it with ranch dressing and chipotle aioli, while Iron Star *(iron starokc.com; 3700 N. Shartel Ave., Oklahoma City, OK; GPS 35.5080, -97.5251)*, a self-styled urban barbecue, offers it fried whole as a side.

» Elsewhere, Martin's Restaurant in Okay serves memorable okra with steaks or seafood *(7121 N. York Rd.,*

Continued on p. 188

Okra, fried whole or seasoned and chopped, is—surprisingly—an Oklahoma thing.

Tex-Mex tacos *al carbon* are made with beef stuffed into crisp taco shells.

GREAT AMERICAN EATING EXPERIENCES

Tex-Mex Food

In a world of mash-ups, none is tastier than Tex-Mex.

Considering you can find tacos in Tokyo and fajitas in France, the world owes thanks to the Hispanic cooks and restaurant owners who developed and adapted the dishes for a broad palate.

From salsa and chips to *queso* dip, the now familiar fare developed in the Texas melting pot (and pans).

The evolution came naturally enough. Texas was once part of Mexico and many of its first citizens had roots south of the border. Over the years, Texans created an entirely new cuisine that, while inspired by Mexico, is something all its own.

For example, Tex-Mex relies more on cheese, chili, and meat than straight Mexican fare. It's often spiced with cumin, which was brought to Texas by immigrants from the Canary Islands, and is more likely to include flour tortillas than the traditional corn.

» Classics & Pioneers

The earliest Tex-Mex pioneers were the so-called chili queens of San Antonio, the Hispanic women who sold pots of chili and tamales in the city's plazas. In the early 1900s, a San Antonio restaurant, noticing their popularity, began serving combo plates with tamales, chili, enchiladas, tortillas, rice, and beans.

Other innovators include Ignacio "Nacho" Anaya, a restaurant owner in the Mexican border town of Piedras Negras, who had the vision to fry corn tortillas into chips, pile them on a platter, and cover them with melted cheese and jalapeños. Other beloved Tex-Mex dishes include tacos *al carbon*, which are tortillas filled with grilled beef; the fried puffy taco, a specialty of San Antonio; and breakfast tacos, typically filled with scrambled eggs, cheese, and chorizo sausage.

A Tex-Mex purist (if there is such a thing) has to venture to Ninfa's on Navigation in Houston, where Maria Ninfa Rodriguez Laurenzo famously put sizzling skirt steak on a griddle and then served a fajita. Some trace the concept to a Laredo restaurant, but Rodriguez popularized it, earning her a national restaurant industry award *(ninfas.com; 2704 Navigation Blvd., Houston, TX; GPS 29.7567, -95.3425)*. A more recent comer, Houston's El Real Tex Mex has won raves since opening in 2011 for its take on vintage Tex-Mex favorites like cheese enchiladas and beef fajitas *(elrealtexmex.com; 1201 Westheimer Rd., Houston, TX; GPS 29.7443, -95.3933)*.

In San Antonio, Mi Tierra has been an institution since 1941. The 24-hour spot near the Mercado has *los trovadores* (strolling musicians) and twinkling lights, but also an on-site bakery. When Bill Clinton was working as a campaign aide in the 1970s, he once ate three meals there in 18 hours *(mitierracafe.com; 218 Produce Row, San Antonio, TX; GPS 29.4250, -98.4998)*.

>> Champion Chains

Dallas likes to claim it invented Tex-Mex, or at least the Tex-Mex chain. Early pioneers like El Fenix were among the first to tout numbered combination platters, and families still line up for the Wednesday night enchilada special there *(elfenix.com; multiple locations)*.

Another early chain, El Chico, helped popularize premade taco shells and the addition of sour cream to help cool off spicy dishes *(elchico.com; multiple locations)*.

Fort Worth's contribution to the genre is Joe T. Garcia's, a rambling family-run institution a few miles south of the Stockyards *(joets.com; 2201 N. Commerce St., Fort Worth, TX; GPS 32.7845, -97.3483)*. While he was in Austin, the chile rellenos at Matt's

El Rancho were a favorite of President Lyndon B. Johnson *(mattselrancho.com; 2613 S. Lamar Blvd., Austin, TX; GPS 30.2451, -97.7792)*.

>> More Mex Than Tex

Go a bit heavier on the Mex at El Paso's famed H&H Coffee Shop, which doubles as a car wash. Have your wheels cleaned while you tickle your palate with spicy fare *(701 E. Yandell Dr., El Paso, TX; GPS 31.7662, -106.4867)*.

Early Tex-Mex expansion took the food beyond the Lone Star State to places like El Rancho Grande in Tulsa, Oklahoma. You'll recognize the restaurant on Route 66 by its classic neon sign *(elranchogrande mexicanfood.com; 1629 E. 11th St., Tulsa, OK; GPS 36.1480, -95.9681)*.

At Mi Tierra in San Antonio, Texas, they've been serving Tex-Mex food 24 hours a day, 7 days a week, for 75 years.

Okay, OK; GPS 35.8433, -95.3153). Or pair it with fried chicken at Eischen's Bar in Okarche, a saloon predating statehood—it first opened in 1896 *(eischensbar.com; 109 S. 2nd St., Okarche, OK; GPS 35.7254, -97.9756).* » Across the border, time your trip to Dallas right and hit Okrapalooza in September. Top city chefs stage an okra-off with their own culinary spins on the veggie *(okrapalooza.com; 7530 E. Grand Ave., Dallas, TX; GPS 32.8103, -96.7292).*

169 OKLAHOMA'S OFFICIAL STATE MEAL

Many states have official foodstuffs, be it a state snack food (Jell-O in Utah) or Massachusetts's famed Boston cream pie.

But only Oklahoma has gone the next step and declared an official state meal—and it's a 12-course whopper: black-eyed peas, chicken-fried steak, corn bread, corn, okra, strawberries, sausage and gravy, barbecue pork, squash, biscuits, grits, and pecan pie.

The repast, which was officially adopted in 1988, makes for a greatest hits of Oklahoma home cooking, with a nod to the state's Native American heritage and to the Deep South roots of many early pioneers.

It's probably obvious, but this is not a light meal. According to CalorieLab, the feast clocks in at a belt-busting 2,700 calories and 125 grams of fat.

Where to Try It

» Though no one offers a state meal as such, a crafty diner can find most of the items on offer at Kd's Southern

Watermelon

Cuisine in Oklahoma City, run by hometown basketball star Kevin Durant *(kdsbricktown.com; 224 Johnny Bench Dr., Oklahoma City, OK; GPS 35.4642, -97.5085).* Likewise, you won't starve at the Boulevard Cafeteria, which offers most, if not every, course of the state meal daily. This Oklahoma City institution, which dates to 1947, makes everything from scratch *(boulevardcafeteria.com; 525 NW 11th St., Oklahoma City, OK; GPS 35.4804, -97.5222).* » You can also find most dishes of the famed meal at Hammett House Restaurant in Claremore on the eastern side of the state *(hammetthouse.com; 1616 W. Will Rogers Blvd., Claremore, OK; GPS 36.3186, -95.6300).*

170 SAND PLUMS

During the Dust Bowl, it is said only one tree continued to bear fruit. It was the sand plum, and its fruit brought rare sweetness to those challenging days, providing an ingredient for syrup, jelly, butter, and occasionally wine. The tree can grow in dry sandy soil, and withstand the relentless prairie winds that devastated the Great Plains during the 1930s.

The tree, sometimes called Chickasaw or Cherokee plum, has a long history in Oklahoma. It was first cultivated by Native Americans, and it still grows wild in bushy hedges and low trees, and in a few commercial orchards.

The cherry-size sand plum ripens to a reddish orange color in late summer. The distinctive flavor is refreshingly tart with a sweet aftertaste. It's sometimes used to make sauces for Asian dishes like stir-fries and egg rolls, and even salsa.

Where to Try It

» Buy sand plum jelly and butter from Kygar Road Market in Ponca City *(kygarmarket.com; 1316 Kygar Rd., Ponca*

Texas barbecue ribs—the state has several regional varieties of the dish.

City, OK; GPS 36.7169, -97.0314).
Experienced foragers can find the
plant in the wild, but it's easier to
drive a half hour outside Oklahoma
City to you-pick Riverside Sand
Plums fields in Luther *(www.river
sidesandplums.com; Luther, OK;
GPS 35.6636, -97.1946)*, the world's
largest commercial producer, or to
Buffalo Creek Berry Farm in Mustang *(9211 S. Sloan Rd., Mustang,
OK; GPS 35.3745, -97.6821)*, just outside Oklahoma City.

171 WATERMELON

As American as apple pie,
watermelon is grown in 44 states. But Oklahoma is so
fond of the crop that in 2007 it declared it the state's
official vegetable.

Vegetable?

The problem was Oklahoma already had an official
fruit, the strawberry, so a state legislator convinced
his colleagues that the refreshing summer treat was a
relative of the cucumber and thus eligible for honored
status as a vegetable.

Debate continues on the issue—there have been
attempts to repeal the designation and classify it as
the state melon or seasonal fruit—but no one denies
the sweet flavor of the state's watermelons.

Residents love the fruit (well, veggie) so much,
they'll eat it for breakfast, lunch, and dinner, and
even on sandwiches. Local varieties include the Black
Diamond, a round melon that can weigh up to 50
pounds, the oblong Royal Sweet, and the yellow-
fleshed Desert King.

Where to Try It

» You can have your fill at the Rush Springs Watermelon Festival, which started in 1948 and is held the
second Saturday of August at the height of the Oklahoma summer *(rushspringswatermelonfestival.com;*

Rush Springs, OK; GPS 34.7860, -97.9506). Patrons
get free, ice-cold slices—more than 50,000 pounds are
purchased from area growers and served to visitors in
the afternoon. The town of Valliant holds its festival
in late July *(valliantchamber.org; Valliant, OK; GPS
34.0046, -95.0919)*.

» From late July to early September, fruit stands
sell melons whole and by the slice. Favorites include
Tumblson's Fruit Stand *(Rush Springs, OK; GPS
34.7901, -97.9563)*, a half mile north of Rush Springs
on U.S. 81, and Williams-Hart Produce & Wholesale
Melons *(4976 U.S. 81, Marlow, OK; GPS 34.7184,
-97.9587)* in nearby Marlow.

★ TEXAS ★

172 TEXAS BBQ TRAIL

Barbecue historians trace Texas's legendary take
on smoked meats and links to German and Czech
immigrant butchers who brought their practices in
meat dressing and prep to the western frontier in
the 1800s. Even today, many Texas barbecue sellers

Watermelons are not new, nor did they originate in America:
The Egyptians **were harvesting them 5,000 years ago.**

Pints of Blue Bell ice cream, one of the nation's favorites, won't stay on the shelf long.

serve sliced beef on butcher paper and sell it by the pound.

Diners are free to gussy up the meal with plain white bread, sliced pickles, onions, and a vinegary sauce, and no one will look twice if you choose to make a sandwich. But just know that the main show is the meat, and eating with the fingers is fine.

Barbecue is found anywhere in the state, but the epicenter is the Texas BBQ Trail, a swath of small towns east and south of Austin. The easiest way to find them is to stick your nose out the window and sniff.

Where to Try It

The trail follows a 75-mile arc from Taylor in the north to Luling in the south (*tourism-tools.com/texasbbq*).

» You'll be following a 60-year-old tradition when you order brisket at Louie Mueller Barbecue in Taylor *(louie muellerbarbecue.com; 206 W. 2nd St., Taylor, TX; GPS 30.5688, -97.4110)*. Or head to Elgin for the famed

sausages at Southside Market & Barbeque *(southside market.com; 1212 U.S. 290 E., Elgin, TX; GPS 30.3501, -97.3859)*.

» Lockhart's Kreuz Market smokes turkey and pork, along with traditional sausage and beef *(kreuzmarket .com; 619 N. Colorado St., Lockhart, TX; GPS 29.8899, -97.6718)*. Others swear by nearby Smitty's Market *(smittysmarket.com; 208 S. Commerce St., Lockhart, TX; GPS 29.8836, -97.6709)*.

» At City Market in Luling, patrons line up to order brisket, pork ribs, or sausage directly from the men working the hot smoky pit *(633 E. Davis St., Luling, TX; GPS 29.6815, -97.6476)*.

173 BLUE BELL CREAMERIES

For all its swagger, Texas has its sweet side, as anyone who has tasted Blue Bell ice cream surely knows.

◇◇◇

Carnivores owe a debt of gratitude to Texas, the nation's *biggest producer* of beef, lamb, and goats.

The ice cream has found its way to such hallowed ground as Camp David in the east and the International Space Station. (NASA scientists from Blue Bell–loving Houston touted it as a way to nudge up astronauts' "happiness quotient.")

The family-owned creamery started in Brenham, Texas, in 1907, and has slowly taken its place among the ice-cream heavyweights. Though it's sold in only 23 states, it is among the country's top three best-selling ice-cream brands (besting Ben & Jerry's).

For Blue Bell fans, it's all about the flavors. Factories in Texas, Oklahoma, and Alabama crank out seasonal, often southern-inspired tastes, from cantaloupe and cream to peach cobbler. Others swear by pistachio almond, banana pudding (made with Nilla wafers), and Dos Amigos, a vanilla swirled with cinnamon-flavored Mexican chocolate.

Where to Try It

» Although Blue Bell is available across the Sunbelt, nothing beats tasting it at the source. The Brenham factory offers tours of its facilities and a scoop at the end *(tours temporarily suspended as of this writing; check the website for updated information: bluebell .com; 1101 S. Blue Bell Rd., Brenham, TX; GPS 30.1628, -96.3781).*

» Two local shops also serve Blue Bell: Downtown's Yumm! Sweets & Eats *(106 E. Alamo St., Brenham, TX; GPS 30.1665 , -96.3975)* and Scoops at Westwood *(scoopsbrenham.com; 2150 U.S. 290, Brenham, TX; GPS 30.1863, -96.5710).*

174 CHICKEN-FRIED STEAK

Why should poultry get all the fun of thick savory breading and panfrying? Beef gets in on the action with a tenderized round steak that's coated in a

Gravy poured over chicken-fried steak is a delicious, Texas-bred meal.

Hungry Texans dig in to their meals (you can be sure they involve meat) at the Big Texan in Amarillo.

batter mixture similar to fried chicken's, cooked in sizzling oil, and served with cream gravy and mashed potatoes.

Some trace chicken-fried steak (CFS, for short) to European immigrants riffing on Austrian Wiener schnitzel. Others note that breading and frying is a time-honored way of making the most of tough meat, a necessity in once hardscrabble Texas.

The town of Lamesa stakes its claim as the home of Texas' original CFS, with the legend that a short-order cook created the dish when he misread orders for fried chicken and steak, combining them into an offbeat, promptly beloved mistake. The town honors the venerable chicken/steak mash-up with a festival—highlights are a chicken-fried steak cook-off and dinner (growlamesa.com; 123 Main St., Lamesa, TX; GPS 32.7252, -101.9520).

Where to Try It

» Texas CFS standouts include Goodson's Cafe in Tomball, which served oil field workers in the 1950s and '60s, but soon attracted diners from farther afield (goodsonscafetomball.com; 27931 Tomball Pkwy., Tomball, TX; GPS 30.0808, -95.6308). Despite its name, Barbecue Inn in Houston also knows its way around CFS (thebarbecueinn.com; 116 W. Crosstimbers Rd., Houston, TX; GPS 29.8285, -95.4002).
» Mary's Cafe in Strawn, west of Fort Worth and Dallas, offers CFS in three sizes. Small is just fine (119 Grant Ave.,

Strawn, TX; GPS 32.5487, -98.4987). Head toward Albany for Fort Griffin General Merchandise Restaurant, where the CFS is so good they opened a second location in Abilene. But you'll want to visit the original, where the owner's likely to seat you (beehivesaloon.com, 525 U.S. 180, Albany, TX; GPS 32.7296, -99.2983).
» Near Fort Worth, check out Babe's Chicken Dinner House (babeschicken.com; multiple locations), although some say Dallas's AllGood Café (allgoodcafe.com; 2934 Main St., Dallas, TX; GPS 32.7843, -96.7807) wears the state's CFS crown.

175 CHILI COOK-OFFS

In Texas, chili is a food-fightin' word. How and who makes the best (and who made it first) is a long-standing and heated topic of debate. About the only thing chili fans will agree on is that the beloved dish does *not* contain beans, and that it pairs best with a longneck beer.

Texas red, as the dish is known, has its roots in spicy range cooking for cowhands on the cattle trails in the 1800s. The chunky beef stews were based on Mexican chili con carne, and the earliest recipes probably used whatever kind of meat was available and seasonings that could be harvested along the trail, like wild garlic, onion, oregano, and chilies. Chili still relies on some of those staples, but it can now contain an

Ready to rumble at the Terlingua International Championship Chili Cookoff in Texas

alchemy of other seasonings like beer, cumin, paprika, or even—somewhat controversially—a dash of cinnamon or chocolate. Some chili also contains sugar and masa, a ground corn flour. Whatever the blend of ingredients, the result usually silences the chili spats—at least for as long as it takes to eat a bowl.

Where to Try It

» For party lovers, it all comes to a boil every November near the desert ghost town of Terlingua, where chili lovers gather for not one, but two chili smackdowns: the Terlingua International Chili Championship (casichili.net; Terlingua, TX; GPS 29.3150, -103.6715), and the Original Terlingua International Championship Chili Cookoff (abowlofred.com; Terlingua, TX; GPS 29.3218, -103.5969). The Terlingua cook-offs can be rowdy affairs, although the chili is unbeatable.

» Others to try: Chilifest (chilifest.org; Snook Rodeo Arena, Somerville, TX; GPS 30.4571, -96.5253), a celebration in Snook, near College Station; the Texas State Open Chili Championship in San Antonio (tradersvillage.com; 9333 Southwest Loop 410, San Antonio, TX; GPS 29.3311, -98.6263); or even the Dallas Kosher Chili Cook-Off (kosherchilicookoff.us; 10909 Hillcrest Rd., Dallas, TX; GPS 32.8962, -96.7890), held in a synagogue parking lot.

» Year-round, get a bowl of red from San Antonio's Institute of Chili food truck (chamoycitylimits.com); and Goodfriend Beer Garden & Burger House in East Dallas (goodfrienddallas.com; 1154 Peavy Rd., Dallas, TX; GPS 32.8390, -96.6965). In Austin, try either 24 Diner (24diner.com; 600 N. Lamar Blvd., Austin, TX; GPS 30.2719, -97.7542) or sports bar Texas Chili Parlor (txchiliparlor.com; 1409 Lavaca St., Austin, TX; GPS 30.2769, -97.7419).

176 CORNY DOG

History may never solve the mystery of which audacious region first dared to batter a hot dog in cornmeal, deep-fry it, and—here's the genius—put it on a stick.

But residents of the Lone Star State are not troubled by that. The creation, they note, is called a corny

Corny dogs—hot dogs battered in cornmeal and deep-fried

(never corn) dog, and the only proper place to eat one is at the Texas State Fair, where Fletcher's serves up 600,000 over the 24 days of the fair.

The basic dog hasn't changed much since 1942, when Fletcher's first started serving the hot and crispy wieners. It's hand-dipped in batter (the recipe is a family secret) and fried in front of patrons. The treat is traditionally enjoyed slathered in bright yellow mustard from large pump dispensers. Though ketchup is available, it is also frowned upon.

Specialty of the House

In 1971, Mariano Martinez and a friend tinkered with a soft-serve ice-cream machine, and soon were rapidly filling margarita orders at Martinez's Dallas restaurant. The original **frozen margarita** machine is in the Smithsonian in D.C., but you can still order the drink from one of the innovator's three Dallas-area restaurants (laharanch.com; multiple locations).

Where to Try It

» The Texas State Fair is really the only place to properly enjoy a corny dog. You'll find several sellers, but only Fletcher's can claim the official dog-on-a-stick. They have several stands; tradition dictates you hit up the one that bellies up to 55-foot Big Tex, near International Boulevard (*Fair Park, Dallas, TX; GPS 32.7787, -96.7578*).

» If you can't make it during the fair, the Dallas-area Burger House also serves a dog worth wagging about (*burgerhouse.com; multiple locations*).

177 DR PEPPER

Dr Pepper is hardly unknown, but mystery still surrounds the soft drink developed by a Waco pharmacist in the 1880s. Just what's in the secret formula? The company will only say it's a unique blend of 23 flavors, and that (despite decades of rumors) prune juice is not one of them.

This much is known: Pharmacist Charles Alderton, inspired by the fruit, spice, and berry scents of the soda fountain where he worked, created a unique flavoring syrup. Customers loved the concoction and soon the pharmacy's owner Wade Morrison was selling the soda far and wide. It became the first major soft drink, predating that upstart Coca-Cola by a year.

And the name? The company says Morrison named it for the father of a girl he was once in love with, a Dr. Charles Pepper of Virginia.

Where to Try It

Though sold around the world, Dr Pepper is the unofficial Texas state drink, and widely available. Although the soda is now sweetened with corn syrup, the central Texas bottler offers special cane-sugar Dr Peppers in vintage-style bottles around the region.

» There's no better place to sip the drink than at Waco's Dr Pepper Museum. Along with an old-time soda fountain and memorabilia, it has a video theater showing vintage Dr Pepper commercials. An old-fashioned soda fountain serves the drink and even Dr Pepper floats

(*drpeppermuseum.com; 300 S. 5th St., Waco, TX; GPS 31.5548, -97.1289*).

178 GULF COAST OYSTERS

The French, who know a thing or two about food, use the word *terroir*—the influence a local environment has on a food, like grapes and cheese. As it just so happens, Texas has wonderful oyster terroir.

Galveston Bay's mixture of salt water and freshwater, and fast and slow currents, offers ideal oyster-growing grounds. The shellfish from the bay is so consistently tasty that much of the harvest is shipped across the country.

Oyster lovers say plump Texas bivalves have a taste all their own. Most come from several different reefs in Galveston Bay. Those from the eastern section tend to be briny, while the western bay yields an oyster fatter and sweeter. Recently, oyster experts, borrowing from the wine world, have designated appellations, specific areas where the shellfish grow—these include Elm Grove, Ladies Pass, and Lone Oak.

Which is best? Belly up to an oyster bar and order a few dozen to see.

Where to Try It

» Favorite Galveston Bay spots include cash-only Gilhooley's (*222 9th St., Dickinson, TX; GPS 29.4944, -94.9197*), a dive bar where children aren't allowed; nearby Topwater Grill (*topwatergrill.com; 815 Ave. O, San Leon, TX;*

The best Texas Gulf Coast oysters are from Galveston Bay, where the mix of salt water and freshwater makes a fertile breeding ground.

GPS 29.4719, -94.9258) is less gritty but just as fun; and Stingaree (stingaree.com; 1295 N. Stingaree Rd., Crystal Beach, TX; GPS 29.4817, -94.6044), a Crystal Beach marina and restaurant, offers Cajun specialties, too.

» Back toward Houston, try Captain Tom's Seafood & Oyster Bar (9651 Cypress Creek Pkwy., Houston, TX; GPS 29.9419, -95.5693). Even fancier: Danton's Gulf Coast Seafood Kitchen (dantonsseafood.com; 4611 Montrose Blvd., Houston, TX; GPS 29.7313, -95.3907), and Brasserie 19 (brasserie19.com; 1962 W. Gray, Houston, TX; GPS 29.7534, -95.4072), which has been called one of the top oyster bars in the nation.

» For oyster overload, head to Fulton north of Corpus Christi in March for Oysterfest. The celebration includes raw oyster–eating competitions, oyster decorating, and shucking contests (fultonoysterfest.org; S. Fulton Beach Rd., Fulton, TX; GPS 28.0635, -97.0339).

179 PAN DE CAMPO

It's the most basic of breads, with some recipes calling for only five ingredients. But *pan de campo* has a history as rich and storied as the American West.

The staple, which translates from Spanish as "camp bread," helped sustain South Texas cowboys on the trail. The cooks, primarily of Mexican descent, simply mixed flour, shortening, baking powder, salt, and hot water into a loaf, and baked the dough in Dutch ovens. The resulting round bread emerged in wheels. It was a versatile dish—sometimes it was prepared in a skillet or even fried. If cowpokes found themselves out on the range without cooking implements, they would wrap the dough around a stick and cook it over open flames.

The simple starch was a perfect accompaniment to stew, or often eaten with butter and blackstrap

Inventive cooks have used *Dr Pepper* to make cakes, baked beans, and meatballs, and even turkey brine.

Sweet potatoes are a food Texas claims as its own, and it celebrates them with the Yamboree.

molasses or honey. Pan de campo finally won a place of honor at the Texas culinary table in 2005, when it was named the official state bread. (The designation didn't come without controversy—some cowboy historians claimed sourdough biscuits or corn bread were just as worthy of recognition.)

But pan de campo prevailed, and today is remembered in cook-offs and campouts as the bread that helped build the Lone Star State.

Where to Try It

≫ Try the made-to-order black pepper and cheddar "cowboy camp bread" at Tejas Steakhouse & Saloon in Bulverde on the grounds of a rodeo (tejasrodeo.com; 401 Obst Rd., Bulverde, TX; GPS 29.7387, -98.4909).
≫ To sample different varieties of the open-range bread, visit the Pan de Campo Cook-Off at the Edinburg American Legion in January (4605 U.S. 281S, Edinburg, TX; GPS 26.2607, -98.1638). Or catch the Cinco de Mayo Festival & Cook-Off in San Juan, which includes a pan de campo category (cityofsanjuantexas .com; 709 S. Nebraska St., San Juan, TX; GPS 26.1939, -98.1615).

180 EAST TEXAS SWEET POTATOES

A lesser known but much celebrated food among Texans in the know is the humble sweet potato, first planted by the Spanish, but with its American roots (arguably) in the Lone Star State. Since 1935, Texas has feted the sweet potato with one of the state's oldest festivals, the Yamboree, in the East Texas town of Gilmer. (Technically, yams and sweet potatoes

◇◇

Houston has *more than 11,000 restaurants,* and residents are more likely to eat out than in any other city.

are different vegetables . . . but it's potayto, potahto when it comes to naming festivals.)

The Yamboree, which runs for four days over the third weekend of October, offers plenty of chances to admire the tubers in all their glory with yam-decorating and cooking contests, and of course, plenty of chances to taste sweet potato pie. Work off your slice at a barn dance or in the fun run called the Tater Trot.

It takes a practiced eye to pick out a prize yam. Winners are displayed in the Yamboree Exhibit Building, with the champion spuds crowned with blue, red, and white ribbons. To those unschooled in the fine points of potato beauty, they all look alike *(yamboree.com; 106 Buffalo St., Gilmer, TX; GPS 32.7298, -94.9449).*

Where to Try It

» Year-round, you can try yam tarts at Lori's Eats and Sweets in Gilmer *(1208 Titus St., Gilmer, TX; GPS 32.7401, -94.9439).*

» You'll also find tasty sweet potato fare in West Texas at Mrs. Kathy's Southern Comforts *(3413 College Ave., Snyder, TX; GPS 32.7080, -100.9191)* and at House of Pies in Houston *(houseofpies .com; two locations).*

181
DELUXE FRUITCAKE

OK, let's skip the fruitcake jokes. If you're one to dismiss the traditional Christmas treat as a doorstop regifted between family members every year, you just haven't tried the right cake.

For more than a century, Collin Street Bakery in Corsicana, between Dallas and Waco, has prepared the DeLuxe fruitcake, a version you'll actually be excited to see on Christmas morning—or any other day of the year.

The key to the DeLuxe fruitcake is, well, the fruit. The bakery uses pineapple and papayas from its own Costa

Rica farms, Pacific Northwest cherries and raisins, and Texas pecans, all held together by a minimum of batter and topped with a glaze.

That, of course, is just the baker's start. Many customers christen their DeLuxe with a liberal splash of cognac, brandy, port, or red wine, to give the cake a warming kick.

Where to Try It

» Collin Street Bakery is open year-round and has six stores around north and central Texas. If you're road-tripping between Dallas and Houston, it's worth a stop for free samples and fresh coffee from the original bakery in downtown Corsicana, just off I-45, or you can order online *(collinstreet.com; multiple locations).*

» For another Texas take on fruitcake, try the Original Ya-hoo! Baking Company in Sherman. Its namesake Ya-hoo! cake is made with pecans, cherries, and chocolate chips. For a true, prideful Lone Star treat, order the cake baked into the shape of the state of Texas *(yahoocake.com; 5302 Texoma Pkwy., Sherman, TX; GPS 33.6908, -96.5805).*

The DeLuxe fruitcake has a low proportion of batter to its fruits and nuts.

ROCKY MOUNTAINS & SOUTHWEST

American Indians, cowboys, mountain men, Mexican Americans, the Basque, and Mormons all contributed to make this region's pantry a diverse one.

MONTANA 202–203	**IDAHO** 215–221
WYOMING 204–205	**UTAH** 221–224
COLORADO 205–211	**ARIZONA** 224–231
NEW MEXICO 211–215	**NEVADA** 231-237

Salsa, chips, and chile rellenos—in New Mexico, food has American, Hispanic, and Pueblo influences.

In Montana, they make the state's dark blue huckleberries into treats like huckleberry pie.

⋆ MONTANA ⋆

182 HUCKLEBERRIES

From Mark Twain and Davy Crockett to the modern music of country star Toby Keith, huckleberries have a long and distinguished place in American folk culture. But just about the only place they're treated with equal respect in the culinary world is western Montana, where the annual berry harvest is cause for much celebration and tasting.

Similar to blueberries in both their dark blue hue and sweet-tart flavor, huckleberries thrive in the Montana Rockies where the volcanic soils, high altitude, abundant summer sunshine and cool nights present almost ideal growing conditions. They are difficult to cultivate commercially (or even in your garden), so "huckleberry hounds" have no choice but to pick them in the wild during the July–September berry season. And huckleberry-hunting can be a dodgy

Surprise

 Set in an old Montana mining town, the **Sweet Palace**—with its Victorian decor awash in pink—produces wonderful confections within its historic walls. This best little candy shop on old Broadway in Philipsburg produces 72 kinds of taffy and 50 flavors of fudge, hand-dipped chocolates, caramels, and truffles (*sweetpalace.com; 109 E. Broadway, Philipsburg, MT; GPS 46.3323, -113.2937*).

pastime: In addition to steep slopes, berry pickers have to keep a sharp eye out for grizzly bears, who also cherish hucks.

As well as eating them raw, Montanans chuck huckleberries into all sorts of things, from pies, jams, and pancakes to salads, sauces, and martinis (why not?).

Where to Try It

» Perched on the edge of Glacier National Park, the Huckleberry Patch kitchen and cannery in Hungry Horse hawks a wide variety of huck items, from fresh-from-the-oven pies and jam to honey and fudge *(huckleberry patch.com; 8868 U.S. 2E, Hungry Horse, MT; GPS 48.3859, -114.0625)*.

» Pancake breakfasts and dessert contests are just part of the huckleberry-centric fun at the Trout Creek annual summer Huckleberry Festival each August *(huckleberryfestival.com; Trout Creek, MT; GPS 47.8368, -115.5982)*.

» Loula's Cafe in Whitefish serves what many connoisseurs consider some of the best huckleberry pie in Montana, including luscious combos like huckleberry-peach and huckleberry-cherry *(loulaswhitefish.com; 300 2nd St. E., Whitefish, MT; GPS 48.4107, -114.3479)*.

183 FLATHEAD CHERRIES

Bings, Rainiers, Vans, Tietons, Lamberts, and Lapins are among the sweet cherry cultivars that thrive in the fertile Flathead Valley in western Montana. The Flathead Valley's first cherry trees were planted in 1893 by farmers who found that the large lake moderated Rocky Mountain temperatures just enough to provide good conditions for cherry farming. They later organized themselves into a cooperative to pack, market, and ship their little red treasures to the rest of the nation via the Great Northern Railway that ran through their valley.

After the pink-white cherry blossoms of spring, the trees burst with fruit during the summer months, the prime season for commercial harvesting and the pick-it-yourself cherry farms around Flathead Lake.

Montanans make a mean cherry pie, but the juice also goes into locally made cider and wine.

Where to Try It

» Every Saturday in July and August, stalls at the Yellowstone Valley Farmers Market in downtown Billings offer fresh Flathead cherries *(yvfm.org; N. 29th St. & 2nd Ave. N., Billings, MT; GPS 45.7830, -108.5066)*.

» One of the Flathead Valley's oldest you-pick spots is Hockaday Orchards, a century-old, family-run operation on the western shore of Flathead Lake *(hockaday orchards.com; Hockaday Ln., Lakeside, MT; GPS 47.9863, -114.1767)*.

» Perched at the confluence of the Flathead River and Flathead Lake, Polson hosts the annual Polson Main Street Flathead Cherry Festival. Held over a weekend in mid-July at the height of the cherry harvest, the event includes pie-eating and pit-spitting contests, a cherry cook-off, and plenty of cherry-based foods and drinks *(flatheadcherryfestival.com; 11 3rd Ave. W., Polson, MT; GPS 47.6933, -114.1635)*.

Specialty of the House

You'll find it in places as far-flung as California and New Zealand, but the **Flaming Orange** was Montana born. Concocted around 1976 at the Chico Hot Springs Resort in Pray, the dessert is a hollowed-out orange filled with chocolate, a special whipped cream, and four different liquors, and then flambéed. When set aflame, the dessert evokes the volcanoes simmering beneath the Yellowstone region. It's still the most requested sweet at the resort's dining room *(chicohotsprings.com; 163 Chico Rd., Pray, MT; GPS 45.3487, -110.6959)*.

Such is the enthusiasm in Montana for *wild huckleberries* **that officials have set a limit of ten gallons per person.**

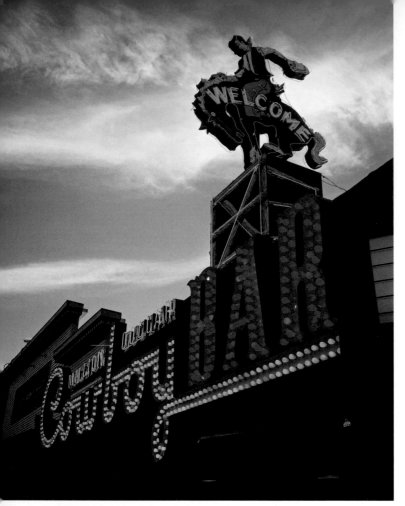

batter and deep-fried (or most expeditiously, just seared on a branding iron)—resulted from the castration of young cattle (a standard practice) combined with the cowboy cook's penchant for not wasting anything.

Where to Try It

» The chuck wagon grub may have moved indoors, but Terry Bison Ranch near Cheyenne still serves a range of cowboy victuals, from Rocky Mountain oysters to bison meatloaf (*terrybisonranch.com; 51 I-25 Service Rd., East Cheyenne, WY; GPS 41.0041, -104.9012*).

» The Million Dollar Cowboy Steakhouse in Jackson gussies up its cowboy cooking into fancy dishes like smoked buffalo bratwurst, cowboy fried chicken with Jack Daniels buttermilk gravy, and prairie harvest elk fillet (*cowboysteakhouse.net; 25 N. Cache Dr., Jackson, WY; GPS 43.4798, -110.7627*).

» Buffalo jerky takes a gourmet turn with flavors like teriyaki and jalapeño cheese at the Wyoming Buffalo Company in Cody (*wyobuffalo.com; 1270 Sheridan Ave., Cody, WY; GPS 44.5258, -109.0627*).

Jackson, Wyoming's Million Dollar Cowboy Steakhouse

★WYOMING★

184 COWBOY COOKING

One seldom heard a discouraging word around cowboy campfires because so many chuck wagon chefs were genius at whipping up tasty fare from whatever happened to be available on the range. They mostly used iron skillets and cauldrons, but Dutch ovens were also popular in the pursuit of quick and easy meals that would disappear down a cowpoke's gullet.

During Wyoming's frontier days, much of the grub was game based, with bison as the main source of either fresh meat or long-lasting staples like buffalo jerky. Famed Rocky Mountain oysters, also called cowboy caviar and calf fries—bull testicles dipped in

185 WYOMING STEWS

Variously called three sisters stew, cowboy stew, or Wyoming stew depending on the ingredients and your point of view, this longtime Wyoming staple combines aspects of Native American and chuck wagon cooking.

Vegetarian varieties are largely derived from the "three sisters" of the Plains Indian garden—corn, beans, and squash. Cowboy cooks tended to add some kind of meat to their medley, in particular salted pork, although beef and lamb were also popular alternatives. The stew can be flavored with a variety of herbs or spices, and you can basically toss all kinds of vegetables into the brew—potatoes, tomatoes, carrots, onions, peppers, celery. A Dutch oven is the preferred cooking vessel, although Wyoming stews can also be prepared in a large pot or cauldron on a stovetop or over a robust campfire.

» Home kitchens are where you're most likely to find Wyoming-style stews. But Luxury Diner in Cheyenne offers a range of homemade soups served inside a frontier-era trolley converted into a diner in 1926 *(facebook.com/LuxuryDiner/timeline; 1401 W. Lincolnway, Cheyenne WY; GPS 41.1272, -104.8288).*

» Check out what's stewing at the Dutch Oven Cook-Off at the August Wyoming State Fair in Douglas *(wystatefair.com; Douglas, WY; GPS 42.7592, -105.3900).*

186 RASPBERRY JAMS

Like much of the northern Rockies, Wyoming is a berry happy state, with a bounty that attracts bears and humans to the mountains each summer in search of the small, sweet fruits that thrive in the high, dry climate and volcanic soils. Wyoming's sweetheart is the raspberry, which grows naturally on talus slopes and is cultivated on farms in the state's more arid regions.

Cascade Canyon on the west side of Jenny Lake in Grand Teton National Park is one of the easier places to come across patches of wild red raspberries *(Rubus idaeus)* in June and July. But be sure to pack bear spray in case the local bruins are also feasting.

Whether harvested from the wild, a you-pick farm, or the local supermarket, Wyomingites have a long tradition of making fresh berries into other food items, in particular jams, jellies, and preserves.

Where to Try It
» Sheridan Farmers Market in Grinnell Plaza in Sheridan is a great place to hunt for homemade Jams and other raspberry condiments. It's open every Thursday early July to late September *(sheridanfarmersmarket.org; Grinnell Plaza, Sheridan, WY; GPS 44.7995, -106.9545).*

» Pick your own raspberries or choose from a selection of raspberry jams, sauces, and syrups at Raspberry deLight Farms in Shoshoni *(raspberrydelightfarms.com; 222 N. Hidden Valley Rd., Shoshoni, WY; GPS 43.1857, -108.2068).*

Specialty of the House

You knew you'd see natural wonders in nature, but at the bar? **Bear Pit Lounge** in the Old Faithful Inn offers several one-of-a-kind libations inspired by Yellowstone's unique geography. A Trip Over the Falls is a gushing blend of Wildrye Distilling spice rum, pineapple, and orange juice with a splash of cream of coconut. If you want something nonalcoholic, a flashy blend of fruit juices called Wyoming Sunset summons the park's vibrant evening skies *(yellowstonenationalparklodges.com).*

★ COLORADO ★

187 MIRASOL CHILIES

Colorado's hottest dining fad (no pun intended) is the copious use of Mirasol chilies in breakfast, lunch, and dinner dishes. Chilies have long been cherished in southeastern Colorado, given the region's proximity to chili-crazed New Mexico, but over the past decade, Denver has also become an enthusiastic user of the Mirasol in restaurants, food trucks, and home kitchens.

Three to five inches long and about two inches wide, the Mirasol boasts a flavor that's almost fruity or berry-like, mild but still savory, in contrast to some of the more piquant peppers.

Colorado cooks use these full-bodied peppers in chicken, fish, potato, and pork dishes as well as in salsa, stew, and chili. Dried Mirasols are one of the main ingredients of traditional mole sauces.

Pueblo remains the main source for homegrown Colorado chilies, especially St. Charles Mesa on the city's eastern fringe. Connoisseurs like to choose their own Mirasols from chili stands and farmers markets in Denver and other cities. You can get them already roasted or

Raspberry jam

Cowboys gather around a chuck wagon for a dinner on the Wyoming range in the 1880s.

roast them yourself before adding them to dishes like chile rellenos, chile verde, burritos, or corn bread.

Where to Try It
» Pueblo's Chile & Frijoles Festival in September celebrates the chili harvest, including the Mirasol, in southern Colorado. Among its many events are a competitive chili and salsa showdown, chili-roasting demonstrations, and a jalapeño-eating contest *(pueblochilefestivalinfo.com; Pueblo, CO; GPS 38.2648, -104.6126).*
» The Morales family runs three popular chili stands around Denver *(denvergreen chili.com/morales-chili-store; multiple locations).*
» Serving green chili by the cup, bowl, and plate—as well as burritos, tamales, *carnitas,* and rellenos laced with green chili—CityGrille puts a gourmet spin on Denver's latest eating obsession *(citygrille.com; 321 E. Colfax Ave., Denver, CO; GPS 39.7402, -104.9828).*

Mirasol chilies, a crucial ingredient in Colorado cooking

188 LAMB

So highly touted is Colorado lamb that, like phony designer watches and handbags, some restaurants that didn't want to pay a premium for the real thing (sometimes double the price of imported Australian lamb) faked it on the menu, the *Denver Post* once reported.

Chefs across the nation rave about the leaner texture, milder flavor, and a higher meat-to-fat ratio of Colorado lamb compared to "gamier" animals from elsewhere in the States and abroad.

Colorado's sheep farmers attribute their success to superior genetic stock combined with natural grazing, abundant sunshine, and strategic grain feeding before the lambs head for market. Several breeds thrive in Colorado, including the Suffolk, Rambouillet, and Columbia. Most are raised on the western slopes of the Rockies, but farms on the eastern plains also rear mighty tasty lambs.

Reputed to be the absolute best meat, spring lamb is found on many Colorado restaurant menus, but local chefs concoct a wide variety of lamb dishes, from traditional chops and stews to exotic curries and gyros.

Where to Try It
» Wyman Living History Museum between Craig and Hayden is the venue for the annual fall Craig Sheep Wagon Days, a tribute to the region's sheep farmers that includes lamb dishes, sheepdog demos, tractor pulls, sheepshearing, and a chance to tour a real sheep wagon, an early, rustic variety of the mobile home *(sheepwagondays.com; 94350 U.S. 40E, Craig, CO; GPS 40.5187, -107.4821).*
» Triple M Bar Ranch lamb chops from southeastern Colorado are one of the specialties at Boulder Cork restaurant in Boulder *(bouldercork.com; 3295 30th St., Boulder, CO; GPS 40.0345, -105.2541).*
» Local Brands Farm and Ranch Markets Co-op in Durango will ship Colorado-raised lamb chops, ribs, and sweetbreads directly to your home *(localbrands farm.com).*

Surprise
Not to be outdone by Colorado's sheep, **goats** are carving their own niche in the Centennial State. Jumpin' Good Goat Dairy in Buena Vista has a national reputation for gourmet goat cheese. Tours between March and October include a cheese tasting, and on the day's later tour, a chance to milk a nanny goat *(jumpingoodgoats.com; 31700 U.S. 24, Buena Vista, CO; GPS 38.8783, -106.1624).*

189 DENVER OMELET

Which came first: the city or the omelet? Nobody knows for sure.

A standard item on restaurant and diner menus around the nation, the Denver, or western, omelet is a simple yet surprisingly tasty blend of eggs, ham, onions, bell peppers, and cheese.

Like many American frontier foods, the exact origin of this breakfast and brunch standby is lost to history. There are those who think it began as an egg sandwich, the omelet wedged between two pieces of bread (toasted or otherwise). Others theorize it evolved from the egg foo yong of Chinese laborers working on the transcontinental railroad. No one is even certain if this variation on the omelet even started in Denver.

No matter, the Colorado capital long ago claimed the eggy delight as its own.

Where to Try It

» Renowned as a place where Colorado's political and business leaders meet for power breakfasts, Boulder's über-elegant Ellyngton's Restaurant in the Brown Palace Hotel cooks up a classic Denver omelet *(brownpalace.com; 321 17th St., Denver, CO; GPS 39.7440, -104.9877).*

» The Eggshell of Cherry Creek in suburban Denver dishes up its Denver omelets with Black Forest ham and smoked Gouda cheese *(theegg shell.com; 235 Fillmore St., Denver, CO; GPS 39.7202, -104.9537).*

190
OSCAR-STYLE STEAK

Colorado's love affair with the cow started in the 1860s, when ranchers Oliver Loving and Charles Goodnight began driving Texas longhorns into the territory along the Goodnight-Loving Trail. Initially the beef fed hungry mining camps

---

Basic Ingredient

Colorado's 2012 legalization of **marijuana** opened up a new world of munchies based on local weed recipes. Colorado's canna- bis chefs have cooked up all kinds of ganja- infused edibles now legally available at pot dispensaries across the state. The mellowed- out menu runs the gamut from truffles and cheesecakes to pizza sauces and olive oil.

---

and military outposts, but as remote settlements like Denver grew into proper towns, steak became an urban favorite.

Along the way, local gourmands developed a taste for highfalutin versions like steak Oscar, a slab of beef covered in crabmeat, asparagus, and béar- naise sauce. Allegedly invented by Oscar Tschirky,

The Denver omelet, a kind of egg, ham, and cheese sandwich

Although western Colorado is arid, peaches, grapes, and cherries are farmed along the Colorado River.

the famous maître d'hôtel of Delmonico's and the Waldorf-Astoria in New York, the culinary mélange has become a staple at Colorado steak houses. Filet mignon is the preferred cut, and although crab is still the ideal crustacean, shrimp and lobster occasionally stand in for their tasty cousin.

Where to Try It

» Served with the standard béarnaise and grilled asparagus, the steak Oscar at Solantro's in Vail also features crab and shrimp *(solantros.com; 333 Bridge St., Vail, CO; GPS 39.6397, -106.3736).*

» Steak House No. 316 in Aspen affords the option of crab or lobster over a variety of meats from Kobe beef and porterhouse to cowboy rib eye and rack of lamb *(steakhouse316.com; 316 E. Hopkins Ave., Aspen, CO; GPS 39.1901, -106.8200).*

» Going where few other Denver chefs have dared, the Keg Steakhouse near Coors Field offers variations on the theme like teriyaki sirloin à la Oscar *(kegsteak house.com; 1890 Wynkoop St., Denver, CO; GPS 39.7543, -104.9973).*

191 GRAND VALLEY ORCHARDS & VINEYARDS

It seems an unlikely place for fruit trees: semiarid western Colorado, where the terrain is rocky, the summers searing, and soaking rainfall a rarity. But in

◇◇◇

At 11,966 feet in the San Juan Mountains of southwestern Colorado, Telluride's *Alpino Vino* (*tellurideskiresort.com*) is the highest altitude restaurant in North America.

the Grand Valley, on the western slope of the Rocky Mountains, a fertile strip along the Colorado River is a patchwork of orchards and vineyards. Mesa County, which encompasses the communities of Palisade, Fruita, Clifton, and Grand Junction, harvests robust crops of peaches, pears, cherries, and grapes every year. Fruit stands line rural roads in the summer, and the area has more than 20 wineries that make local vintages from their own grapes and other fruit.

Where to Try It

» Grand Junction's Downtown Farmers Market, held every Thursday evening in summer, sells fruit and produce from more than a dozen local farms (downtown gj.org; Main St., Grand Junction, CO; GPS 39.0673, -108.5577). Over in Palisade, the farmers market is every Sunday in summer, and farmers peddle fresh cherries, apricots, and peaches (facebook.com/palisade farmersmarket; 3rd & Main Sts., Palisade, CO; GPS 39.1103, -108.3509).

» The Palisade Fruit & Wine Byway has three possible routes, and all wind you through Colorado River Valley scenery and past the area's vineyards, orchards, and farm market stands. Don't be in a rush on this drive—stop off along the way for a wine tasting at one of more than a dozen tasting rooms, a tour of a farm or orchard, or just to pick up some fresh-picked cherries or peaches (or preserves and pie fillings) from a fruit market (visitpalisade.com /portfolio-item/fruit-wine-trail; Palisade, CO; multiple locations).

» In Grand Junction, Alida's Fruits offers Colorado fruits, dried and dipped in chocolate and vanilla crème. There are also un-candied dried peaches, apricots, apples, and cherries for sale—the perfect trail snack for Rocky Mountain hikes (alidas fruits.com; 419 Main St., Grand Junction, CO; GPS 39.0673, -108.5654).

» Carlson Vineyards, above the town of Palisade, makes more than 15 distinctive wines from the vineyards on its own property, or minutes away. A classic Carlson vintage is the Tyrannosaurus Red, a dry red made from Lemburger grapes that thrive in the high altitude of western Colorado. Or for a sweeter wine, try the Palisade Peach, made entirely from Palisade-grown peaches (carl sonvineyards.com; 461 35 Rd., Palisade, CO; GPS 39.0719, -108.4063).

★ NEW MEXICO ★

192 NEW MEXICO'S SOUTHWESTERN CUISINE

One of the country's most distinctive regional cuisines, New Mexican food is a fusion of Hispanic, Pueblo, and American culinary traditions, ingredients, and cooking techniques. For more than 400 years, settlements along the upper Rio Grande Valley have acted as literal melting pots for this tasty tradition.

Chile relleno is one of the most distinctive dishes— an elongated green poblano pepper filled with cheese, then coated with egg batter and either deep-fried or panfried until crispy on the outside. Red or green salsa—normally mild rather than spicy so that diners can savor the subtle flavors—completes the ensemble. *Carne adovada* is another New Mexico favorite, tender chunks of pork slow cooked in a red chili sauce. It easily holds up as a stand-alone dish, but it can also serve as a flavorsome filling in burritos, enchiladas, and tacos.

Continued on p. 214

Sopaipillas, deep-fried dough puffs served with honey

The Buckhorn Exchange in Denver is the place to go for a meal of mountain game like elk, quail, or duck.

GREAT AMERICAN EATING EXPERIENCES

Mountain Game & Fish

The natural bounty of the Rocky Mountains has always been part of the regional culinary scene. From the Shoshone to the Cheyenne, the region's Native peoples consumed a wide variety of wild game, a gastronomic tradition quickly adopted by the European trappers, explorers, and settlers who arrived from the 18th century onward.

Lewis and Clark recorded their daily trail food, which included deer, elk, bison, and wild turkey, as well as squirrel, bear, bighorn sheep, pronghorn, and even otter. Beyond roasting meat over an open fire, the expedition cooks often concocted more elaborate victuals like buffalo dumplings and sausages.

The tradition endures into modern times, in both home kitchens and restaurants that feature game dishes. No one would think of eating otter these days, but bison and elk are found on menus throughout the region. Once driven to the brink of extinction, bison are now farmed in an effort to keep up with demand for their lean, flavorful, slightly gamy meat.

Fishing is also a Rocky Mountain tradition, a pastime that has yielded both tasty meals and a rich literary tradition of books like the famed *A River Runs Through It and Other Stories* by Norman Maclean (1976), and Colorado author John Gierach's 1986 ode, *Trout Bum*. Trout has always been the region's primary game fish, but salmon, walleye, catfish, whitefish, and perch also thrive in the Rockies' rivers and lakes.

≫ Montana's Bison Burgers

Montana is home to the National Bison Range and dozens of ranches that raise the lumbering creatures.

Free range and hormone free, and renowned for having less fat and fewer calories than other meats, bison has grown into a popular burger alternative in West Yellowstone at eateries like the Geyser Grill *(615 Highway Ave., West Yellowstone, MT; GPS 44.6637, -111.1116)*, and the Slippery Otter Pub *(139 N. Canyon St., West Yellowstone, MT; GPS 44.6620, -111.0994)*, which offers bison burgers with a choice of American, Swiss, cheddar, or pepper jack cheese.

» Wyoming Elk

Jackson's influx of affluent West and East Coasters has brought sophisticated dining to the west Wyoming city and elevated elk to a new level of gourmet fare. Local, a restaurant and bar on Jackson's historic town square, offers spicy elk sausage as part of its charcuterie board *(localjh.com; 55 N. Cache St., Jackson, WY; GPS 43.4802, -110.7623)*. The menu at the Blue Lion restaurant on Miller Park in Jackson features grilled elk tenderloin and grilled wasabi elk fillet *(bluelionrestaurant.com; 160 N. Millward St., Jackson, WY; GPS 43.4811, -110.7648)*.

» Wild Trout in Wyoming & Colorado

One of the holy grails of Rockies fly-fishing, the Medicine Bow Mountains are the source of several trout-rich streams in south-central Wyoming. Medicine Bow Anglers out of Saratoga, Wyoming, offers guided float and wade fishing on the upper North Platte and other local rivers *(medicinebowanglers .com)*. In downtown Saratoga, the historic Hotel Wolf sometimes serves trout as a special, or if you catch your own and gut it, they'll cook it for you *(wolfhotel .com; 101 E. Bridge St., Saratoga, WY; GPS 41.4548, -106.8077)*. Farther south, Littleton-based Colorado Trout Hunters offers fully guided trips—for beginners or veteran fly-fishers *(coloradotrouthunters.com)*. Numerous rich fishing spots around Colorado include Rocky Mountain National Park, the South Platte River, and private lakes in the high Rockies.

» Colorado Wild Game Restaurants

The bounty of the Rockies has featured on Denver restaurant menus for more than a century and a half. Opened in 1893 and the recipient of Colorado's first liquor license, the Buckhorn Exchange serves buffalo, elk, quail, and duck *(buckhornexchange.com; 1000 Osage St., Denver, CO; GPS 39.7322, -105.0048)*. The Fort Restaurant in suburban Morrison takes the wild dining experience to another level with a wide variety of wilderness eats, including elk chops, grilled quail, barbecued duck quesadillas, buffalo sirloin steak medallions, braised bison tongue, and quail eggs wrapped in buffalo sausage—all of it served inside a reproduction of Bent's Old Fort *(thefort.com; 19192 Rte. 8, Morrison, CO; GPS 39.6290, -105.1925)*.

Wild trout, a river catch in the Rocky Mountains in south-central Wyoming

One of the most durable New Mexico dishes, sopaipillas are deep-fried dough puffs filled with various savories as an appetizer, a main course, or sugar-coated and served with ice cream or honey for dessert.

Where to Try It

≫ Owned and operated by the same family since 1953, the Shed is a Santa Fe eating institution renowned for its use of local chilies in dishes like carne adovada *(sfshed.com; 113 ½ E. Palace Ave., Santa Fe, NM; GPS 35.6874, -105.9370).*

≫ Blending two New Mexican food icons, Garcia's Kitchen in Albuquerque offers a sopaipilla stuffed with carne adovada. They also serve sopaipillas and carne adovada with eggs for breakfast *(garciaskitchen.com; multiple locations).*

≫ One of Santa Fe's most atmospheric venues, La Fonda on the Plaza, tenders gourmet chile rellenos, red chili pork tamales, and enchiladas topped with red or green chilies in a romantic courtyard setting *(lafondasantafe .com; 100 E. San Francisco St., Santa Fe, NM; GPS 35.6866, -105.9378).*

≫ Lodged inside an 1849 adobe overlooking Mesilla's plaza in Las Cruces, the Double Eagle offers modern takes on New Mexican classics like green chili cheese wontons and ahi tuna tartar nachos, flatbread with cilantro-jalapeño butter, and seafood chile rellenos *(double-eagle-mesilla.com; 2355 Calle de Guadalupe, Mesilla, NM; GPS 32.2745, -106.7952).*

193 CHILI PEPPERS

The fiercest debate in New Mexico isn't about whether you support the Aggies or Lobos, but if you prefer red or green. Chilies, that is. Aficionados figure your pepper palate has to swing one way or the other.

The irony is that they both derive from the same plant. Green chilies are younger, not fully ripe, and used more like a vegetable in traditional dishes like chile relleno, the popular stuffed pepper creation (see p. 211). They must be used at once or else frozen because they spoil quickly.

Red chilies are fully mature, dried or roasted, and often ground into a powder that's used like a spice. *Ristras*—those strings of drying chilies you see hanging in New Mexico homes, shops, and restaurants—double as edibles and decorative items.

Chili relleno—a stuffed and fried green poblano pepper

The Spanish introduced capsicum chilies to the Rio Grande Valley more than 400 years ago. They were quickly adopted by the region's Pueblo Indians and over the centuries the various groups evolved their own unique varieties.

In the early 1900s, Las Cruces horticulturist Fabian Garcia developed the first standardized chili pod, New Mexico No. 9. Garcia's groundbreaking cultivar led to the Hatch, Big Jim, Sandia, Anaheim, and other local chilies (cue New Mexico's half-billion-dollar chili industry), each boasting its own unique flavor profile and heat level.

Where to Try It

» One of the best places to buy (and try) a wide variety of locally grown hot things is the Viva New Mexico Chile Festival in Los Lunas. In addition to a salsa contest and chili cook-off, the three-day event invites chili farmers to vend their green and red treasures at numerous stalls around the festival grounds (vivachilefestival.com; Los Lunas, NM; GPS 34.8287, -106.7622).
» Sandia Chile Company inside the Village Farmers Market in Albuquerque sells a wide variety of New Mexico chili products, including fresh-roasted green Hatch and red Sandia chilies, as well as chili pods, seeds, powder, and sauce (sandiachile.bravesites.com; 607 Osuna Rd. NE, Albuquerque, NM; GPS 35.1512, -106.6169).

194 BISCOCHITOS

The Land of Enchantment is renowned for its piquant foods. But New Mexicans also have a sweet tooth, especially when it comes to the biscochito (or bis-cochos, as they call them in southern New Mexico), butter cookies flavored with anise and cinnamon. Anyone who's lived in the state more than two or three generations probably has a family recipe passed down from a beloved abuela (grandmother) or tía (aunt), prepared with loving care on birthdays, weddings, graduations, holidays, and other special occasions, or perhaps just as a school lunch snack.

The state's official cookie, the

Biscochitos

biscochito might be a throwback to Spanish colonial days, but there are many modern variants that add all sorts of tasty new ingredients to the ancient recipes. Traditional accompaniments include hot chocolate and peach compote.

Where to Try It

» Golden Crown Panaderia, a neighborhood bakery near Old Town Albuquerque, offers a mouthwatering choice of blue corn, chocolate, cappuccino, and even sugar-free biscochitos (goldencrown.biz; 1103 Mountain Rd. NW, Albuquerque, NM; GPS 35.0956, -106.6583).
» Lemon, chocolate chip, red chili, and pecan count among the titillating flavors at Celina's Biscochitos in Albuquerque (celinasbiscochitos.com; 404 Osuna Rd. NW, Ste. A, Los Ranchos de Albuquerque, NM; GPS 35.1534, -106.6393).
» Frontier Mart in Corrales sells Osito's Biscochitos, made from an old Las Cruces family recipe (biscochitos .net; 3677 Corrales Rd., Corrales, NM; GPS 35.2178, -106.6247).

★IDAHO★

195 RUSSET POTATOES

Developed in New England and first established in Colorado, the russet potato didn't gain celebrity until Idaho farmers discovered its affinity for the Snake River Valley, with

A loaded baked potato, courtesy of Idaho's favorite crop

Where to Try It

» Potato sack races, tuber tosses, tugs-of-war over a potato "mash pit," and the Miss Russet beauty contest highlight September's Idaho Spud Day in Shelley, on the banks of the Snake River *(idaho spudday.com; Shelley, ID; GPS 43.3840, -112.1221).*

» "Burgers on the side" is the motto of the Boise Fry Company, which specializes in gourmet french fries and dipping sauces *(boisefrycompany.com; multiple locations).*

» The 1950s-style Westside Drive-In on State Street offers Boise's best (and strangest) selection of spud dishes, including a Greek spud with olives, feta, and tomato relish; mashed potatoes with gravy; potato salad; curly fries; and Westside's famous Idaho ice-cream potato *(cheflou .com; 1929 W. State St., Boise, ID; GPS 43.6257, -116.2150).*

volcanic soil, sunny days, and cool nights similar to the humble spud's original Andes homeland.

Though it's neither native to Idaho nor naturally occurring, the state has lovingly embraced the potato as its own. So much so that many folks think of the russet as the quintessential Idaho potato. Pioneering botanist Luther Burbank—considered the father of the Idaho potato—"invented" the russet in 1873 while experimenting with seedlings from an Early Rose variety during attempts to make the plant more disease-resistant.

The variety draws its name from its brown skin color, but the beloved russet is also known for its substantial bulk, creamy white flesh, low water content, and general lack of "eyes" compared to other varieties. Copious starch makes the russet ideal for mashed or baked potatoes, but their large size also renders this potato perfect for slicing into french fries.

196 HASSELBACK POTATOES

Named after the Stockholm hotel where it was first concocted in the 1950s, the Hasselback potato in its original form was nothing more than an accordion-sliced baked potato with crispy outside and soft interior. With their large size and creamy texture, Idaho spuds proved the ideal vessel for the Hasselback and it wasn't long before Snake River Valley

Surprise

Idahoans have probably been distilling potatoes into alcohol for the past century, but surprisingly, a premium **vodka** industry emerged only recently. Spirits by Idaho distilleries like Grand Teton Distillery *(tetondistillery .com)* and 44 North *(44northvodka.com)* are reaping awards as America's best domestic vodkas and the world's best potato vodkas.

You say potato, *Lewis and Clark said wapato.* It's a wild tuber they ate that's found west of the Rockies and that was once a staple of Northwest American Indian cooking.

cooks were creating their own variations on the Scandinavian theme.

Modern recipes call for all sorts of different stuffings, from basic butter, sour cream, and chives to cheese, bacon bits, and herbal concoctions. Professional cooks use special Hasselback cutting boards with a dip in the middle that keeps the potato firmly in place during the slicing process, available to the general public via online shopping websites.

Where to Try It

Hasselback potatoes are rarely found in Idaho restaurants, but spud lovers can try the recipes at home by investing in a bag of genuine local potatoes.

» The U-Pick Red Barn in Idaho Falls sells unwashed spuds for 25 cents a pound in 25-, 50-, and 100-pound burlap sacks (*upickredbarn.com; 2726 Rollandet St., Idaho Falls, ID; GPS 43.4731, -112.0434*).

» The Idaho Potato Commission website features a recipe for classic Hasselback potatoes (*idahopotato.com*).

197 REED'S DAIRY ICE CREAM

Gorilla Munch, Gavin's Mess, and Grasshopper are just a few of the 49 flavors churned out by Reed's In Idaho Falls, a small local dairy that has evolved into a national ice-cream lover's phenomenon thanks to online sales and fast, efficient modern shipping.

Incredibly rich and smooth, the velvety concoction is the brainchild of Alan Reed, a second-generation Idaho Falls dairy farmer who as a young man dreamed of making world-famous ice cream. Long before organic was trendy, he decided to raise his Holstein cows without hormones, antibiotics, or other additives and make natural dairy products from their milk.

Reed's basic recipe was passed down from his grandmother; many of the initial flavors were suggested by family, friends, and farmhands. Although the business has grown exponentially since he made his first batch in the early 1980s, the process is still just a step removed from homemade. Despite growing demand, Reeds continues to make no more than 240 pints a day.

Ice-cream cone

Where to Try It

» Anyone passing through Idaho Falls can lick to their heart's content at the Reed's Dairy Ice Cream Parlor on West Broadway, adjacent to the farm where the cows are raised and milked twice a day (*reedsicecream .com; 2660 W. Broadway, Idaho Falls, ID; GPS 43.4970, -112.0844*).

» Everyone else, order online at *reedsicecream.com*, and fair warning: It's not cheap!

198 FINGER STEAKS

Boise's great culinary claim to fame, finger steaks, are thin slices of beef dipped in batter and deep-fried.

According to local legend, a former U.S. Forest Service butcher by the name of Milo Bybee launched them at the capital city's Torch Lounge in the late 1950s and they soon became a local passion. Such is their popularity that one suggestion for the design of Idaho's state quarter was that it have something to do with finger steaks. (Luckily, cooler heads prevailed and a peregrine falcon appears on the state quarter instead.)

Although they originally created a convenient way to utilize table scraps, finger steaks have risen in stature over the years to the point where some Idaho restaurants feature them as a specialty gourmet item. Chefs use various cuts of beef and batter that often features a secret blend of herbs and spices.

Rather than cooked all the way through, the perfect finger steak should display just a touch of pink in the middle.

Bagging potatoes on
Idaho Spud Day in Shelley, Idaho

During the Trailing of the Sheep Festival in Ketchum, Idaho, the animals return to the lowlands before winter.

Where to Try It

» Sockeye Grill & Brewery in west Boise batters its finger steaks in their own Hell-Diver Pale Ale beer and recommends munching them with barbecue sauce made with their Power House Porter beer *(sockeyebrew.com; 3019 N. Cole Rd., Boise, ID; GPS 43.6324, -116.2751).*
» On Main Street in downtown Boise, the BrickYard serves its gourmet "steak sticks" with smoked blue cheese, béarnaise, and demi-glace dipping sauces *(brickyardboise.com; 601 Main St., Boise, ID; GPS 43.6144, -116.2011).*
» Owned by three generations of the Werner family, Smitty's Pancake & Steak House in Idaho Falls serves finger steaks for lunch and dinner just yards from the Snake River *(smittys-if.com; 645 W. Broadway, Idaho Falls, ID; GPS 43.4935, -112.0464).*

199 TRAILING OF THE SHEEP FESTIVAL

Set between the snowcapped Sawtooth Mountains and the lava desert called the Craters of the Moon, Idaho's Wood River Valley has always been perfect sheep country. By the end of the 19th century, the valley was world renowned for both its wool and lamb meat. The annual Trailing of the Sheep Festival, which plays out every October in Ketchum and Hailey, honors the region's shepherding traditions and strives to preserve that heritage for future generations.

The weekend includes a lamb barbecue in Ketchum, outdoor lamb feast in Hailey, lamb cooking classes, and lamb every which way at gourmet restaurants in both towns—like lamb meatloaf, lamb sliders, lamb kebabs, and lamb *ragù*. The music and dance of the Basque immigrants who played such a large part in Idaho sheep history is another big part of the festival scene.

The weekend culminates with a "trailing of the sheep" through Ketchum, during which thousands of the animals are herded through the town's streets as part of the traditional transfer of sheep from highlands to lowlands before winter arrives *(trailing ofthesheep.org).*

Where to Try It

Even when the festival isn't in full swing, there are plenty of places to purchase cuts of the region's lamb, or try the valley's lamb dishes.

» Hailey's Wood River Farmers' Market sells locally produced sheep cheese, and organic cuts of lamb in the
summer (*wrfarmersmarket.org; Main & Carbonate Sts.,
Hailey, ID; GPS 43.5207, -114.3165*).
» The Wood River Sustainability Center in Hailey, a
year-round farmers market, sells lamb chops, leg of
lamb, lamb roasts, and even has a smoked lamb meatball Italian sub on its lunch menu (*wrsustainability
center.com; 308 S. River St., Hailey, ID; GPS 43.5169,
-114.3146*).
» Order the braised northern Rockies lamb shank at the
Ketchum Grill, and chase it with some of the restaurant's
house-made ice cream or sorbet (*ketchumgrill.com; 520
East Ave., Ketchum, ID; GPS 43.6832, -114.3642*).

★UTAH★

200 JELL-O

Utah's official state snack, Jell-O brand gelatin has
become so synonymous with Mormon cooking that
Salt Lake City and the surrounding region is sometimes called the Jell-O belt.

The quintessential instant American dessert, Jell-O
is easy to make in large batches suitable for big
Mormon families. In fact, annual consumption runs
twice the national average in Utah, where it's
widely considered an ideal family food. Given
its long shelf life, it also segues into the Latter-
day Saint tradition of each family storing a
year's supply of food at home. The wiggly,
jiggly substance became Utah's official snack
in 2001 after a statewide petition drive and surprisingly serious debate in the state legislature.

Cooks know Jell-O is also highly adaptable
and lends itself to almost endless variations of
"salad" or dessert (also popular in the Midwest;
see sidebar p. 157) when mixed with everything
from fruit to candy. The most iconic form and
a staple of Mormon cookbooks is green Jell-O
salad, which blends lime gelatin, crushed pineapple, cottage cheese, and whipped cream.

It doesn't stop at culinary art: Utah also stages
Jell-O carving contests. And for special events,
locals have been known to grease their summer
Slip'N Slides with Jell-O rather than water.

see sidebar p. 157

Surprise

Hawaiian haystacks are a favorite at
potlucks among Utah's Mormon cooks.
The culinary mash-up involves a mound of rice
covered in gravy and heaped with chicken,
diced tomato, celery, bell pepper, onion, shredded coconut, canned pineapple bits (hence the
name), and more. The mound is crowned with
crispy chow mein noodles and grated cheese.

Where to Try It
» One of the many bizarre midway foods you can
munch at September's Utah State Fair in Salt Lake City
is deep-fried lime Jell-O (*utahstatefair.com; 155 N. 1000
W., Salt Lake City, UT; GPS 40.7722, -111.9211*).
» *LDS Living* magazine's website offers an entire page
of gelatinous recipes, including lemon Jell-O cake, layered Jell-O salad, chocolate raspberry Jell-O pie, and
Jell-O pops (*ldsliving.com*).

201 BREAD PUDDING

Utah homemakers and chefs have taken the Mormon
pioneer practice of not wasting a single scrap of food

Bread pudding, a frontier-era concoction of Mormon cooks in Utah

and transformed it into a yummy statewide dessert tradition. Resourceful frontier-era cooks made their bread puddings by blending stale bread with milk, eggs, sugar, and lard into a simple yet tasty after-dinner treat. Modern chefs have turned the once modest dessert into a gourmet confection by combining fresh bread with things like custard, caramel, berries, and indulgent sauces.

Where to Try It

» Kneaders Bakery & Cafe, with locations throughout Utah, sells hot raspberry or apple cinnamon streusel bread pudding, all with homemade vanilla bean sauce (kneaders.com; multiple locations).

» Ogden's Union Grill, in the city's historic railroad station, serves homemade bread pudding with a topping of caramel sauce and fresh whipped cream (uniongrill ogden.com; 2501 Wall Ave., Ogden, UT; GPS 41.2207, -111.9796).

202 FRY SAUCE

Utah's favorite condiment is fry sauce, a savory blend of ketchup, mayonnaise, and a blend of spices.

Almost every Utah restaurant and fast-food chain has its own unique ratio, a secret recipe closely guarded by the owners and chef. Originally called pink sauce, it has an appearance and consistency similar to Thousand Island dressing's. Although fry sauce can be used on hamburgers and hot dogs—and conceivably dripped on your breakfast eggs—its primary raison d'être is as a complement to french fries, tater tots, and onion rings.

Where to Try It

» Don Carlos Edwards allegedly invented fry sauce after opening Salt Lake City's first Arctic Circle restaurant in 1950. His original fry sauce is now available at more than 60 Arctic Circle locations in Utah and neighboring states, which collectively pump out around 120 gallons per day (and you can purchase a bottle of the sauce to go). Although the exact blend has never been revealed, it's rumored that buttermilk is among the covert ingredients in the AC sauce (acburger.com; multiple locations).

» Another oldie but goodie, Hires Big H drive-ins make and dispense their own supersecret-recipe fry sauce at three locations in and around Salt Lake City (hiresbigh .com; multiple locations).

In Utah, it's fry sauce you dunk your curly fries in, and the recipe is a secret.

203 UTAH SCONES

Banish all thoughts that Utah scones (also called Mormon scones) are kin to the more familiar British variety. The latter is basically a quick bread made with baking powder as the leavening agent and served at afternoon tea with clotted cream and jam as the primary condiments. On the other hand, Utah scones are deep-fried balls of yeast dough.

Born of the Western frontier, they are often compared to Navajo fry bread or New Mexican sopaipillas. As a breakfast item, freshly fried Utah scones are smothered in butter, honey, or powered sugar. Taking them deeper into the day, they can also be used as the outer "shell" of Navajo tacos, filled with ground beef or shredded chicken, refried beans, lettuce, cheese, and salsa.

» Utah's family-owned Sconecutter restaurant chain offers a variety of scone-based dishes from honey butter, apple, and cinnamon scones to scone sandwiches, chocolate sconenuts, and Navajo tacos (*sconecutter.com; multiple locations in central Utah*).

» Just off I-15 on the south side of Salt Lake City, Midvale Mining Cafe has been serving homemade Utah scones for more than 30 years (*390 W. 7200 S., Midvale, UT; GPS 40.6209, -111.9011*).

204 PASTRAMI BURGER

Piles of pastrami heaped onto a beef patty, topped with cheese, lettuce, tomato, and onion, drizzled in Thousand Island dressing, and then shoved in a sesame-seed bun has become a standard item on many Utah restaurant menus. But unlike so many other dishes that have become Utah standards, the pastrami burger is not a Mormon invention. The hybrid sandwich made its way to Utah via a couple of Greek-American chefs (John Katzourakis and Jim Katsanevas) who learned how to make it in Southern California before starting their own Salt Lake City restaurant in the 1970s. Almost lost on a menu that included traditional Greek items like gyros and souvlaki kebabs, the pastrami burger struggled at first but eventually became the star of their citywide Crown Burgers chain, and a juicy culinary darling copied by dozens of restaurants around the state.

Where to Try It

» If you don't see pastrami burgers on the menu at the seven Crown Burgers locations around Salt Lake

A Utah scone, fried and served with honey and powdered sugar

City, that's because they call it the Crown Burger (*crown-burgers.com; multiple locations*).

» Hook & Ladder Company Fire Station No. 13 in Salt Lake City serves its pastrami burgers in a vintage drive-in atmosphere (*1313 California Ave., Salt Lake City, UT; GPS 40.7402, -111.9286*).

Basic Ingredient

It's dubbed the Beehive State for the Mormon symbol of industriousness, but Utah produces some pretty great **honey**, too. The arid climate translates into higher sugar content in the sweet food. Salt Lake City's Honey Stop sells a dozen-plus varieties from local beekeepers (*thehoneystop.com; 159 E. 800 S., Salt Lake City, UT; GPS 40.7520, -111.8956*).

205 FUNERAL POTATOES

Once upon a time, funeral potatoes may have been strictly something you made for the wake of a deceased friend or family member. But the savory dish has spread to potlucks, picnics, and other occasions, and well beyond the Mormon sphere into Utah's general population.

Like so many Mormon specialties, funeral potatoes are an eclectic treat that combines many different

The pasta-based frog eye salad is less alarming than you expect.

food groups into a single, easy-to-make meal. The casserole includes shredded frozen or fresh potatoes, canned cream of chicken soup, and sour cream topped with crumbled cornflakes and is then baked until molten. But there are infinite variations. Some cooks sprinkle tortilla chips across the top instead of cornflakes; others spice things up by adding onions, chili peppers, or salsa.

Where to Try It

» Contests to choose the best funeral potatoes are a staple of the Utah State Fair, held every September in Salt Lake City (*utahstatefair.com; 155 N. 1000 W., Salt Lake City, UT; GPS 40.7722, -111.9211*).
» The Chuck-a-Rama restaurant chain offers funeral potatoes as part of its Sunday "Home Cookin' With All the Fixin's" dinner buffet (*chuck-a-rama.com; multiple locations*).

206 FROG EYE SALAD

Disclaimer: No amphibians are harmed in the making of this salad. It's actually a pasta-based casserole and a mainstay of Mormon potlucks and Thanksgiving dinners throughout the Rocky Mountain and Intermountain regions. In fact, a 2014 survey by Google and the *New York Times* determined that frog eye salad was the most searched Turkey Day recipe in four western states with large Mormon populations.

The frog's eye of the title derives from the tiny *acini de pepe* pasta that serves as the dish's main ingredient. When boiled to the right consistency, the little pasta balls do resemble (and feel like) something through which a frog may have peered at the world. The pasta gets chilled, doused in pineapple juice, and then mixed with crushed pineapple, mandarin orange segments, and finally whipped cream. Some cooks add coconut or marshmallows to the mix for a final result that isn't far removed from traditional ambrosia salad.

Where to Try It

» Even in Utah, frog eye salad is rare on restaurant menus. One exception is Utah's Chuck-a-Rama buffet chain, where frog eye is sometimes featured at the salad bar (*chuck-a-rama.com; multiple locations*).
» Mormon Mavens in the Kitchen, a culinary blog founded and run by LDS women, offers a classic frog eye salad recipe on its website (*mormonmavens.blog spot.com/2013/04/frog-eye-salad.html*).

★ARIZONA★

207 CHILTEPIN CHILIES

Much of America's chili culture (and cultivation) originated south of the border. Not so in Arizona. Here, in

Morton harvests around *half a million tons* of salt each year along the south shore of Utah's Great Salt Lake.

the rocky, cactus-studded wilderness near Tucson, the mother of all peppers, chiltepins—thought to be the origin of all chili peppers—grow wild.

The small but feisty, pea-size pepper packs quite a punch. On the official Scoville heat scale, the chiltepin scores a scorching 50,000–100,000 units—well ahead of the jalapeño and trailing only the habanero in overall heat. In addition to spicing foods, the chiltepin was integral to the "medicine cabinet" of indigenous people on both sides of the border, used to treat headaches, rheumatism, stomach ailments, and more.

Where to Try It

» Tucson's hip Downtown Kitchen & Cocktails infuses its fish tacos and slow-braised beef cheek tacos with chiltepin-based salsa (downtownkitchen.com; 135 S. 6th Ave., Tucson, AZ; GPS 32.2205, -110.9683).
» Chiltepin chili features in a number of the regionally inspired drinks at Exo Roast Company coffee shop in Tucson, including the chiltepin latte, ice toddy, and cold brew (exocoffee.com; 403 N. 6th Ave., Tucson, AZ; GPS 32.2265, -110.9688).

208 SONORAN HOT DOG

A hybrid hound with an international résumé, the Sonoran hot dog is definitely a breed apart. Something like this was bound to happen when the humble American hot dog traveled to Mexico, with its zest for spicy foods and exotic flavors. Sonorans wrapped the frankfurter in bacon before stuffing it into a thicker bun, and then smothered it with pinto beans, chopped tomatoes, onions, jalapeño sauce, mayonnaise, and mustard.

No one expected the amped-up dog to make much noise when it slipped back across the border. But in short order it became one of Arizona's favorite

Continued on p. 228

Arizona's pea-size chiltepin chilies are used in everything from tacos to lattes.

People line up for Indian fry bread—sour milk leavened, deep-fried, and eaten on its own or used as a taco shell.

GREAT AMERICAN EATING EXPERIENCES
Native American Fare

Traditional Native American foods vary greatly from region to region and go back to the source. The differences depend on what was available from nature or what crops indigenous groups of a given area were able to cultivate.

As one of North America's more sophisticated farming cultures, the people of the Southwest supplemented their hunting and gathering with several crops—corn, beans, and squash in particular. Maize was especially useful as a stand-alone food or source of cornmeal that could be used in other dishes. Southwest Indians also cooked a lot with cactus, especially the prickly pear and saguaro, as well as the desert-dwelling tepary bean. Today, the region still carries a rich tradition of Native American dishes.

›› Fry Bread
Ubiquitous throughout the Southwest, fry bread is a traditional Native American quick bread. It's normally leavened with baking powder or soured milk rather than yeast, and fried or deep-fried in oil or lard. Eat it on its own with butter, honey, or even jam, or as the base for Indian tacos. Although it's the official state bread of South Dakota, fry bread originated during the middle of the 19th century in the Navajo lands of northern Arizona.

Nowadays, Phoenix is the hotbed of fry bread, especially places like the Fry Bread House, which in 2012 received an "America's Classics" award from the James Beard Foundation for its nurturing of Native American cuisine *(1003 E. Indian School Rd., Phoenix, AZ; GPS 33.4943, -112.0606).* Near Tucson, members of the Tohono O'odham tribe sell fry bread with all the fixings at stalls outside Mission San Xavier del Bac (sanxaviermission.org; 1950 W. San Xavier Rd., Tucson, AZ; GPS 32.1070, -111.0078).

>> Authentic Eateries

Scattered around the Southwest are a handful of venues serving Native American dishes, from food trucks and roadside stalls to sophisticated resorts and restaurants. One of the most authentic indigenous eateries is the Desert Rain Café on the Tohono O'odham Reservation in southern Arizona, where every dish contains at least one traditional ingredient, such as cholla buds, tepary beans, or saguaro cactus (desertraincafe.com; Tohono Plaza, Main St., Sells, AZ; GPS 31.9146, -111.8878).

In neighboring Utah, Provo's Black Sheep Cafe puts a gourmet spin on Native American favorites with dishes like posole soup with braised pork, hominy, and red chili broth, and Navajo tacos with pinto beans, green chili sauce, and cilantro lime rice (blacksheepcafe.com; 19 N. University Ave., Provo, UT; GPS 40.2342, -111.6591).

>> Indian Tacos

Made with a flat piece of fry bread rather than a curved corn tortilla, Indian tacos look more like tostadas than tacos you typically find in a Mexican restaurant. Beyond that, regional and tribal variations abound. Oklahoma-style Indian tacos consist of fry bread topped with ground beef, pinto beans, shredded cheese, diced tomato, shredded lettuce, jalapeño peppers, sour cream, and salsa. Tim's Drive Inn in suburban Warr Acres is the place to munch delicious Indian tacos in the Oklahoma City metro area (5037 N. MacArthur Blvd., Warr Acres, OK; GPS 35.5218, -97.6192). September's annual Oklahoma State Fair in the state capital features food trucks and stalls with Indian tacos (okstatefair.com; 333 Gordon Cooper Blvd., Oklahoma City, OK; GPS 35.4711, -97.5724).

>> Tepary Beans

Among the age-old legends spun by the Tohono O'odham people of southern Arizona is a story about how the Milky Way is composed of billions of tepary beans. One of the most drought-resistant crops on the entire planet, teparies thrive in the super-arid Sonoran Desert climate. The beans are used in salads, dips, and stews and as filler for fry bread or tortillas. Harvested in the fall, they come in various colors, but white and brown are the most common. At Tucson's Barrio Cuisine Native American bistro, tepary hummus complements other indigenous favorites like fry bread, calabacitas (a squash-based vegetable side dish), and sweet Yaqui bread pudding for dessert (barriocuisine.com; 188 E. Broadway Blvd., Tucson, AZ; GPS 32.2212, -110.9672). The Courtyard Café at the Heard Museum in Phoenix features tepary bean hummus with fry bread and a tepary veggie wrap (heard.org; 2301 N. Central Ave., Phoenix, AZ; GPS 33.4724, -112.0722).

In Arizona, tepary beans are turned into hummus and eaten with fry bread.

mobile meals. Aficionados in Phoenix and Tucson argue about which among the scores of *hotdogueros* (hot dog vendors) makes the best Sonorans. Fans often travel miles out of their way to feast at their favorite stand. Even food critics love it. "The Sonoran dog brings together all the important food groups in one meal that spans many cultures in the most delicious way possible," crooned the *Tucson Weekly*.

Where to Try It

≫ The Sonoran dogs at Tucson's El Güero Canelo have reached something approaching legendary status, especially the two-frank Sammy variation *(elguero canelo.com; multiple locations)*.

≫ Trimming things down to the bare essentials, Ruiz Hot-Dogs in Tucson serves nothing more than Sonoran dogs and drinks from a van parked beside a tent *(22nd St. & 6th Ave., Tucson, AZ; GPS 32.2068, -110.9685)*.

≫ Nogales Hot Dogs, the Phoenix hot spot for the alternative wieners, sets up nightly at the corner of North 20th Street and East Indian School Road *(GPS 33.4948, -112.1021)*.

Sonoran hot dogs, an ambitious mix of frankfurter, bacon, beans, and other fixings.

209 FRESH DATES

Native to the Fertile Crescent in the Middle East, date palms flourish in hot, desert environments, a fact that Arizona farmers didn't ignore when they were pondering plants that might thrive in their own arid wilderness.

Arizona's dates—mostly grown in the Gila River Valley between Yuma and Phoenix—trace their roots to 11 Medjool palms imported to the United States from Morocco in the 1920s. As sweet as candy and easy to pack, dates became a sought-after souvenir for those crossing the Southwest desert by car, bus, or train. They're also incredibly healthy, low in both fat and sodium, and high in fiber and minerals. While Medjools continue to dominate the desert groves, other dates have crept into the Arizona mix, including Halawi, Thoory, and Khadrawy.

Where to Try It

≫ Created as a railroad whistle-stop in the 1920s in the aptly named community of Dateland, Dateland Date Gardens hawks both raw dates and a variety of fruity spin-offs like date milkshakes, butter, and steak sauce *(dateland.com; 1737 S. Ave. 64 E, Dateland, AZ; GPS 32.7994, -113.5404)*.

≫ Sphinx Date Company in Scottsdale specializes in fruit and products made from Black Sphinx dates, a small, sweet hybrid of the Medjool that developed spontaneously in Arizona *(sphinxdateranch .com; 3039 N. Scottsdale Rd., Scottsdale, AZ; GPS 33.4833, -111.9258)*.

≫ In downtown Yuma, a regional souvenir shop called Basket Creations and More sells gourmet gift boxes of Bard dates stuffed with pecans, almonds, apricots, walnuts, coconut, pistachios, and chocolate *(basketcreationsyuma.com; 245 S. Main St., Yuma, AZ; GPS 32.7234, -114.6179)*.

During the growing season, Yuma, Arizona, ships out a million boxes of winter lettuce a day to the rest of the country.

210 YUMA LETTUCE DAYS

Everything you always wanted to know about lettuce is the focus of Yuma Lettuce Days, which unfolds each February at the University of Arizona Agriculture Center on the western edge of Yuma.

A fresh-from-the-field salad bar featuring locally grown head, leaf, and romaine lettuce is one of the main attractions. But the leafy shindig also boasts celebrity chefs, cooking demonstrations, live music, and a "spinach trial" growing plot (with 80 varieties) that pays homage to Yuma's other big cash crop. On the serious side, the festival organizes lectures and demonstrations on lettuce irrigation, cultivation, management, and automated technologies (*yumalettucedays.com; 6425 W. 8th St., Yuma, AZ; GPS 32.7124, -114.7062*).

Fed by water from the nearby Colorado River, Yuma County produces about 90 percent of the winter lettuce grown in the United States each year during a short but very fertile season that runs from November to March. During that time, about 1,000 trucks packed with 1,000 boxes of lettuce depart Yuma each day bound for supermarkets and restaurants around the nation.

Where to Try It

» In addition to the festival, the Yuma Visitors Bureau offers "Field to Feast" tours of lettuce and vegetable growing areas January through March, an adventure that includes lunch and a chance to pick lettuce (*visit yuma.com; 201 N. 4th Ave., Yuma, AZ; GPS 32.7273, -114.6226*).

◇◇

In addition to lettuce, Yuma is *Arizona's top producer* **of broccoli, cauliflower, lemons, tangerines, watermelons, cantaloupes, and wheat.**

211 ARIZONA SOUTHWEST SPECIALTIES

Although it doesn't yet carry the same cachet as Tex-Mex (see pp. 186–187) or New Mexico cuisine (see pp. 211, 214), Arizona has developed its own distinct culinary traditions and unique dishes.

Foremost is the chimichanga—a deep-fried burrito packed with beans, rice, cheese, and some sort of meat, and covered in guacamole, sour cream, and salsa. It's a widely debated point, but local legend holds that Tucson restaurateur Monica Flin invented the chimichanga in the 1920s when she inadvertently dropped a burrito into a deep fryer and decided it tasted pretty good. By the 1950s, it was standard at many southern Arizona eateries and spreading through the Southwest.

Carne seca (dried meat) is another Arizona favorite, although it probably came across the border from Sonora where it has a long tradition as *vaquero* (cowboy) cuisine. Sometimes described as shredded jerky, the rehydrated meat is often mixed with chili peppers, tomatoes, onion, and eggs to make *machaca,* a great stand-alone dish or a filling for tacos, burritos, and other tortilla-wrapped treats.

Where to Try It

» Macayo's Mexican Kitchen, which started in Phoenix, is one of a handful of restaurants that pioneered the chimichanga and still serves it the original way *(macayo.com; multiple locations).*
» In addition to being the place where Monica Flin famously fumbled her burrito, Tucson's El Charro Café makes a pretty mean carne seca, too *(elcharrocafe.com; flagship location: 311 N. Court Ave., Tucson, AZ; GPS 32.2257, -110.9745).*

212 ARIZONA SALSA TRAIL

The upper Gila River region has long been dominated by cotton, copper, and cattle. But in recent

Basic Ingredient

Native to the Arizona desert, the very **prickly pear cactus,** or nopal, has been a common ingredient of Southwest cuisine (and medicine) new and ancient. Tasting like a mild pickle and packed with antioxidants, the plant is versatile. Its green pads add character to salads, soups, and chili; and the purple pears are blended into juice, smoothies, and ice cream.

years the area has added a fourth *C*—cuisine, reflecting the valley's growing repute for excellent Mexican food.

Many of the best restaurants are strung like dried chilies along Arizona's Salsa Trail, a 120-mile stretch of U.S. 70 between the old copper mining town of Globe and the New Mexico border.

Mormons pioneered many of the small towns along the upper Gila, but demographic shifts over the past century brought waves of Hispanic migrants and their delicious foods. Eateries range from roadside taco stalls and country stores to proper sit-down affairs along historic main streets. You can verily eat your way along the route, starting with huevos rancheros or fresh tortillas for breakfast, tamales or tacos at lunch, and then something even more substantial for dinner like carne asada or green chili *burro* (a large burrito) cooked enchilada style. Many of the menus reflect old family recipes and nearly every restaurant along the route has its own secret salsa. For more information on the Salsa Trail, including a map with addresses of the restaurants, visit *salsatrail.com.*

Where to Try It

» Worthy eateries along the trail: Husband-wife-run La Casita Cafe in Thatcher *(3338 W. Main St., Thatcher, AZ; GPS 32.8493, -119.7558),* where owner Ray Villalobos does all the cooking; in Solomon, La Paloma

---

One of the nation's most remote eateries, the Grand Canyon's Phantom Ranch Canteen is a *7.8-mile hike* from the nearest parking lot.

Chateaubriand, a high-end Vegas steak often served with a prime piece of lobster

Restaurant *(5183 E. Clifton St., Solomon, AZ; GPS 32.8128, -109.6278),* one of the valley's oldest Mexican eateries, renowned for shrimp fajitas, tasty margaritas, and fried ice-cream dessert; and another family-run establishment, El Coronado *(409 W. Main St., Safford, AZ; GPS 32.8333, -109.7117),* winner of numerous awards for its homemade salsa.

» The Salsa Challenge Tent with its recipe competitions and chili-eating contests is the place to hang during Safford's annual September SalsaFest *(salsa trail.com; 1111 Thatcher Blvd., Safford, AZ; GPS 32.8345, -109.7196).*

★NEVADA★

213 CHATEAUBRIAND

Like shrimp cocktail, chateaubriand came to Las Vegas in the 1950s, but it's always sat at the opposite end of the city's dining table—an upscale meal to treat VIPs and high rollers rather than a way to lure your average Joe through the casino doors.

The high-end steak became a staple of supper clubs, known as gourmet rooms, both on and off the Strip. The dish derives its name from the early 19th-century French writer, diplomat, and epicurean François-Auguste-René, vicomte de Chateaubriand, in whose kitchen the carnivorous treat was first developed.

In its original form, chateaubriand was a choice cut of beef tenderloin seared, cooked rare to medium rare, and served with a savory wine sauce.

But as with so many things, Las Vegas has whisked the dish to a whole new decadent place. The steak is still prepared in the traditional way, but a chateaubriand Vegas-style almost always includes a prime piece of lobster, too—swanky surf and turf. And because it's usually made for two, rather than solo servings, chateaubriand has become the ultimate Las Vegas anniversary or hot date (or mob tête-à-tête) meal. Sadly for high rollers and spendthrifts, the near extinction of gourmet rooms in modern times means the dish is relatively hard to find these days.

Shrimp cocktail was invented to lure patrons into Vegas casinos.

Where to Try It

» Chateaubriand is still a lavish production at Hugo's Cellar in the Four Queens Hotel & Casino. Starting with a rose for the lady as you take your seats, the three-stage extravaganza includes salad prepared tableside by a tuxedo-clad waiter, followed by steak and lobster, and finished with either cherries jubilee or bananas Foster for two (*hugoscellar.com; 202 Fremont St., Las Vegas, NV; GPS 36.1698, -115.1433*).

» Moved lock, stock, and red velvet booths from the old Barbary Coast casino hotel, Michael's at South Point continues the tradition of excellent chateaubriand established by owner Michael Gaughan at the original location (*southpointcasino.com; 9777 Las Vegas Blvd. S., Las Vegas, NV; GPS 36.1127, -115.1731*).

» Inside the Venetian, celebrity chef Emeril Lagasse's Delmonico Steakhouse serves its naturally raised Angus chateaubriand with potatoes and asparagus (*emerils restaurants.com; 3355 Las Vegas Blvd. S., Las Vegas, NV; GPS 36.1214, -115.1696*).

214 SHRIMP COCKTAIL

Given its ubiquitous presence on restaurant menus around the globe, it's easy to forget that shrimp cocktail first became a star in Las Vegas. Northern California restaurateur Italo Ghelfi is credited with introducing the dish to the Nevada desert in 1959, a few years after he helped found the Golden Gate Casino.

It was such a simple concept: a tulip-shaped glass filled with chilled shrimp, a wedge of lemon, and a tangy, tomato-based sauce. Sold at half a buck a shot, it was clearly a loss leader—a way of luring people into the casino in the hopes they would gamble after they gulped their cocktail.

But the dish evolved into a local eating phenomenon. Nearly 60 years down the road, the Golden Gate moves around 2,000 shrimp cocktails a day and has served more than 40 million since it was first introduced.

Where to Try It

» Served at Du-par's Restaurant & Bakery just off the main casino floor, the Golden Gate dish now sells for $3.99. When adjusted for inflation, that's actually cheaper than the 1950s price. And cocktail connoisseurs can munch it 24 hours a day, seven days a week. Don't bother to ask for the sauce recipe: After all these years, it's still a closely guarded secret (*du-pars .com; 1 Fremont St., Las Vegas, NV; GPS 36.1713, -115.1462*).

» Aquaknox seafood restaurant at Las Vegas's Venetian hotel puts a Latin spin on this seafood standard, a shrimp ceviche cocktail with a spicy *sangrita* sauce (*aquaknox.net; 3355 Las Vegas Blvd. S., Las Vegas, NV; GPS 36.1214, -115.1696*).

215 VEGAS ALL-YOU-CAN-EAT BUFFETS

Along with slots and showgirls, buffets are a Vegas mainstay. In bygone days, they were dirt cheap and fairly uninspiring. But in modern times, the casino-hotel buffet has evolved into an alternative form of gourmet dining—with price tags to match.

El Rancho Vegas created the first all-you-can-eat meal in the early 1940s, a cornucopian spread called the Chuck Wagon Buffet that promised "every variety of hot and cold entrée to appease the howling coyote in your innards" for just a buck.

Both the price and standard stayed low until 2010, when the Wicked Spoon restaurant in the Cosmopolitan hotel launched a gourmet version that (in the words of *Forbes* magazine) "ushered in the new era of the upscale Vegas buffet by ditching the giant bowls of salad and cocktail shrimp" in favor of selections normally found in only the best restaurants, from basil goat cheese *panna cotta* with pine nut brittle and blackberry gel, *salade Niçoise* with quail eggs, and whole roasted lamb to a dozen kinds of sorbet and gelato.

Where to Try It

» The spread at the Wicked Spoon in the Cosmopolitan hotel is definitely not your grandfather's Vegas buffet (*cosmopolitanlasvegas.com; 3708 Las Vegas Blvd. S., Las Vegas, NV; GPS 36.1097, -115.1738*).

» Often voted the city's best buffet, the Bacchanal Buffet at Caesars Palace offers another sumptuous spread, more than 500 dishes for breakfast, lunch, and dinner including special stations for meats, seafood, Mexican, Italian, and Asian cuisine (*caesars.com; 3570 Las Vegas Blvd. S., Las Vegas, NV; GPS 36.1162, -115.1745*).

» Another foodie favorite, the Bellagio Buffet features a fee-added unlimited drinks option and a chef's table

experience with caviar and a variety of chef-selected dishes made tableside (*bellagio.com; 3600 Las Vegas Blvd. S., Las Vegas, NV; GPS 36.1127, -115.1767*).

» The recently revamped Excalibur Buffet serves a global breakfast spread that includes huevos rancheros, breakfast pizza, Greek yogurt, French crepes, and cheese blintzes (*excalibur.com; 3850 Las Vegas Blvd. S., Las Vegas, NV; GPS 36.0989, -115.1755*).

» The Garden Court Buffet in downtown Vegas's Main Street Station casino hotel is one of only a handful of restaurants that still offers bargain buffets for breakfast, lunch, and dinner. At last check, you could bag an

The dessert spread at the Bacchanal Buffet at Caesars Palace in Las Vegas

The table at Louis' Basque Corner in Reno, Nevada, is spread with hearty dishes like Basque beans, sweetbreads, and soups.

Racks of ribs at the Nugget Rib Cook-Off in Sparks, Nevada

best sauce, and attendees get to vote on the People's Choice award. The cook-off includes the Rib Eating Championship, dominated by the world's top-ranked professional eater, Joey Chestnut, who set a world record at the event in 2013 by gobbling down 13.76 pounds of St. Louis–style pork ribs in just 12 minutes (*nuggetribcookoff.com; 1100 Nugget Ave., Sparks, NV; GPS 39.5333, -119.7571*).

Where to Try It

>> Beyond the cook-off, there's another must-try for rib meat in the vicinity. Even the name is a mouthful—Kinder's Meats, Deli, & BBQ—but the longtime Reno joint (opened in 1946) is celebrated for its tequila lime ribs (*kindersbbqreno.com; 3600 Warren Way #107, Reno, NV; GPS 39.4909, -119.8048*).

endless dinner for under $12 (*mainstreetcasino.com; 200 N. Main St., Las Vegas, NV; GPS 36.1741, -115.1450*).

216 SPARKS RIB COOK-OFF

Among the first Europeans who settled in the Truckee Meadows region of northwestern Nevada were cattlemen who swapped stock with wagon trains headed for California. Sparks, Nevada, honors that pioneer heritage with the beastly popular Best in the West Nugget Rib Cook-Off over Labor Day weekend, billed as the nation's largest festival devoted to ribs.

Competitions and food stalls collectively serve about 230,000 pounds of ribs to half a million hungry meat-eaters over six days.

Staged in the city's revamped Victorian Square area, the alfresco event pits two dozen rib maestros around the nation, including longtime attendees like the Chicago BBQ Company, Famous Dave's of Minnesota, Checkered Pig from Virginia's Blue Ridge Mountains, and Armadillo Willy's from California. In addition to the best overall ribs, judges also name the

217 VINTAGE "RAT PACK" RESTAURANTS

Wherever they landed, the famous fivesome of Frank Sinatra and his crew (Dean Martin, Joey Bishop, Peter Lawford, and Sammy Davis, Jr.) established regular hangouts, and Las Vegas was one of them. During their long sojourns performing, playing, and moviemaking in the Nevada desert, the so-called Rat Pack famously frequented Piero's and the Golden Corral restaurants, both just off the Strip.

Where to Try It

>> Near the old Desert Inn, where members of the Rat Pack often performed, Piero's Italian Cuisine was both a showbiz haunt and a mob lair where the Feds occasionally nabbed their most wanted men. In addition to hot and cold antipasti and hearty Italian soups, the menu includes classic Italian dishes like saltimbocca, veal scaloppine, and linguine (*pieroscuisine.com; 355 Convention Center Dr., Las Vegas, NV; GPS 36.1320, -115.1560*).
>> Frank and the gang were also regulars at the Golden Steer Steakhouse, opened in 1958 and one of the city's oldest meateries. In addition to prime rib, the Sahara Avenue restaurant also serves Italian specialties

Nevada's oldest drinking establishment is the Genoa Bar, which *opened in 1853* in gold rush–era Genoa.

and offers private rooms to those trying to elude the paparazzi (*goldensteerssteakhouselasvegas.com; 308 W. Sahara Ave., Las Vegas, NV; GPS 36.1440, -115.1611*).

218 BASQUE CUISINE

The 19th-century Basques who came west with all the rest hoping to find gold or silver quickly recognized northern Nevada as a perfect landscape for grazing sheep. And when they didn't find shiny metal, they established sheep farms on the outskirts of Winnemucca, Elko, Reno, and Carson City.

One of the ways they kept their Old World culture alive was food, a tradition that has endured into the 21st century in both restaurants and food festivals along the I-80 corridor.

Basque kitchens often took root in residential hotels where Basque workers boarded. Dining was normally family-style at long wooden tables. That's still the case today at most of Nevada's Basque eateries, where the menus might include lamb chops, oxtail stew, tripe stewed with pig's feet, chicken with garbanzo beans, beef tongue, sweetbreads, chorizo sausages, and the occasional paella.

Where to Try It

» Over Fourth of July weekend, Elko's National Basque Festival includes plenty of food stalls and a sheepherder's bread-baking contest (*elkobasqueclub.com; 1601 Flagview Dr., Elko, NV; GPS 40.8462, -115.7604*).

» Elko's Toki Ona Bar & Restaurant, one of the state's newer Basque eateries, offers tasty lamb, pork, and beef dishes as well as Basque chorizo omelets at breakfast (*eattokiona.com; 1550 Idaho St., Elko, NV; GPS 40.8412, -115.7524*).

» Lodged inside Reno's old Lincoln Hotel is thoroughly old-style Louis' Basque Corner. Lamb or beef entrées are served with French bread, Basque beans, and a hearty soup (*louisbasquecorner.com; 301 E. 4th St., Reno, NV; GPS 39.5308, -119.8101*).

» Launched by two Basque brothers in 1960, J.T. Basque in Gardnerville features offbeat Iberian items like roast rabbit, pig's feet with tripe, and a Basque-American cocktail called Picon Punch (*jtbasquenv.com; 1426 U.S. 395, Gardnerville, NV; GPS 38.9406, -119.7487*).

It was once Frank Sinatra and his Rat Pack gracing the interior of Piero's Italian Cuisine in Las Vegas, Nevada.

WEST

Fresh fruit and lots of seafood—this is the bounty of the Pacific states. Throw in Asian influence, coffee, and some sourdough bread, and you have the West's cuisine in a nutshell.

WASHINGTON
240–247

OREGON
247–255

CALIFORNIA
255–264

HAWAII
265–274

ALASKA
274–277

Rainbow chard, ready for sale at California's Point Reyes Farmers Market

To give it a smoky, sweet flavor, salmon gets roasted on a wet cedar plank.

★ WASHINGTON ★

219 ALDER- & CEDAR-PLANK-SMOKED SALMON

In Washington, salmon is a keystone species that helps maintain the ecosystem—and the state's culture. The majestic fish has played an important role in Native American traditions of the Pacific Northwest, and has remained a de facto symbol of the region. The time-honored Northwest Native American method of cooking it with cedar or alder wood best captures salmon's essence while imparting a smoky and sweet flavor to the fish. Soak a cedarwood or alderwood plank in water, and then place halved salmon skin-side down on the wood. Roast it in the oven or grill over an open fire, and the wood infuses the salmon with a lush aroma reminiscent of the area's evergreen fauna.

Where to Try It

>> Cooked to flaky perfection and served alongside roasted, seasonal veggies, the cedar-plank salmon at Palisade is a Seattle classic (palisaderestaurant.com; 2601 W. Marina Pl., Seattle, WA; GPS 47.6303, -122.3914).

>> Ivar's Salmon House, part of a local franchise in existence since 1938, roasts sockeye salmon on cedar in a coat of brown sugar spice rub, and serves it with corn bread pudding and Washington blackberries (ivars.com; 401 NE Northlake Way, Seattle, WA; GPS 47.6536, -122.3240).

>> Held each fall on the grounds of the Leavenworth National Fish Hatchery, the three-day Wenatchee River Salmon Festival celebrates the return of the salmon to the sea from their freshwater spawning grounds. There's food and educational events, including the Tribal Village, a collaborative project of Native American tribes throughout the Northwest showcasing traditional fishing and cooking of salmon as well as storytelling and

handicrafts *(salmonfest.org; 12790 Fish Hatchery Rd., Leavenworth, WA; GPS 47.5583, -120.6747).*

» If you want to try your hand at using wood planks, Chef John Howie ships kiln-dried western red cedar and alder boards around the country *(plankcooking.com).*

220 PACIFIC SHELLFISH

Briny Olympia oysters; tender Penn Cove mussels; buttery scallops; sweet-tasting, speedy razor clams that disappear two feet under sand in a moment; and even long, mild-flavored geoduck clams—this is the shellfish bounty offered up by Washington State's great Northwest Pacific. Washington's love affair with shellfish goes so deep that one of its public universities, Evergreen State College, heralds the vaguely phallic geoduck (pronounced gooey-ᴅᴜᴄᴋ) as its mascot.

There are myriad ways of preparing the state's abundant shellfish, using the Columbia Valley's white wine or pan-Asian spices, but its freshness is really its crowning quality.

Where to Try It

» Seafood reigns at Seattle restaurants. Chef Zoi Antonitsas changes her menu nightly, but her Seattle eatery Westward always draws its inspirations from the ocean, with fresh seafood fare like Treasure Cove manila clams steamed in Rainier beer and green garlic, and smoked clam dip *(westwardseattle .com; 2501 N. Northlake Way, Seattle, WA; GPS 47.6517, -122.3287).* Cutters Crabhouse features fresh produce and seafood from neighboring Pike Place Market in entrées like Asiago-and-almond-crusted scallops and blue cheese–sprinkled mussels

Oysters from the Walrus & the Carpenter in Seattle

from Penn Cove *(cutterscrabhouse.com; 2001 Western Ave., Seattle, WA; GPS 47.6105, -122.3442).* At Anchovies & Olives, an Italian-inspired seafood restaurant, sample the fresh oysters from Pickering Passage in the southern end of Puget Sound, in a sauce of scallions, minced shallots, and vinegar *(ethanstowellrestaurants .com; 1550 15th Ave., Seattle, WA; GPS 47.6146, -122.3127).* From Skookum Inlet to Hood Canal, the oyster menu at the Walrus & the Carpenter reads like the maritime map of western Washington *(thewalrus bar.com; 4743 Ballard Ave. NW, Seattle, WA; GPS 47.6635, -122.3801).*

» Hailing from a South Vietnam village, Xinh Dwelley began her career as a teenager, cooking for American GIs and later became famous around Olympia for her oyster stew and mussels cooked in a Vietnamese-style curry seasoned with lemongrass, cayenne, coconut milk, and ground peanuts. You can try it at her restaurant Xinh's Clam and Oyster House *(xinhsrestaurant.com; 221 W. Railroad Ave., Shelton, WA; GPS 47.2126, -123.1023).*

» In July, experience the oddly shaped culinary star of the region at the Allyn Days Geoduck Festival, where seafood fans can sample shellfish delicacies as well as a thousand

Washington State produces *90 percent of all American red raspberries,* **up to 76 million pounds per year.**

pounds of chewy geoduck prepared by local chefs (*allynwa.org; Allyn Waterfront Park, Rte. 3, Allyn, WA; GPS 47.3849, -122.8274*).

221 PAN-ASIAN CUISINE

Long before fusion became a tired fad elsewhere, Washingtonians were mixing aromas and flavors from different Asian nations to create uniquely Pacific Northwestern dishes like radicchio-studded soba noodles and shiitake mushrooms in a red wine soy reduction.

Waves of immigrants from Japan, Korea, Vietnam, Laos, Thailand, China, and other Asian countries have profoundly changed the culinary landscape of Washington, imbuing the state's palate with searing chili, sweet basil, vibrant cilantro, fresh ginger, and other staples of the Asian pantry.

Where to Try It

» The annual Dragon Fest celebration, in Seattle's International District, includes a popular $2 Food Walk, which lets you sample bites from restaurants representing various Asian countries (*cidbia.org; Seattle, WA; GPS 47.5987, -122.3239*).

» Year-round, the deli of the historic Asian grocer Uwajimaya is another great place to taste how different Asian cuisines come together in Seattle, with treats like a fruit custard crepe in a cone, spam *musubi,* and Korean soft tofu soup (*uwajimaya.com; flagship location: 600 5th Ave. S., Seattle, WA; GPS 47.5969, -122.3270*).

» Among the most established pan-Asian eateries is Seattle's Wild Ginger, where you can try butter lettuce cups stuffed with Thai-spiced seabass, *laksa* (spicy Malaysian noodle soup), and Cambodian-style short ribs (*wildginger.net; 1401 3rd Ave., Seattle, WA; GPS 47.6088, -122.3375*).

» In the quaint port town of Edmonds, check out black cod pickled in sake along with avocado rice, Taiwanese-style ribbon noodles with braised beef, and snap pea risotto at Bar Dojo (*bardojo.com; 8404 Bowdoin Way, Edmonds, WA; GPS 47.8062, -122.3468*).

A fried shrimp appetizer at Edmonds, Washington's Bar Dojo, which specializes in pan-Asian cuisine

222 THE TERIYAKI SHOP

More than a burger or sandwich joint, Washingtonians turn to teriyaki for some fast food—beef, chicken, pork, or better yet, Washington's staple, salmon, marinated in soy sauce and sweet mirin rice wine and charred over open flames. In Washington, Koreans own many of its teriyaki shops, putting their own spin on the dish by adding ginger and garlic to the marinades. The resulting flavored-soaked meats come infused with a refreshingly sweet flair. Not surprisingly, the teriyaki that's come to be known as "Seattle style" takes on Korean influences and adds sugar and pineapple juice for extra sweetness, and cornstarch for a thicker sauce.

The Washington teriyaki restaurant is a humble, comforting establishment, often no more than just a couple of plastic tables where you stop by for a quick lunch of the eponymous dish. Other popular items you'll find include *bibimbap,* a Korean staple of rice mixed with ground beef, boiled spinach, bean sprouts, and pickled veggies; and Nepalese *momo* dumplings.

Really, you can't go very far without seeing a place serving some variation of the teriyaki dish. In fact, you can take me out to a ball game . . . and buy me veggie wieners topped with teriyaki-glazed onion. That's how you roll in Seattle, where Mariners fans garnish even their ballpark snack with triple garlic sauce by hometown favorite chef Tom Douglas (*seattle.mariners.mlb .com; Safeco Field, 1250 1st Ave. S., Seattle, WA; GPS 47.5914, -122.3323*).

Where to Try It
» Toshi's Teriyaki Grill, opened in 1976, claims to be the originator of Seattle-style teriyaki (*toshisgrill.com; 16212 Bothell Everett Hwy., Mill Creek, WA; GPS 47.8517,*

A bowl of pho, Vietnamese beef noodle soup, from Pho Bac

-122.2186). Wanna Teriyaki & Burger is another one of Seattle's favorites (*wannateriyaki.com; 1513 SW Holden St., Seattle, WA; GPS 47.5334, -122.3546*).

223 PHO

Though Vietnamese in origin, pho (pronounced FUH) may as well have been created for the rainy weather of Seattle. The dish has the winning combination of rice noodles and thinly sliced meat in hearty beef broth, garnished with cilantro, scallions, bean sprouts, and basil—perfect to warm the body and fortify the soul on the gloomiest of days.

Washington's love affair with pho began in 1975, when an influx of Vietnamese war refugees first brought their culture and cuisine to the local landscape. Today, pho is an everyday staple not just among the nearly 70,000-strong Vietnamese in Washington, but all over the Pacific Northwest. There are a staggering 45 restaurants in the Emerald City with pho in the name—just 10 fewer than Starbucks—and many more that serve the dish, not to mention the countless pho specialists all over the Evergreen State.

Where to Try It
» Pho Bac, which began as a sandwich shop in 1982, is credited for introducing the soup to the city, and

---

Surprise

You may associate **lentils** with the Middle East or India, but this ancient bean is harvested abundantly closer to home, in eastern Washington. Pullman even hosts a festival for it, with the world's largest bowl of lentil chili (350 gallons!) parceled out to attendees for free (*lentilfest.com; Washington State University, Pullman, WA; GPS 46.7319, -117.1544*).

At Westward in Seattle, you can eat Pacific shellfish while looking out over Lake Union.

continues to expand with its network of franchises run by family members or friends of the family *(thephobac .com; multiple locations).*

» Another ubiquitous Washington State institution is Than Brothers *(thanbrothers.com; multiple locations).*

» For a hipper version, try Ba Bar's upscale duck confit pho paired with a Nguyen Dynasty, a gin-and-rhubarb creation finished with prosecco *(babarseattle .com; 550 12th Ave., Seattle, WA; GPS 47.6069, -122.3165).*

» Other faves among locals: Vien Dong Restaurant in Tacoma *(3801 S. Yakima Ave., Takoma, WA; GPS 47.2230, -122.4432),* Lynnwood's Phoenix *(14007 Rte. 99, Lynwood, WA; GPS 47.8709, -122.2745),* and Spokane's Pho Van *(2909 N. Division St., Spokane, WA; GPS 47.6847, -117.4115).*

224 COFFEEHOUSES

It may be unthinkable today to imagine your day without your morning latte, but the proliferation of Italian-style coffee drinks in America owes its existence to Seattle-born Starbucks. The behemoth began in 1971 as a purveyor of freshly roasted beans and brewing equipment in the city's foodie capital, Pike Place Market, and since then Seattle has proselytized its coffeehouse culture across America.

But don't think Washington is all about finicky Seattleites ordering from snooty baristas. From the trendiest cafés to one-person, drive-through shacks to cozy neighborhood hangouts with fireplaces, its coffee culture is as diverse as the selection of brews.

Where to Try It

» Where can you not smell coffee? America's most caffeinated city has an endless supply of noteworthy cafés, like the nonprofit Street Bean Coffee *(streetbean.org; 2711 3rd Ave., Seattle, WA; GPS 47.6173, -122.3493);* Espresso Vivace *(espressovivace.com; flagship location: 532 Broadway E., Seattle, WA; GPS 47.6238, -122.3206),* where coffee bags come with a "born-on" stamp; arts-focused Zeitgeist *(zeit geistcoffee.com; 171 S. Jackson St., Seattle, WA; GPS 47.5990, -122.3319),* where you can also catch an indie film screening; and Bauhaus *(bauhaus.coffee; multiple locations),* where the coffee is strong and the Wi-Fi free.

» Monorail Espresso has the distinction of introducing America's first mobile latte cart in 1980 *(520 Pike St., Seattle, WA; GPS 47.6153, -122.3260).*

The heart pretty much symbolizes Seattle's relationship with coffee.

Rainier cherries

» Washington's coffee culture extends far beyond Seattle's city limits, with countless suburban espresso drive-throughs and ubiquitous cafés. In Spokane, coffee connoisseurs congregate at Roast House, recognized with a 2014 Good Food Award for supporting sustainability and social justice by using shade-grown, fair-trade crops (*roasthousecoffee.com; 423 E. Cleveland Ave., Spokane, WA; GPS 47.6846, -117.4037*).

225 RAINIER CHERRIES

There are cherries, and then there are Rainier cherries. The yellow drupe that blushes red is named after Washington State's iconic mountain and trumps all its cherry cousins in taste and appearance. A cross between the bing and Van cultivars and developed

Surprise

Stale hot dogs, sugary sodas . . . forget what you know about gas station food. Spokane's **Rocket Market** has gourmet items, top-notch wine, and specialty health foods. Fill up the tank and grab obscure vintages, locally brewed kombucha (fermented tea), and homemade pastries (*rocketmarket.com; 726 E. 43rd Ave., Spokane, WA; GPS 47.6144, -117.3995*).

in 1952, Rainiers are extra sweet and have succulent flesh that adds extra chewiness with each bite. People aren't the only ones in love with the fruit, though. Birds feast on it, destroying up to a third of the state's crop and making Rainiers a rare summer treat. Undeterred by the higher price tags, Washingtonians look forward to the Rainier season each summer—and so should you.

Where to Try It

» Go straight to the source by picking them yourself at Hauck's Orchard in Ferndale (*haucksorchard.com; 1920 Harksell Rd., Ferndale, WA; GPS 48.9069, -122.5843*); Barrett Orchards in Yakima (*treeripened.com; 1209 Pecks Canyon Rd., Yakima, WA; GPS 46.6184, -120.5739*); Stutzman Ranch in Wenatchee (*thestutzmanranch.com; 2226 Easy St., Wenatchee, WA; GPS 47.4871, -120.3926*); or Mead's Cherry Hill (*cherryhillwa.com; 18207 N. Sands Rd., Mead, WA; GPS 47.8230, -117.2654*).

» If you want the finished product, order a slice of cherry pie at Twede's Café in North Bend, also known as the Twin Peaks café for its role in the cult TV series (*twedescafe.com; 137 W. North Bend Way, North Bend, WA; GPS 47.4951, -121.7868*).

★OREGON★

226 MARIONBERRY PIE

Dubbed the "Cabernet of blackberries" for their earthy, rich flavor, marionberries accentuate sorbets and jellies with their deep purple hue. But no other dish highlights the Oregon berries' tart, complex taste better than the marionberry pie, a beloved state dessert. Topped with crumbles or crisscrossed with a lattice crust, this treat is an American classic with an Oregonian twist.

Where to Try It

» Streusel pies and turnovers featuring marionberries keep Four and Twenty Blackbirds Bakery in Ashland a

With 35 coffee shops per 100,000 residents, Seattle has ten times the number of cafés per capita than the national average.

Goat cheese, one of the options on the Oregon Cheese Trail

227 OREGON CHEESE TRAIL

Few road trips will let you experience the diverse climates and landscapes of Oregon better than visiting the state's many creameries. Follow the cheese trail and you'll get to taste everything from pungent chèvres to mild Bries, and you'll realize that not only wines get to have terroirs, the gustatory fingerprints left by a particular place's environment. Cheesemakers of Oregon use milk from grazing cows and goats that give each dairy product distinct flavors from the varying soils and grasses of the state *(oregoncheese guild.org)*.

Where to Try It

» Start your cheese trail journey at Portland's urban cheesemonger, the Ancient Heritage Dairy, which produces the soft-ripened cow and sheep's milk Adelle and the raw-milk, earthy Hannah in its creamery in the so-called Artisan Corridor (Northeast Grand Avenue and Martin Luther King Jr. Boulevard on Portland's eastside), chockablock with foodie businesses *(ancient heritagedairy.com; 1311 SE 7th Ave., Portland, OR; GPS 45.5135, -122.6587)*. Then head out to Tillamook, the "land of cheese, trees, and ocean breeze." Here, at the Tillamook County Creamery Association, you can take a free tour of its factory where over 170,000 pounds of cheese are made daily *(tillamook.com; 4175 Rte. 101, Tillamook, OR; GPS 45.4845, -123.8443)*.

» Come for the single-source cheddar and stay for the ice cream at the Face Rock Creamery in Bandon on the

local favorite *(420blackbirdsbakery.us; 130 A St., Ashland, OR; GPS 42.1998, -122.7125)*.

» If you can't commit to a whole pie, you can sample the marionberry danish at Chalet Restaurant & Bakery in Newport *(chaletrestaurantandbakery.com; 2026 N. Coast Hwy., Newport, OR; GPS 44.6522, -124.0529)*.

» If you love a marionberry pie so much that you want to scarf it down in seconds, try your luck at the end-of-summer Oregon State Fair in Salem, where contestants vie to make masses of fruit and dough disappear before the eyes of cheering spectators *(oregonstatefair.org; Oregon State Fairgrounds, 2330 17th St. NE, Salem, OR; GPS 44.9591, -123.0070)*. Or for a fresh sample of the indigenous berry, stop by July's Oregon Berry Festival in Portland *(oregonberryfestival.com; 721 NW 9th Ave., Portland, OR; GPS 45.5283, -122.6806)*.

» Out-of-towners will appreciate ordering a variety of marionberry pies and cobblers from the Willamette Valley Pie Company in Salem *(wvpie.com; 2994 82nd Ave. NE, Salem, OR; GPS 44.9676, -122.8911)*.

Basic Ingredient

Oregon's beer boom would be impossible without the state's **hops,** an important flavoring agent. With 14 types grown in the Willamette Valley alone, Oregon is an ideal place to experiment with beer, and the fall Sisters Fresh Hop Festival celebrates a lineup of local brews *(sisterscountry.com; Village Green Park, Sisters, OR; GPS 44.2890, -121.5493)*.

Oregon produces *over a billion pears a year—* **enough to wrap around the world twice.**

rugged Oregon coast (*facerockcreamery.com; 680 2nd St. SE, Bandon, OR; GPS 43.1191, -124.4050*).

» Southern Oregon's Rogue Creamery in Central Point captures the beauty of its mountainous surroundings in its handcrafted and buttery TouVelle, a nutty love child of cheddar, jack, and Gouda. Also be sure to try the creamery's savory blue cheeses, which are carefully aged in caves to create their characteristic blue veins. The Oregonzola is a clever nod to Gorgonzola's Italian roots, but it is mellower than the original, with a rich butter flavor complemented by hints of fruit (*roguecreamery.com; 311 N. Front St., Central Point, OR; GPS 42.3763, -122.9206*).

228 SEA SALT

Sure, every coastal state has access to sea salt, but few others have the dramatic history or high expectations from the everyday ingredient as Oregon.

When the historic Lewis and Clark expedition was exploring the western territory, Clark dispatched five men with a critical mission: Find salt needed to preserve their meat. For weeks these men spent day and night boiling seawater on an Oregon beach. Finally, they returned to camp with 28 gallons of what Lewis described as "excellent, fine, strong & white" salt, enough for the remainder of the journey.

Today, the clean Oregon seawater salt has been elevated to a sought-after staple of world-renowned chefs.

Where to Try It

» Former software marketing exec Ben Jacobsen drove up and down the West Coast to collect seawater from 25 spots before he found Oregon's Netarts Bay, where the seawater yielded perfect crystals with delicate texture and balanced salinity. Savor the resulting salt—infused with smoked chili, local coffee, or as pure flakes in the Jacobsen Salt Company tasting room in Portland (*jacobsensalt.com; 602 SE Salmon St., Portland, OR; GPS 45.5141, -122.6595*).

Continued on p. 252

Oregon's sea salt—Lewis and Clark discovered it long before today's gourmet chefs.

Burgers have a strong California connection—the state is the birthplace of both McDonald's and In-N-Out Burger.

GREAT AMERICAN EATING EXPERIENCES
All-American Burgers

Born in the U.S.A.—well, not quite. It is said that the all-American hamburger actually originated on the docks of the German harbor city that gave it its name. Today, the burger is a quintessentially American food, a marriage of Old World roots and New World efficiency that has been thoroughly assimilated, mass produced, innovated, and exported around the globe.

The basic formula of a grilled meat patty between two halves of a bun, which Louis' Lunch in New Haven claims to have originated in 1900 (see p. 32), has spun countless variations. And dare to try to find the best burger in America and you get more than 26 million results on Google.

Amid all this choice beef, you'll discover peculiar geographic iterations, from spiced up in the Southwest to smoked by Okies.

Here, we start where the oh-so-fast version turned the humble hamburger into a love-hate national obsession, in California.

» California Eatin'

The Golden State gave the world McDonald's, when two brothers started a restaurant in their name in San Bernardino in the 1940s. The eatery's so-called Speedee Service System harbingered the birth of the modern burger—and fast food—by simplifying the menu, making the kitchen an assembly line, and having customers self-serve.

Today, fans of McDonald's can take a selfie in front of the two, original golden arches and order from employees in 1950s-style hats and bolo ties at the oldest existing branch in Downey, California, that opened in 1953 (mcdonalds.com; original location: 10207 Lakewood Blvd., Downey, CA; GPS 33.9474, -118.1177).

McDonald's isn't the only burger behemoth in California. In-N-Out Burger, a still privately owned chain, has a cultlike following among those who can reach its 300-some locations. Aficionados prize In-N-Out classics like Animal Style, a mustard-grilled beef patty piled with grilled onions (in-n-out.com; original location: 13800 Francisquito Ave., Baldwin Park, CA; GPS 34.0676, -117.9737).

» South Carolina Gold

Endearingly called the "caviar of the South," pimento cheese spread is a beloved staple in South Carolina (see sidebar p. 90) found in kitchens and on menus—and, of course, crowning a burger. Especially around Columbia, you will find pimento cheeseburgers in popular places like Rosewood Dairy Bar (3003 Rosewood Dr., Columbia, SC; GPS 33.9884, -81.0004). A contemporary take on the southern barbecue house, the Southside Smokehouse in Landrum melts homemade pimento cheese between brioche buns with fried green tomatoes (southsidesmokehouse .com; 726 S. Howard Ave., Landrum, SC; GPS 35.1640, -82.1825).

» Onions in Oklahoma

The Sooner State likes to fry juicy onions into golden ribbons alongside beef on the grill. At Johnnie's Grill, a greasy spoon since the 1940s, hamburgers take on a smoky flavor thanks to the hickory sauce in addition to the charred onion (301 S. Rock Island Ave., El Reno, OK; GPS 35.5311, -97.9523). Sid's Diner uses spatulas to mash Spanish white onions directly into sizzling beef patties (300 S. Choctaw Ave., El Reno, OK; GPS 35.5312, -97.9551).

» Hot in New Mexico

Crank up the heat of the sizzling patty with a fiery kick of roasted green chilies and salsa in New Mexico. The state is so proud of its spicy spin on the burger that it touts a Green Chile Cheeseburger Trail (newmexico.org). Noteworthy stops include the Buckhorn Tavern in San Antonio (buckhornburgers.com; 68 U.S. 380,

San Antonio, NM; GPS 33.9178, -106.8674), whose chef beat celeb chef Bobby Flay in a cook-off; and Santa Fe Bite (santafe

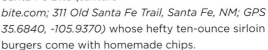

bite.com; 311 Old Santa Fe Trail, Santa Fe, NM; GPS 35.6840, -105.9370) whose hefty ten-ounce sirloin burgers come with homemade chips.

» Midwestern Classic

Lionized by the stoner classic flick *Harold & Kumar Go to White Castle,* the Kansas-based national chain is a midwestern classic that popularized the square, bite-size slider (whitecastle.com; multiple locations).

New Mexico's favorite burger is smothered in green chilies and cheese.

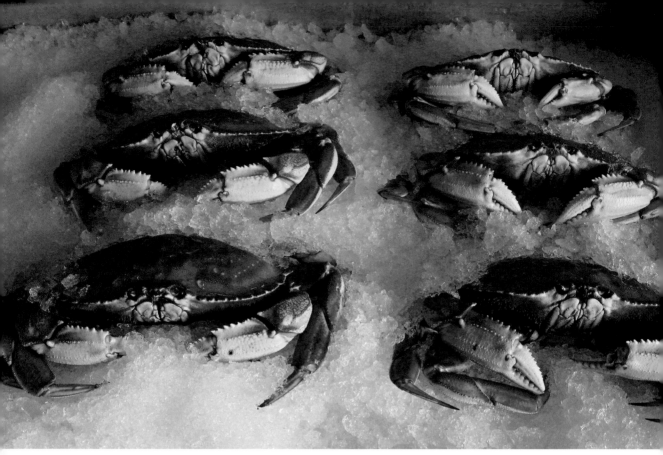

Oregon's Dungeness crabs have ten legs and sweet, tender meat.

》 The Meadow in Portland stocks more than 100 different sorts of gourmet salts (atthemeadow.com; multiple locations).

》 Sample both Oregon's artisan salt and see how important it is to West Coast foodies at September's Feast Portland, one of the best gourmet gatherings in the country, where chefs show off how to turn the most basic of condiments into culinary fireworks (feastportland.com).

229 DUNGENESS CRAB

Hailed as a "meal the gods intended only for the pure in palate" by renowned chef and cookbook author James Beard, the Dungeness crab is a West Coast delicacy prized for its tender and sweet meat. The name comes from the minuscule fishing village of Dungeness in Washington State, but this ten-legged shellfish found from Alaska's Aleutian Islands down to Santa Barbara and even in the Gulf of

Mexico has the distinction of being Oregon's official state crustacean. Abundant in number and resilient to fishing, the crab has a good sustainable seafood rating from consumer watchdog Seafood Watch—so get cracking!

Where to Try It

》 Local Ocean Seafoods in Newport is a go-to place for fresh seafood on the Oregon coast, with Dungeness crab po'boys fixed with green chili avocado puree and terrific Brazilian moqueca de peixe stew using rockfish, wild shrimp, coconut milk, and of course Dungeness crab (localocean.net; 213 SE Bay Blvd., Newport, OR; GPS 44.6321, -124.0491).

》 Newport's Ocean Bleu at Gino's Fish Market and Café turns locally caught crustaceans into pineapple salsa–topped patties and a crab "cocktail" over lettuce (oceanbleuseafoods.com; 808 SW Bay Blvd., Newport, OR; GPS 44.6274, -124.0562).

》 Across the state border, Dockside Grill in Sequim, Washington, near the town of Dungeness serves mean crab fritters (*docksidegrill-sequim.com; 2577 W. Sequim Bay Rd., Sequim, WA; GPS 48.0625, -123.0414*). And October's Dungeness Crab & Seafood Festival in Port Angeles, Washington, celebrates the acclaimed shellfish with food, art, music, Native American handicrafts, and games like Grab-a-Crab Tank Derby over three days (*crabfestival.org*).

230 WILD MUSHROOMS

The moody climate of the Pacific Northwest is made for mycophiles. Prized porcini, woodsy matsutake, delicate chanterelles, and meaty shiitake are just some of the wild mushrooms that thrive in the wet climate. In Oregon, you will even find winter white truffles, long considered a European indulgence. Once dismissed as inferior to its European cousins, Oregon's truffles have come a long way and are now recognized for their hardy, fragrant umami (a savory taste understood not to be quite like any other). Cooked or eaten raw, these forest treasures brighten up the palate even on the grayest Northwest day.

Where to Try It

» At the January Oregon Truffle Festival, held in Eugene, you can sample the luxurious white truffle in myriad preparations and even have your pooch trained to sniff out the underground tuber (*oregon trufflefestival.com*).

» Yachats, an intimate, picturesque coastal town, celebrates wild forest mushroom cuisine along with wine and beer tastings and live music. There are also seminars on how to grow your own culinary mushrooms during the annual Village Mushroom Fest, held in October (*yachats.org*).

» On the 209-acre grounds of the Mount Pisgah Arboretum in Eugene, you can buy fresh, dried, and growing mushrooms as well as kits and tinctures during the autumn Mushroom Festival (*mountpisgaharboretum.com; 34901 Frank Parrish Rd., Eugene, OR; GPS 44.0074, -122.9807*).

Surprise

🍽 Buffalo jerky, elk salami, smoked rabbit . . . the Holland family at **Southern Oregon Fine Meats** in Medford, Oregon, turns environmentally responsible meat and wild game into all kinds of products you may not expect from the crunchy Northwest. This old-fashioned butcher shop is a local institution where you might encounter hunters dropping off bears and antelope to be processed. You can also pick up German products like loaves of rye *Landbrot* and spaetzle noodles (*southernoregonmeats.com; 885 Shafer Ln., Medford, OR; GPS 42.2973, -122.8801*).

» As a fourth-generation family business, the Joel Palmer House in Dayton has turned the family's passion for mushroom hunting into a fine-dining establishment, with dishes like three-mushroom tarts and candy cap mushroom crème brûlée (*joelpalmerhouse.com; 600 Ferry St., Dayton, OR; GPS 45.2179, -123.0796*).

231 WEST COAST DOUGHNUTS

Savory or sweet, topped with tried-and-true chocolate or powdered sugar, or decked out in unexpected fixings like porcini mushrooms, the West Coast doughnut—of which Oregon is particularly proud—is a destination decadence. These artisan creations, which have spread beyond state boundaries, prove doughnuts are

Shiitake mushrooms

◇◇

Along with Washington's Dungeness crab, only two other states, *Maryland and Louisiana,* have state shellfish.

more than just the sum of starch, hot oil, and sugar. West Coast doughnut shops elevate this winning formula to a whole new level of culinary ecstasy.

Where to Try It

» A bakery that never sleeps, Voodoo Doughnut has become a must-visit Portland attraction, famous for its outlandish garnishes like bubblegum powder, grape dust, lavender sprinkles, and cayenne pepper (*voodoo doughnut.com; flagship location: 22 SW 3rd Ave., Portland, OR; GPS 45.5227, -122.6729*).

» If fried chicken, blueberry bourbon basil, and passion fruit cocoa nibs sound enticing as doughnut flavors, head to Portland's Blue Star Donuts (*bluestardonuts .com; multiple locations*).

» At Pip's Original Doughnuts in Portland, try to resist popping a dozen of the fried-to-order mini doughnuts decorated with candied bacon bits, Himalayan sea salt, Nutella, and other exciting garnishes (*4759 NE Fremont St., Ste. C, Portland, OR; GPS 45.5484, -122.6138*).

» Farther afield in Seattle, Top Pot Doughnuts is proud of its "hand-forged" creations like the Feather Boa, a cake doughnut slathered in pink or chocolate icing and topped with coconut shavings (*toppotdoughnuts .com; flagship location: 2124 5th Ave., Seattle, WA; GPS 47.6152, -122.3411*).

» At Tacoma's Legendary Doughnuts, the caramel sea salt–glazed pretzel doughnuts and bear claws filled with peanut butter and jelly are hard to resist (*legendary doughnuts.com; multiple locations*).

» Down in San Francisco, Rich Table's savory fried balls dusted with dried porcini powder have become an institution (*richtablesf.com; 199 Gough St., San Francisco, CA; GPS 37.7748, -122.4228*).

232 FRUIT LOOP

Just an hour outside Portland in Hood River County awaits a tasty road trip along the so-called Fruit Loop. The nation's largest pear-growing region, this fertile land is perfect for a culinary excursion along the Columbia River and contains fruit stands, orchards, farms, and wineries along a 35-mile path.

Where to Try It

» Pick up pear butter, Merlot jelly, and jalapeño jam, along with fresh seasonal fruits at Packer Orchards and Bakery in Hood River (*packerorchardsandbakery .com; 3900 Rte. 35, Hood River, OR; GPS 45.6124, -121.5320*).

» While you're in Hood River, make time for Apple Valley Country Store with oven-fresh fruit pies, local ice cream, and country-style barbecue on festival weekends; you can easily kill a whole afternoon here (*applevalleystore.com; 2363 Tucker Rd., Hood River, OR; GPS 45.6540, -121.5485*).

» More than 80 varieties of apples and pears await at Mount Hood's Mt. View Orchards, where you can pick your own spoils, go on a hayride, or simply admire the stunning views of the mountain (*mtvieworchards .com; 6670 Trout Creek Ridge Rd., Mount Hood, OR; GPS 45.5369, -121.6229*).

» Family-owned since 1911, Kiyokawa Family Orchards near Mount Hood is an American institution, with a founder who bounced back from forced internment during World War II to set up a thriving farm where you can attend events like heirloom apple and Asian pear tastings (*mthoodfruit.com; 8129 Clear Creek Rd., Parkdale, OR; GPS 45.4954, -121.5967*).

A box of Portland's decadent Voodoo doughnuts

Food carts in Portland, Oregon, serve up everything from hot dogs to Turkish *döner* kebabs.

233 FOOD CART PODS

Other cities have food trucks; Portland has "pods" of food carts, microcosms of global cuisines in lively clusters. Some are as tiny as 3 stands, others can contain upwards of 60.

Portland's street food has worldly savoir faire that can impress even the most jaded gourmand—think Korean-spiced pulled pork, gourmet ramen, and Venezuelan stews. You can't walk very far without running into a group of food carts. Go with an open mind and you'll discover dozens of dishes you might never try otherwise.

Where to Try It

» Notable pods include Alder pod, where more than 60 carts pack two downtown city blocks with favorites like Nong's Khao Man Gai's Thai ginger chicken *(SW 10th & Alder St., Portland, OR; GPS 45.5208, -122.6817).*
» If you want to burn off some calories first, bike along the Springwater Corridor cycling path to Cartlandia, where you'll find dozens of food carts along with a bar

with 18 taps of beer *(cartlandia.com; 8145 SE 82nd Ave., Portland, OR; GPS 45.4635, -122.5793).*
» Not to be confused with Cartlandia, the renovated Cartopia pod offers good grub along with an eclectic lineup of Sunday night films projected outside *(1201 SE Hawthorne Blvd., Portland, OR; GPS 45.5122, -122.6536).*
» Go to *foodcartsportland.com* for a handy map of the city's pods.

★ CALIFORNIA ★

234 SAN FRANCISCO SOURDOUGH BREAD

A loaf of bread can encapsulate a city's spirit, and no other baked good comes closer to representing San Francisco than the tangy sourdough bread. Different yeasts, water, and even air contribute to unique tastes of fermented bread, and the San Francisco variety is known for its sharp acidity.

The Acme Bread Company in San Francisco bakes up a variety of artisanal breads, including the city's classic sourdough.

Popularized during the gold rush days when miners subsisted all day on a single loaf, the San Francisco sourdough at once embodies the city's humble origin and its epicurean finesse. Light and fluffy inside a crunchy crust, the sourdough is a perfect accompaniment to the city's specialty cioppino and other seafood dishes, but really, this bread knows how to play well with all kinds of food.

Where to Try It

» The Boudin family, originally from France, has been making sourdough since 1849—and claims it is baking its signature sourdough from the original starter, more than 150 years old (*boudinbakery.com; multiple locations*).

» The Acme Bread Company in Berkeley kicked off the Bay Area's artisanal breadmaking by creating leavened sourdough from wild wine grape yeast. Most San Francisco groceries and markets carry Acme's sourdough, but head to the Ferry Building Marketplace for the full range of the bakery's breads (*acmebread.com; 1 Ferry Building #15, San Francisco, CA; GPS 37.7953, -122.3929*).

» Tartine Bakery, the leader in San Francisco's new generation of bakeries, continues the city's sourdough pedigree with its country bread (*tartinebakery.com; 600 Guerrero St., San Francisco, CA; GPS 37.7614, -122.4241*).

◇◇

The lactic acid bacteria responsible for the San Francisco sourdough bread's tang are named *Lactobacillus sanfranciscensis*—in honor of the foggy city.

» Neighborhood favorite Arizmendi Bakery flirts with fun variants like fig-fennel sourdough and sourdough croissants (arizmendibakery.com; flagship location: 1331 9th Ave., San Francisco, CA; GPS 37.7633, -122.4664).
» And diners seated at communal tables at Lazy Bear, a new kid on the block in the city's gourmet supper club scene, break fresh sourdough bread before a long night of a dozen-plus courses (lazybearsf.com; 3416 19th St., San Francisco, CA; GPS 37.7604, -122.4197).

235 MEYER LEMON CAKE

Championed by celeb and home cooks alike, the yolk-colored Meyer lemon is much juicier and has more complex taste notes than the regular lemon, with more bitterness and less sourness, and balanced with sweetness. Its edible rind tends to be too weak to endure long journeys, making the thin-skinned fruit all the more prized. Sorbet, soufflé, salsa . . . Californians love using this little fruit that can in many recipes, but few dishes highlight its tart and sweet aroma better than the Meyer lemon cake, made with pureed whole fruits and, for a tart, California almonds in the crust.

Where to Try It

» Soft pound cake made with Meyer lemons wins over visitors at Pavel's Bäckerei in Pacific Grove (219 Forest Ave., Pacific Grove, CA; GPS 36.6201, -121.9180).
» Depending on the month, La Jolla's Nine-Ten restaurant pairs its Meyer lemon tarts in crunchy, caramelized crusts with sorbet or ricotta (nine-ten.com; 910 Prospect St., La Jolla, CA; GPS 32.8471, -117.2753).
» Della Fattoria in Petaluma adds extra richness with rosemary and olive oil in its Meyer lemon loaf—make sure you order in advance (dellafattoria.com; 141 Petaluma Blvd. N., Petaluma, CA; GPS 38.2349, -122.6410).
» For a modern variant, try the Tesla pâte de fruit at San Francisco's Tout Sweet Pâtisserie, which makes a creamy concoction of passion fruit, yuzu, and Meyer lemon (toutsweetsf.com; 170 O'Farrell St., San Francisco, CA; GPS 37.7867, -122.4073).

» If you're lucky enough to visit when the fruit is in its spring season, you may sample the cake at the temple of Californian cuisine, Berkeley's Chez Panisse (chezpanisse.com; 1517 Shattuck Ave., Berkeley, CA; GPS 37.8795, -122.2689).

236 CIOPPINO

Boil down the Pacific Ocean's bounty into a single bowl, and you have cioppino. Bringing together fresh Dungeness crab, scallops, clams, shrimp, mussels, and chunks of fish, this dish has an unmistakable Italian fingerprint, with a tomato-based broth and a name that originated from the Ligurian dialect of Genoa, meaning "to chop." Once made by Italian fishermen around North Beach in San Francisco, this red soup is now a coastal staple.

Where to Try It

» Sotto Mare Oysteria and Sea Food Restaurant claims to serve San Francisco's "best damn cioppino," sparing no olive oil, red chili, garlic, or crabmeat (sottomare sf.com; 552 Green St., San Francisco, CA; GPS 37.7997, -122.4083).
» Woodhouse Fish Company makes a similar claim and has its own fervent following (woodhousefish.com; flagship location: 2073 Market St., San Francisco, CA; GPS 37.7675, -122.4284).
» The oldest surviving seafood restaurant in San Francisco, The Old

Meyer lemons

Cioppino, a dish of crab, scallops, clams, shrimp, and mussels stewed in a tomato broth, originated in San Francisco.

Clam House has been serving cioppino in its off-the-beaten-path Bayview location since 1861 *(theoldclam housesf.com; 299 Bayshore Blvd., San Francisco, CA; GPS 37.7430, -122.4049)*.

» Farther afield and south of the city, Phil's Fish Market is so confident of the quality of its spicy stew that it lists the recipe on the website *(philsfishmarket.com; 7600 Sandholdt Rd., Moss Landing, CA; GPS 36.8033, -121.7877)*.

237 SAN FRANCISCO CHINESE FOOD

With more than one in five residents claiming Chinese heritage, San Francisco has no shortage of excellent food from the Middle Kingdom. From tongue-searing Sichuan to diminutive dim sum, you can taste just about every Chinese culinary tradition in San Francisco.

Though fascinating and visually captivating, the city's Chinatown, America's oldest, is not the place where the local Chinese community dines. Head out to the outer boroughs of Sunset and Richmond, and you'll be rewarded with authentic experiences.

Where to Try It

» Dim sum joints abound, but few have elevated Hong Kong's answer to tapas like Yank Sing and its steamed dumplings *(yanksing.com; 101 Spear St., San Francisco, CA; GPS 37.7925, -122.3933)*.

Specialty of the House

Whether a slapdash concoction of leftovers or a carefully crafted summer alfresco lunch, **Cobb salad** is a complete meal in itself. Diced greens, tomato, hard-boiled egg, chicken breast, crispy bacon, and blue cheese dressing was invented at Los Angeles's now defunct Brown Derby restaurant in the 1930s, but it now graces tables all over the land.

» Shanghai specialties like dumplings that pop with soupy goodness in your mouth are best at Kingdom of Dumpling (kingofchinesedumpling.com; 1713 Taraval St., San Francisco, CA; GPS 37.7423, -122.4845).
» Old Mandarin Islamic Restaurant serves favorites of the Uighur ethnic minority and other halal-keeping Chinese folks like lamb skewers and chicken swimming in tear-inducing spicy sauce (3132 Vicente St.; San Francisco, CA; GPS 37.7383, -122.5007).
» Taiwan takes a best-of-China approach to cooking, and you can sample the island's famed beef noodle soup and fried chicken at Taste of Formosa (2428 Clement St.; San Francisco, CA; GPS 37.7822, -122.4854).

238 ARTISAN CHOCOLATES

Brussels, Oaxaca, Zürich . . . Santa Cruz? If the United States' West Coast sounds like an odd place to find excellent chocolate, think again. A number of artisan producers have been creating world-class confections, putting to rest the notion that U.S. sweets are only the oversugared, mass-produced sort sold in drug stores.

Marrying quality cacao with surprising ingredients like bacon, West Coast sweetmakers show what happens when you mix the American, can-do spirit with world-class tastes.

Where to Try It

» After learning from master chocolatiers in France and Belgium, Richard Donnelly returned to Santa Cruz to make small-batch truffles and chocolate bars. The best among his extensive line of chocolates are multicultural inventions like bars infused with Chinese five spices, cardamom, smoky spicy chipotle, as well as out-of-this-world sea salt–caramel chocolate bars (donnelly chocolates.com; 1509 Mission St., Santa Cruz, CA; GPS 36.9667, -122.0397).
» In the heart of San Francisco's hip epicenter, the Mission District, Dandelion Chocolate makes its production completely transparent by keeping the chocolate factory open to the public seven days a week—and in addition to watching the workers handcraft single-origin bars, you must try the frozen hot chocolate, a velvety concoction (dandelionchocolate.com; 740 Valencia St., San Francisco, CA; GPS 37.7610, -122.4218).
» For more than three decades, family-owned Fran's in Seattle has been selling handmade sweets, including its

signature salted caramel, topped with gray or smoked sea salt (franschocolates.com; multiple locations).

239 LOS ANGELES KOREAN FOOD

More than 350,000 Korean Americans call Los Angeles County home—no wonder dishes like kimchi (fermented napa cabbage), dolsot bibimbap (seasonal veggies mixed with rice and pepper sauce in a hot stone bowl), and bulgogi (grilled, thin sirloin) are now part of the mainstream food scene in the Southern California metropolis.

Korean food, featuring generous doses of fiery red chili pepper, pickled vegetables, and marinated meat, has long been an underdog among Asian cuisines in North America. But thanks to the increasing popularity of Koreatown, in the very heart of L.A., this spicy cuisine has become among the most beloved culinary heritages of the West Coast. Instead of merely copying everything from the mother country, Los Angeles Korean food has

Banchan—small, tapas-like plates of Korean food

WELCOME TO DAN

three things to

1 TASTE CHOCOLATE

We use only two ingredients in our chocolate: cocoa beans and cane sugar, so you can taste the nuances of each bean, harvest, and roast
Pro tip: try the samples from left to right.

2 TALK

We are
actually
here. Si
flag us c

ours! We love showing guests around the factory. All of our tours are free. Please RSVP on Eventbrite:

ery Wednesday, Thursday, and Friday, 6-6:20 PM

production and cafe teams lead these tours. Today's tour:

d by:

9|27

For: 1. Takeshi   4.
2.   5.
3.

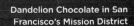
Dandelion Chocolate in San Francisco's Mission District

evolved on its own, exporting dishes like L.A. *galbi,* barbecue beef short ribs marinated in sweet soy sauce and cut into strips, back to Seoul.

Where to Try It

>> Koreatown has no shortage of authentic restaurants, and Kang Ho Dong Baekjeong, in an art deco drive-through complex, is popular for its prime ribs, sliced brisket, and its own invention, cheesy egg soufflé—all cooked right on the tabletop grill *(3465 W. 6th St. #20, Los Angeles, CA; GPS 34.0637, -118.2972).*

>> In addition to grilled meat, Soowon Galbi is a good place to sample *banchan,* the tapas-like plates served for free at the beginning of any authentic Korean meal *(soowongalbi.net; 856 S. Vermont Ave., Los Angeles, CA; GPS 34.0564, -118.2912).*

>> At BCD Tofu House, try the comfort food of hot soft tofu soup seasoned with hot pepper sauce and toppings of your choice like shrimp or pork belly *(bcdtofu.com; multiple locations in California and nationwide).*

240 BURRITOS

Everyone in California agrees a burrito is a solid cylinder of tortilla stuffed with meat and sauce—and that's where the consensus ends.

Northern Californians pledge their allegiance to the Mission style, involving flash-steaming a white or wheat tortilla and topping it with rice; refried, pinto, or black beans; stewed or grilled meat; and salsa. The meat can range from barbecued pork to beef tongue to cubed chicken to beef simmered in chocolaty mole. Roll up your sleeves, prepare to get messy, and order a super burrito: You'll find guacamole, fresh cheese, and sour cream filling out a dish that's as crowded as the San Francisco district that gave it its name, the Mission.

San Diegans, on the other hand, are so confident of their style's iconic status that they named their dish the California burrito. Chunks of beefsteak meet cheese, *pico de gallo* salsa, sour cream, and french fries inside this Southern California style of burrito.

Los Angeles burritos rarely use rice, and fillings can run the gamut from shrimp to Asian-style meats and for breakfast, eggs and sausage.

So which is best? Golden Staters will never agree—so you'll have to try them all.

Where to Try It

>> For Mission style in San Francisco, some locals believe the unassuming Taqueria La Cumbre to be the birthplace of the massive burrito *(taquerialacumbre.com; 515 Valencia St., San Francisco, CA; GPS 37.7645, -122.4215).* The cash-only Taquerias El Farolito sates revelers until the wee hours with its impressive array of fillings—from grilled veggies to beef *(multiple locations).* La Taqueria is an honest taco and burrito joint with little frill and all the flavors *(facebook .com/lataqsf; 2889 Mission St., San Francisco, CA; GPS 37.7508, -122.4180).*

>> For Southern California variations in San Diego, Lolita's Taco Shop has been serving award-winning local favorites like monster burritos that require both hands and a huge appetite for over three decades *(lolitasmexicanfood.com; multiple locations).*

Manuel's Original El Tepeyac Café's Hollenbeck burrito, covered in a *chili verde*

Garlic ice cream aficionados memorialize their day at the Gilroy Garlic Festival.

Or go a little fancier with the combo lobster burrito and shrimp taco at El Zarape (*elzarape.menutoeat.com; 4642 Park Blvd., San Diego, CA; GPS 32.7617, -117.1464*). » At Manuel's Original El Tepeyac Café in L.A., try the famous Hollenbeck (named for the division of L.A. police officers that once consumed it in huge quantities), filled with pork simmered in tomato-based *chile verde* (*manuelseltepeyac.com; 812 N. Evergreen Ave., Los Angeles, CA; GPS 34.0478, -118.1975*).

241 GILROY GARLIC FESTIVAL

Once misunderstood (too ethnic!) or even reviled (stinky!), the boldly flavored *Allium sativum* has come a long way to become an essential part of the American pantry. Hardneck or softneck, sautéed or freshly minced, garlic adds an unmatchable oomph to any dish. And no place in America wears its garlic pride like the agricultural city of Gilroy, just south of Silicon Valley. The number of people in this self-proclaimed "garlic capital of the world" nearly triples every July as it celebrates the annual Gilroy Garlic Festival. In its Gourmet Alley, dozens of vendors spare no flavor as they prepare scampi, calamari, pasta, sandwiches, satays, and other dishes, while chefs take to the stage to face one another in Food Channel–style cook-offs (*gilroygarlicfestival.com; Christmas Hill Park, Gilroy, CA; GPS 36.9967, -121.5833*).

Where to Try It

If you miss the Gilroy Garlic Festival, never fear—the city has other venues, open year-round, where you can shop for and sample all things garlic.
» You can stop by Garlic World, a rural emporium combining a vegetable stand, gourmet deli, and gift shop featuring fresh produce, dried fruits, nuts, and honey in addition to everything garlic (*garlicworld.com; 4800 Monterey Hwy., Gilroy, CA; GPS 36.9715, -121.5532*).
» If raw garlic leaves you cold, try the roasted white bulb and garlic soup at Garlic City Café (*7461 Monterey Rd., Gilroy, CA; GPS 37.0076, -121.5694*).

242 AVOCADOS

Spiced up in a dip or laid out like a flower atop salads, blended into a smoothie or folded into a jumbo burrito, the avocado is a delectable mash-up of contradictions: both refreshing and creamy, subtle yet distinctive, rich but healthy, a fruit most often treated like a vegetable. No state can lay claim to the American avocado more than California, home to 90 percent of the nation's crop. Green with a grassy scent, the avocado is equally beloved by vegetarians and meat lovers, and no place is better than California to sample it, straight up or garnishing another dish.

Where to Try It

» Where *not* to try it is more like the question when the fatty fruit is so ubiquitous throughout California. But for a special pilgrimage, consider visiting fall's California Avocado Festival in Carpinteria, now into its third decade of celebrating everything Hass, Fuerte, and Zutano with guacamole contests, food vendors, and concerts *(avofest.com; Carpinteria, CA; GPS 34.3975, -119.5199).*

» At Fallbrook's Avocado Festival in spring, the young and young at heart compete in their best homemade avocado-shaped racers, and of course food vendors offer a broad array of avocado-centric goodies *(fall brookchamberofcommerce.org; Fallbrook, CA; GPS 33.3821, -117.2513).*

Avocados

» For grown-up fun, September's Avocado & Margarita Festival in Morro Bay beckons *(avomargfest.com; Morro Bay, CA; GPS 35.3656, -120.8531).*

243 FISH TACOS

Given San Diego's proximity to the sea and to Mexico, it's natural that the city should know how to expertly wrap excellent seafood in a tortilla. Fried in beer batter or grilled over an open flame, drenched in fiery salsa or topped with cabbage, fish tacos come in various flavors and colors, but they all have one thing in common: They're something you must try while you're in the Southern California city.

Where to Try It

» Track down the Mariscos German Lonchera taco truck, purveyor of the classic, succulent whitefish and shredded cabbage–topped corn tortilla, along with a complementary cup of tomato seafood soup *(3269 Beyer Blvd., San Diego, CA; GPS 32.5675, -117.0632).*

» Aside from the spicy, briny fish tacos, try the smoked fish burrito and fresh shrimp ceviche at Oscars Mexican Seafood *(oscarsmexicanseafood.com; 703 Turquoise St., San Diego, CA; GPS 32.8081, -117.2608).*

» Touted as San Diego's godfather of fish tacos, Ralph Rubio claims to have introduced the dish to America in 1983 at his fish taco stand in Mission Bay *(rubios.com; multiple locations).*

Pasadena-based amateur horticulturist Rudolph Hass *earned only $5,000* from his namesake avocados, which he patented in 1935.

San Diego's favorite fusion: a fish taco, combining Mexican, American, and coastal food influences

★ HAWAII ★

244 MUSUBI

No other state knows how to take Spam to epicurean heights like Hawaii. The popular snack of Spam musubi is composed of a slice of canned Spam and a block of rice wrapped into a bite-size morsel by a piece of dried seaweed.

Ever present beside gas station cash registers, at convenience stores, and in supermarkets, musubi has evolved far from its raw fish–topped, Japanese inspiration, *nigiri*. Modern musubis tout a variety of toppings. On Kauai, you'll find Göteborg (beef and pork summer sausage) instead of Spam. Elsewhere, toppings like chicken *katsu* (cutlets), grilled tofu, and charred fish give multicultural twists to this road trip staple.

Where to Try It
» Healthier variants are at Mana Bu's in Honolulu, where you'll find 35 different kinds of musubi, including brown rice with eel and baked salmon *(hawaiimusubi.com; 1618 S. King St., Honolulu, HI; GPS 21.2970, -157.8354)*. Also in Honolulu, try Spam musubi with avocado and bacon, or try musubi with mayonnaise-seasoned salmon instead of Spam at Musubi Cafe Iyasume *(tonsuke.com /eomusubiya.html; multiple locations)*.
» At Mark's Place on Kauai, sample Korean-style fried chicken or beef teriyaki musubi *(marksplacekauai.com; 1610 Haleukana St., Lihue, HI; GPS 21.9600, -159.3937)*. And in Hilo on the Big Island, Kawamoto Store has a good selection of Hawaiian, Filipino, Japanese, and Chinese dishes along with musubis *(kawamotostore.com; 784 Kilauea Ave., Hilo, HI; GPS 19.7163, -155.0789)*.

245 SHAVE ICE

How special can mounds of ground ice doused with bright-colored syrup be? Pretty special when you're in the Aloha State.

Hawaiians take their shave ice seriously and harbor strong feelings about who makes the best summery

Continued on p. 268

Apples, nectarines, apricots—they're all for sale at farmers markets in the West.

GREAT AMERICAN EATING EXPERIENCES
Fruits, Nuts & Berries

» Califruitopia

Sunbaked California is America's indisputable fruit bowl. Though set back by the recent drought, the Golden State continues to produce 99 percent of all American almonds, dates, figs, kiwis, pistachios, pomegranates, and walnuts—not to mention more than 90 percent of the plums, nectarines, apricots, and strawberries grown in the United States.

Go on a road trip to take in the abundance. Around the oasis town of Palm Springs, sweet dates grow plentifully. Sip a thick date shake at Hadley Fruit Orchards *(hadleyfruitorchards.com; 48980 Seminole Dr., Cabazon, CA; GPS 33.9234, -116.8072)* or make a meal of bacon-wrapped dates stuffed with blue cheese, jalapeño, and prosciutto (and see 119 varieties of dates amid random biblical kitsch)

at the retro-cool Shields Date Garden *(shieldsdate garden.com; 80225 Rte. 111, Indio, CA; GPS 33.7068, -116.2666)*.

Health-packed almonds have become a prized crop, and you can celebrate this nutty wonder every February at Northern California's century-old Capay Valley Almond Festival, which brings together dessert contests and food stalls *(esparto regionalchamber.com; multiple locations)*.

Of course, California is also the capital of farmers markets frequented by locals spoiled for choice. You'll find an ever changing cornucopia of fruits and nuts, from pluots to persimmons and way beyond. San Joaquin Certified Farmers Market around Stockton *(sjcfarmersmarket.com; multiple locations)* and the San Francisco Ferry Plaza *(ferrybuildingmarketplace.com; 1 Ferry Building, San Francisco, CA; GPS 37.7957, -122.3934)* are just a couple of the many notable ones.

≫ All-Washington Apples

Washington State is America's clear leader in cultivating all things Red Delicious, Gala, and Honeycrisp, producing more than ten billion handpicked apples each year—or enough to circle the Earth 29 times. Touted by Ralph Waldo Emerson as the "American fruit," these red, green, and yellow orbs are at their best when freshly plucked at the orchards of eastern Washington fed by Cascade Mountain waters.

Start your juicy journey at the Washington Apple Commission Visitor Center in Wenatchee where you can gather tips on which farms to visit *(bestapples.com; 2900 Euclid Ave., Wenatchee, WA; GPS 47.4700, -120.3255)*. West of the mountains in Lynden, pick your own Jonagolds and Sansas at Lynden's BelleWood Acres, which has its own distillery making apple-based vodka *(bellewoodfarms.com; 6140 Guide Meridian Rd., Lynden, WA; GPS 48.8640, -122.4859)*.

≫ Berry Oregon & Hazelnuts

Whether turned into pralines, starring in chocolate truffles, baked in tortes, mixed into coffee, or spread on toast, hazelnuts add unmistakable sophisticated nuttiness. Oregon produces more than 90 percent of the filberts (the state's name for hazelnuts) cultivated in the United States. Celebrations honoring the state's official nut include a December hazelnut festival in Mount Angel that combines hazelnut-laced treats with a German holiday market *(hazelnutfest.com; 500 Wilco Hwy. NE, Mount Angel, OR; GPS 45.0646, -122.7979)*.

The state also boasts an abundance of marionberries, blackberries, blueberries, raspberries, and strawberries. The LifeWise Oregon Berry Festival in Portland celebrates summer with fresh-fruit vendors and berry-themed food booths, and a gala dinner prepared by the foodie city's

acclaimed chefs *(oregonberryfestival.com; Portland, OR; GPS 45.5283, -122.6806)*.

≫ Alaska's Last Fruit Frontier

Don't let the state's frosty reputation delude you. Alaska is another berry haven, with nutritious wild blueberries and salmonberries used in candy, jam, and even wine. Treat yourself to a berry pie at the century-old Roadhouse in the end-of-the-road town Talkeetna *(talkeetnaroadhouse.com; 13550 E. Main St., Talkeetna, AK; GPS 62.3229, -150.1151)* or the famous three-berry crisp at the summer-only Sheep Mountain Lodge, 60 miles northeast of Anchorage in Sutton *(sheepmountain.com/restaurant; 17701 Glenn Hwy., Sutton, AK; GPS 61.8125, -147.4982)*.

≫ Hawaii Fruit-O

Taste homegrown tropical fruits in Hawaii, home to America's most distinct ecosystem. Coconuts, pineapples, passion fruit, acai, and 100 varieties of bananas (though not all of them edible) flourish on the lush isles. The Kapiolani Community College Farmers Market on Oahu *(hfbf.org; 4303 Diamond Head Rd., Honolulu, HI; GPS 21.2709, -157.7994)* and the Hilo Farmers Market on the Big Island *(hilofarmersmarket.com; Kamehameha Ave. & Mamo St., Hilo, HI; GPS 19.7234, -155.0848)* offer great opportunities to see them lined up side by side.

Salmonberries, native to Alaska

The vivid, syrupy shades of Hawaiian shave ice

treat. The texture of the ice matters—when done right, it feels smooth, like fluffy snow on the tip of your tongue—as do the flavors, which the best shave ice joints make from scratch.

Whether you opt for *lilikoi* (passion fruit) or tamarind (a strong spice), matcha green tea or Thai iced tea, don't leave the islands without sinking your mouth into these frosty piles of delicious slush.

Where to Try It

» Waiola grocery's flagship location, inside a 1940s mom-and-pop store, started selling shave ice in 1999 and is a local institution. Don't forget to add adzuki red beans or a "snow cap"—sweetened condensed milk *(waiolashaveice.com; flagship location: 2135 Waiola St., Honolulu, HI; GPS 21.2924, -157.8286).*

» Try the Matsumoto, a trinity of lemon, pineapple, and coconut, at the eponymous shop on the North Shore of Oahu *(matsumotoshaveice.com; 66-087 Kamehameha Hwy., Haleiwa, HI; GPS 21.5911, -158.1028).*

» Off the beaten tourist path in Honolulu, Shimazu Store does all the standard flavors and then some, like crème brûlée and red velvet cake *(330 N. School St., Honolulu, HI; GPS 21.3199, -157.8584).*

» On Maui, six branches of Ululani's Hawaiian Shave Ice *(ululanisshaveice.com; multiple locations)* serve this frozen treat with Hawaii-specific ingredients like Roselani vanilla ice cream, while Local Boys *(local boysshaveice.com; two locations)* is proud to use Hawaiian cane sugar along with what the store boasts as the largest selection of shave ice flavors in Hawaii.

» In addition to shave ice, Kauai's Ono Ono Shave Ice sells ice cream, acai desserts, and *halo-halo,* the Filipino interpretation of shave ice loaded with beans, jam, or Jell-O *(4-1292 Kuhio Hwy., Kapaa, HI; GPS 22.0740, -159.3190).*

246 LUAU FARE

The luau, or Hawaiian feast accompanied by entertainment, will fill you up with such traditional dishes as *kalua* pig, salted pork slow roasted all day in a mesquite-fueled underground pit. Other staples include *lomilomi* salmon (a salad of fresh tomatoes, onions, and shredded salmon), *laulau* (pork steamed in taro leaf), *kulolo* (taro pudding with grated coconut), *pipikaula* (salted beef jerky), and poi (a paste made of the taro root common across Polynesia). These labor-intensive dishes aren't affectations for tourists, but an everyday expression of Hawaii's unique culture.

Where to Try It

» Plenty of resorts offer luaus, but you can enjoy even better food while rubbing shoulders with local residents in unpretentious neighborhood joints. Helena's Hawaiian Food *(helenashawaiianfood.com; 1240 N. School St., Honolulu, HI; GPS 21.3309, -157.8651)* and Ono Hawaiian Foods *(onohawaiian foods.com; 726 Kapahulu Ave., Honolulu, HI; GPS 21.2801, -157.8142)* are two Honolulu favorites.

» You can dine in or have a whole luau sent to the mainland from Young's Fish Market in Honolulu *(youngsfishmarket.com; 1286 Kalani St., Honolulu, HI; GPS 21.3216, -157.8763).*

» In addition to the luau fare, Kauai's Pono Market serves *manju* pastries filled with red bean paste, apple, coconut, or sweet potato, as well as some mean fried chicken *(4-1300 Kuhio Hwy., Kapaa, HI; GPS 22.0742, -159.3188)*.

» For a glimpse at how Hawaii's culinary tradition continues to evolve, check out the Hawaii Food & Wine Festival featuring a roster of more than 100 internationally renowned culinary personalities alongside homegrown chefs. The annual festival celebrates the rich bounty and culinary diversity of the islands on Oahu, Maui, and the Big Island over three weekends in August and September *(hawaiifoodandwinefestival.com; multiple locations)*.

247 POKE

Deriving from Hawaiian for "to slice," *poke* today means cubes of raw fish marinated in myriad ways, often served atop white rice. Ahi tuna, cured octopus, salmon, and other kinds of fresh fish get generously seasoned with onions, soy sauce, sesame oil, and seaweed. Real poke is hard to make anywhere but Hawaii because it calls for *inamona,* a relish that requires roasting Hawaii *kukui* nuts, or candlenuts, which adds a rich nutty flavor to the dish.

Though the seafood dish can now be found in high-end restaurants of all stripes in Hawaii, the best comes from humble, by-the-pound fish markets where you'll see stacks of containers brimming with fresh poke, made with varying degrees of spiciness, and from all sorts of fish.

Where to Try It

» The best bet is to follow the crowd. Most places that serve the popular "plate lunch," a Hawaiian staple consisting of a scoop or two of rice accompanied by macaroni salad and a main dish, will have excellent poke. Honolulu's Ono Seafood *(747 Kapahulu Ave., Honolulu, HI; GPS 21.2809, -157.8139)* and Alicia's Market *(aliciasmarket.com;*

267 Mokauea St., Honolulu, HI; GPS 21.3244, -157.8849), and Tanioka's in Waipahu *(taniokas.com; 94-903 Farrington Hwy., Waipahu, HI; GPS 21.3841, -158.0011)* are some of Oahu's standouts.

» Locals praise Kauai's Koloa Fish Market *(5482 Koloa Rd., Koloa, HI; GPS 21.9048, -159.4636)*. On the Big Island, they also love Umeke's poke bowls and local

Poke—chunks of raw fish marinated and seasoned, often served with rice

lunch plates *(umkespoke 808.com; 75-143 Hualalai Rd. #105, Kailua-Kona, HI; GPS 19.6384, -155.9911).*

» Surprisingly, on Maui, a branch of the Foodland supermarket chain gets all the local love *(foodland .com; 1881 S. Kihei Rd., Kihei, HI; GPS 20.7321, -156.4525).*

248 SAIMIN

Drawing ingredients, flavors, and inspirations from Chinese, Japanese, Filipino, Portuguese and Korean cuisines, saimin is the Hawaiian history of migration boiled down to a bowl of noodle soup.

The dish is composed of egg noodles in piping hot meat or fish broth, garnished with *char siu* (Chinese barbecue pork), linguica (Portuguese sausage), surimi (Japanese imitation crab meat), and a number of other optional toppings, including the islands' favorite luncheon meat, Spam. It may not have the hipster popularity of ramen noodles, but this comfort food is a tried-and-true Hawaiian staple. Even local McDonald's have sold it.

Where to Try It

» Try saimin with chewy udon (a thick, wheat noodle), and pork dumplings at Honolulu's noodle soup specialist Palace Saimin *(palacesaimin.com; 1256 N. King St., Honolulu, HI; GPS 21.3272, -157.8701).* Also in Honolulu, both saimin and ramen shine at Yotteko-ya *(1960 Kapiolani Blvd., Honolulu, HI; GPS 21.2900, -157.8325).*

» On Maui, try Tasty Crust *(1770 Mill St., Wailuku, HI; GPS 20.8924, -156.4996)* and Sam Sato's, famous for its dry saimin *(1750 Wili Pa Loop, Wailuku, HI; GPS 20.8933, -156.5002).* And Fumi's Kitchen on the Big Island is another local favorite *(m.fumiskitchenkona .com; 75-5799 Alii Dr., Kailua-Kona, HI; GPS 19.6354, -155.9898).*

Saimin—egg noodles in broth, topped with meat and seafood

249 MALASADAS

Simply rolled in sugar or filled with delectable creams, these yeast doughnuts are a Madeiran dish that became popular with sugar plantation workers in the 19th century, and have since evolved into a proud Hawaiian treat that's easily found at food festivals. *Malasadas* may derive from the Portuguese word for "undercooked," but these rich, delicious deep-fried balls of yum almost always taste like perfection.

Where to Try It

» Don't leave Honolulu without waiting in line at Leonard's Bakery for a golden ball filled with custards made with chocolate, *lilikoi,* or *haupia* (traditional coconut milk pudding). The bakery claims it was the first to introduce malasadas to an adulatory Hawaii audience in the 1950s *(leonardshawaii .com; 933 Kapahulu Ave., Honolulu, HI; GPS 21.2848, -157.8132).*

» Also on Oahu, the unassuming Agnes' Portuguese Bake Shop in Kailua only does the classic, plain kind, made to order from scratch *(46 Hoolai St., Kailua, HI; GPS 21.3951, -157.7449).*

» On Maui, check out Home Maid Bakery *(homemaid bakery.com; 1005 Lower Main St., Wailuku, HI; GPS 20.8995, -156.4886),* which makes malasadas only before 10 a.m. and after 4 p.m., and Komoda Store and Bakery *(3674 Baldwin Ave., Makawao, HI; GPS 20.8540, -156.3106),* famed for its guava cream malasadas. Fifty-cent malasadas at Hanalima Bakery on Kauai *(hanalimabaking.com; 4495 Puhi Rd., Lihue, HI; GPS 21.9666, -159.3958)* and lilikoi-iced ones at Punalu'u Bake Shop on the Big Island *(bakeshophawaii .com; 5642 Mamalahoa Hwy., Naalehu, HI; GPS 19.0653, -155.6083)* round out the other island favorites.

250 KONA COFFEE

Hailing from the highlands of Ethiopia, the *Coffea arabica* came a long way via Brazil to find a perfect home in the mineral-rich volcanic soil of Hawaii.

As the only state with significant coffee cultivation, Hawaii has made a name for itself for its superior Kona beans from the southwest coast of the Big Island. Grown at elevations between 500 and 2,500 feet within a mile-wide strip known as the Kona coffee belt, Kona coffee has a reputation for being mild and sweet, like the island's climate, with a hint of chocolate.

Where to Try It

» In addition to shipping across the country, both Greenwell Farms (*greenwellfarms.com; 81-6581 Mamalahoa Hwy., Kealakekua, HI; GPS 19.5112, -155.9220*) and Hilo Coffee Mill (*hilocoffeemill.com; 17-995 Volcano Hwy., Mountain View, HI; GPS 19.5639, -155.0882*) welcome visitors to their working coffee farms.

» In Honolulu, you can taste expert espresso drinks made from Hawaiian beans at Kai Coffee Hawaii (*kaicoffeehawaii.com; 2424 Kalakaua Ave., Honolulu, HI; GPS 21.2759, -157.8249*).

251 MACADAMIA NUTS

Rich in energy and high in dietary fiber, minerals, and antioxidants, macadamia nuts might be the healthiest guilty pleasure you'll ever pop in your mouth. And there's a reason why this luxurious kernel is also known as the Hawaii nut. With more than 700 macadamia nut farms accounting for nearly three-quarters of the world's production, Hawaii sets the gold standard for macadamias around the globe.

The island macadamia boasts a sweet, buttery flavor complementing its creamy texture. Good things come to those who wait: A planted tree can take as long as 12 years to start bearing good nuts, and even then, the macadamia is never picked from the tree but patiently anticipated until it ripens fully and falls to the ground. To keep the nuts fresh,

workers only have 24 hours to husk them once they're harvested.

Macadamias are well worth the fuss. Salted or covered in chocolate, this handsome Hawaiian nut easily trumps its competitors in taste and appearance.

Where to Try It

» The five-acre homestead of Purdy's Natural Macadamia Nuts on Molokai welcomes visitors to sample fresh-from-the-shell nuts or honey made from macadamia blossoms (*molokai-aloha.com/macnuts; 4 Lihi Pali Ave., Hoolehua, HI; GPS 21.1743, -157.0572*).

» What began as a roadside stand is now the working Tropical Farms, with a brick-and-mortar shop and guided tours that even Oahu locals take to learn about the cultivation process and the best way to crack the nuts (*macnutfarm.com; 49-227A Kamehameha Hwy., Kaneohe, HI; GPS 21.5104, -157.8513*).

» Generous with free samples, Hamakua Macadamia Nut Company on the Big Island stocks all sorts of nut-related products, including Spam-flavored macadamias (*hawnnut.com; 61-3251 Maluokalani St., Waimea, HI; GPS 20.0490, -155.8356*).

252 PINEAPPLE

Though pineapples were only commercially planted in the late 19th century, the tropical fruit immediately

Pineapple

◇◇◇

Hawaii is the only state to commercially grow *both cacao and vanilla.*

Classic luau foods include *laulau* (pork steamed in taro leaf) and *lomilomi,* a salad of salmon, tomatoes, and onions.

Early Russian fish traders brought to Alaska the salmon pie, a fish, rice, and veggie pastry in a golden shell.

flourished on the warm and sunny Hawaiian Islands. For better or worse, Hawaii's modern history is interlinked with that of pineapple cultivation, which played a role in attracting workers from all over the world and causing the United States to annex Hawaii.

Where to Try It

≫ Get free samples, plus lessons in history and agriculture on the Maui Pineapple Tour (*mauipineappletour .com/tours*). You can also take farm tours of the Maui Tropical Plantation (*mauitropicalplantation.com; 1670 Honoapiilani Hwy., Wailuku, HI; GPS 20.8492, -156.5071*).
≫ In addition to a fun train ride for little ones and popular gardens, Dole Plantation on Oahu serves soft-serve ice cream flavored with the yellow fruit (*dole-plantation .com; 64-1550 Kamehameha Hwy., Wahiawa, HI; GPS 21.5259, -158.0375*).

★ALASKA★

253 RUSSIAN SALMON PIE

Alaskans call salmon pies *pirok, perok,* or *peroche*— all variations on the Russian word for "pie." Inherited from Alaska's early Russian fur traders, this hearty, 18th-century dish consists of rice, mushrooms, cabbage, and, of course, salmon that's been poached, baked, grilled, or seared. The stuffing is layered inside flaky puff pastry or buttery brioche, and baked to a full golden glory.

Where to Try It
≫ Veteran chef Kirsten Dixon has been championing Alaska cuisine for over 20 years and continues to show

off her version of the salmon pie, which involves healthier brown rice, at Winterlake Lodge in Skwentna. But note that you won't get to the backcountry location without the help of a water taxi or floatplane (*within thewild.com/lodges/winterlake; Skwentna, AK; GPS 61.9869, -152.0769*). You can find a recipe online in the *Alaska Dispatch News (adn.com)* by Googling "Kirsten Dixon salmon pie."

» Try variations on this local favorite at special events like Fairbanks's Golden Days, the 60-plus-year-old festival held in July honoring the state's gold rush heritage (*fairbankschamber.org; multiple locations*).

254 AKUTAQ

If you never considered seal oil and shredded fish as dessert, think again. *Akutaq, ackutuk* . . . there are many ways to spell the dessert, but the meaning remains the same in Yupik, an indigenous language of Alaska: something mixed together.

So-called Eskimo ice cream, traditional akutaq combines fresh berries such as blueberries, cranberries, salmonberries, cloudberries, or crowberries with whipped-up animal tallow like seal oil or moose fat, and sometimes even throws in salmon and caribou meat. A more modern update substitutes the animal fat with vegetable shortening and adds extra sugar.

Where to Try It

» Don't hesitate if an Alaskan invites you to try the dish. You may never get another chance to sample akutaq because this homemade treat is rarely served in commercial places. The Festival of Native Arts, held every spring at the University of Alaska Fairbanks, is among those rare occasions (*facebook.com/festivalof nativearts; University of Alaska, Fairbanks, AK; GPS 64.8570, -147.8231*).

» If you can get your hands on some reindeer, caribou, or moose fat and some seal, walrus, or whale oil, go for it yourself. Find the recipe at *alaskaweb.org/food /akutaq.html*.

Basic Ingredient

The Atlantic Ocean is home to one kind of salmon, while five varieties of **wild salmon** roam the Pacific waters. The scarcest and biggest: Alaska's state fish, the chinook, or king, salmon, with a pure, clear-ocean taste. Others include sockeye, or red, salmon often used in sushi; coho, touting a firm texture perfect for poaching; and chum, or keta, salmon.

255 BANNOCK

Flour, baking powder, lard, and sugar—these are the makings of tried-and-true comfort food, and in Alaska, these ingredients become a hearty snack called bannock or fry bread. Made in a pan over an open fire, baked in an oven, or even deep-fried in a vat of oil, the bannock comes in different forms. Think of it as a cooler, subarctic cousin of funnel cakes and beignets.

Where to Try It

» Make bannock yourself by going to *dhss.alaska.gov* and searching "nellie's recipes" from an Alaska cookbook of traditional foods.

» You'll find Alaska-inspired dishes at the Alaska Native Heritage Center's café in Anchorage (*alaska native.net; 8800 Heritage Center Dr., Anchorage, AK; GPS 61.2329, -149.7166*). And if you're lucky, you just might meet the famous fry bread vendor Garfield Katasse at special occasions like Celebration, the biannual Native American festival in Juneau (*sealaska heritage.org/celebration*).

256 REINDEER

Less gamy than venison and as delicate as veal, reindeer meat has been a major source of food (and clothing) for some Alaska native cultures for centuries. You'll find the fine-grained, mild-tasting meat as steaks and smoked sausages around the state. The domesticated

Though not commercially available, *reindeer milk has a fat content of 22 percent—six times that of cow's milk.*

cousin of the caribou is also among the healthiest forms of protein—low in fat and high in essential fatty acids and vitamin B$_{12}$.

Where to Try It

» Snow Goose Restaurant in Anchorage mixes free-range reindeer with ground chuck to make seared meatloaf topped with mushroom sauce and fried onions (*alaskabeers.com; 717 W. 3rd Ave., Anchorage, AK; GPS 61.2196, -149.8958*).

» Those traveling through the state might taste reindeer as part of a breakfast skillet on the scenic Alaska Railroad (*alaskarailroad.com*) or in reindeer chili aboard Princess Cruises (*princess.com*).

» For out-of-staters, Alaska's Indian Valley Meats ships reindeer sausages, hot dogs, and caribou medallions (*indianvalleymeats.com*).

257 ALASKA SALMON BAKE

This Alaska dining event is all about the salmon—and much more. This all-you-can-eat repast usually features slow-roasted prime rib, beer-battered cod, baked beans, potatoes au gratin, and, of course,

Salmon grilled over an open fire at a salmon bake

Alaska salmon, grilled over a fragrant wood fire. Filling enough for a hardworking frontier explorer or just a visitor equipped with a hearty appetite, this summer dining event is all about seconds—and thirds, and fourths . . .

Where to Try It

» Several venues have been offering similar meals for decades. A True Alaskan Experience in Fairbanks (*akvisit.com; Fairbanks, AK; GPS 64.8371, -147.7742*), the Denali Park Salmon Bake (*denaliparksalmonbake.com; Mile 238.5, George Parks Hwy., Denali National Park and Preserve, AK; GPS 63.7447, -148.8965*), and Gold Creek Salmon Bake in Juneau (*bestofalaskatravel.com; 1061 Salmon Creek Ln., Juneau, AK; GPS 58.3318, -134.4680*) are among the many places where you can enjoy Alaska feasts prepared before your eyes.

» If you're averse to all-you-can-eat styles but want the variety, check out July's Copper River Wild! Salmon Festival in Cordova, the yearly cook-off where local chefs compete for the title "King of Salmon" (*copper riverwild.org; Mt. Eyak Ski Area, Cordova, AK; GPS 60.5507, -145.7499*).

258 KING CRAB LEGS

Caught in the cold, pristine waters of Alaska, king crab legs are succulent and savory, not to mention impressive in scale. Served hot or cold, these huge claws are filled with firm, juicy meat that packs in the flavors of the sea.

Crab lovers can savor some ten varieties caught in Alaska, from the sweet, white-meat snow crab to blue king, found in small populations around a few islands. But the most prized is the red king, the largest of all king crabs whose legs can span up to six feet.

These creatures aren't easy to catch—fishing in search of these giant crustaceans in Alaska's icy, treacherous waters is one of America's truly dangerous jobs. The difficulty, combined with high demands from Asia, makes these delicacies all the dearer.

Take note: The season to trap them is short, starting in October and ending around January, to ensure sustainability.

King crab legs—catching them is treacherous, but the reward is a succulent, juicy meat.

Where to Try It

≫ Every May, the Kodiak Crab Festival celebrates one of Alaska's most sought-after food items over five days of bacchanal, with cooking demonstrations by Alaska chefs using locally harvested seafood and wild greens (kodiakchamber.org; Kodiak, AK; GPS 57.7885, -152.3987).

≫ A James Beard Foundation classic restaurant, the family-owned Gustavus Inn serves from-scratch meals championing local catches such as steamed king crab fresh from the nearby strait, and foraged herbs (gustavusinn.com; 1270 Gustavus Rd., Gustavus, AK; GPS 58.4138, -135.7315).

≫ Longtime Alaska resident Tracy LaBarge shares her fascination with crabbing by serving up fresh-from-the-sea crab legs and crab bisque at her King Crab Shack, a Juneau institution (kingcrabshack.com; 406 S. Franklin St., Juneau, AK; GPS 58.2974, -134.4022).

259 ALASKA HALIBUT

Beloved for its sweet flavor, firm texture, and brilliantly white color, the halibut is among the most prized fish today. Alaska boasts more than a century of commercial halibut fishing, with the greatest concentration of the Pacific fish found in the Gulf of Alaska. No wonder that Alaskans make the most of the halibut's versatility, smoking it over fragrant wood, grilling it in an herb crust, and poaching the tender cheeks, considered the sweetest, most flavorful part of the fish.

Now strictly regulated to ensure the survival of the species, looking for wild halibut involves traversing great distances, as far as the Bering Sea. The largest of all the flatfish, halibuts can exceed nine feet and weigh in at 500 pounds.

Where to Try It

≫ Ludvig's Bistro in Sitka serves locally sourced seafood highlighted with Mediterranean flavors, with such popular menu items as fresh halibut served with sautéed oyster mushrooms and a lauded seafood chowder (ludvigsbistro .com; 256 Katlian St., Sitka, AK; GPS 57.0511, -135.3413).

≫ Enjoy halibut at its purest and freshest in the ceviche served with corn and bright orange chili at Seven Glaciers restaurant at a mountaintop luxury resort in Girdwood (alyeskaresort.com; 1000 Arlberg Ave., Girdwood, AK; GPS 60.9704, -149.0987).

> ### Surprise
>
> Just a few degrees from the tundra of the Arctic Circle, in the historic mining town of Fox, Alaska, Silver Gulch is the nation's **northernmost brewery.** Enjoy brews like smooth, malty Fairbanks Lager at the end of a long summer day—or in the middle of a very long winter night (silvergulch.com; 2195 Old Steese Hwy., Fox, AK; GPS 64.9779, -147.5436).

INDEX

Boldface indicates illustrations.

A

Abbott's Lobster in the Rough, Noank, CT 34, **34**
Acme Bread Company, San Francisco, CA 256, **256**
Akutaq (Alaskan dessert) 275
Alabama 114–115
  catch-and-cook restaurants 114, **115**
  soul food 118
  southern-style potato salad 114–115
Alaska 274–277
  akutaq (dessert) 275
  bannock (fry bread) 275
  beer 277
  blueberries 267
  halibut 277
  king crab legs 276–277, **277**
  reindeer 275–276
  Russian salmon pie **274,** 274–275
  salmon bake 276, **276**
  salmonberries 267, **267,** 275
Alder-plank-smoked salmon 240–241
Alligator 99
Almonds 266
Alpino Vino, Telluride, CO 210
Al's #1 Italian Beef, Chicago, IL 149, **149**
Amish foods
  Ohio 136
  Pennsylvania **52,** 52–53, **53, 54,** 54–55
Apizza **31,** 31–32
Apples
  Appalachian apple stack cake (KY) **106,** 106–107
  apple pie (NY) 43
  cider (NH) 16, **16**
  hard cider **66,** 66–67, **67**
  Monticello, VA 79–80, **80**
  Washington 267
  West Virginia **82–83,** 85
Applewood Farmhouse Grill, Sevierville, TN 110, **110**
Area 51, NV 233
Arizona 224–231
  chiltepin chilies 224–225, **225**
  fresh dates 228
  prickly pear cactus 230
  Salsa Trail 230–231
  Sonoran hot dog 225, 228, **228**
  southwest specialties 226–227, **227,** 230
  Yuma Lettuce Days 229, **229**
Arkansas 117–120
  chocolate gravy and biscuits 120

fried dill pickles 117, 120, **120**
possum pie 120, **121**
rice 120
Asian cuisine
  pan-Asian cuisine (WA) 242, **242**
  pho (WA) 243, **243,** 246
  San Francisco, CA 258–259
  steamed dumplings **6**
Avocados 264, **264**

B

Bacchanal Buffet, Caesars Palace, Las Vegas, NV 233, **233**
Bachelor Farmer, Minneapolis, MN 153, **154–155**
Bacon 109–110, **110**
Bacon cheeseburger **front cover**
Bagels 35, **35,** 38
Bahr, Cory 7
Baked beans 24–25
Bananas Foster 126
Bannock (fry bread) 275
Bar Dojo, Edmonds, WA 242, **242**
Barbecue **96,** 96–97, **97**
  Kansas City 97, 163, **163**
  North Carolina 97, **97**
  soul food **118,** 119
  Sparks, NV 236, **236**
  Tennessee 96–97, 119
  Texas **189,** 189–190
Basque cuisine **234–235,** 237
Beans
  Boston baked beans (MA) 24–25
  field peas (SC) 92
  frijoles (NM) 215
  lentils (WA) 243
  tepary beans (AZ) 227, **227**
Bear Pit Lounge, Yellowstone NP 205
Beef
  beef on weck (NY) **42,** 43
  burnt ends (KS) **180,** 180–181
  cheesesteak (PA) **48,** 48–49
  chicken-fried steak (TX) 191, **191,** 194
  finger steaks (ID) 217, 220
  Italian beef sandwich (IL) 148–149, **149**
  loose meat sandwich (IA) **158,** 158–159
  pit beef (MD) 69
  see also Hamburgers; Steak and steak houses
Beer
  Alaska 277
  hops (OR) 248
  National Bohemian beer (MD) 71
  New Hampshire 14–15, **15**
  Wisconsin 144

Beer cheese
  Beer Cheese Trail (KY) 107
  Bierkäse (WI) 161
Beignets 123, **123, 124–125,** 126
Ben & Jerry's ice cream 21, **21**
Bendix Diner, NJ **58–59**
Berries 152, 266–267, **267**
  see also specific types of berries
Bierkäse (beer cheese) 107, 161
Big Texan, Amarillo, TX 191, **192–193**
Birch beer 60
Biscochitos (cookies) 215, **215**
Biscuits
  and chocolate gravy (AR) 120
  Tennessee 110–111, **111, 112–113**
Bison burgers
  Montana 212–213
  North Dakota **164,** 167
Black-and-white cookies 39, **39,** 42
Black-and-white milkshakes 27
Blue Bell creameries, TX **190,** 190–191
Blue crabs 65
Blue Gate Restaurant, Shipshewana, IN 137, **137**
Blueberries
  blueberry pancakes **front cover**
  blueberry pie (ME) 11, **11**
  wild blueberries (ME) 10
Boiled peanuts 90–91, **91**
Bologna 132
Boston baked beans 24–25
Boston cream pie **23,** 23–24
Bowens Island Restaurant, Charleston, SC **92,** 93
Bread
  bannock (AK) 275
  Mormon scones (UT) 222–223, **223**
  pan de campo (TX) 197–198
  San Francisco sourdough bread (CA) 255–257, **256**
  "throwed" rolls (MO) 163
  zwiebach (KS) 183
Bread pudding **221,** 221–222
Bristow Tabouleh Fest, OK 183–184, **184**
Brooklyn Farmacy & Soda Fountain, Brooklyn, NY 27, **27**
Brown Hotel, Louisville, KY 107–108, **108**
Brunswick stew 78–79, **79**
Buckeye candy 135, **135**
Buckhorn Exchange, Denver, CO **212,** 213
Buckwheat
  ployes (ME) 13
  Preston County Buckwheat Festival (WV) 85
Buffalo wings 43

Buffets 232–233, **233**
Burgoo (stew) 105, **105**
Burnt ends (beef brisket) **180,** 180–181
Burritos **262,** 262–263
Butter cake 159, **159,** 162
Buttermilk 60

C

Cabinets (frappes) 27
Cactus 230
Café Du Monde, New Orleans, LA 123, **123**
Cajun cuisine
  Delaware 64
  Louisiana 121, **121**
Cakes
  Appalachian apple stack cake (TN) **106,** 106–107
  Boston cream pie (MA) **23,** 23–24
  DeLuxe fruitcake (TX) 199, **199**
  gooey butter cake (MO) 159, **159,** 162
  king cake (LA) 126, **126**
  kuchen (SD) 173, **173**
  Meyer lemon cake (CA) 257
  Smith Island cake (MD) 69–70, **70**
Calabash-style seafood **88,** 88–89
California 255–264
  artisan chocolates 259, **260–261**
  avocados 264, **264**
  burritos **262,** 262–263
  California roll 264
  cioppino 257–258, **258**
  Cobb salad 258
  doughnuts 254
  farmers markets **238, 266**
  fish tacos 264, **265**
  fruits, nuts & berries 266–267
  Gilroy Garlic Festival 263, **263**
  hamburgers **250,** 250–251, **251**
  Los Angeles Korean food 259, **259,** 262
  Meyer lemon cake 257
  Meyer lemons 257, **257**
  San Francisco sourdough bread 255–257, **256**
  San Francisco Chinese food 258–259
Candy
  Idaho Candy Company, Boise 217
  Valomilk candy (KS) 180
  see also Chocolate
Cantaloupes 137
Cantler's Riverside, Annapolis, MD 69, **69**
Catch-and-cook restaurants 114, **115**
Catfish 115–116, **116,** 117

Cedar-plank-smoked salmon
    240, 240–241
Chard **238**
Charlie Parker's, Springfield, IL
    148, **148**
Charlie the Butcher, Buffalo, NY
    42, 43
Chateaubriand **231,** 231–232
Chauncey Creek Lobster Pier,
    Kittery Point, ME **10,** 11
Cheddar cheese 141–143
Cheerwine (soft drink) 89, **89**
Cheese
    Beer Cheese Trail (KY) 107
    Bierkäse (WI) 161
    cheddar cheese (WI) 141–143
    cheese curds (WI) 141–143, **142**
    Oregon Cheese Trail **248,**
        248–249
    Palmetto Cheese (SC) 90
    saganaki (IL) 151
    Vermont Cheese Trail 16–20,
        17, 18–19
Cheese straws 117, **117**
Cheeseburgers
    Green Chile Cheeseburger
        Trail, NM 251, **251**
    pimento cheeseburgers (SC)
        251
Cheesecake **38,** 39
Cheesesteak **48,** 48–49
Cherries
    cherry pie (MI) 130–131
    flathead cherries (MT) 203,
        203
    National Cherry Festival,
        Traverse City, MI 130, **130**
    Rainier cherries (WA) 247,
        247
Chicago, IL
    Frango mints 151
    Greektown 151
    horseshoe sandwich 148
    hot dogs 138–139, **139**
    Italian beef sandwich 148–149
    pierogi 161
    pizza 40–41, **41,** 145, **145,** 148
    steak houses 150–151, **151**
Chicken
    buffalo wings (NY) 43
    chicken and dumplings (DE)
        64, **64**
    fried chicken (KS) 180
    fried chicken (KY) **86,**
        108–109, **109**
Chicken-fried steak 191, **191,** 194
Chili
    Cincinnati chili (OH) **134,**
        134–135
    Texas chili cook-offs **194,**
        194–195
Chili peppers **back cover**
    chiltepin chilies (AZ) 224–225,
        225

Mirasol chilies (CO) 205, 208,
    208
New Mexico **214,** 214–215
Chinese food **6,** 258–259
Chippers (chocolate-covered
    potato chips) 166, **166**
Chislic (meat on a stick) **172,**
    172–173
Chocolate
    artisan chocolates (CA) 259,
        260–261
    buckeye candy (OH) 135, **135**
    Chippers (ND) 166, **166**
    chocolate gravy and biscuits
        (AR) 120
    Frango mints (IL) 151
    Goo Goo Clusters (TN) 111, 114
    MoonPies (TN) 111, 114, **114**
    Pennsylvania **50,** 51
    Chocolate chip cookies 25
Cider
    hard cider **66,** 66–67, **67**
    New Hampshire 16, **16**
Cincinnati, OH
    chili **134,** 134–135
    goetta (breakfast sausage
        loaf) 161
Cioppino 257–258, **258**
Citrus **2–3,** 103, **103**
City Tavern Restaurant,
    Philadelphia, PA 49, **49**
Clams
    clam cakes (RI) **29,** 29–30
    clam shacks (MA) **24,** 25
    clambakes (MA) 21–22
    clams casino (RI) 28
    quahogs & stuffies (RI) 28, **28,**
        29
    steamers (ME) 11–12
Cobb salad 258
Cobblers **98,** 98–99
Coca-Cola 94–95
Coffee
    coffee milk (RI) 28–29
    coffeehouses (WA) **246,**
        246–247
    Kona coffee (HI) 271
Collard greens **118**
Colorado 205–211
    Denver omelet 209, **209**
    goats 208
    Grand Valley orchards &
        vineyards **210,** 210–211
    lamb 208
    marijuana 209
    Mirasol chilies 205, 208, **208**
    Oscar-style steak 209–210
    wild game restaurants **212,** 213
    wild trout 213
"Concrete" (frozen custard) 162
Coney dogs 128, **138,** 139
Connecticut 31–35
    apizza **31,** 31–32, 41
    hamburgers **32,** 32–33

hot lobster rolls **34,** 34–35
oysters **33,** 33–34
Cookies
    biscochitos (NM) 215, **215**
    black-and-white cookies (NY)
        39, **39,** 42
    chocolate chip cookies (MA)
        25
Corn
    corn bread (TN) 110–111, **111,**
        112–113
    corn chowder (NH) 15
    corn pudding (VA) 76, **76**
    fried cornmeal mush (IN) 140,
        140
    grilled corn **back cover**
    johnnycakes (RI) 30
    Midwest 140
    native sweet corn (New
        England) 15
    popcorn (IL) 149–150, **150**
    sweet corn (NE) 176, **176**
Corny dogs **195,** 195–196
Cowboy cooking 204, **204,**
    206–207
Cownose rays 77
Crabs
    blue crabs (MD) 65
    crab cakes (MD) 65, **65,** 68
    crab houses (MD) **68,** 69, **69**
    crab Louis (WA) 241
    crab shacks **back cover**
    Dungeness crabs (OR) **252,**
        252–253
    king crab legs (AK) 276–277,
        277
    she-crab soup (SC) 91–92
    soft-shell crabs (MD) **46,**
        68–69
    stone crab (FL) 99, **99,**
        100–101, 102
Cranberries **22,** 22–23
Crawfish boil 126–127, **127**
Creole food
    Delaware 62
    Louisiana 121–122
Cuban sandwiches & specialties
    102, 102–103
Cudighi (sausage sandwich)
    131–132, **132**
Czech pastries 160, **160**

D
Dallas, TX
    chicken-fried steak 194
    chili cook-offs 195
    corny dogs 196
    fried okra 188
    margaritas 195
    steak houses 179
    Tex-Mex food 187
    tortilla soup 194
Dandelion Chocolate, San
    Francisco, CA 259, **260–261**

Dates 228
Deep-dish pizza 40–41, **41,** 145,
    145, 148
Delaware 61–64
    chicken dishes 64, **64**
    fried oysters **61,** 61–62
    frozen custard **63,** 63–64
    po'boys 62
    pretzel salad 63
    scrapple 52, 53
    vinegar french fries **62,** 63
Delis 35, **36–37**
Deluxe fruitcake 199, **199**
Denver omelet 209, **209**
Detroit, MI
    Coney dogs 128, **138,** 139
    paczki (Polish pastry) 161
    pickles 133–134
    Vernors ginger ale 133
Dill pickles, fried 117, 120, **120**
Diners **56,** 56–57, **58–59**
Disco fries 61
District of Columbia 71–76
    Ethiopian food 71, **71,** 74
    food trucks **72–73, 75,**
        75–76
    half-smokes **74,** 74–75
Dorothy Lynch dressing 174–175
Doughnuts
    apple cider doughnuts (NH) 16,
        16
    Dunkin' Donuts (MA) 23
    malasadas (HI) 270
    potato doughnuts (ME) 14
    West Coast doughnuts (OR)
        253–254, **254**
Dr Pepper 196, **196,** 197
Dungeness crab **252,** 252–253
Dunkin' Donuts 23
Dutch letters (pastries) **157,**
    157–158
Dutch lettuce salad 158
Dye's Gullah Fixin's, Hilton Head,
    SC 90, **90**

E
Egg creams 27, **27**
El Reno Fried Onion Burger Day,
    OK 184
Elk 213
Elk jerky 182, **182**
Eskimo Pies 158
Ethiopian food 71, **71,** 74
Ethiopic Restaurant, Washington,
    D.C. 71, **71**

F
Farmers markets **238, 266**
Field peas 92
Finger steaks 217, 220
Fish
    Alaska halibut 277
    Alaska salmon bake 276,
        276

catch-and-cook restaurants
(AL) 114, **115**
fish fry dinners (WI) 143, **143**
fish tacos (CA) 264, **265**
fried catfish (MS) 115–116, **116**
Great Lakes whitefish (MI) 132
poke (HI) **269,** 269–270
rockfish (MD) 70–71
Rocky Mountains 212–213, **213**
Russian salmon pie (AK) **274,**
274–275
smoked salmon (WA) **240,**
240–241
Fish tacos 264, **265**
Flaming Orange (dessert) 203
Flathead cherries 203, **203**
Floribbean cuisine 104
Florida 99–104
alligator 99
Cuban sandwiches &
specialties **102,** 102–103
Floribbean cuisine 104
key lime pie 102, **102**
oranges & citrus **2–3,** 103, **103**
seafood 104
stone crabs 99, **99, 100–101,**
102
Food trucks
District of Columbia **72–73, 75,**
75–76
Portland, OR 255, **255**
Frango mints 151
Frappes 27
French-Canadian foods **14,** 14–15
French fries
disco fries (NJ) 61
French Fry Feed (ND) 169
poutine (NH) 14
vinegar french fries (DE) **62,**
63
Fried catfish 115–116, **116**
Fried chicken
Kansas 180
Kentucky **86,** 108–109, **109**
soul food 118, 119, **119**
Fried cornmeal mush 140, **140**
Fried dill pickles 117, 120, **120**
Fried green tomatoes 115
Fried okra 185, **185,** 188
Fried oysters **61,** 61–62
Fried shrimp **242**
Frijoles 215
Fritos 196
Frog eye salad 224, **224**
Frozen treats
"concrete" (MO) 162
frozen custard (DE) **63,** 63–64
frozen lemonade (RI) 30, **30**
frozen margaritas (TX) 195
shave ice (HI) 265, 268, **268**
see also Ice cream
Fruit 266–267, **267**
California 266–267
cobblers (GA) **98,** 98–99

Fruit Loop, OR 254
see also specific fruits
Fruitcake 199, **199**
Fry bread
Arizona **226,** 226–227
bannock (AK) 275
Fry sauce 222, **222**
Funeral potatoes 223–224

G
Game
elk jerky (KS) 182, **182**
Medford, OR 253
reindeer (AK) 275–276
Rocky Mountains **212,** 212–213
Garlic 263, **263**
Geechee culture 89–90, **90**
Geno's Steaks, Philadelphia, PA
48, **48**
Georgia 94–99
Coca-Cola 94–95
fruit cobblers **98,** 98–99
peaches 95, **95,** 98
pecans 94, **94**
soul food 119
Vidalia onions 98
German foods 161
German-Russian foods
North Dakota 167
Runza (NE) **175,** 175–176
Gilroy Garlic Festival, CA 263,
263
Ginger ale 133
Goats 208
Goetta (breakfast sausage loaf)
161
Golden Delicious apples **82–83,**
85
Goo Goo Clusters 111, 114
Gooey butter cake 159, **159,** 162
Goose 153
Grand Canyon, AZ 230
Grand Valley, CO **210,** 210–211
Grapefruit **103**
Great Lakes whitefish 132
Green Chile Cheeseburger Trail,
NM 251, **251**
Grits **93,** 93–94
Ground bologna sandwiches 132
Gullah/Geechee Cultural
Heritage Corridor, SC 89–90,
90

H
Half-smokes **74,** 74–75
Halibut 277
Ham
Cuban sandwiches (FL)
102–103
horseshoe sandwich (IL) 148,
148
Taylor ham (NJ) 60
Tennessee 109
Virginia ham 76–77, **77**

Hamburgers **250,** 250–251, **251**
bacon cheeseburger **front**
cover
bison burgers (MT) 212–213
bison burgers (ND) **164,** 167
California **250,** 250–251
Connecticut **32,** 32–33
fried onion burgers (OK) 184,
251
Green Chile Cheeseburger Trail
(NM) 251, **251**
Juicy Lucy (MN) 152, **152**
White Castle 182, 251
Hamtramck, MI 161
Hard cider 16, **66,** 66–67, **67**
Harvey Houses, Kansas 181, **181**
Hasselback potatoes 216–217
Hawaii 265–274
fruit 267
Kona coffee 271
luau fare 268–269, 274
macadamia nuts 271
malasadas 270
musubi 265
passion fruit 269
pineapple 271, **271,** 274
poke (raw fish) **269,** 269–270
saimin 270, **270**
shave ice 265, 268, **268**
Hawaiian haystacks 221
Hazelnuts 267
Hershey's Chocolate World,
Hershey, PA **50,** 51
Hiram's Roadstand, Fort Lee, NJ
57, 60
HobNob supper club, Racine, WI
144, **144**
Hominy Grill, Charleston, SC 93,
93
Honey 223
Hootenanny (baked pancake) 81
Hops 248
Horseshoe sandwich 148, **148**
Hot Brown sandwich 107–108,
108
Hot dogs **138,** 138–139, **139**
Chicago style 138–139, **139**
corny dogs (TX) **195,** 195–196
Detroit Coney dogs **128, 138,**
139
half-smokes (DC) **74,** 74–75
Kansas City style 139
New Jersey 57, **57,** 60
New York 42–43, **44–45,** 138
Rhode Island style 139
shot from cannon (NE) 177
Sonoran hot dog (AZ) 225,
228, **228**
Houston, TX
chicken-fried steak 194
DeLuxe fruitcake 199
Gulf Coast oysters 197
restaurants 198
steak 179

sweet potatoes 199
Tex-Mex food 187
Huckleberries **202,** 202–203

I
Ice cream **26,** 26–27
Ben & Jerry's (VT) 21, 21
Blue Bell creameries (TX) 190,
190–191
Eskimo Pies (IA) 158
ice-cream cones (MO) 159
Kansas State University 182
Mount Rushmore (SD) 173
Reed's Dairy Ice Cream Parlor,
Idaho Falls, ID 217, 217
Ice tea 116
Idaho 215–221
finger steaks 217, 220
Hasselback potatoes 216–217
Idaho Candy Company, Boise
217
Reed's Dairy Ice Cream Parlor,
Idaho Falls 217, **217**
russet potatoes 215–216, **216,**
218–219
Trailing of the Sheep Festival,
Ketchum **220,** 220–221
vodka 216
Illinois 144–151
Chicago style hot dogs 138–139,
139
deep-dish pizza 40–41, **41,** 145,
145, 148
Frango mints 151
horseshoe sandwiches 148,
148
Italian beef sandwiches
148–149, **149**
Morton Pumpkin Festival
144–145, **146–147**
pierogi 161
popcorn 149–150, **150**
saganaki (flaming cheese) 151
steak houses 150–151, **151**
In-N-Out Burger **250,** 251, **251**
Indian tacos 227
Indiana 136–140
cantaloupes 137
fried cornmeal mush 140, **140**
persimmons 136, **136**
pierogi 161
sugar cream pie 137, **137**
Tipton County Pork Festival 137,
140
Iowa 156–159
Dutch letters (pastries) **157,**
157–158
Dutch lettuce salad 158
Eskimo Pies 158
Jell-O 157
kolache (Czech pastry) 160
loose meat sandwiches **158,**
158–159
mushrooms 156

pork tenderloin sandwiches 156–157

steak houses 179

Italian beef sandwiches 148, 149, **149**

J

Jaarsma Bakery, Pella, IA **157,** 158

Jefferson, Thomas
apples 66–67, 79, 80
Gadsby's Tavern 76
ice cream 173
pawpaws 80

Jell-O 157, 221

Jerky, elk 182, **182**

Johnnycakes 30

Juicy Lucy (hamburger) 152, **152**

Juneberry pie 168, **168**

Junior's, Brooklyn, New York **38,** 39

K

Kansas 180–184
burnt ends **180,** 180–181
elk jerky 182, **182**
fried chicken 180
Harvey Houses 181, **181**
Kansas State University ice cream 182
potatiskorv (Swedish sausage) 182–183
Valomilk candy 180
wheat 183
White Castle 182
zwieback (dinner roll) 183

Kansas City, MO
barbecue 97, 163, **163,** 180
hot dogs 139
steak houses 179

Katz's Delicatessen, New York, NY 35, **36–37**

Kentucky 104–109
Appalachian apple stack cake **106,** 106–107
barbecue 96
Beer Cheese Trail 107
fried chicken **86**
goetta (breakfast sausage loaf) 161
Hot Brown sandwich 107–108, **108**
Kentucky Fried Chicken 108–109, **109**
mint juleps & Derby fare **104,** 104–105, **105**
sweet sorghum syrup 106

Key lime pie 102, **102**

KFC 108–109, **109**

Kielbasa (Polish boy) sandwich 160–161

King cake 126, **126**

King crab legs 276–277, **277**

King's Arms Tavern, Williamsburg, VA 78, **78**

Kolache (Czech pastry) 160, **160**

Kona coffee 271

Kool-Aid **174,** 175

Korean food 259, **259,** 262

Kringle (pastry) 140–141, **141**

Kuchen (cake) 173, **173**

Kutztown Folk Festival, Kutztown, PA **front cover, 54,** 55

L

Lamb
Colorado 208
Trailing of the Sheep Festival, Ketchum, ID **220,** 220–221

Lambert's Cafe's, Sikeston, MO 163

Las Vegas, NV
all-you-can-eat buffets 232–233, **233**
chateaubriand **231,** 231–232
shrimp cocktail 232, **232**
vintage "Rat Pack" restaurants 236–237, **237**

Leeks, wild 81, **81**

Lemonade, frozen 30, **30**

Lemons 257, **257**

Lentils 243

Lettuce
Dutch lettuce salad (IA) 158
Yuma Lettuce Days (AZ) 229, **229**

Lobster
hot lobster rolls (CT) **34,** 34–35
lobster rolls (ME) **8,** 11
Maine **10,** 10–11

Loose meat sandwiches **158,** 158–159

Los Angeles, CA
burritos 262, **262,** 263
Cobb salad 258
Korean food 259, **259,** 262

Louis' Basque Corner, Reno, NV **234–235,** 237

Louis' Lunch, New Haven, CT 31, **32,** 32–33, 250

Louisiana 121–127
bananas Foster 126
beignets 123, **123, 124–125,** 126
Cajun food 121, **121**
crawfish 127
crawfish boil 126–127, **127**
Creole food 121–122
king cake 126, **126**
muffuletta sandwich 123
po'boy sandwiches **122,** 122–123
ya-ka-mein ("yock") soup 122

Loveless Cafe, Nashville, TN 110–111, **112–113**

Luau fare 268–269, 274

M

Macadamia nuts 271

Maid-Rite, Muscatine, IA **158,** 159

Maine 10–14
blueberries 10
blueberry pie 11, **11**
lobster **10,** 10–11
lobster rolls **8,** 11
Moxie (soft drink) 12, **12**
ployes (buckwheat pancakes) 13
potatoes 13–14
steamers (clams) 11–12
whoopie pies 12–13, **13**

Malasadas (doughnuts) 270

Manuel's Original El Tepeyac Café, Los Angeles, CA **262,** 263

Maple syrup **20,** 20–21

Margaritas 195

Marijuana 209

Marionberry pie 247–248

Marshmallow Fluff 25, **25,** 28

Martha Lou's Kitchen, Charleston, SC **4,** 119, **119**

Maryland 65–71
crab cakes 65, **65,** 68
crab houses **68,** 69, **69**
National Bohemian beer 71
pit beef 69
rockfish 70–71
Smith Island cake 69–70, **70**
soft-shell crabs **46,** 68–69

Massachusetts 21–28
Boston baked beans 24–25
Boston cream pie **23,** 23–24
chocolate chip cookies 25
clam shacks **24,** 25
clambakes 21–22
cranberries **22,** 22–23
Dunkin' Donuts 23
frappes 27
Marshmallow Fluff 25, **25,** 28

McDonald's 250–251

Meat pies **175,** 175–176

Memphis, TN
barbecue 96–97
soul food 119

Mennonite foods
Pennsylvania **52,** 52–53, **53, 54,** 54–55
South Dakota 173–174
zwieback (KS) 183

Meyer lemon cake 257

Meyer lemons 257, **257**

Michigan 130–134
cherries **130**
cherry pie 130–131
cudighi (sausage sandwich) 131–132, **132**
Detroit Coney dogs **128, 138,** 139
Great Lakes whitefish 132

ground bologna sandwiches 132

hard cider 67

paczki (Polish pastry) 161

pannukakku (baked pancake) 131

pasties 131, **131**

pickles **133,** 133–134

Vernors ginger ale 133

Milk 142

Milkshakes 27

Million Dollar Cowboy Steakhouse, Jackson, WY 204, **204**

Minnesota 152–156
goose 153
Juicy Lucy (hamburger) 152, **152**
Scandinavian foods 153, **154–155,** 156
wild berries 152
wild rice 152–153, **153**

Mint juleps **104,** 104–105

Mirasol chilies 205, 208, **208**

Mississippi 115–117
cheese straws 117, **117**
fried catfish 115–116, **116**
Mississippi mud pie 116–117
sweet ice tea 116

Missouri 159–163
"concrete" (frozen custard) 162
gooey butter cake 159, **159,** 162
ice-cream cones 159
Kansas City barbecue 97, 163, **163**
Kansas City hot dogs 139
Lambert's Cafe's "throwed" rolls 163
St. Louis-style pizza 41, 162
steak houses 179
toasted ravioli 162

Montana 202–203
bison burgers 212–213
Flaming Orange (dessert) 203
flathead cherries 203, **203**
huckleberries **202,** 202–203
Sweet Palace, Philipsburg 202

Monticello, VA
apples 79–80
hard cider 66–67
pawpaws 80

MoonPies 111, 114, **114**

Mormon (Utah) scones 222–223, **223**

Morton Pumpkin Festival, IL 144–145, **146–147**

Moxie (soft drink) 12, **12**

Mud pies 116–117

Muffuletta sandwich 123

Mushrooms
Iowa 156
Oregon 253, **253**

Musubi 265

N

Nathan's Famous, Brooklyn, NY 42, **44–45**

National Bohemian beer 71

Native American foods **226,** 226–227, **227**

Nebraska 174–180
Dorothy Lynch dressing 174–175
hot dogs 177
Kool-Aid **174,** 175
popcorn 149
Reuben sandwiches 176–177, **177,** 180
Runza (meat pie) **175,** 175–176
steak houses 179
sweet corn 176, **176**

Nevada 231–237
Basque cuisine **234–235,** 237
chateaubriand **231,** 231–232
Little A'Le'Inn, Alamo 233
shrimp cocktail 232, **232**
Sparks rib cook-off 236, **236**
Vegas all-you-can-eat buffets 232–233, **233**
vintage "Rat Pack" restaurants 236–237, **237**

New Hampshire 14–16
apple cider 16, **16,** 67
corn 15
corn chowder 15
French-Canadian fare **14,** 14–15
hard cider 67
poutine 14
pumpkins **15,** 15–16
tourtière (pork pie) 14–15

New Haven, CT
hamburgers **32,** 32–33, 250
oysters 34
pizza 31–32, 41

New Jersey 55–61
birch beer 60
buttermilk 60
diners **56,** 56–57, **58–59**
disco fries 61
hot dogs 57, **57,** 60
ice cream 26
saltwater taffy 55, **55**
scrapple 53
scungilli 56
Taylor pork roll sandwiches 60, **60**
tomato pie (pizza) 40, 41, 55–56

New Mexico 211–215
biscochitos (cookies) 215, **215**
chili peppers **214,** 214–215
frijoles 215
Green Chile Cheeseburger Trail 251, **251**
southwestern cuisine **200,** 211, **211,** 214

New Orleans, LA 7

New York 35–45
bagels 35, **35,** 38
beef on weck **42,** 43

black-and-white cookies 39, **39,** 42

black-and-white milkshakes 27

buffalo wings 43

cheesecake **38,** 39

egg creams 27, **27**

hard cider **66,** 67

New York City delis 35, **36–37**

New York City hot dogs 42–43, **44–45**

New York City water 38

Orange County Apple Pie Trail 43

pizza 40

Waldorf salad 35

Nopal (prickly pear cactus) 230

Nordic foods
Minnesota 153, **154–155,** 156
North Dakota 168–169, **169, 170–171**
potatiskorv (KS) 182–183

North Carolina 88–89
barbecue 97, **97**
Calabash-style seafood **88,** 88–89
Cheerwine 89, **89**
soul food 119

North Dakota 166–172
bison burgers **164,** 167
Chippers (chocolate-covered potato chips) 166, **166**
French Fry Feed, Grand Forks 169
German-Russian foods 167
Juneberry pie 168, **168**
Scandinavian cuisine 168–169, **169, 170–171**
summer sausage 169, 172

Nuts
almonds (CA) 266
boiled peanuts (SC) 90–91, **91**
hazelnuts (OR) 267
macadamia nuts (HI) 271
peanuts (VA) 78, **78,** 79

O

Ohio 134–136
Amish cooking 136
buckeye candy 135, **135**
Cincinnati chili **134,** 134–135
goetta (breakfast sausage loaf) 161
Polish boy (kielbasa) sandwich 160–161
sauerkraut balls 136
Somali restaurants 135

Oklahoma 183–189
Bristow Tabouleh Fest 183–184, **184**
El Reno Fried Onion Burger Day 184
fried okra 185, **185,** 188
hamburgers 251

Native American fare 227
official state meal 188
Oklahoma State Sugar Art Show, Tulsa 188
Pops gas station 185
sand plums 188–189
Sonic drive-ins 184
steak houses 179
watermelon **188,** 189

Okra, fried 185, **185,** 188

Old country cuisine **160,** 160–161, **161**

Onions, Vidalia 98

Orange County Apple Pie Trail, NY 43

Oranges
Flaming Orange (dessert) 203
Florida **2–3,** 103, **103**

Oregon 247–255
berries 267
doughnuts 253–254, **254**
Dungeness crabs **252,** 252–253
Fruit Loop 254
hazelnuts 267
hops 248
marionberry pie 247–248
Oregon Cheese Trail **248,** 248–249
Portland food carts 255, **255**
sea salt 249, **249,** 252
wild game 253
wild mushrooms 253, **253**

Oscar-style steak 209–210

Oysters
Calabash-style seafood (NC) **88,** 88–89
Connecticut **33,** 33–34
fried oysters (DE) **61,** 61–62
Gulf Coast oysters (TX) 196–197, **197**
South Carolina **92,** 92–93
Washington **241**

P

Pacific shellfish **241,** 241–242, **244–245**

Paczki (Polish pastry) 161

Palmetto Cheese 90

Pan-Asian cuisine 242, **242**

Pan de campo (bread) 197–198

Pancakes
blueberry pancakes **front cover**
buckwheat (WV) 85
hootenanny (WV) 81
johnnycakes (RI) 30
pannukakku (MI) 131
ployes (ME) 13
pumpkin pancakes (IL) 144
pumpkin pancakes (NH) 15
wild rice (MN) 153

Pannukakku (baked pancake) 131

Parker's Restaurant, Boston, MA 23, **23**

Passion fruit 269

Pasta
frog eye salad (UT) 224, **224**
toasted ravioli (MO) 162

Pasties 131, **131**

Pastrami burger 223

Pawpaws 80–81

Peaches 95, **95,** 98

Peanut butter
buckeye candy (OH) 135, **135**
Reese's Peanut Butter Cups (PA) 51

Peanuts
boiled peanuts (SC) 90–91, **91**
Virginia 78, **78,** 79

Pecans 94, **94**

Pennsylvania 48–55
cheesesteak **48,** 48–49
chocolate **50,** 51
ice cream 26
Pennsylvania Dutch/Amish food **52,** 52–53, **53, 54,** 54–55
pepper pot soup 49, **49**
potato chips 51, **51,** 54
pretzels 50–51
scrapple 52–53
whoopie pies 54

Pepper pot soup 49, **49**

Pepperoni rolls 81, 84, **84**

Persimmons 136, **136**

Pho 243, **243,** 246

Pickles
fried dill pickles (AR) 117, 120, **120**
Michigan **133,** 133–134

Pie
apple pie (NY) 43
blueberry pie (ME) 11, **11**
Boston cream pie (MA) **23,** 23–24
cherry pie (MI) 130–131
Juneberry pie (ND) 168, **168**
key lime pie (FL) 102, **102**
marionberry pie (OR) 247–248
Mississippi mud pie 116–117
possum pie (AR) 120, **121**
Runza (NE) **175,** 175–176
Russian salmon pie (AK) **274,** 274–275
sugar cream pie (IN) 137, **137**
tourtière (NH) 14–15

Pierogi 161, **161**

Piero's Italian Cuisine, Las Vegas, NV 236, **237**

Pimento cheeseburgers 251

Pineapple 271, **271,** 274

Pinto beans 215

Pit beef 69

Pizza **40,** 40–41, **41**
apizza (CT) **31,** 31–32, 41
Chicago deep-dish pizza (IL) 40–41, **41,** 145, **145,** 148
St. Louis–style (MO) 41, 162
tomato pie (NJ) 40, 41, 55–56

Ployes (buckwheat pancakes) 13
Po'boy sandwiches
 Delaware 62
 Louisiana **122,** 122–123
Poke (raw fish) **269,** 269–270
Polish foods 160–161
Popcorn
 Illinois 149–150, **150**
 Nebraska 149
Pops gas station, Arcadia, OK 185
Pork
 barbecue **96,** 96–97, **97**
 pork tenderloin sandwiches
 (IA) 156–157
 Taylor pork roll sandwiches
 (NJ) 60, **60**
 Tipton County Pork Festival
 (IN) 137, 140
 tourtière (NH) 14–15
 see also Sausage
Portland, OR
 cheese 248
 doughnuts 254, **254**
 food carts 255, **255**
 Oregon Berry Festival 248,
 267
 sea salt 249, 252
Possum pie 120, **121**
Potatiskorv (Swedish sausage)
 182–183
Potato chips
 chocolate-covered (ND) 166,
 166
 Pennsylvania 51, **51,** 54
Potatoes
 funeral potatoes (UT)
 223–224
 Hasselback potatoes (ID)
 216–217
 Maine 13–14
 potato salad (AL) 114–115
 russet potatoes (ID) 215–216,
 216, 218–219
 see also French fries
Poutine 14
Preston County Buckwheat
 Festival, WV 85
Pretzel salad 63
Pretzels 50–51
Prickly pear cactus 230
Providence, RI
 coffee milk 29
 frozen lemonade 30
 hot dogs 139
 pizza 41
Pumpkins
 Morton Pumpkin Festival (IL)
 144–145, **146–147**
 New Hampshire **15,** 15–16

R

Rainier cherries 247, **247**
Ramps (wild leeks) 81, **81**
Raspberry jams 205, **205**

"Rat Pack," vintage Las Vegas
 restaurants 236–237, **237**
Ravioli, toasted 162
Red Arrow Diner, NH **14,** 14–15
Reed's Dairy Ice Cream Parlor,
 Idaho Falls, ID 217, **217**
Reese's Peanut Butter Cups 51
Reindeer 275–276
Reuben sandwiches 176–177, **177,**
 180
Rhode Island 28–30
 Awful Awful ice cream drink
 27
 cabinet (frappe) 27
 clam cakes **29,** 29–30
 clams casino 28
 coffee milk 28–29
 frozen lemonade 30, **30**
 hot dogs 139
 johnnycakes 30
 pizza 41
 quahogs & stuffies 28, **28,** 29
Rice 120
Rocket Market, Spokane, WA
 247
Rockfish 70–71
Rocky Mountain game & fish
 212, 212–213, **213**
Runza (meat pie) **175,** 175–176
Russ & Daughters, New York, NY
 35, 38
Russet potatoes 215–216, **216,**
 218–219
Russian foods
 chislic (SD) **172,** 172–173
 German-Russian fare (ND) 167
 Runza (NE) **175,** 175–176
 Russian salmon pie (AK) **274,**
 274–275

S

Saganaki (flaming cheese) 151
Saimin 270, **270**
Salad
 Cobb salad (CA) 258
 Dorothy Lynch dressing (NE)
 174–175
 Dutch lettuce salad (IA) 158
 frog eye salad (UT) 224, **224**
 pretzel salad (DE) 63
 southern-style potato salad
 (AL) 114–115
 Waldorf salad (NY) 35
Salmon
 Alaska salmon bake 276, **276**
 Russian salmon pie (AK) **274,**
 274–275
 smoked salmon (WA) **240,**
 240–241
Salmonberries **267,** 275
Salsa Trail, AZ 230–231
Salt
 sea salt (OR) 249, **249,** 252
 Utah 224

Saltwater taffy 55, **55**
San Francisco, CA
 artisan chocolates 259, **260–261**
 burritos 262
 Chinese food 258–259
 cioppino 257–258, **258**
 crab Louis 241
 doughnuts 254
 farmers markets 266–267
 Meyer lemon cake 257
 sourdough bread 255–257, **256**
Sand plums 188–189
Sauerkraut balls 136
Sausage
 cudighi (MI) 131–132, **132**
 goetta (OH) 161
 half-smokes **74,** 74–75
 Polish boy (kielbasa) sandwich
 160–161
 pork sausage (TN) 109–110, **110**
 potatiskorv (KS) 182–183
 summer sausage (ND) 169, 172
Scandinavian foods
 Minnesota 153, **154–155,** 156
 North Dakota 168–169, **169,**
 170–171
 potatiskorv (KS) 182–183
Scrapple 52, 52–53, **53**
Scungilli (conch) 56
Sea salt 249, **249**
Seafood
 Calabash-style seafood (NC)
 88, 88–89
 catch-and-cook restaurants
 (AL) 114, **115**
 cioppino (CA) 257–258, **258**
 Florida 104
 Pacific shellfish (WA) **241,**
 241–242, **244–245**
 see also specific foods
Seattle, WA
 artisan chocolates 259
 coffeehouses 247, **247**
 crab Louis 241
 doughnuts 254
 Pacific shellfish 241, **244–245**
 Pan-Asian cuisine 242
 pho 246
 smoked salmon 240
 teriyaki 243
Serviceberries 168, **168**
Shave ice 265, 268, **268**
She-crab soup 91–92
Shelburne Farms, VT 17, **17**
Shellfish, Pacific **241,** 241–242,
 244–245
Shrimp
 fried shrimp (WA) **242**
 shrimp cocktail (NV) 232, **232**
 South Carolina **92,** 92–93, **93**
Smith Island cake 69–70, **70**
Smithfield ham 77, **77**
Smoked salmon **240,** 240–241
Soda fountains 26–27, **27**

Soft-shell crabs **46,** 68–69
Somali restaurants 135
Sonic drive-ins 184
Sonoran hot dog 225, 228, **228**
Soul food **118,** 118–119, **119**
Soup
 cioppino (CA) 257–258, **258**
 pepper pot soup (PA) 49, **49**
 pho (WA) 243, **243,** 246
 saimin (HI) 270, **270**
 she-crab soup (SC) 91–92
 tortilla soup (TX) 194
 va-ka-mein ("vock") soup (LA)
 122
Sourdough bread 255–257, **256**
South Carolina 89–94
 barbecue 97
 boiled peanuts 90–91, **91**
 field peas 92
 grits **93,** 93–94
 Gullah/Geechee Cultural
 Heritage Corridor 89–90,
 90
 Palmetto Cheese 90
 she-crab soup 91–92
 shrimp & oysters **92,** 92–93
 soul food **4,** 119, **119**
South Dakota 172–174
 chislic (meat on a stick) **172,**
 172–173
 ice cream 173
 kuchen (cake) 173, **173**
 Mennonite foods 173–174
 sunflower seeds 173
Southern foods
 barbecue **96,** 96–97, **97**
 soul food **118,** 118–119, **119**
 southern-style potato salad
 (AL) 114–115
Southwestern cuisine
 Arizona 230
 Native American foods **226,**
 226–227, **227**
 New Mexico **200,** 211, **211,** 214
Spam 265
Sparks Rib Cook-Off, NV 236,
 236
Spokane, WA
 coffee 247
 crab Louis 241
 pho 246
 Rocket Market 247
Squirrel 84
St. Louis, MO
 butter cake 159, **159,** 162
 "concrete" (frozen custard) 162
 gooey butter cake 159, **159,** 162
 pizza 41, 162
 toasted ravioli 162
 World's Fair 159
Starbucks 246
Steak and steak houses 178–179,
 179
 chateaubriand (NV) **231,**
 231–232

chicken-fried steak (TX) 191, **191,** 194
Illinois 150–151, **151**
Oscar-style steak (CO) 209–210
Texas 179, 191, **192–193**
Steamers (clams) 11–12
Stew
　Brunswick stew (VA) 78–79, **79**
　burgoo (KY) 105, **105**
　Wyoming 204–205
Stone crab 99, **99, 100–101,** 102
Sugar art 188
Sugar cream pie 137, **137**
Summer sausage 169, 172
Sunflower seeds 173
Supper clubs 143–144, **144**
Sushi 264
Sweet corn
　Nebraska 176, **176**
　New England 15
Sweet ice tea 116
Sweet Palace, Philipsburg, MT 202
Sweet potatoes **198,** 198–199
Sweet sorghum syrup 106

T

Tabouleh 183–184, **184**
Tacos
　fish tacos (CA) 264, **265**
　Indian tacos (OK) 227
　Tex-Mex food **186,** 186–187
Taylor Grocery & Restaurant, Taylor, MS 116, **116**
Taylor pork roll sandwiches 60, **60**
Tennessee 109–114
　bacon & pork sausage 109–110, **110**
　barbecue 96–97
　biscuits & corn bread 110–111, **111, 112–113**
　MoonPies, Goo Goo Clusters & other sweets 111, 114, **114**
　soul food 119
Tepary beans 227, **227**
Teriyaki 243
Tex-Mex food **186,** 186–187, **187**
Texas 189–199
　barbecue **189,** 189–190
　Blue Bell creameries **190,** 190–191
　chicken-fried steak 191, **191,** 194
　chili cook-offs **194,** 194–195
　corny dogs **195,** 195–196
　DeLuxe fruitcake 199, **199**
　Dr Pepper 196, **196,** 197
　East Texas sweet potatoes **198,** 198–199
　Fritos 196
　frozen margaritas 195
　Gulf Coast oysters 196–197, **197**
　pan de campo (bread) 197–198

steak houses 179, 191, **192–193**
Tex-Mex food 186–187, **187**
tortilla soup 194
Thrasher's french fries **62,** 63
"Throwed" rolls 163
Tipton County Pork Festival 137, 140
Toasted ravioli 162
Toll House Inn, Whitman, MA 25
Tomato pie (pizza) 40, 41, 55–56
Tortilla soup 194
Tourtière (pork pie) 14–15
Trailing of the Sheep Festival, Ketchum, ID **220,** 220–221
Trenton, NJ
　pizza 40, 41, 55
Taylor pork roll 60
Trout 213, **213**

U

Utah 221–224
　bread pudding **221,** 221–222
　frog eye salad 224, **224**
　fry sauce 222, **222**
　funeral potatoes 223–224
　Hawaiian haystacks 221
　honey 223
　Jell-O 221
　Native American fare 227
　pastrami burger 223
　salt 224
　Utah scones 222–223, **223**

V

Valomilk candy 180
Vermont 16–21
　Ben & Jerry's ice cream 21, **21,** 26–27
　cheese 16–20, **17, 18–19**
　hard cider 67
　maple syrup **20,** 20–21
Vernors ginger ale 133
Versailles Restaurant, Miami, FL 103, **103**
Vidalia onions 98
Vinegar french fries **62,** 63
Vineyards
　Grand Valley, CO 210–211
　Virginia 79
Virginia 76–80
　apple tasting at Monticello 79–80, **80**
　Brunswick stew 78–79, **79**
　corn pudding 76, **76**
　cownose rays 77
　hard cider 66–67
　peanuts 78, **78,** 79
　Virginia ham 76–77, **77**
　wine 79
Vodka 216
Voodoo Doughnut, Portland, OR 254, **254**

W

Waldorf salad 35
Washington 240–247
　alder- & cedar-plank-smoked salmon **240,** 240–241
　apples 267
　artisan chocolates 259
　coffeehouses **246,** 246–247
　crab Louis 241
　doughnuts 254
　lentils 243
　Pacific shellfish **241,** 241–242, **244–245**
　pan-Asian cuisine 242, **242**
　pho 243, **243,** 246
　Rainier cherries 247, **247**
　Rocket Market, Spokane 247
　teriyaki 243
Washington, DC *see* District of Columbia
Water 38
Watermelon **188,** 189
West Virginia 80–85
　Golden Delicious apples **82–83,** 85
　hootenanny (baked pancake) 81
　pawpaws 80–81
　pepperoni rolls 81, 84, **84**
　Preston County Buckwheat Festival 85
　ramps (wild leeks) 81, **81**
　squirrel 84
Westward, Seattle, WA 241, **244–245**
Wheat 183
White Castle 182, 251
Whitefish 132
Whoopie pies 12–13, **13,** 54
Wild berries 152
Wild game 253
Wild mushrooms 253, **253**
Wild rice 152–153, **153**
Wine
　Grand Valley, CO 210–211
　Virginia 79
Wisconsin 140–144
　beer 144
　beer cheese 161
　cheddar cheese & cheese curds 141–143, **142**
　fish fries 143, **143**
　kolache (Czech pastry) 160
　kringle (pastry) 140–141, **141**
　milk 142
　supper clubs 143–144, **144**
Woodman's (clam shack), Essex, MA **24,** 25
Wyoming 204–205
　Bear Pit Lounge, Yellowstone NP 205
　cowboy cooking 204, **204, 206–207**
　elk 213

raspberry jams 205, **205**
stews 204–205
wild trout 213, **213**

Y

Ya-ka-mein ("yock") soup 122
Yams *see* Sweet potatoes
Yellowstone NP 205
Yuma Lettuce Days, AZ 229, **229**

Z

Zwieback (dinner roll) 183

ILLUSTRATIONS CREDITS

FRONT COVER (bacon cheeseburger), Scott Suchman; (blueberry pancakes), Malte Jaeger/laif/Redux Pictures; (ice-cream stand), Gabriela Herman/Gallery Stock **BACK COVER** (peppers), David Cavagnaro/Visuals Unlimited/Corbis; (crab house), Scott Suchman; (ears of corn), getcloser/Shutterstock

FRONT MATTER 2-3, Standret/Shutterstock; 4, Peter Frank Edwards/Redux; 6, Karin Dreyer/Blend Images/Corbis **NORTHEAST** 8, Scott Suchman; 10, Jane Shauck/Alamy; 11, bonchan/Shutterstock; 12, Jo Moser Photography/StockFood; 13, Beth Segal/StockFood; 14, AP Photo/Elise Amendola; 15 (UP), iStock.com/EasyBuy4u; 15 (LO), Courtesy Smuttynose Brewing Company; 16, iStock.com/huePhotography; 17, Matz Sjoberg/Robert Harding World Imagery; 18-19, Sabin Gratz/Vermont Cheese Council; 20, Ben Stechschulte/Redux Pictures; 21, Stan Tess/Alamy; 22, My Number/Alamy; 23, Beth Galton, Inc./StockFood; 24, Aurora Photos/Alamy; 25, Courtesy Durkee-Mower, Inc.; 26, Christopher Robbins/Digital Vision/Getty Images; 27, Phil Kline/Redux Pictures; 28, eye-blink/Shutterstock; 29, Envision/Corbis; 30, AP Photo/Steven Senne; 31, Hub/laif/Redux Pictures; 32, Mike Franzman; 33, iStock.com/Maksud_kr; 34, Susan Pease/DanitaDelimont.com; 35, 13 Photo/Redux Pictures; 36-7, Bryan Thomas/Redux Pictures; 38, Don Hogan Charles/The New York Times/Redux Pictures; 39, Mark Thomas/StockFood; 40, Natan Dvir Xinhua/eyevine/Redux Pictures; 41 (UP), Judith Collins/Alamy; 41 (LO), Felix Choo/Alamy; 42, Ginny Rose Stewart/The New York Times/Redux Pictures; 44-5, Mike Segar/Reuters **MID-ATLANTIC** 46, Andrew Scrivani/The New York Times/Redux Pictures; 48, Mark Peterson/Redux Pictures; 49, John Greim/Loop Images/Corbis; 50, Lissandra Melo/Shutterstock; 51, iStock.com/cveltri; 52, Charles Douglas Peebles/the food passionates/Corbis; 53, Kim Stallknecht/Redux Pictures; 54, Gabriela Herman/Gallery Stock; 55, Michael C. Gray/Shutterstock; 56, Scott Suchman; 57, Vintage Images/Getty Images; 58-9, Car Culture/Getty Images; 60, iStock.com/Ezume Images; 61, Jim Wilson/The New York Times/Redux Pictures; 62, D. Trozzo/Alamy; 63, iStock.com/TheCrimsonMonkey; 64, Scott Suchman; 65, Scott Suchman; 66, Courtesy of the Harvest Moon Cidery at Critz Farms, Cazenovia, NY; 67, images72/Shutterstock; 68, Scott Suchman; 69, AP Photo/Patrick Semansky; 70, Karen Kasmauski/National Geographic Creative; 71, Scott Suchman; 72-3, Scott Suchman; 74, Jon Hicks/Corbis; 75, Scott Suchman; 76, Tina Rupp/StockFood; 77, Rich-Joseph Facun/Reuters/Corbis; 78, 167/Richard Nowitz/Ocean/Corbis; 79, Taylor Mathis/StockFood; 80, Simon Reddy/Alamy; 81, Valery121283/Shutterstock; 82-3, RosalreneBetancourt 9/Alamy; 84, Foodcollection/the food passionates/Corbis **SOUTH** 86, Keller & Keller Photography/StockFood; 88, Paul Poplis/StockFood; 89, Courtesy of the Carolina Beverage Corporation; 90, Milton Morris; 91, David R. Frazier Photolibrary, Inc./Alamy; 92, Peter Frank Edwards/Redux; 93 (UP), Philip Scalia/Alamy; 93 (LO), Peter Frank Edwards/Redux; 94, Andre Baranowski/StockFood; 95, Allen Creative/Steve Allen/Alamy; 96, ilumus photography/Alamy; 97, Peter Frank Edwards/Redux Pictures; 98, Rachel Ballard/StockFood; 99, Jim Damaske/Tampa Bay Times/ZUMA Wire/ZUMA Press, Inc/Alamy; 100-101, Barbara P. Fernandez/Redux Pictures; 102, iStock.com/JMichl; 103 (UP), Russell Kord/Alamy; 103 (LO), A. and I. Kruk/Shutterstock; 104, John Clines/Getty Images; 105, Brian Yarvin/StockFood; 106, Glane23/https://en.wikipedia.org/wiki/Stack_cake#/media/File:Apple_Stack_Cake.jpg/http://creativecommons.org/licenses/by/2.0/legalcode; 107, Michael Cogliantry/StockFood; 108, Michael Ventura/Alamy; 109, Peter Frank Edwards/Redux Pictures; 110, RosalreneBetancourt 10/Alamy; 111, Marie C Fields/Shutterstock; 112-3, Gregor Lengler/laif/Redux Pictures; 114, Courtesy of MoonPie; 115, Richard Nowitz/National Geographic Creative; 116, Phillip Parker; 117, Ian Garlick/StockFood; 118, Erik S. Lesser/The New York Times/Redux Pictures; 119, Peter Frank Edwards/Redux Pictures; 120, Shane Luitjens/Alamy; 121 (UP), Kath Hale/www.cookbookwall.com; 121 (LO), Michael Mohr/Redux Pictures; 122, Michael Mohr/Redux; 123, David R. Frazier Photolibrary, Inc./Alamy; 124-5, Robyn Beck/AFP/Getty Images; 126, Arina Habich/Alamy; 127, Blend Images/Alamy **MIDWEST** 128, Joe Vaughn/Redux Pictures; 130, AP Photo/The Record-Eagle, Keith King; 131, Simon Brown/StockFood; 132, Russell Cooper, flickr.com/bellzatk; 133 (LO), Fanfo/Shutterstock; 134, Rosa-Betancourt 0 people images/Alamy; 135, Courtesy The Buckeye Chocolate Company; 136, jiangdi/Shutterstock; 137, RosalreneBetancourt 8/Alamy; 138, Joe Vaughn/Redux Pictures; 139, iStock.com/Lauri Patterson; 140, Martina Urban/StockFood; 141, Keller & Keller Photography/StockFood; 142, Kim Karpeles/Alamy; 143, Nicole Malena Photography; 144, Universal Images Group (Lake County Discovery Museum)/Alamy; 145, Multhaupt/laif/Redux Pictures; 146-7, AP Photo/Peoria Journal Star, Ron Johnson; 148, RosalreneBetancourt 3/Alamy; 149, Beth Rooney/Getty Images; 150, iStock.com/huePhotography; 151, Andrew Woodley/Alamy; 152, Kristi Sauer; 153, IngridHS/Shutterstock; 154-5, Allen Brisson Smith/Redux Pictures; 157, Sharon Lee; 158, Josh Thompson; 159, Jackie Alpers; 160, Michael Stravato/Redux Pictures; 161, Olha Afanasieva/Alamy; 163, D. Trozzo/Alamy **GREAT PLAINS** 164, Tate

GREAT AMERICAN EATING EXPERIENCES:
Local Specialties, Favorite Restaurants,
Food Festivals, Diners, Roadside Stands, and More

Prepared by the Book Division

Hector Sierra, *Senior Vice President and General Manager*
Lisa Thomas, *Senior Vice President and Editorial Director*
Jonathan Halling, *Creative Director*
Marianne R. Koszorus, *Design Director*
Barbara A. Noe, *Senior Editor*
R. Gary Colbert, *Production Director*
Jennifer A. Thornton, *Director of Managing Editorial*
Susan S. Blair, *Director of Photography*
Meredith C. Wilcox, *Director, Administration and Rights Clearance*

Staff for This Book

Lawrence M. Porges, *Editor*
Olivia Garnett, *Project Editor*
Carol Clurman, *Text Editor*
Elisa Gibson, *Art Director*
Moira Haney, *Senior Photo Editor*
Larry Bleiberg, Karen Carmichael, Katherine Cancila, Maryellen Kennedy Duckett, Chaney Kwak, April White, Joe Yogerst, *Contributing Writers*
Sophie Massey, Marlena Serviss, *Researchers*
Allie Fahey, *Editorial Assistant*
Marshall Kiker, *Associate Managing Editor*
Mike O'Connor, *Production Editor*
Rock Wheeler, *Rights Clearance Specialist*
Katie Olsen, *Design Production Specialist*
Nicole Miller, *Design Production Assistant*
Jennifer Hoff, *Manager, Production Services*
Rahsaan Jackson, *Imaging*

Since 1888, the National Geographic Society has funded more than 12,000 research, exploration, and preservation projects around the world. National Geographic Partners distributes a portion of the funds it receives from your purchase to National Geographic Society to support programs including the conservation of animals and their habitats.

For more information, please call 1-800-647-5463 or write to the following address:

National Geographic Partners, LLC
1145 17th Street NW
Washington, DC 20036-4688 USA

Become a member of National Geographic and activate your benefits today at natgeo.com/jointoday.

For information about special discounts for bulk purchases, please contact National Geographic Books Special Sales: ngspecsales@ngs.org

For rights or permissions inquiries, please contact National Geographic Books Subsidiary Rights: ngbookrights@ngs.org

Library of Congress Cataloging-in-Publication Data

Great American eating experiences : local specialties, favorite restaurants, food festivals, diners, roadside stands, and more / foreword by Andrew Nelson, contributing editor, National Geographic Traveler magazine. -- 1st edition.
    pages cm
  Includes index.
  ISBN 978-1-4262-1639-8 (pbk. : alk. paper)
  1. Food service--United States--Directories. 2. Restaurants--United Statesv--Directories. I. National Geographic Society (U.S.)
   TX907.2.G737 2016
   647.9573--dc23

                               2015033599

Printed in China
16/RRDS/1

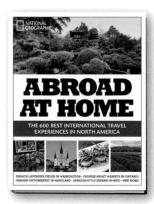
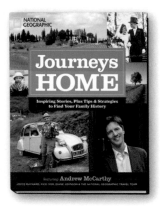
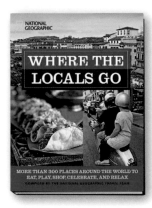